COMPUTER SYSTEM PERFORMANCE MODELING IN PERSPECTIVE

A Tribute to the Work of Professor Kenneth C. Sevcik

Advances in Computer Science and Engineering: Texts

Editor-in-Chief: Erol Gelenbe *(Imperial College)*
Advisory Editors: Manfred Broy *(Technische Universitaet Muenchen)*
Gérard Huet *(INRIA)*

Published

Vol. 1 Computer System Performance Modeling in Perspective:
A Tribute to the Work of Professor Kenneth C. Sevcik
edited by E. Gelenbe (Imperial College London, UK)

Advances in Computer Science and Engineering: Texts — Vol. 1

Computer System Performance Modeling in Perspective

A Tribute to the Work of Professor Kenneth C. Sevcik

editor

Erol Gelenbe
Imperial College, UK

Imperial College Press

Published by

Imperial College Press
57 Shelton Street
Covent Garden
London WC2H 9HE

Distributed by

World Scientific Publishing Co. Pte. Ltd.
5 Toh Tuck Link, Singapore 596224
USA office: 27 Warren Street, Suite 401-402, Hackensack, NJ 07601
UK office: 57 Shelton Street, Covent Garden, London WC2H 9HE

British Library Cataloguing-in-Publication Data
A catalogue record for this book is available from the British Library.

COMPUTER SYSTEM PERFORMANCE MODELING IN PERSPECTIVE
A Tribute to the Work of Professor Kenneth C. Sevcik
Advances in Computer Science and Engineering: Texts — Vol. 1

Copyright © 2006 by Imperial College Press

All rights reserved. This book, or parts thereof, may not be reproduced in any form or by any means, electronic or mechanical, including photocopying, recording or any information storage and retrieval system now known or to be invented, without written permission from the Publisher.

For photocopying of material in this volume, please pay a copying fee through the Copyright Clearance Center, Inc., 222 Rosewood Drive, Danvers, MA 01923, USA. In this case permission to photocopy is not required from the publisher.

ISBN 1-86094-661-5
ISSN 1793-2408

Printed in Singapore by World Scientific Printers (S) Pte Ltd

Preface

This book is a tribute to the many contributions that Kenneth C. Sevcik made both as a scholar, and a mentor to numerous young researchers, that was planned on the occasion of his 60th birthday. The project for the book was launched at the end of 2004. Unfortunately it only appears in print after his untimely death due to delays in bringing together the various contributions and in producing the volume.

Ken, who was a very good friend and highly distinguished and respected colleague, passed away on October 4, 2005. We dedicate this book to Ken's memory and to his wife Carmen who encouraged and very warmly supported him for many years.

Prof. Sevcik received his B.S. in 1966 from Stanford University and his Ph.D. in 1971 from the University of Chicago. He joined the Computer Science Department at the University of Toronto as an Assistant Professor in 1971, rose to the rank of Professor, and was Chair of the Department from 1990 to 1992. He served as Director of the Computer Systems Research Institute (CSRI) and on the Governing Council of the University of Toronto. Ken was a founder of the field of computer system performance. During a career that spanned some thirty-five years, he made major scientific and technical contributions to computer system performance evaluation and greatly influenced its practice. Several papers in this volume underline some of these contributions and recall his role as an advisor and mentor to numerous post-graduate and Ph.D. students. His seminal work not only covers queueing network models, but also includes important contributions to database systems through his work on grid files and on database system performance. He was one of the first members of the ACM SIGMETRICS Board of Directors and of IFIP Working Group 7.3. He was honoured with the SIGMETRICS Achievement Award in 2004. He graduated more than 50 M.Sc. and 20 Ph.D. students who, individually and collectively, have in turn made a major impact on the field of Computer Science and on the academic world in general.

The first paper in this volume is written by four of his very prominent students and it describes with accuracy, affection and respect, how Ken worked with his graduate students and what he contributed to them. It is followed by three papers which outline some of Ken's salient contributions and puts them into the broader perspective of its impact on the work of others. The remaining ten papers provide novel technical contributions based on the recent research of the authors in the field of stochastic models, computer and network performance evaluation and system modeling.

By balancing brief personal reminiscences with an overview of some of Ken's important contributions, and with ongoing or recent research work, we pay homage to Ken as an individual who was warm and caring, rigorous, and was also an inquisitive, creative and productive scholar.

Erol Gelenbe
Imperial College London

Contents

Preface   v

Chapter 1   **Ken Sevcik as an Advisor and Mentor**   1
Ed Lazowska, Satish Tripathi, John Zahorjan and Derek Eager

Chapter 2   **Shadow Servers and Priority Scheduling**   7
Jeffrey P. Buzen

    1. Introduction 7
    2. Single Class Models 8
    3. Multi-Class Models 8
    4. Importance of Priorities 9
    5. The Shadow Server Approximation 10
    6. Extensions 12
    7. Comments on Significance 13
    References 14

Chapter 3   **On the Chronology of Dynamic Allocation Index Policies: The Pioneering Work of K. C. Sevcik**   15
Ed Coffman

    1. Introduction 15
    2. Sevcik's Smallest-Rank-First Index Policy 16
    3. Background and Chronology 17
    4. Examples 18
    5. Concluding Remarks 19
    References 19

Chapter 4	**Operational Analysis**	**21**
	Peter J. Denning	

    1. Introduction 21
    2. Dead Cows 21
    3. Dead Cows in Markovian Queueing Networks 22
    4. The Birth of Operational Analysis 24
    5. The Fundamental Assumptions of Operational
       Analysis 25
    6. Controversy 28
    7. Salute 29
    8. An Historical Footnote 29
    References (Published) 29
    References (Unpublished Technical Reports) 30
    Appendix — Operational Analysis: A Fable 31

Chapter 5	**Function Approximation by Random Neural Networks with a Bounded Number of Layers**	**35**
	Erol Gelenbe, Zhi-Hong Mao and Yan-Da Li	

    1. Introduction 35
    2. The GNN and Its Extensions 36
       2.1. The BGNN model 38
    3. Approximation of Functions of One Variable by the GNN
       with a Bounded Number of Layers 40
       3.1. Technical premises 41
       3.2. BGNN approximation of continuous functions of
           one variable 44
       3.3. CGNN approximation of continuous functions of
           one variable 46
    4. Approximation of Continuous Functions of s Variables . 49
    5. Conclusions 53
    References 54
    Appendix: Proof of Technical Lemmas 56

Chapter 6	**The Achilles' Heel of Computer Performance Modeling and the Model Building Shield**	**59**
	Vittoria De Nitto Personè and Giuseppe Iazeolla	

    1. Introduction 59
    2. The Current Status of Model Building 60
    3. System Multilevel Description 61
       3.1. The system vertical description 62
       3.2. The system horizontal description 63
       3.3. The system software description 64

          4. The Multilevel Model Building Method 68
             4.1. The top-down bottom-up process 68
          5. Comparison with Existing Approaches 71
          6. Conclusions 72
          Acknowledgment 72
          References 73

Chapter 7 **Wireless Network Simulation:**
           Towards a Systematic Approach   **75**
           Satish K. Tripathi, J. Jobin and Michalis Faloutsos

           1. Introduction 76
           2. Background and Model 78
           3. Description of Our Framework 79
              3.1. System parameters 79
              3.2. Performance metrics 80
              3.3. Our framework 81
           4. Experimental Results 82
              4.1. Parameters that affect steady state utilization . . . 82
              4.2. The significance of steady state arrival rate 86
              4.3. Discussion and applications 87
           5. Homogeneity 90
              5.1. Related work 91
              5.2. Metrics for comparison 92
           6. Evaluation 92
              6.1. Cell shape (number of neighbors) 92
              6.2. User speed 96
              6.3. User bandwidth requirement 97
           7. Conclusion 98
           References 99

Chapter 8 **Location- and Power-Aware Protocols**
           for Wireless Networks with Asymmetric Links   **101**
           Guoqiang Wang, Yongchang Ji, Dan C. Marinescu,
           Damla Turgut and Ladislau Bölöni

           1. Introduction and Motivation 102
           2. Related Work 104
           3. The Model of the System 106
           4. m-Limited Forwarding 110
              4.1. Simulation study 112
           5. Routing Protocol 118
              5.1. Neighbor discovery 119
              5.2. Location and power update 120
              5.3. Route discovery 120

	5.4. Route maintenance	121
6.	MAC Protocol	121
	6.1. Topological considerations	121
	6.2. A solution to the hidden node problem	124
	6.3. Node status	126
	6.4. Medium access model	126
	6.5. A simulation study	128
7.	Cross-Layer Architecture	130
8.	Work in Progress	131
9.	Summary	132
	Acknowledgments	133
	References	133

Chapter 9 Multi-Threaded Servers with High Service Time Variation for Layered Queueing Networks 137
Greg Franks, Murray Woodside and Jerry Rolia

1.	Introduction	137
2.	Residence Time Expressions	138
	2.1. MVA waiting time expressions	139
3.	Accuracy and Computation-Time Comparisons	141
4.	Example Case Studies	143
	4.1. Systems management example	143
	4.2. Electronic bookstore example	144
5.	Conclusions	148
	Acknowledgments	150
	Appendix A. Marginal Probabilities	150
	Appendix B. de Souza e Silva and Muntz Approximation	152
	References	152

Chapter 10 Quantiles of Sojourn Times 155
Peter G. Harrison and William J. Knottenbelt

1.	Introduction	156
2.	Time Delays in the Single Server Queue	158
	2.1. Waiting time distribution in the M/G/1 queue	158
	2.2. Busy periods	159
	2.3. Waiting times in LCFS queues	160
	2.4. Waiting times with Processor-Sharing discipline	162
3.	MM CPP/GE/c G-Queues: Semi-Numerical Laplace Transform Inversion	162
4.	Time Delays in Networks of Queues	166
	4.1. Open networks	167
	4.2. Closed networks	169

		4.2.1	Cyclic networks 173
		4.2.2	Paths with service rates all equal 174
	5.	Passage Times in Continuous Time Markov Chains . . . 174
		5.1. First passage times in CTMCs 174
		5.2. Uniformization 175
		5.3. Hypergraph partitioning 176
		5.4. Parallel algorithm and tool implementation 177
		5.5. Numerical example 179
	6.	Passage Times in Continuous Time Semi-Markov Processes 182
		6.1. First passage times in SMPs 183
		6.2. Iterative passage time algorithm 185
		6.3. Laplace transform inversion 186
		6.4. Implementation 187
		6.5. Numerical example 187
	7.	Conclusion 190
	References 191

Chapter 11 Asymptotic Solutions for Two Non-Stationary Problems in Internet Reliability   195
Yaakov Kogan and Gagan Choudhury

1. Introduction 195
2. Poisson Approximation for the Number of Failed Routers 197
3. Asymptotics of Lost Bandwidth 200
References 204

Chapter 12 Burst Loss Probabilities in an OBS Network with Dynamic Simultaneous Link Possession   205
Tzvetelina Battestilli and Harry Perros

1. Introduction 205
2. Problem Description 208
3. A Queueing Network Model for an OBS Path 209
   3.1. The arrival process 211
4. The Decomposition Algorithm 213
   4.1. An example 213
      4.1.1 Analysis of sub-system 1 213
      4.1.2 Analysis of sub-system 2 215
      4.1.3 The iterative procedure 216
   4.2. The decomposition algorithm 217
   4.3. Calculation of the burst loss probability 219
5. Numerical Results 220

	6. Conclusions	223
	References	224

Chapter 13   **Stochastic Analysis of Resource Allocation in Parallel Processing Systems**   **227**
Mark S. Squillante

1. Introduction 227
2. Model of Parallel Processing Systems 230
3. Analysis of Dynamic Spacesharing 232
    3.1. Irreducibility and stability criterion 235
    3.2. Special case: Exponential model parameters 235
    3.3. Performance measures 237
4. Analysis of Memory Reference Behavior 239
    4.1. Program behavior models 240
    4.2. Intra-locality memory overhead 244
    4.3. Inter-locality memory overhead 245
        4.3.1 Calculation of N_I^* 246
        4.3.2 Calculation of C_I 247
    4.4. Total memory overhead 250
5. Conclusions 250
Acknowledgment 251
References 251

Chapter 14   **Periodic Task Cluster Scheduling in Distributed Systems**   **257**
Helen Karatza

1. Introduction 257
2. Model and Methodology 260
    2.1. System and workload models 260
    2.2. Scheduling strategies 262
    2.3. Performance metrics 263
    2.4. Model implementation and input parameters . . . 263
3. Simulation Results and Performance Analysis 264
    3.1. Normal distribution case 264
    3.2. Uniform distribution case 271
4. Conclusions and Future Research 273
References 273

CHAPTER 1

Ken Sevcik as an Advisor and Mentor

Ed Lazowska
University of Washington, USA

Satish Tripathi
University at Buffalo, USA

John Zahorjan
University of Washington, USA

Derek Eager
University of Saskatchewan, USA

Ken Sevcik joined the Computer Science faculty at the University of Toronto in 1971, following his doctoral studies at the University of Chicago and his bachelor's studies at Stanford. Like many of Toronto's early hires in Computer Science, Ken was persuaded by then-chair Tom Hull to "give it a try for a couple of years," which became a career.

The four of us are privileged to have been among Ken's early Ph.D. students — numbers 2, 3, 5, and 8 of his 22 Ph.D. students as of 2004 (see Table 1). Ken also graduated 50 M.Sc. students as of 2004 (see Table 2), and the 7 of his 22 Ph.D. students who pursued academic careers have given him, thus far, 61 Ph.D. grandchildren, 86 great grandchildren, 32 great great grandchildren, and 2 great great great grandchildren (see Fig. 1) — a total of 203 Ph.D. descendants in all!

As faculty members ourselves, we often reflect on the characteristics that made Ken such a successful advisor and mentor, and try as best we can to emulate them.

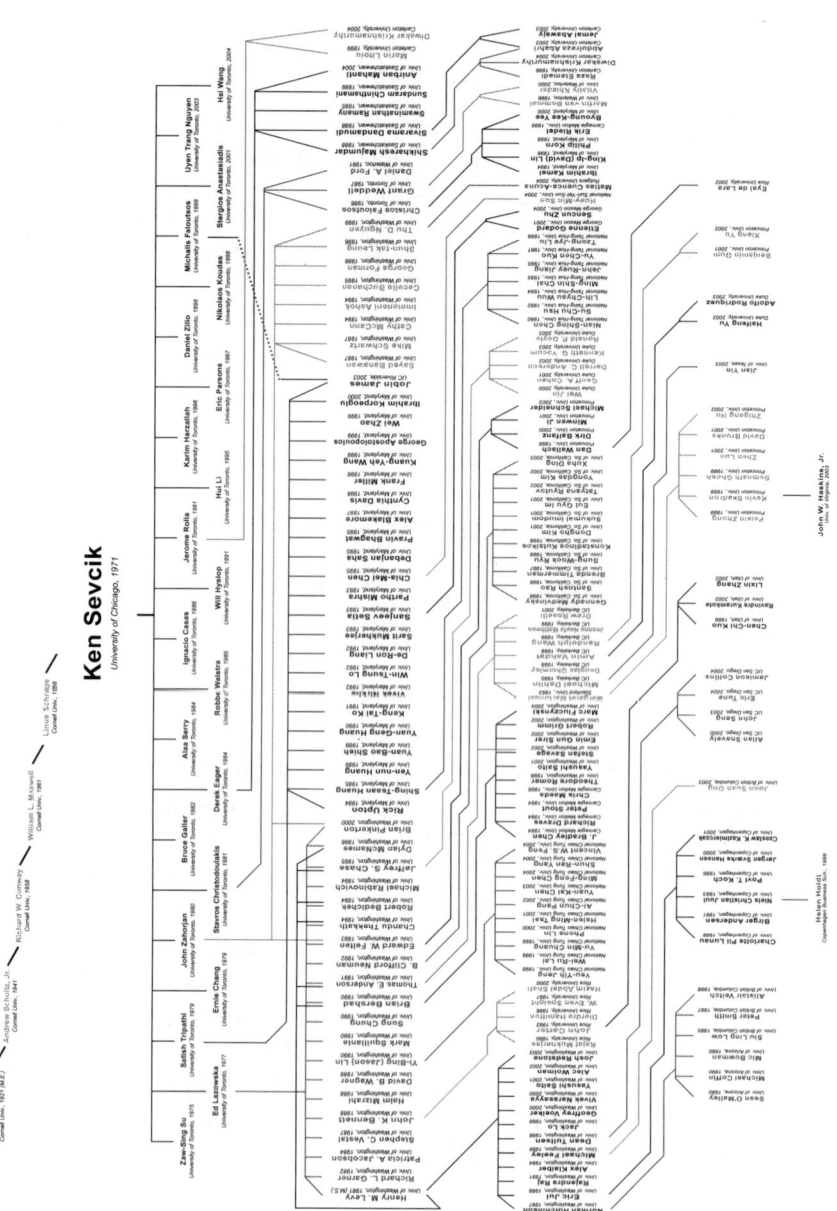

Fig. 1. Ken Sevcik's Ph.D. genealogy.

Table 1. Ken Sevcik's Ph.D. students.

1. Su, Zaw-Sing, *Dynamic Scheduling with Preemption: A Deterministic Approach* (1975)
2. Lazowska, Edward D., *Characterizing Service Time and Response Time Distributions in Queueing Network Models of Computer Systems* (1977)
3. Tripathi, Satish K., *On Approximate Solution Techniques for Queueing Network Models of Computer Systems* (1979)
4. Chang, Ernie, *Decentralized Algorithms in Distributed Systems* (1979)
5. Zahorjan, John, *The Approximate Solution of Very Large Queueing Network Models* (1980)
6. Christodoulakis, Stavros, *Estimating Selectivities in Data Bases* (1981)
7. Galler, Bruce, *Concurrency Control Performance Issues* (1982)
8. Eager, Derek, *Bounding Algorithms for Queueing Network Models of Computer Systems* (1984)
9. Serry, Alaa, *An Analytical Approach to Modelling IMS Systems* (1984)
10. Walstra, B. Robbe J., *Iterative Analysis of Networks of Queues* (1985)
11. Casas-Raposo, Ignacio, *PROPHET: A Layered Analytical Model for Performance Prediction of Database Systems* (1986)
12. Hyslop, William, *Performance Prediction of Relational Database Management Systems* (1991)
13. Rolia, Jerome, *Predicting the Performance of Software Systems* (1991)
14. Li, Hui, *Software Approaches to Memory Latency Reduction on NUMA Multiprocessors* (1995)
15. Harzallah, Karim, *Impact of Memory Contention in Large Scale Multiprocessors* (1996)
16. Parsons, Eric, *Coordinated Allocation of Processors and Memory in Multiprocessor Operating Systems* (1997)
17. Zilio, Daniel, *Physical Database Design Decision Algorithms and Concurrent Reorganization for Parallel Database Systems* (1998)
18. Koudas, Nikolaos, *Fast Algorithms for Spatial and Multidimensional Joins* (1998)
19. Faloutsos, Michalis, *The Greedy, The Naive, and The Optimal Multicast Routing: From Theory to Internet Protocols* (1998) [co-supervised with A. Banerjea]
20. Anastasiadis, Stergios, *Supporting Variable Bit-Rate Streams in a Scalable Continuous Media Server* (2001) [co-supervised with M. Stumm]
21. Nguyen, Uyen Trang, *Congestion Control for Multipoint Communications in ATM Networks* (2003) [co-supervised with I. Katzela]
22. Wang, Hai, *Concise and Accurate Data Summaries for Fast Approximate Query Answering* (2004)

Ken was open and approachable. When you met Ken, whether for the first time or the thousandth, you could count on being received with a smile. No matter how busy Ken was, while you were talking with him that conversation had his full attention. No matter how naïve what you had to say was, he gave full consideration (before gently pointing out what might be wrong with it).

Table 2. Ken Sevcik's M.Sc. students.

1. Tran, Tuan Khan, *The Response Time Distributions of Some Computer Scheduling Disciplines* (1972)
2. Lester, Eleanor A., *The Investigation of Service Time Distributions* (1973)
3. Lazowska, Edward D., *Scheduling Multiple Resource Computer Systems* (1974)
4. Lam, Lettice Hung, *Comparison of Three Logical Views of Data in Hospital Information Systems* (1974)
5. Schumacher, Helmut, *The Synthesis of Optimal Decision Trees from Decision Tables* (1974)
6. Tripathi, Satish, K., *Approximate Models of Multi-Programmed Computer Systems with Paging* (1975)
7. Lum, Wade C., *Data Collection, Reduction and Analysis of Computer System Measurement* (1975)
8. Cheung, Stephen Chun-Lap, *A Computer Method for Cyclical Scheduling of Shift Workers* (1975)
9. Shen, Helen, *The Effect of Interarrival Times in Scheduling* (1975)
10. Spirk, Franz, *An Analysis of Different Deadlock Control Schemes* (1975)
11. Lin, Hing-Lung, *Closed Queueing Network Models: Computational Algorithms with Application to Computer System Performance Evaluation* (1976)
12. Dubien, Ronald J., *Extending a Commercial Database System to Provide Data Independence* (1977)
13. Kienzle, Martin G., *Measurements of Computer Systems for Queueing Network Models* (1977)
14. Kidd, Robert John, *A Common Model for Multi-Key Access Performance Evaluation* (1978)
15. Lai, Chi Sang, *Patient Identification and Record Linkage* (1979)
16. Au, Matthew, *Some Properties of Queueing Network Models* (1981)
17. Bell, Barbara, *Database System Performance Prediction: The First Two Levels of a Multi-level Modelling Framework* (1981)
18. Casas-Raposo, Ignacio, *Analytic Modelling of Database Systems: The Design of a System 2000 Performance Predictor* (1981)
19. Eager, Derek, *Robust Concurrency Control in Distributed Databases* (1981)
20. Bobrowski, Christoph, *The Principle of Maximum Entropy in Some Computer System Modelling Problems* (1983)
21. Vopalensky, Jan, *The Scheduling Problem in Distributed Computer Systems: Its Definition and Partial Solution* (1983)
22. Martin, Vickie, *SPIRAL ONE — Dynamic Hashing Scheme* (1983)
23. Aldwinckle, John, *A Scheduler for UNIX* (1984)
24. Gelblum, Michael, *Some Results of the File Placement Problem* (1984)
25. Rolia, Jerome, *Performance Estimates for Multi-tasking Software Systems* (1987)
26. Coatta, Terry, *Queueing Networks with State-Dependent Service Rates* (1987)
27. Clark, Graeme, *Performance Properties of the FDDI Token Ring* (1987)
28. MacLean, Richard, *Performance Characteristics of the FDDI Token Ring Priority Mechanism* (1989)
29. Lee, Jei-min, *Concurrency Control Through Hierarchical Synchronization* (1989)
30. LeBel, Edgar, *Sparse Undistributed Memory: A Local Storage Model for Pattern Matching* (1990)
31. Cupit, Brian, *Parse Tree Based Revision Control and Program File Compression* (1990)
32. Verma, Raj, *A Metric Approach to Isolated Word Recognition* (1991)

Table 2. (*Continued*)

33.	Srikantiah, Nandini, *Processor Scheduling in Hierarchical NUMA Multiprocessors* (1991)
34.	Bacque, Ben, *SUPERMON: Flexible Hardware for Performance Monitoring* (1991) [co-supervised with K. C. Smith]
35.	Marwood, Simon, *Performance Comparison of Concurrency Control Techniques in Partitioned Systems* (1993)
36.	Wu, Chee Shong, *Processor Scheduling in Multiprogrammed Shared Memory Computer Systems* (1993)
37.	Larson, Johan, *Domain-Partitioned Parallel Sort-Merge Join* (1995)
38.	Wang, Corina, *An Adaptive Rendering and Display Model for Networked Applications* (1996) [co-supervised with M. van de Panne]
39.	Tam, Anita, *Performance Prediction for Parallel Applications* (1996)
40.	Anastasiadis, Stergios, *Parallel Application Scheduling on Networks of Workstations* (1996)
41.	Soreanu, Gabriel, *A Comparative Study of Interconnection Networks in Large-Scale Multiprocessors* (1996)
42.	Wang, Hai, *Approximate MVA Algorithms for Solving Queueing Network Models* (1997)
43.	Gibbons, Richard, *A Historical Application Profiler for Use by Parallel Schedulers* (1997)
44.	Kennedy, Brett, *Declustering Spatial Data for Range and Join Queries* (1999)
45.	Piegaze, Peeter, *Incorporating Time into Computer Cartography: A Digital Atlas of History* (2001)
46.	Lu, Jingjing, *Fast Algorithms for Distance-Based Spatial Queries* (2001)
47.	Garcia Arellano, Christian, *Quantization Techniques for Similarity Search in High-Dimensional Data Spaces* (2002)
48.	Tjioe, Wei, *Finding Structure in Data* (2003)
49.	Pham, Hang, *Accurate Two-Dimensional Histograms for Fast Approximate Answers To Queries on Real Data* (2004)
50.	Dong, Junfeng, *Indexing High-Dimensional Data for Main Memory* (2004)

Ken was incredibly conscientious. As a student, you need many things from your advisor (including many things you do not know you need, but you do). You could count on Ken to provide these, both the good (e.g., introducing you to the community at conferences) and the bad (e.g., insisting that your thesis really did need another chapter's worth of work before it was complete). You could count on him looking out for your welfare, even when the effort to do so benefited him at most extremely indirectly.

Ken led by example. He engaged in all the aspects of the work that a student had to learn to do, as well as those carried only by the advisor. He set high standards for his students, and even higher ones for himself.

Ken was always open to new ideas and new approaches, and eager to learn new things. His willingness to tackle new problem areas was evident from the titles of the Ph.D. and M.Sc. theses that he supervised: scheduling theory, queueing network modeling techniques, distributed algorithms, database management systems, applications of performance models, multiprocessor architecture, multiprocessor operating systems, communication network protocols, computer system performance measurement, file structures, spatial databases, and many more.

Finally, Ken managed to be our friend as well as our advisor, without letting either of those relationships interfere with the other. This is at the heart of the immense respect we have for him, both professionally and personally. In the final tally, how well one has done as an advisor is reflected in how much one's students have learned. We owe Ken a terrific debt for the lessons he gave us about performing and leading research, and about how to lead our lives.

CHAPTER 2

Shadow Servers and Priority Scheduling

Jeffrey P. Buzen

12 Mountain Laurels, Nashua, NH 03062, USA

jeffbuzen@comcast.net

Queuing network models have been applied to the analysis of computer system performance since the early 1970s. Shortly after their introduction, a number of major extensions to the underlying mathematical theory were developed by a worldwide community of researchers. Among the most important of these new extensions was the ability to represent priority scheduling at CPUs. Sevcik's shadow server approximation, which appeared in 1977, provided the first computationally viable technique for analyzing the effect of CPU priority scheduling within a queuing network model. The shadow server approximation is based on a powerful and intuitively appealing heuristic. It provided a solution to an important open problem and contributed substantially to the practical success of commercial modeling tools based on the theory of queuing networks.

1. Introduction

For researchers investigating the performance of large scale computer systems, the 1970s could well be characterized as the decade of queuing network models. The mathematical foundation for this period of intensive research was established in the 1960s through the work of Jackson[12] and Gordon and Newell.[11] However, these important results were not applied immediately to the analysis of computer performance, and they remained unknown within the computer science community for several years.

All this changed early in 1971 with the introduction of the central server model for multi-programmed computer systems[4,5] and the convolution algorithm for queuing network evaluation.[5,6] These developments demonstrated that queuing network models were exceptionally well suited for analyzing and predicting computer system performance. As a result, hundreds of papers on this general topic were published during the next decade and beyond by a worldwide community of researchers. The work of Ken Sevcik on shadow server approximations for priority scheduling represents a highly significant contribution to this body of research.

2. Single Class Models

The original central server model of 1971 was a single class model, intended to represent a multi-programmed computer system processing a single workload. The workload could be associated with a backlog of batch jobs waiting in an input queue, or the cyclic flow of requests and responses associated with interactive users at time sharing terminals, or an open stream of transactions generated by users of an online transaction processing application. Each of the three workload types was represented in a different manner, but only one workload type could be present in a given central server model. This constraint was due to the fact that the closed form solutions derived by Jackson and by Gordon and Newell were limited to single class queuing networks.

Priority scheduling was not a critical concern for users of these models since the most important application of priorities is to regulate CPU access in systems where batch jobs, time sharing users and online transaction processing applications are all executing concurrently. Such systems were quite rare in the early 1970s. As a result, the central server model could be applied successfully in a number of practical situations without providing a detailed representation of CPU dispatching priorities.

3. Multi-Class Models

The steady state solutions derived by Jackson and by Gordon and Newell in the 1960s were extended to include multi-class queuing networks in a landmark paper published in 1975 by Baskett, Chandy, Muntz and Palacios.[2] That same year, Reiser and Kobayashi[14] published a multi-class extension to the single class convolution algorithm[5,6] I developed in 1971, making it computationally feasible to evaluate the new multi-class queuing networks. This set the stage for extending the central server model so it could be capable of handling multiple workloads in a single model.

On the commercial side, powerful new systems capable of concurrently processing multiple streams of batch, time sharing and transaction processing workloads were becoming increasingly common. Understanding how these workloads interacted with one another, and with the physical and logical resources available in the underlying computational platform, became a major practical concern for system administrators and professional performance analysts.

It would seem that the central server model, extended mathematically to handle multiple customer classes and evaluated numerically by the new multi-class convolution algorithm, would be ideally suited for evaluating these emerging computer systems. However, two important mechanisms that have a major influence on system performance could not be represented in the closed form solution derived by Baskett, Chandy, Muntz and Palacios. These mechanisms were the queuing delays that arriving transactions encounter when memory becomes full ("passive resource" queuing) and the impact of priority scheduling on queuing delays at the CPU.

Fortunately, viable approximations for the memory queuing problem had already been developed by Brandwajn[3] and Courtois.[10] Extending these single class approximations to multi-class networks is a complex undertaking,[13] but at least the groundwork had been established. On the other hand, no satisfactory approximation was available for priority scheduling in queuing networks as 1975 came to a close.

4. Importance of Priorities

Priority scheduling can be implemented to manage queues at both I/O devices and CPUs. However, I/O priorities usually have minimal impact on the performance of a well-tuned system. The reason is that I/O queues are usually kept relatively short to maintain good performance. This is done by distributing heavily accessed files across multiple volumes, and purchasing additional disks if necessary. Keeping I/O queues short helps to avoid the catastrophic effect that long I/O queues can have on overall performance. As a side effect, short queues also reduce the influence that priority scheduling algorithms can exert.

A related consideration is that priority queuing for I/O devices is almost always implemented with a non-preemptive (head-of-line) algorithm. Preempting an I/O operation in mid-course is difficult to accomplish and can create substantial overhead. Use of non-preemptive priorities further reduces the influence that priority scheduling algorithms can exert. With short queues and non-preemptive priorities, the impact of priority scheduling on I/O device response time is almost always a second order effect.

In contrast, priority scheduling at CPUs was absolutely critical to the design of large mainframe computers in the 1970s. One of the design principles underlying these systems is that CPUs represent extremely expensive components that need to be kept busy as much as possible to justify the costs involved. However, keeping CPU utilization near 100% in systems that are dedicated to online applications results in unacceptably long queuing delays for the CPU.

To resolve the conflict between high CPU utilization and acceptable online response time, large mainframes typically run a mix of high priority online workloads and low priority batch workloads. Since CPUs can be scheduled using a preemptive resume dispatcher, the presence of low priority batch jobs will have a negligible impact on CPU response times for high priority online workloads. Moreover, low priority batch jobs can then soak up most available CPU cycles, performing useful work and justifying the heavy investments enterprises make in new hardware.

System administrators and performance analysts are of course concerned about the impact that multiple workloads have as they contend with one another for system resources. The multi-class central server model of the mid-1970s was ideally suited for analyzing such questions. However, without a means of representing CPU priority scheduling, these models would be neglecting an important first order effect and would be inadequate for the task at hand. It was at this point that Ken Sevcik became interested in the priority scheduling problem for queuing networks.

5. The Shadow Server Approximation

Sevcik begins his analysis of priority scheduling[15] by developing a series of upper and lower bounds that bracket the exact solution. This in itself is noteworthy since many researchers attack such problems with the goal of deriving one — and only one — solution. Sevcik's systematic examination of a range of multiple bounds provides considerable insight into the underlying mechanisms that regulate performance in systems with priority scheduling.

The first series of examples considered by Sevcik consists of single class models where all low priority workloads are simply deleted. Note that deleting low priority workloads has no effect on the CPU response time of the remaining high priority workload since low priority workloads generate no CPU interference under preemptive resume. On the other hand, low priority workloads do interfere with high priority workloads when they contend for I/O devices (which employ first come, first served scheduling). To account for this, I/O service times for the remaining high priority workload must be stretched out to represent the extra delays that would have been generated at the I/O devices by the deleted low priority workloads. By using alternative formulas for computing stretch-out at I/O devices, Sevcik is able to derive upper and lower bounds on the performance of the high priority workload.

Sevcik then considers multi-class models where both high and low priority workloads are represented by separate workloads. In these models, I/O contention does not require any special treatment since all I/O activity is explicitly represented. However, the model still must be adjusted to account for preemptive resume priority scheduling at the CPU.

The first approximation utilized by Sevcik to represent priority scheduling is to simply assume that the CPU is scheduled according to a processor sharing algorithm (rather than a preemptive resume priority algorithm). The model is easily solved using the known multi-class solution.[2] This approximation is pessimistic for high priority performance (providing a lower bound on throughput) since there is interference at the CPU from low priority workloads under processor sharing. Conversely, the approximation is optimistic for low priority performance (providing an upper bound on throughput) since low priority workloads have better access to the CPU under processor sharing than they do under preemptive-resume priorities.

The next approximation in this sequence refines the treatment of CPU processing for the high priority workload. This is accomplished by completely offloading all CPU processing demands generated by the lower priority workloads. Thus, only the high priority workload uses the CPU. This provides an excellent estimate of CPU response for the high priority workload (since low priority workloads are invisible under preemptive resume scheduling). However, this approach raises the question of what to do with the CPU processing demands generated by the lower priority workloads.

At this point Sevcik makes a particularly insightful proposal, which is to add new "shadow servers" to the original queuing network model and to direct the lower priority workloads to these new servers. In the general case where there are N priority levels, Sevcik's approach results in the addition of $N - 1$ new shadow servers, one dedicated to each priority level (except for the highest priority level, which is still processed by the original CPU).

Once the new shadow servers have been added, the next issue to consider is how to stretch out the service times at these servers to represent interference from higher priority workloads. Here again, Sevcik proposes a range of stretch-out factors, yielding both upper and lower bounds on performance.

6. Extensions

One of the advantages of the approach that Ken Sevcik employed when developing the shadow server approximation is that it is readily extensible. In particular, a range of alternate algorithms can be used to stretch out the service times for low priority shadow servers. Two different approximations were presented in Sevcik's original 1977 paper. The first was to assume no stretch out all, and to simply set the service times at the lower priority servers equal to the original unmodified CPU service times. This has the effect of totally ignoring the degradation due to preemption by higher priority workloads. As a result, the throughput rates of lower priority workloads are overestimated, providing an upper bound on low priority throughput. This in turn overestimates the I/O contention experienced by higher priority workloads, and provides an upper bound on high priority throughput.

A second and more accurate (but more complex) approximation is to compute stretch out by dividing the original service times of lower priority workloads by one minus the sum of the utilizations of all higher priority workloads. For example, if the highest priority workload has a CPU utilization of 50%, one can assume that, on average, every other CPU cycle is consumed by that workload. Thus, it will take twice as long for the CPU requests at the next lower priority to be completed. This can be represented by dividing the service times of these lower priority requests by 1–0.50 (which is equivalent to multiplying service times by 2.0).

To continue with this example, suppose the workload with the second highest priority has a CPU utilization of 25%. The first two highest priority workloads must then have a combined CPU utilization of 75%. Together, they consume three out of every four available CPU cycles. This leaves only one cycle in four available for lower priorities, resulting in a stretch-out factor of 4.0 (equivalent to dividing original service times by 1–0.75). This procedure for computing stretch-out produced the most accurate approximation in Sevcik's 1977 paper.

An alternative approach not considered in that paper is known as Response Time Preservation or RTP.[1] With RTP, the service times are multiplied by factors that yield response times which have the same ratios to one another as are found in the exact solution to an M/M/1 queue with preemptive resume priority scheduling. In the simple case of an open queuing network with no memory constraints, RTP yields exactly the same CPU response times that would be obtained by modeling the CPU as an isolated M/M/1 queue with preemptive resume priority scheduling. Note that dividing service times by one minus the utilization of all higher priority workloads does not yield this result.

Of course, in order to apply RTP in this case it is necessary to know the exact solution of an M/M/1 queue with preemptive-resume priority scheduling. This is a well known result in classical queuing theory. However, symmetric multiprocessor systems (SMPs) had become quite common by the late 1970s. To apply RTP to multiprocessor systems, it was necessary to obtain an exact solution to the previously unsolved case of M/M/n queues with preemptive-resume priority scheduling. Once this solution was obtained,[9] it was a straightforward matter to integrate it into the central server model by following Sevcik's shadow server approach and using RTP.

7. Comments on Significance

The shadow server approximation is important for a number of reasons. First, it leveraged the power of existing queuing network solutions by mapping a model that had no closed form solution into a "shadow model" that could be solved using standard techniques. Evaluation of the "shadow model" then provided a reasonably good approximation to the original intractable model. This general paradigm has wide applicability.

A second important point is that the shadow server approach was presented in a generalized and flexible context along with a number of alternate approximations. The idea of presenting a range of alternative approximations, each with its own level of accuracy and complexity, is important because it often leads to extensible solutions that can be refined by other researchers conducting follow-on research. This was indeed true in the case of the shadow server approximation.

Yet another point is that the shadow server approximation is based on a powerful insight about the dynamics of preemptive resume priority scheduling. It is well known that low priority workloads are essentially invisible to higher priority workloads under preemptive resume scheduling. Moving from this observation to a hierarchy of shadow servers, each dedicated to a separate priority level, constitutes a highly creative leap of imagination.

Finally, the shadow server approximation came along at just the right time for researchers interested in applying the central server model to real world problems. When combined with multi-class queuing networks,[2] the multi-class extension to the convolution algorithm,[14] and the decomposition approach to modeling memory queuing[3,10] the shadow server approximation became part of the core of the original BEST/1 modeling package.[7,8] For this reason, I would like to add a personal note of appreciation on this special occasion. Thanks Ken!

References

1. S. C. Agrawal, J. P. Buzen and A. W. Shum, Response time preservation: A general technique for developing approximate algorithms for queuing networks, *Proc. ACM Sigmetrics Conference* (August 1984), 63–77.
2. F. Baskett, K. M. Chandy, R. R. Muntz and J. Palacios, Open, closed and mixed networks with different classes of customers, *J. ACM* **22**(2) (April 1975), 248–260.
3. A. Brandwajn, A model of a time sharing system solved using equivalence and decomposition methods, *Acta Informatica* **4**(1) (1974), 11–47.
4. J. P. Buzen, Analysis of system bottlenecks using a queuing network model, *Proc. ACM SIGOPS Workshop on System Performance Evaluation* (April 1971), 82–103.
5. J. P. Buzen, Queuing network models of multiprogramming, Ph.D. Dissertation, Harvard University, Cambridge, MA, May 1971.
6. J. P. Buzen, Computational algorithms for closed queuing networks with exponential servers, *Comm. ACM* **15**(9) (September 1973), 527–531.
7. J. P. Buzen, R. P. Goldberg, A. M. Langer, E. Lentz, H. S. Schwenk, D. A. Sheetz and A. W. Shum, BEST/1: Design of a tool for computer system capacity planning, *AFIPS Conference Proc.*, Vol. 47, 1978 National Computer Conference (June 1978), 89–97.
8. J. P. Buzen, A queuing network model of MVS, *ACM Computing Surveys* **10**(3) (September 1978), 319–331.
9. J. P. Buzen and A. Bondi, The response time of priority classes under preemptive-resume in M/M/n queues, *Operations Research* **31**(3) (May 1983), 456–465.
10. P. J. Courtois, *Decomposability: Queuing and Computer System Applications* (Academic Press, NY, 1977).
11. W. J. Gordon and G. F. Newell, Cyclic queuing systems with restricted queue lengths, *Operations Research* **15**(2) (April 1967), 266–277.
12. J. R. Jackson, Jobshop-like queuing systems, *Management Science* **10**(1) (October 1963), 131–142.
13. E. D. Lazowska and J. Zahorjan, Multiple class memory constrained queuing networks, *Proc. ACM Sigmetrics Conf.* (May 1982), 130–140.
14. M. Reiser and H. Kobayashi, Queuing networks with multiple closed chains: Theory and computational algorithms, *IBM Journal of Research and Development* **19** (May 1975), 283–294.
15. K. C. Sevcik, Priority scheduling disciplines in queuing network models of computer systems, *Proc. IFIP Congress '77* (August 1977), 565–570.

CHAPTER 3

On the Chronology of Dynamic Allocation Index Policies: The Pioneering Work of K. C. Sevcik

Ed Coffman

*Department of Electrical Engineering, Columbia University,
1312 Mudd Bldg., 500 W. 120th St., New York, NY 10027, USA
egc@ee.columbia.edu*

Kenneth Sevcik's pioneering result in stochastic scheduling theory seems to be the first dynamic allocation index policy for problems of bandit type. The Sevcik *rank* was the precursor of the much celebrated Gittins *index* that appeared about a year later. We present the main result, put it in the context of the research on these problems in the late sixties to mid seventies, and give a number of illustrations extending those of Sevcik.

1. Introduction

For the present purposes, stochastic scheduling theory refers to the optimal scheduling of jobs on ≥ 1 processors subject to the constraints that all jobs are available at the outset (no arrivals), but job running times are *not* known in advance, only the distribution from which they are independently sampled. (See work by Weiss[17] and Nino Mora[11] for surveys of the field.) Optimality can have several meanings, but the one adopted here is perhaps the most common: minimum expected total loss (or maximum expected total gain/reward), where each job carries its own loss rate. The problem acquires depth only if preemptions are allowed, so that advantage can be taken of elapsed running times to change the jobs currently being run on the processors. For technical reasons often associated with the analysis of preemptive scheduling, preemptions are allowed only at multiples of a basic interval $\delta > 0$, which may be taken as small as desired. Bounded job running times is also a technical requirement. With no significant loss in generality, we assume that running times are multiples of the basic intervals of duration δ. Finally, it will help focus on essentials if we adopt δ as the time unit.

Sevcik's early work on this problem focused on the single-processor case with constant loss rates and no-cost preemptions. The general model allows for multiple classes, each associated with a loss rate and a running-time distribution. His main result is quite elegant, sufficiently so that it can be stated with very little mechanism.

2. Sevcik's Smallest-Rank-First Index Policy

Sevcik's algorithm.

To decide at (integer) time $t \geq 0$ the job to schedule in $[t, t+1]$, compute for each unfinished job j, as a function of i,

$$R_j(t,i) := \frac{E[\min\{i, \text{remaining running time of job } j\}]}{k_j \times \Pr\{\text{job } j \text{ completes within the next } i \text{ time units}\}}$$

and then the extremum, or *rank* of job j,

$$R_j(t) = \min_{i \geq 1} R_j(t,i).$$

By Sevcik's algorithm, the job scheduled during $[t, t+1]$ must be one having least rank. Ties can be broken arbitrarily, but for convenience we will assume that they are broken in favor of the job with lowest index.

Remark. Note that, since the ranks of waiting jobs do not change, a job, say j, with least rank at time t, can be run throughout $[t, t+i_0]$, where i_0 is the largest $i \geq 1$ such that job j has the least rank throughout $[t, t+i]$.

Theorem. Sevcik's algorithm minimizes the expected total loss

$$\sum_j k_j \times \text{expected completion time of job } j.$$

In modern parlance, the reciprocal of Sevcik's term rank is called an *index*,[a] which is to be maximized, so after a trivial problem reformulation, Sevcik's algorithm becomes an index policy. Sevcik gave a rather lengthy inductive proof of the above result, but with the developments in the theory over the past 30 years, it is possible to give at least three other distinct proofs.[5]

---

[a]This use of "index" is not to be confused with our earlier, standard use in enumeration.

3. Background and Chronology

This result was apparently the earliest in the modern index theory of bandit problems, whose origins, up until recently, were credited to the independent, but later result of Gittins and Jones.[6] In their more general dynamic allocation problem, which originated with Bellman,[1] the jobs are usually called processes or projects that operate over a potentially infinite time horizon, and the objective is to maximize the expected total *discounted* reward. In successive time units during which a process operates, the states are determined by a given finite Markov chain (the states of processes not operating in any interval do not change). To fit stochastic scheduling into this model, the state of a process can be taken as the number of time units already received. Each transition is of the form $i \to i+1$, $i \geq 0$, or $i \to s$, where s is an absorbing, job completion state. Transition probabilities are determined by the hazard rates. This problem is easily seen to be subject to a dynamic programming formulation, but the dimensionality of the problem makes solutions within this framework much less efficient than an index policy like that of Sevcik.

The rank/index for the stochastic scheduling problem described here would normally be regarded as equivalent to a Gittins index. The confusion in historical credits seems to be a consequence of the limited communication one often finds between separate (albeit cognate) scientific disciplines. While citations of the journal publication of Sevcik's result[14] and the proceedings publication of the Gittins and Jones result[6] are both dated 1974, Sevcik's result traces back to the publication in August, 1971 of a (still available) Ph.D. thesis[13] in computer science at the University of Chicago, whereas the work of Gittins and Jones traces back to a talk given at a statistics meeting in 1972.

The work of a number of authors can be mentioned as being preliminary to Sevcik's result. The earliest work is that of Olivier,[12] which dealt with versions of the same general problem, but fell short of actually propounding an index policy. Other early papers (with the same shortcoming) include those by Konheim and his colleagues (Chazan *et al.*[4] and Konheim[9]). For other, closely related early work subsequent to that of Sevcik, see work by Klimov,[8] Harrison,[7] Tcha and Pliska,[16] Meilijson and Weiss,[10] Bruno and Hofri[3] and Bruno *et al.*[2]; for more recent work, see the bibliography compiled by R. R. Weber www.statslab.cam.ac.uk/~rrw1/stoc_sched/gittins.bib.

4. Examples

A well-known case, with an easy separate proof, has each class distribution function reduced to a single atom, so running times are effectively known in advance. Sevcik's index rule reduces to Smith's[15] classic rule whereby jobs are run in increasing order of the ratio of running time to loss rate.

Superficially, the SERPT (shortest expected remaining processing time) rule is an intuitive candidate for optimality in the case of equal loss rates. But Sevcik gives a counterexample containing the following special case. Job 1 has running time 1 with probability p and K_1 with probability $1-p$; job 2 has the (deterministic) running time K_2. Normalize the common loss rates to 1. Assuming K_2 is less than $p + (1-p)K_1$ (the expected running time of job 1), then SERPT requires that job 2 be run to completion. The expected total loss is

$$E_1 = 2K_2 + p + (1-p)K_1.$$

But running job 1 for one time unit first, preempting it if it does not complete, and then running job 2 (before finishing job 1) gives

$$E_2 = 1 + p + (2-p)K_2 + (1-p)K_1,$$

which in fact is less than E_1 if $pK_2 > 1$. Roughly speaking, in appropriate regions of the parameter space, an optimal policy must make (relatively) small investments of time when they lead to job completions with sufficiently high probability, despite the fact that SERPT would call for a different decision.

Next, consider the following wide class of practical examples where there is but one class, a unit loss rate, and a distribution with hazard rate $\{h_i\}$, where h_i, $i \geq 0$, is the conditional probability that a job will complete after receiving $i+1$ time units, given that it has already run for i time units. In this case, one finds that Sevcik's rank/index is simply the reciprocal hazard rate. If the hazard rate is monotone increasing, then the Sevcik rule simply runs the jobs non-preemptively. Now suppose the hazard rate is monotone decreasing to some point $k > 0$, and is monotone increasing thereafter. At the outset, jobs lose their least-index status as soon as they begin to run. In this case, the jobs are run round-robin one time unit at a time until they depart, or until all that remain have received exactly k time units of service. Beyond that point, jobs are run non-preemptively, as in the previous example. From these examples, it is easy to piece together the possible sample paths for any $\{h_i\}$, bearing in mind that, at some point, $\{h_i\}$ must increase to 1, since running times are bounded.

Note that, when multiple running jobs have the same index and decreasing hazard rates, the limit, as the time unit shrinks to 0, of Sevcik's algorithm becomes classical processor sharing. Clearly, the geometric distribution (or the exponential distribution in the above continuous limit) is an indeterminate singular point of Sevcik's algorithm.

This discussion is easily extended to differing, constant loss rates; the index now incorporates constant factors (the loss rates) into the hazard rates. Note that, when running jobs have decreasing hazard rates, the "shares" in processor sharing are proportional to loss factors.

5. Concluding Remarks

Sevcik's result typifies those elegantly simple results that make researchers slap their foreheads in frustration, and say: "Why didn't I think of that?" It cannot only lay claim to historical primacy, but to the essential unification of numerous modern scheduling policies within a framework of stochastic optimization. Sevcik long since moved on to seminal work in other areas of Computer Science (as is evidenced by the papers in this volume), but he has left behind a cornerstone of stochastic scheduling theory and the theory of dynamic allocation index policies.

References

1. R. Bellman, A problem in the sequential design of experiments, *Sankhia* **16** (1956), 221–229.
2. J. L. Bruno, E. G. Coffman and D. B. Johnson, On batch scheduling of jobs with stochastic service times and cost structures on a single server, *J. Comp. Sys. Sci.* **12** (1976), 319–335.
3. J. L. Bruno and M. Hofri, On scheduling chains of jobs on one processor with limited preemptions, *SIAM J. Comput.* **4**(4) (1975), 478–490.
4. D. Chazan, A. Konheim and B. Weiss, A note on time-sharing, *J. Combinatorial Theory* **5**(4) (1968), 344–369.
5. E. Frostig and G. Weiss, Four proofs of Gittins's multiarmed bandit theorem, available on the Internet (1999).
6. J. C. Gittins and D. M. Jones, A dynamic allocation index for the sequential design of experiments, in *Progress in Statistics (European Meeting of Statisticians, 1972)*, ed. J. Gani (North-Holland, Amsterdam, NL, 1974), pp. 241–266.
7. J. M. Harrison, Dynamic scheduling of a multiclass queue, discount optimality, *Operations Research* **23** (1975), 270–282.
8. G. P. Klimov, Time sharing service systems, I, *Theory of Probability and Applications* **19** (1974), 532–551.

9. A. G. Konheim, A note on time-sharing with preferred customers, *Z. Wahrschienlichkeitstheorie u. Verw. Geb.* **9** (1968), 112–130.
10. I. Meilijson and G. Weiss, Multiple feedback at a single server station, *Probability Theory and Related Fields* **5** (1977), 195–205.
11. J. Nino Mora, Stochastic scheduling, in *Encyclopedia of Optimization*, Vol. V, eds. C. Floutas and P. Pardalos (Kluwer, Dordrecht, 2001), pp. 367–372.
12. G. Olivier, Optimale zeitzuteilung fuer wartende rechenaufgaben, *Elektron. Rechenanlagen* **9**(5) (1967), 218–224.
13. K. C. Sevcik, *The use of service time distributions in scheduling*, Ph.D. thesis, University of Chicago, August 1971.
14. K. C. Sevcik, Scheduling for minimum total loss using service time distributions, *Journal of the ACM* **21** (1974), 66–75.
15. W. E. Smith, Various optimizers for single stage production, *Naval Res. Log. Quart.* **3** (1956), 59–66.
16. D. Tcha and S. R. Pliska, Optimal control of single server queueing networks and multi-class m/g/1 queues with feedback, *Operations Research* **25** (1975), 248–258.
17. G. Weiss, A tutorial in stochastic scheduling, in *Scheduling Theory and Its Applications*, eds. P. Chretienne, E. Coffman, J. Lenstra and Z. Liu (Wiley, Canada, 1995).

CHAPTER 4

Operational Analysis

Peter J. Denning
*Computer Science Department,
Naval Postgraduate School,
Monterey, CA 93943, USA
pjd@nps.edu*

Operational analysis is a branch of queueing network models. It derives the basic equations for calculating throughput, response time, and congestion from fully operational assumptions. These assumptions, applicable in any finite observation period, require that all variables be directly measurable and all modeling assumptions be directly testable. In this framework, the steady-state stochastic limit theorems become operational laws that hold in every observation period. The resulting model applies in many cases where stochastic models do not. Operational analysis was created during the late 1970s to explain why Markovian queueing network models worked so well for real computer and network systems, even though the systems violated almost all the assumptions of the Markovian model. Operational analysis considerably simplifies the theory needed to deal with practical queueing systems and gives an indisputable edge to teaching, understanding, and communicating about queueing networks.

1. Introduction

In 1975, Jeff Buzen and I discovered we shared a concern about a fundamental problem we observed in the field of performance analysis. This article is about that concern, what we did about it, and a key role that Ken Sevick played in the outcome.

2. Dead Cows

My friend and teacher, Fernando Flores, likes to tell his business clients the story of Pasteur and the dead cows. In the 1870s the French sheep and cattle industry was being decimated by anthrax and France's economic position was in grave peril. At the time, the farmers were completely baffled by the mounting toll of dead cows and sheep; the cause, anthrax, had not yet been identified and named. Although a few researchers, including Pasteur, believed that a microbe might be the cause, the theory that diseases could be caused by microbes was so much at odds with conventional thinking that few physicians accepted it; Pasteur could not even persuade surgeons to wash their hands and use clean instruments. Finally, in 1882, Pasteur was challenged to "put up or shut up" by a French veterinarian. Pasteur vaccinated 25 of a group of 50 sheep with his anthrax vaccine; all 50 then received a lethal dose of anthrax. Every one of the vaccinated sheep survived without symptoms and every one of the unvaccinated sheep died within three days. Pasteur became a national hero. From that time forward, the medical profession came to believe in the germ theory of disease and in vaccinations to prevent disease. Within two years, anthrax was virtually eliminated from the French cattle and sheep industry.

Flores aimed his story at entrepreneurs: if you want to make an innovation that people will care about and value, look for the dead cows.

3. Dead Cows in Markovian Queueing Networks

Network-of-queues models were very attractive for computing systems and networks. They directly represent systems of servers in which jobs circulate. When a job arrives at a server, it waits in queue and then receives an interval of service before departing for another server. The state of the system at any given time is a vector $\boldsymbol{n} = (n_1, \ldots, n_K)$ saying how many jobs are queued at each server. Randomness arises in these systems because the length of service during a visit to a server, and the next server visited after a departure, are not known. The randomness is described by a service distribution at each server and by a probability distribution of next server after a departure.

The traditional stochastic model (SM) for such systems assumes that the process by which the system moves through its states is Markovian: the successive service times are independent, successive transitions between servers are independent, the service distributions are exponential, and the system reaches a steady state.

A few tests during the 1960s and 1970s of the fit between these models and the throughput and response times of real systems were highly encouraging. For example, in 1965 Alan Scherr of MIT showed that the simple two-server "machine repairman" model could be used to predict quite accurately the throughput and response time of the first time-sharing systems. Forest Baskett observed similar fits between models and measurements on systems at the University of Texas in the early 1970s.

Although they had the right structure, queueing network models were unattractive because of the high computation needed to calculate performance quantities with them. In the 1950s, Jackson, and again in the 1960s Jackson, Gordon, and Newell showed that the equilibrium state probability distribution of a network of queues model decomposed into a product form when arrivals and service times were all exponentials. Although the product form was much simpler to evaluate than numerically solving the balance equations, the computations were still intractable for all but the smallest systems. Thus testing the model was limited to small systems. In 1971, Jeff Buzen demonstrated a breakthrough: a quadratic algorithm for evaluating the product form. Suddenly performance analysts could compare models with large, real systems. In a long line of experimental studies, performance analysts concluded that these models would typically get throughput correct to within 10% of the observed value, and response time to within 25% of the observed value. Soon thereafter blossomed the now-flourishing industry of system performance evaluation and capacity planning.

But depite their empirical success, these models presented a serious problem. While performance analysts repeatedly found users interested in their queueing models, they constantly faced skepticism because no one trusted the models' assumptions. The models assumed that a system was in equilibrium; measurements in real systems showed constantly shifting measures and parameters at different times of day and days of the week. The models assumed that inter-server job transitions were independent; in real systems transitions correlated with previous transitions. The models assumed that the service times at the servers were exponentially distributed; real systems had distinctly non-exponential service distributions, including many with very long tails. This presented a troubling paradox: the real world of computing systems consistently violated all the model assumptions, and yet the models agreed remarkably closely with observed throughput and response time.

This paradox was not a simple annoyance; it was standing in the way of business. Jeff Buzen and his partners, who were establishing a company (BGS Systems) to build and market performance prediction and capacity planning tools for the computing industry, knew this first hand. Distributed computing systems and networked systems were increasingly common and the performance and capacity questions for these systems were high on the minds of designers and users. Business executives were prepared to invest significantly in performance prediction and capacity planning — their customers demanded it — and yet they felt it unsafe to invest in technology based on what appeared to be black magic, technology whose limits were not understood.

To sidestep the skepticism, pragmatists pressed an empirical argument: "So what if the model assumptions don't hold? We can show empirically that the equations from the models work well, and that should be good enough for practical performance analysts." But business people weren't buying that argument. Did the empirical models rest on still hidden, deep principles? Or where they *ad hoc*? No one knew what the limits of the models might be or for which real systems they might fail. In other words, dead cows littered the intellectual landscape of performance modeling.

4. The Birth of Operational Analysis

Several of us were concerned about this and had started independent searches for a "vaccine." Dick Muntz and John Wong published a paper in the 1974 Princeton Conference showing that some of the formulas, including those for utilization, response time, and throughput, held in the limit for very general networks.[11] Jeff Buzen and I started to discuss this in 1975. We were struck by the parallels in our thinking and decided to collaborate. Jeff had already drafted papers, published in 1976, about fundamental laws (utilization, throughput, and response time) that were always true because of the way they were defined for collected data.[2,3] Jeff suggested the term "operational analysis" to differentiate the approach from stochastic analysis. With my students I worked on a series of technical reports applying this form of analysis to multiprogrammed virtual memory systems in 1975.[1,14–16] Jeff and I published a series of papers taking operational analysis into queueing networks beginning in 1977[4–7,13] I followed up with versions for *American Scientist* in 1991.[8,9]

The operational approach goes to fundamentals. In validating models, analysts substitute measured, operational values of parameters for the model's stochastic parameters. We wondered whether the direct substitution of measured values might be equivalent to interpreting the product form as the solution to a broader class of systems than the Markovian assumptions suggested. Could we find another set of assumptions that give the same equations but apply to large classes of real systems?

Queueing theory gives various limit theorems relating basic quantities for systems in equilibrium. For example, the utilization of a server is the product of the arrival rate and the mean service time ($U = XS$). In those days, we would "prove" this by solving a system's equations for utilization as a function of time and then taking the limit as time becomes infinite. Because students found it difficult to follow the mathematical details of such a proof, we would also offer an "intuitive" explanation based on how we would verify the limit theorem through an experiment. The intuitive explanation was this. If we observe a server for a period of time T, we can measure the number of service completions, C, and the total busy time, B. We can then empirically define the utilization as $U = B/T$, the mean service time as $S = B/C$, and the throughput as $X = C/T$. But with these definitions, it is *always* true that $U = XS$. The limit theorem of stochastic theory becomes an operational law when applied directly to the measured data.

We quickly found that several other limit theorems are also laws in the same way. For example, Little's law is $N = RX$, for mean number N in the system and mean response time R of the system. The forced flow law in a network is $X_i = XV_i$ where X_i is the throughput at server i, X the system throughput, and V_i the mean number of visits by a job to server i. The time sharing response time law is $R = N/X - Z$, where N is the number of users and Z is the average think time between submitting new commands. The memory space-time law says $XY = M$, where Y is the mean space-time per job and M is the total amount of memory used by jobs.

Jeff and I decided to see if we could start there, rather than finish there. Instead of concluding that $U = XS$ is true of systems in the limit, why not start with the observation that $U = XS$ is *always* true because of the way we define our measurements? In other words, $U = XS$ is a law that holds for all observation periods, including but not limited to those in Markovian equilibrium.

We found this so compelling that we then asked: Can we build a queueing theory that starts from the operational laws and avoids making any Markovian or equilibrium assumptions? To our delight we were able to do this. Operational Analysis (OA) became a vaccine whose new interpretation of systems prevented the death of trust in models (the cows).

5. The Fundamental Assumptions of Operational Analysis

We insisted that all assumptions we would make in our theory be operational, meaning that one can design an experiment to observe all the quantities we define. The experimental measurements would always be calculated in a given, arbitrary observation period of length T.

We insisted on testability, not because we advocated that everything be tested, but because we wanted the theory to be founded on behaviors that people can easily visualize. We often made an analogy with an old argument in physics where field theory replaced action-at-a-distance. One could explain the electrical attraction of two charged particles as an action over a distance (Coulomb's law); or one could say that one particle moves in the electric field of the other. The electric field was operational: one can imagine a small particle placed at any point in the field, and from the field direction and intensity one could say how the particle would move (a Δx in the next Δt). We fully realized that the large state spaces of networked systems would preclude actually testing all the assumptions, but we wanted to state them in a way that anyone wishing to understand the experiment would know exactly what we meant.

For queueing systems, the states $\boldsymbol{n} = (n_1, \ldots, n_K)$ are vectors giving the number of jobs queued up at each server. Stochastic modeling assigns an equilibrium probability $p(\boldsymbol{n})$ to each state. Operational analysis instead interprets the $p(\boldsymbol{n})$ as the proportions of time that the system spends in state $\boldsymbol{n}$. We called these $p(\boldsymbol{n})$ the *state occupancies*.

We re-formulated the familiar balance equations among the equilibrium $p(\boldsymbol{n})$ into balances of state transitions: entries = exits. We called this assumption *flow balance*. Entries and exits from states are observable and can be measured. Because the numbers of entries and exits need not match, we said that it is only an assumption that they are equal. We calculated the error that would arise in a solution of the balance equations when flow is not balanced in the real system. We showed that in long observation periods of systems with finite state spaces, the error caused by flow balance is negligible.

Because we wanted the balance equations to conform to the operational laws, we wanted the state transitions of the system to coincide with job completions at the individual servers. In other words, we wanted state transitions to correspond one-one with inter-server job transitions. This was easily accomplished with a second assumption: that each state change is caused by exactly one job completion. We called this assumption *one-step behavior*. As with flow balance, we calculated the error caused by this assumption and showed that in most real systems the error would be negligible.

With these two assumptions, the balance equations are mathematically identical to the equilibrium state probability equations of the same system interpreted as Markovian. We needed a third operational assumption to reduce these equations to the same form from which Jackson, Gordon, and Newell obtained the product form solution. This happened when we assumed that the rate of transitions between two states is identical to the rate of job-flow between the servers causing the transitions. We called this assumption *homogeneity*. As with the other two assumptions, we could calculate the error caused by this assumption. Unlike the other two assumptions, however, we could not show that the homogeneity error is negligible. In fact, in some systems, homogeneity introduces considerable error.

Under the homogeneity assumption, the configuration of queue lengths in the rest of the system does not affect the completion rate of a server, and hence that rate can be measured by studying the server in isolation from all other servers. Thus the homogeneity assumption is equivalent to an assumption that a server has the same completion rate (for a given queue length) in an on-line measurement as it will in an off-line measurement. For this reason we also called the homogeneity assumption the "on-line equals off-line" assumption.

Taken together, the three assumptions allowed us to reduce the balance equations and conclude that the state occupancies obey the same product form structure as had been found by Jackson, Gordon, and Newell.

We thus arrived at the same mathematical form as the Markovian theory, but with a completely operational interpretation. In addition to dealing directly with measured parameters, the operational interpretation can be applied in any finite observation period. It allows us to calculate the error caused by any of the three key assumptions. We had found a way to formulate queueing network theory so that the product form solution holds for finite intervals in which the system is flow balanced, one step, and homogeneous. Therefore, all the algorithms for solving product form networks could be used with confidence in many practical situations where their validity was dubious according to Markovian assumptions.

We found that operational analysis was less satisfactory for more complex systems such as an $M/G/1$ queue. Although we were able to formulate operational assumptions for the famous Pollaczek–Khinchtine formula for the mean queue length, the assumptions were more complex and harder to understand. The mathematics of transform analysis, which are well known in stochastic modeling, got to the same result more quickly.

6. Controversy

The new theory attracted a lot of attention — from strong praise to strong criticism. In 1979, Ken Sevcik summarized the best and worst of the assessments about operational analysis (OA) and stochastic modeling (SM) as follows[12]:

- "OA offers nothing but tautologies."
- "OA makes SM obsolete."
- "OA is a smokescreen for trivially deriving the obvious from the known."
- "SM is a security blanket used to smother intuition by those who lack it."

The most popular criticism focused on the homogeneity assumption, which the critics believed to be fundamentally equivalent to the exponential assumption. Ken attacked this criticism head on. In 1979 (with Maria Klawe) he gave several examples of deterministic systems that are flow-balanced, one-step, and homogeneous — but obviously not Markovian. That was a turning point in the acceptance of operational analysis as a valid alternative to the traditional queueing theory. Many skeptics came on board after that. Ken drew several conclusions about the debate in 1979:

> OA invokes a different level of abstraction from the SM: the two systems have the same symbols but interpret them differently. SM refers to probabilistic ensembles of system behaviors; OA refers to one behavior at a time. OA is more obviously relevant to real systems than SM. OA generates confidence in applying models by offering assumptions that are understandable and testable. OA and SM are complementary approaches. OA offers much that is new; SM isn't obsolete.

After that, the debate became more philosophical. What does it mean to model? How are the approaches of SM and OA to creating and interpreting system models the same? Different? A hot example of this kind was the use of the models for performance prediction. The traditional practice of SM was to assume that the same stochastic process governs both the base and future observation periods. Therefore, one estimates the parameters from data in the base period and extrapolates them to the future period. Jeff and I argued that this practice didn't depend on an underlying SM. All it depended on was extrapolation of parameters to the future period. In any observation period, the computation of performance metrics from parameters uses algorithms that do not care whether the product form solution comes of operational or stochastic assumptions.

In 1981 I was present at a debate between Jeff Buzen and his critics. Neither the OA believers nor the SM believers were able to muster any argument that would change minds. Afterwards I wrote a fable to satirize the debate and suggest that the two sides may never come to an accord. A copy is attached as an appendix.

Despite their differences, the OA and SM believers did have one major point of agreement: almost everyone found it *much* easier to teach queueing networks to beginning students when starting with the operational interpretation. I was able to teach queueing network basics to undergraduate computer science students in about two weeks of an operating systems class, compared to almost a whole course for Markovian theory. By thinking in the operational framework, my OS students developed a much better "feel" for how the models worked and their scopes of applicability. Ken Sevcik experienced the same thing with his students. Jeff Buzen experienced it in teaching his clients how the models work and why they can be trusted. Operational analysis gave an indisputable edge to teaching, understanding, and communicating about queueing networks. Because of this Ken embraced operational analysis to explain queueing theory in his best-selling book, which became the leading book in the field for many years.[10] More recent authors, such as Menascé and Almeida, have adopted operational analysis as their pedagogic tool for the same reason.

7. Salute

So I salute Ken Sevcik, whose insight at a critical point turned the tide in our favor and showed the skeptics that homogeneity was indeed a new assumption, more primitive and broader in scope than Markovian assumptions. Ken helped clear the field of its dead cows.

8. An Historical Footnote

When we formulated operational analysis, "queueing" had two "e's" in it. Microsoft Office spell checker now claims that "queuing" is the proper spelling. I tell recalcitrant editors that queueing is the only word in English with five consecutive vowels. So far this argument has prevailed.

References (Published)

1. G. Balbo and P. Denning, Homogeneous approximations of general queueing networks, *Proc. Int. Symp. on Computer Performance Measurement, Modelling, and Evaluation*, Vienna, Austria (North-Holland Publishing Co., 1979).
2. J. Buzen, Fundamental laws of computer system performance, *Proc. IFIP-SIGMETRICS Int. Symp. on Computer Performance Modeling, Measurement, and Evalaution*, Cambridge, MA (March 1976), 200–210.

3. J. Buzen, Operational analysis: The key to the new generation of performance prediction tools, *Proc. IEEE COMPCON 76*, Washington, DC (September 1976), 166–171.
4. J. Buzen and P. Denning, Measuring and calculating queue length distributions, *IEEE Computer* **13**(4) (April 1980), 33–44.
5. J. Buzen and P. Denning, Operational treatment of queue distributions and mean value analysis, *Computer Performance* **1**(1) (June 1980), 6–15.
6. P. Denning and J. Buzen, Operational analysis of queueing networks, *Proc. 3rd Int. Symp. on Modelling and Performance Evaluation of Computer Systems* (North-Holland Publishing Co., 1977), 151–172.
7. P. Denning and J. Buzen, The operational analysis of queueing network models, *Computing Surveys* **10**(3) (September 1978), 225–261 [Reprinted in *CMG Transactions*, Summer 1994, 29–60].
8. P. Denning, Queueing in networks of computers, *American Scientist* **79**(3) (May–June 1991), 206–209.
9. P. Denning, In the Queue: Mean Values, *American Scientist* **79**(5) (September–October 1991), 402–403.
10. E. Lazowska, J. Zahorjan, G. Scott Graham and K. Sevcik, *Quantitative System Performance* (Prentice-Hall, 1984).
11. R. Muntz and J. Wong, Asymptotic properties of closed queueing network models, *Proc. 8th Princeton Conf. on Information Sciences and Systems*, Dept. EECS, Princeton University (1974), 348–352.
12. K. C. Sevcik and M. Klawe, Operational analysis versus stochastic modelling of computer systems, *Proc. of Computer Science Statistics: 12th Annual Symp. on the Interface*, Waterloo, Canada (May 1979), 177–184.

References (Unpublished Technical Reports)

13. J. Buzen and P. Denning, Operational analysis of Markov chains, File Memorandum PD78.1 (May 1978).
14. P. Denning and K. Kahn, Some distribution free properties of throughput and response time, Purdue University, CS Dept., CSD-TR-159 (May 1975), 28 pp.
15. P. Denning, Operational laws of system performance, File Memorandum PD75.6 (June 1975), 8 pp.
16. P. Denning, Asymptotic properties of multiprogrammed response, File Memorandum PD75.11 (August 1975), 13 pp.

Appendix — Operational Analysis: A Fable

Peter J. Denning
Version of 30 Jan 1991

Operational queueing theory was controversial among queueing theorists. A popular criticism was that the operational assumption of homogeneity — service rates of servers do not depend on total system state — was nothing more than an exponential service-time assumption in disguise. That criticism was neatly dispelled by Ken Sevick and Maria Klawe, whose examples of operationally-deterministic systems in no sense satisfied an exponential service time assumption, but satisfied product form solutions. Another criticism was that one cannot make predictions of a future system's performance without assuming the present and future systems are manifestations of the same underlying stochastic process. Buzen said that stochastic processes had nothing to do with it; he argued that prediction in practice operates as a process of extrapolating present to future parameter values and then using a validated model to calculate future performance measures. Such logic did little to assuage some critics, who maintained that operational analysis denied the existence of stochastic processes.

In 1981, I witnessed a debate between Buzen and his critics. I was struck by the symmetry of their arguments. Each started with his domain as the ground and claimed that the other was in effect performing unneeded, error-inducing mappings to get to the same answer. They were both describing the same loop from different angles! This prompted me to write the following little fable.

A Tale of Two Islands

Once upon a time there were two islands. The citizens of Stochasia had organized their society around a revered system of mathematics for random processes. The citizens of Operatia had organized their society around a revered system for experimentation with nondeterminate physical processes. Both societies were closed. Neither would ever have known of the other's existence had it not been for the events I shall now describe.

At a moment now lost in the mists of antiquity, a great sage of Stochasia posed this problem: Given a matrix of transition probabilities, find the corresponding equilibrium probability distribution of occupying the possible states. He worked out the solution, which he engraved on stones. Ever since, whenever they encounter a problem in life, the Stochasians phrase it in these terms and, using the stones, they find and implement its solution.

At a moment now lost in the mists of antiquity, a great sage of Operatia posed this problem: Having observed a matrix of transition frequencies, calculate the corresponding distribution of proportions of time of occupying the possible states. He worked out the solution, which he engraved on stones. Ever since, whenever they encounter a problem in life, the Operatians phrase it in these terms and, using the stones, they find and implement its solution.

In a recent time there was an anthropologist who specialized in islands. He discovered these two islands from photographs taken by an orbiting satellite. He went to visit Stochasia, where he learned the secrets of their stones. He also visited Operatia, where he learned the secrets of their stones.

Struck by the similarities, the anthropologist asked the elders of each island to evaluate the approach used by the other island. In due course, each island's elders reached a decision.

The elders of Operatia told the anthropologist: "The Stochasians are hopelessly confused. They have developed a highly indirect approach to solving the problem posed by our great sage. First, they transform the problem into an untestable domain by a process we would call 'abstraction'. Using their stones, they find the abstract answer corresponding to the abstract problem. Finally, they equate the abstract answer with the real world by a process we would call 'interpretation.' They make the audacious claim that their result is useful, even though the two key steps, abstraction and interpretation, can nowise be tested for accuracy. Indeed, these two steps cannot be tested even in principle! Our stones tell us elegantly how to calculate the real result directly from the real data. No extra steps are needed, and nothing untestable is ever used."

The elders of Stochasia told the anthropologist: "The Operatians are hopelessly confused. They have developed a highly indirect approach to solving the problem posed by our great sage. First, they restrict the problem to a single case by a process we would call 'estimation'. Using their stones, they estimate the answer corresponding to their estimate of the problem. Finally, they equate the estimated answer with the real world by a process we would call 'induction.' They make the audacious claim that their result is useful, even though the two key steps, estimation and induction, are nowise error free. Indeed, these two steps cannot be accurate even in principle! Our stones tell us elegantly how to calculate the general answer directly from the parameters. No extra steps are needed, and nothing inaccurate is ever used."

The anthropologist believed both these arguments and was confused. So he went away and searched for new islands.

Some years later, the anthropologist discovered a third island called Determia. Its citizens believe randomness is an illusion. They are certain that all things can be completely explained if all the facts are known. On studying the stones of Stochasia and Operatia, the elders of Determia told the anthropologist: "The Stochasians and Operatians are both hopelessly confused. Neither's approach is valid. All you have to do is look at the real world and you can see for yourself whether or not each state is occupied. There is nothing uncertain about it: each state is or is not occupied at any given time. It is completely determined."

Later, he told this to an Stochasian, who laughed: "That's nonsense. It is well known that deterministic behavior occurs with probability zero. Therefore, it is of no importance. How did you find their island at all?" Still later, he told this to an Operatian, who laughed: "I don't know how to respond. We have not observed such behavior. Therefore it is of no importance. How did you find their island at all?"

The anthropologist believed all these arguments and was profoundly confused. So he went away and searched for more new islands. I don't know what became of him, but I heard he discovered Noman. (Noman is an island.)

CHAPTER 5

Function Approximation by Random Neural Networks with a Bounded Number of Layers

Erol Gelenbe*

*Department of Electrical & Electronic Eng.,
Imperial College, London SW7 2BT, UK
e.gelenbe@imperial.ac.uk*

Zhi-Hong Mao[†] and Yan-Da Li[‡]

*Department of Automation, Tsinghua University,
Beijing 100084, P. R. China
†maozh@jerry.au.tsinghua.edu.cn*

This paper discusses the function approximation properties of the "Gelenbe" random neural network (GNN).[5,6,9] We use two extensions of the basic model: the bipolar GNN (BGNN)[7] and the clamped GNN (CGNN). We limit the networks to being feedforward and consider the case where the number of hidden layers does not exceed the number of input layers. With these constraints we show that the feedforward CGNN and the BGNN with s hidden layers (total of $s + 2$ layers) can uniformly approximate continuous functions of s variables.

1. Introduction

A novel neural network model — the GNN or "Gelenbe's Random Neural Network"[5,6,9] — has had significant applications in various engineering areas,[7,8,10–15] using the network's learning algorithm[9] or its ability to act as an optimizing network. These random neural networks differ significantly from standard connexionist models in that information travels between

---

*Supported by the Office of Naval Research and NAWC under Contract Nos. N00014-97-1-0112, N61339-97-K-005 and N61339-00-K-002.
‡Supported by the National Science Foundation of the P. R. of China under Grant No. 69682010.

neurons in this model in the form of random spike trains, and the network state is represented by the probability distributions that the n neurons in the network are excited. These models have a mathematical structure which is significantly different from that of the sigmoidal connexionist model, the Hopfield model, or the Boltzman machine.[3] Thus the approximation capability of these networks also needs to be established in a manner distinct from that of previous models.[4] In particular, the "Gelenbe" random neural network model[5,6,9] does not use sigmoid functions which are basic to the standard models' approximation capabilities.

In recent work[16] we have studied the approximation of arbitrary continuous functions on $[0,1]^s$ using the GNN. We have shown that the clamped GNN and the bipolar GNN[7] have the universal approximation property, using a constructive method which actually exhibits networks constructed from a polynomial approximation of the function to be approximated. However, the constructions in Ref. 16 place no restrictions on the structure of the networks except for limiting them to being feedforward. For instance, in Ref. 16 we were not able to limit the size of the network as a function of other meaningful characteristics such as the number of input variables or the number of layers.

In this paper we will discuss the design of GNN approximators with a bounded number of layers. In Sec. 2, a brief introduction to the GNN and the bipolar GNN (BGNN) is given. In Sec. 3, we establish the technical premises for our main results. Then, in Sec. 4, we prove the universal approximation capability of the feedforward BGNN and CGNN when the number of hidden layers does not exceed the number of input variables. The last section presents conclusions.

2. The GNN and Its Extensions

Consider a GNN[5,6,9] with n neurons in which "positive" and "negative" signals circulate. The ith neuron's state is represented at any time t by its "potential" $k_i(t)$, which is a non-negative integer. In the RNN[5,6] signals in the form of spikes of unit amplitude circulate among the neurons. Positive signals represent excitation and negative signals represent inhibition. Each neuron's state is a non-negative integer called its potential, which increases when an excitation signal arrives, and decreases when an inhibition signal arrives. An excitatory spike is interpreted as a "+1" signal at a receiving neuron, while an inhibitory spike is interpreted as a "−1" signal. Neural potential also decreases when the neuron fires. Thus a neuron i emitting a spike, whether it be an excitation or an inhibition, will lose potential of one unit, going from some state whose value is k_i to the state of value $k_i - 1$. In general, this is a "recurrent network" model, i.e., a network which is allowed to have feedback loops of arbitrary topology.

The state of the n-neuron network at time t, is represented by the vector of non-negative integers $k(t) = (k_1(t), \ldots, k_n(t))$, where $k_i(t)$ is the potential or integer state of neuron i. We will denote by k and k_i arbitrary values of the state vector and of the ith neuron's state. Neuron i will "fire" (i.e., become excited and send out spikes) if its potential is *positive*. The spikes will then be sent out at a rate $r(i) \geq 0$, with independent, identically and exponentially distributed inter-spike intervals. Spikes will go out to some neuron j with probability $p^+(i,j)$ as excitatory signals, or with probability $p^-(i,j)$ as inhibitory signals. A neuron may also send signals out of the network with probability $d(i)$, and $d(i) + \sum_{j=1}^{n}[p^+(i,j) + p^-(i,j)] = 1$.

Exogenous excitatory signals arrive to neuron i in a Poisson stream of rate $\Lambda(i)$. Similarly exogenous inhibitory signals arrive to neuron i in a Poisson stream of rate $\lambda(i)$. These different Poisson streams for $i = 1, \ldots, n$ are independent of each other. To simplify the notation, in the sequel we will write:

$$\omega^+(i,j) = r(i)p^+(i,j), \tag{1}$$
$$\omega^-(i,j) = r(i)p^-(i,j). \tag{2}$$

The state transitions of the network are represented by Chapman–Kolmogorov equations[1] for the probability distribution:

$$p(k,t) = Prob[k(t) = k], \tag{3}$$

where $k = (k_1, \ldots, k_n)$ denotes a particular value of the state vector.

Let $\lambda^+(i)$ and $\lambda^-(i)$ denote the average arrival rates of positive and negative signals to each neuron i. The key results about the GNN developed in Refs. 5, 6 and 9 are summarized below.

Theorem 1. (Proposition 1 in the Appendix of Ref. 9.) *There always exists a non-negative solution* $(\lambda^+(i) \geq 0, \lambda^-(i) \geq 0)$ *to the equations*:

$$\lambda^+(i) = \Lambda(i) + \sum_{j=1}^{n} q_j \omega^+(j,i), \tag{4}$$

$$\lambda^-(i) = \lambda(i) + \sum_{j=1}^{n} q_j \omega^-(j,i), \tag{5}$$

for $i = 1, \ldots, n$, where

$$q_i = \frac{\lambda^+(i)}{r(i) + \lambda^-(i)}. \tag{6}$$

The next important result concerns the stationary joint probability distribution of network state:

$$p(k) = \lim_{t \to \infty} p(k, t). \tag{7}$$

Theorem 2. (Theorem 1 of Ref. 5.) *For an n-neuron GNN, let the vector of neuron potentials at time t be $k(t) = (k_1(t), k_2(t), \ldots, k_n(t))$, and let $k = (k_1, k_2, \ldots, k_n)$ be an n-vector of non-negative integers. Then if the q_i in (6) satisfy $0 \leq q_i < 1$, the stationary joint probability of network state is given by:*

$$p(k) = \prod_{i=1}^{n}(1 - q_i)q_i^{k_i}. \tag{8}$$

Note that if the conditions of Theorem 2 are satisfied, then the stationary probability distribution of the state of neuron i denoted by $p(k_i) = \lim_{t \to \infty} p(k_i(t) = k_i)$, is given by:

$$p(k_i) = (1 - q_i)q_i^{k_i} \tag{9}$$

and

$$q_i = \lim_{t \to \infty} \text{Prob}\{k_i(t) > 0\}. \tag{10}$$

2.1. *The BGNN model*

In order to represent bipolar patterns taking values such as $\{+1, -1\}$, and to strengthen the associative memory capabilities of the GNN, in some early work Gelenbe, Stafylopatis and Likas[7] extended the original model by introducing the artifact of "positive and negative" neurons. The resulting Bipolar GNN (BGNN) can also be viewed as the coupling of two complementary standard GNN models.

In the BGNN the two types of neurons have opposite roles. A positive neuron behaves exactly as a neuron in the original GNN. A negative neuron has a completely symmetrical behavior, namely, only negative signals can accumulate at this neuron, and the role of positive signals arriving to a negative neuron is to eliminate negative signals which have accumulated in a negative neuron's potential. A positive signal arriving to a negative neuron

i cancels a negative signal (adds +1 to the neuron's negative potential), and has no effect if $k_i = 0$.

This extension is in fact mathematically equivalent to the original GNN described above, with respect to the specific form taken by the stationary solution (Theorems 1 and 2). However, the use of both positive and negative neurons allows the BGNN to become a convenient universal approximator for continuous functions because of the possibility of using both positive and negative valued functions of the input variables. Let P and N denote, respectively, the indices of the positive and negative neurons in the network. In the BGNN the state of the network is represented by the vector $k(t) = (k_1(t), \ldots, k_n(t))$ so that $k_i(t) \geq 0$ if $i \in P$ and $k_i(t) \leq 0$ if $i \in N$.

In the BGNN, the emission of signals from a positive neuron is the same as in the original GNN. Similarly, a negative neuron may emit negative signals. A signal leaving negative neuron i arrives at neuron j as a negative signal with probability $p^+(i,j)$ and as a positive signal with probability $p^-(i,j)$. Also, a signal departs from the network upon leaving neuron i with probability $d(i)$. Other assumptions and denotations are retained as in the original model.

Let us consider a BGNN with n nodes. Since negative signals account for the potential of negative neurons, we will use negative values for k_i if neuron i is negative. If we take into account the distinction between positive and negative neurons, Theorems 1 and 2 can be summarized as follows for the BGNN. The flow of signals in the network is described by the following equations:

$$\lambda^+(i) = \Lambda(i) + \sum_{j \in P} q_j \omega^+(j,i) + \sum_{j \in N} q_j \omega^-(j,i), \tag{11}$$

$$\lambda^-(i) = \lambda(i) + \sum_{j \in P} q_j \omega^-(j,i) + \sum_{j \in N} q_j \omega^+(j,i), \tag{12}$$

and

$$q_i = \frac{\lambda^+(i)}{r(i) + \lambda^-(i)}, \quad i \in P, \tag{13}$$

$$q_i = \frac{\lambda^-(i)}{r(i) + \lambda^+(i)}, \quad i \in N. \tag{14}$$

Using a direct extension of the results for the conventional GNN, it can be shown that a non-negative solution $\{\lambda^+(i), \lambda^-(i), i = 1, \ldots, n\}$ exists to the above equations. If the $q_i < 1$, $i = 1, \ldots, n$, then the steady-state joint probability distribution of network state is given by[7]:

$$p(k) = \prod_{i=1}^{n}(1-q_i)q_i^{|k_i|}, \qquad (15)$$

where the quantity q_i is the steady-state probability that node i is "excited." Note the $|k_i|$ exponent in the above product form, since the k_i's can be positive or negative, depending on the polarity of the ith neuron. In the following we will consider how the BGNN, as well as a simpler extension of the feedforward (i.e., non-recurrent) GNN, can be used to approximate arbitrary continuous functions.

Another extension of the GNN — the clamped GNN (CGNN) — will be introduced in Sec. 3.3.

3. Approximation of Functions of One Variable by the GNN with a Bounded Number of Layers

All feedforward models considered in this section are guaranteed to have an unique solution for the $q_i, i = 1, \ldots, n$ as a result of Theorems 2 and 3 of Refs. 6 and 9. Thus from now on we do not revisit this issue.

Consider a continuous function $f : [0,1]^s \mapsto R$ of an input vector $X = (x_1, \ldots, x_s)$. Since an $[0,1]^s \mapsto R^w$ function can always be separated into a group of w distinct functions $[0,1]^s \mapsto R$, we will only consider outputs in one dimension. The remainder of this paper is therefore devoted to how a continuous function $f : [0,1]^s \mapsto R$ can be approximated by neural networks derived from the GNN model. To approximate f, we will construct s-input, 1-output, L-layer feedforward GNNs. We will use the index (l, i) for the ith neuron at the lth layer. Furthermore, when we need to specify this, we will denote by M_l the number of neurons in the lth layer.

The network under consideration is organized as follows:

- In the first layer, i.e., the input layer, we set $\Lambda(1,i) = x_i$, $\lambda(1,i) = 0$, $r(1,i) = 1$, so that $q_{1,i} = x_i$, for $i = 1, \ldots, s$.
- In the lth layer $(l = 2, \ldots, L)$, $\Lambda(l,i)$, $\lambda(l,i)$, and $r(l,i)$ are adjustable parameters, and $q_{l,i}$ is given by

$$q_{l,i} = \frac{\Lambda(l,i) + \sum_{1 \leq h < l}\sum_{1 \leq j \leq M_h} q_{h,j}\omega^+((h,j),(l,i))}{\lambda(l,i) + r(l,i) + \sum_{1 \leq h < l}\sum_{1 \leq j \leq M_h} q_{h,j}\omega^-((h,j),(l,i))}, \qquad (16)$$

where the connection "weights" $\omega^+(\cdot,\cdot)$ and $\omega^-(\cdot,\cdot)$ are also adjustable parameters.

- In the Lth or output layer there is only one neuron. As suggested in Refs. 5 we can use the output function

$$A_{L,1} = \frac{q_{L,1}}{1 - q_{L,1}} \tag{17}$$

whose physical meaning is that it is the average potential of the output neuron as the output of the network. In this manner, we will have $A_{L,1} \in [0, +\infty)$, rather than just $q_{L,1} \in [0, 1]$.

3.1. *Technical premises*

Before we proceed with the developments concerning GNN approximations we need some technical results. They are similar to some technical results used in Ref. 16 concerning continuous and bounded functions $f : [0,1] \mapsto R$ for a scalar variable x. The generalization to $f : [0,1]^s \mapsto R$ is direct and will be examined in Sec. 4. The proofs are given in the Appendix.

Lemma 1. *For any continuous and bounded $f : [0,1] \mapsto R$ and for any $\epsilon > 0$, there exists a polynomial*

$$P(x) = c_0 + c_1\left(\frac{1}{1+x}\right) + \cdots + c_m\left(\frac{1}{1+x}\right)^m, \quad 0 \leq x \leq 1, \tag{18}$$

such that $\sup_{x \in [0,1]} |f(x) - P(x)| < \epsilon$ is satisfied.

The second technical result concerns the relationship between polynomials of the form (18) and the GNN.

Lemma 2. *Consider a term of the form*

$$\frac{1}{(1+x)^v},$$

for $0 \leq x \leq 1$, and any $v = 1, 2, \ldots$. There exists a feedforward GNN with a single output neuron $(v + 1, 1)$ and input $x \in [0, 1]$ such that

$$q_{v+1,1} = \left(\frac{1}{1+x}\right)^v. \tag{19}$$

The following lemma shows how an arbitrary polynomial of the form (18) with non-negative coefficients can be realized by a feedforward GNN.

Lemma 3. *Let $P^+(x)$ be a polynomial of the form (18) with the restriction that $c_v \geq 0$, $v = 1, \ldots, m$. Then there exists a feedforward GNN with a* single output neuron (O) such that:

$$q_O = \frac{P^+(x)}{1 + P^+(x)}, \qquad (20)$$

so that the average potential of the output neuron is $A_O = P^+(x)$.

The fourth technical result will be of use in proving the approximating power of the "clamped GNN" discussed below.

Lemma 4. *Consider a term of the form*

$$\frac{x}{(1+x)^v},$$

for $0 \leq x \leq 1$, and any $v = 1, \ldots, m$. There exists a feedforward GNN with a single output neuron $(v+1, 1)$ and input $x \in [0,1]$ such that

$$q_{v+1,1} = \left(\frac{x}{1+x}\right)^v. \qquad (21)$$

We state without proof another lemma, very similar to Lemma 3, which uses terms of both forms of $1/(1+x)^v$ and $x/(1+x)^v$ to construct polynomials. Its proof uses Lemmas 3 and 4, and follows exactly the same lines as Lemma 3.

Lemma 5. *Let $P^o(x)$ be a polynomial of the form*

$$P^o(x) = c_0 + \sum_{v=1}^{m} \left[c_v \frac{1}{(1+x)^v} + d_v \frac{x}{(1+x)^v} \right], \quad 0 \leq x \leq 1, \qquad (22)$$

with non-negative coefficients, i.e., $c_v, d_v \geq 0$, $v = 1, \ldots, m$. Then there exists a feedforward GNN with a single output neuron (O) such that:

$$q_O = \frac{P^o(x)}{1 + P^o(x)}, \qquad (23)$$

so that the average potential of the output neuron is $A_O = P^o(x)$.

The next lemma is a technical premise of Lemma 7.

Lemma 6. *For any $\left(\frac{1}{1+x}\right)^i$ ($0 \leq x \leq 1, i = 1, 2, \ldots$) and for any $\epsilon > 0$, there exists a function*

$$P_1(x) = b_0 + \frac{b_1}{x + a_1} + \frac{b_2}{x + a_2} + \cdots + \frac{b_r}{x + a_r}, \quad 0 \leq x \leq 1, \qquad (24)$$

where $a_k > 0$, $k = 1, \ldots, r$, such that $\sup_{x \in [0,1]} \left| \left(\frac{1}{1+x}\right)^i - P_1(x) \right| < \epsilon$ is satisfied.

Proof. We proceed by induction. For $i = 1$, the conclusion obviously holds. Now assume it is true for $i = j$, i.e., for any $\epsilon > 0$, there exists a

$$P^{(j)}(x) = b_0^{(j)} + \frac{b_1^{(j)}}{x + a_1^{(j)}} + \frac{b_2^{(j)}}{x + a_2^{(j)}} + \cdots + \frac{b_m^{(j)}}{x + a_m^{(j)}}, \quad 0 \leq x \leq 1, \quad (25)$$

where $a_k^{(j)} > 0$, $k = 1, \ldots, m$, such that $\sup_{x \in [0,1]} \left| \left(\frac{1}{1+x} \right)^j - P^{(j)}(x) \right| < \epsilon$.
Then for $i = j + 1$,

$$\left(\frac{1}{1+x} \right)^{j+1} = \left(\frac{1}{1+x} \right)^j \left(\frac{1}{1+x} \right) = b_0^{(j)} \frac{1}{1+x} + \sum_{k=1}^{m} \frac{b_k^{(j)}}{x + a_k^{(j)}} \frac{1}{1+x}. \tag{26}$$

When $a_k^{(j)} \neq 1$,

$$\frac{b_k^{(j)}}{x + a_k^{(j)}} \frac{1}{1+x} = \frac{b_k^{(j)}}{a_k^{(j)} - 1} \left(\frac{1}{1+x} - \frac{1}{x + a_k^{(j)}} \right), \tag{27}$$

which is in the form of (24). When $a_k^{(j)} = 1$,

$$\left(\frac{1}{1+x} \right)^2 = \lim_{\eta \to 0} \frac{1}{(1 - \eta + x)(1 + \eta + x)}$$

$$= \lim_{\eta \to 0} \frac{1}{2\eta} \left(\frac{1}{1 - \eta + x} - \frac{1}{1 + \eta + x} \right), \tag{28}$$

which can be arbitrarily approximated by a function of the form (24).

Therefore $\left(\frac{1}{1+x} \right)^{j+1}$ can also be approximated by a function in the form of (24). Through mathematical induction, the conclusion holds for any $i = 1, 2, \ldots$. □

The following lemma is the preparation for the construction of a single-hidden-layered BGNN for the approximation of a one-dimensional continuous function.

Lemma 7. *For any continuous function $f : [0, 1] \mapsto R$ and for any $\epsilon > 0$, there exists a function $P_1(x)$ in the form of (24) such that $\sup_{x \in [0,1]} |f(x) - P_1(x)| < \epsilon$ is satisfied.*

Proof. This is a direct consequence of Lemmas 1 and 6. □

3.2. BGNN approximation of continuous functions of one variable

The technical results given above now pave the way for the use of the Bipolar GNN (BGNN) with a bounded number of layers. Specifically in Theorem 4, we show that a BGNN with a single hidden layer can uniformly approximate functions of one variable. The multivariable case is discussed in Sec. 4.

Let us first recall a result from Ref. 16 concerning the case when the number of layers is *not* bounded.

Theorem 3. *For any continuous function* $f : [0,1] \mapsto R$ *and any* $\epsilon > 0$, *there exists a BGNN with one positive output neuron* $(O, +)$, *one negative output neuron* $(O, -)$, *input variable* x, *and output variable* $y(x)$ *such that:*

$$y(x) = A_{O,+} + A_{O,-}, \tag{29}$$

$$A_{O,+} = \frac{q_{O,+}}{1 - q_{O,+}}, \tag{30}$$

$$A_{O,-} = \frac{-q_{O,-}}{1 - q_{O,-}}, \tag{31}$$

and $\sup_{x \in [0,1]} |f(x) - y(x)| < \epsilon$. *We will say that the BGNN's output uniformly approximates* $f(x)$.

Proof. The result is a direct application of Lemmas 1 and 3. Apply Lemma 1 to f and express the approximating polynomial as $P(x) = P^+(x) + P^-(x)$ so that the coefficients of $P^+(x)$ are non-negative, while the coefficients of $P^-(x)$ are negative:

$$P^+(x) = \sum_{i=1}^{m} \max\{0, c_i\} \left(\frac{1}{1+x}\right)^i, \tag{32}$$

$$P^-(x) = \sum_{i=1}^{m} \min\{0, c_i\} \left(\frac{1}{1+x}\right)^i. \tag{33}$$

Now simply apply Lemma 3 to obtain the feedforward GNN with an output neuron $(O, +)$ whose value is

$$q_{O,+} = \frac{P^+(x)}{1 + P^+(x)}, \tag{34}$$

and the average potential of the output neuron is $A_{O,+} = P^+(x)$. Similarly, using the non-negative polynomial $|P^-(x)|$ construct a feedforward BGNN which has positive neurons throughout, except for its output neuron, along the ideas of Lemma 4. Its output neuron $(O, -)$ however is a negative neuron, yet all the parameter values are the same as those prescribed in Lemma 4 for the output neuron, as they relate to the polynomial $|P^-(x)|$. Thus, the output neuron takes the value

$$q_{O,-} = \frac{|P^-(x)|}{1 + |P^-(x)|}, \tag{35}$$

and the average potential of the output neuron is $A_{O,-} = -|P^-(x)|$, completing the proof. □

The next theorem shows the approximation capability of a BGNN with a *single* hidden layer.

Theorem 4. *For any continuous function $f : [0,1] \mapsto R$ and any $\epsilon > 0$, there exists a BGNN of three layers (only one hidden layer), one positive output neuron $(O, +)$, one negative output neuron $(O, -)$, input variable x, and output variable $y(x)$ determined by (29) such that $\sup_{x \in [0,1]} |f(x) - y(x)| < \epsilon$.*

Proof. The result is obtained by using Lemma 7. Applying Lemma 7 to f we express the approximating function as $P_1(x) = P_1^+(x) + P_1^-(x)$ so that the coefficients of $P_1^+(x)$ are non-negative, while the coefficients of $P_1^-(x)$ are negative:

$$P_1^+(x) = \max\{0, b_0\} + \sum_{k=1}^{r} \max\{0, b_k\} \frac{b_k}{x + a_k}, \tag{36}$$

$$P_1^-(x) = \min\{0, b_0\} + \sum_{k=1}^{r} \min\{0, b_k\} \frac{b_k}{x + a_k}. \tag{37}$$

Now construct a BGNN of three layers: one output layer with one positive output neuron $(O, +)$ and one negative output neuron $(O, -)$ in it, one input layer with one input neuron $(1, 1)$ in it, and one hidden layer with r neurons $(2, 1), \ldots, (2, r)$ in it. Now set:

- $\Lambda(1,1) = x$, $\lambda(1,1) = 0$, $r(1,1) = 1$, $d(1,1) = 0$;
- $\omega^+((1,1),(2,k)) = 0$, $\omega^-((1,1),(2,k)) = 1/r$,
  $r(2,k) = a_k/r$, $\Lambda(2,k) = a_k/r$, $\lambda(2,k) = 0$, for $k = 1, \ldots, r$;
- $p^+((2,k),(O,+)) = p^-((2,k),(O,+)) = (\max\{b_k, 0\}r)/(2a_k^2 C_{\text{MAX}})$,
  $p^+((2,k),(O,-)) = p^-((2,k),(O,-)) = (|\min\{b_k, 0\}|r)/(2a_k^2 C_{\text{MAX}})$,
  for $k = 1, \ldots, r$, where $C_{\text{MAX}} = \max\{1, |b_0|, \frac{|b_k|r}{a_k^2}, k = 1, \ldots, r\}$;

- $\Lambda(O, +) = \lambda(O, +) = \max\{b_0, 0\}/(2C_{\text{MAX}})$, $r(O, +) = 1/(2C_{\text{MAX}})$,
  $\Lambda(O, -) = \lambda(O, -) = |\min\{b_0, 0\}|/(2C_{\text{MAX}})$, $r(O, -) = 1/(2C_{\text{MAX}})$.

It is easy to see that $q_{1,1} = x$, and that

$$q_{2,k} = \frac{a_k}{a_k + x}, \quad k = 1, \ldots, r, \tag{38}$$

$$q_{O,+} = \frac{\frac{P^+(x)}{2C_{\text{MAX}}}}{\frac{1}{2C_{\text{MAX}}} + \frac{P^+(x)}{2C_{\text{MAX}}}} = \frac{P^+(x)}{1 + P^+(x)}, \tag{39}$$

$$q_{O,-} = \frac{\frac{|P^-(x)|}{2C_{\text{MAX}}}}{\frac{1}{2C_{\text{MAX}}} + \frac{|P^-(x)|}{2C_{\text{MAX}}}} = \frac{|P^-(x)|}{1 + |P^-(x)|}. \tag{40}$$

Therefore, $A_{O,+} = P^+(x)$, $A_{O,-} = -|P^-(x)|$, and $y(x) = P_1(x)$, completing the proof. □

3.3. CGNN approximation of continuous functions of one variable

We can also demonstrate the approximating power of a normal feedforward GNN by just adding a "clamping constant" to the average potential of the output neuron. We call this extension the "clamped GNN (CGNN)" since the additive constant c resembles the clamping level in an electronic clamping circuit. Let us first see the corresponding result from our previous work.[16]

Theorem 5. *For any continuous function $f : [0, 1] \mapsto R$ and any $\epsilon > 0$, there exists a GNN with two output neurons $(O, 1)$, $(O, 2)$, and a constant c, resulting in a function $y(x) = A_{O,1} + A_{O,2} + c$ which approximates f uniformly on $[0, 1]$ with error less than ϵ.*

Proof. Use Lemma 1 to construct the approximating polynomial (18), which we write as $P(x) = P^+(x) + P^-(x)$, where $P^+(x)$ only has non-negative coefficients c_v^+, while $P^-(x)$ only has non-positive coefficients c_v^-:

$$c_v^+ = \max\{0, c_v\},$$
$$c_v^- = \min\{0, c_v\}.$$

Notice that

$$-\frac{1}{(1+x)^i} = 1 - \frac{1}{(1+x)^i} - 1 = \sum_{j=1}^{i} \frac{x}{(1+x)^j} - 1,$$

so that

$$P^-(x) = \sum_{v=1}^{m} |c_v^-| \sum_{j=1}^{v} \frac{x}{(1+x)^j} + \sum_{v=1}^{m} c_v^-. \tag{41}$$

Call $c = c_0 + \sum_{v=1}^{m} c_v^-$ and for some $d_v \geq 0$ write:

$$P(x) = c + \sum_{v=1}^{m} \left[c_v^+ \frac{1}{(1+x)^v} + d_v \frac{x}{(1+x)^v} \right]. \tag{42}$$

Let us write $P(x) = c + P^*(x) + P^o(x)$ where both $P^*(x)$ and $P^o(x)$ are polynomials with non-negative coefficients, and

$$P^*(x) = \sum_{v=1}^{m} c_v^+ \frac{1}{(1+x)^v},$$

$$P^o(x) = \sum_{v=1}^{m} d_v \frac{x}{(1+x)^v}.$$

Then by Lemma 5 there are two GNNs whose output neurons $(O,1), (O,2)$ take the values:

$$q_{O,1} = \frac{P^+(x)}{1 + P^+(x)},$$

$$q_{O,2} = \frac{P^o(x)}{1 + P^o(x)}.$$

Clearly, we can consider that these two GNNs constitute one network with two output neurons, and we have $y(x) = c + P^*(x) + P^o(x) = P(x)$, completing the proof. □

This result can be extended to the CGNN with only one output neuron by applying Lemma 5. However, let us first consider the manner in which a positive "clamping constant" $c > 0$ can be added to the average potential of an output neuron of a GNN using the ordinary structure of the network.

Remark 1 (Adding a Positive Clamping Constant). Consider a GNN with an output neuron $\hat{q}$ and an input vector x which realizes the function $\hat{q}(x) = P(x)$. Then there is another GNN with output neuron $Q(x)$ which, for real $c > 0$ realizes the function:

$$Q(x) = \frac{P(x) + c}{1 + P(x) + c} \tag{43}$$

and hence whose average potential is $P(x) + c$. More generally we can exhibit a GNN with output neuron $Q_1(x)$ whose average potential is $bP(x) + c$, for $b > 0$, $c > 0$.

Proof. The proof is by construction. We first take the output of the neuron of the original network (whose firing rate is denoted $2r$), and feed it into a new neuron with probability 0.5 as an excitatory signal and with probability 0.5 as an inhibitory signal. We set the firing rate of the new neuron to r, and introduce additional exogenous inhibitory and excitatory arrivals to the new neuron, both of rate rc. As a result we have:

$$Q(x) = \frac{rP(x) + rc}{r + rP(x) + rc},$$

$$= \frac{P(x) + c}{1 + P(x) + c}.$$

As a result, the new neuron's average potential is:

$$\frac{Q(x)}{1 - Q(x)} = P(x) + c$$

and we have thus been able to obtain a new neuron with an added positive "clamping constant" c with respect to the average potential $P(x)$ of the original neuron. The extension to a neuron with average potential $bp(x)+c$ is straightforward. Let the additional neurons firing rate be $R > 0$ rather than r and take its exogenous excitatory and inhibitory arrival rates to be Rc. We then obtain:

$$Q(x) = \frac{rP(x) + Rc}{R + rP(x) + Rc},$$

$$= \frac{\frac{r}{R}P(x) + c}{1 + \frac{r}{R}P(x) + c},$$

so that if we call $b = r/R$ this leads to an average potential of $bP(x) + c$.
□

Theorem 6. *For any continuous function $f : [0,1] \mapsto R$ and any $\epsilon > 0$, there exists a GNN with one output neuron (O), and a constant c, resulting in a function $y(x) = A_O + c$, which approximates f uniformly on $[0,1]$ with error less than ϵ.*

Proof. Use Lemma 1 to construct the approximating polynomial of (18), which we write as $P(x) = P^+(x) + P^-(x)$, where $P^+(x)$ only has non-negative coefficients c_v^+, while $P^-(x)$ only has non-positive coefficients c_v^-:

$$c_v^+ = \max\{0, c_v\},$$
$$c_v^- = \min\{0, c_v\}.$$

Notice that

$$-\frac{1}{(1+x)^i} = 1 - \frac{1}{(1+x)^i} - 1 = \sum_{j=1}^{i} \frac{x}{(1+x)^j} - 1,$$

so that

$$P^-(x) = \sum_{v=1}^{m} |c_v^-| \sum_{j=1}^{v} \frac{x}{(1+x)^j} + \sum_{v=1}^{m} c_v^-. \quad (44)$$

Call $c = c_0 + \sum_{v=1}^{m} c_v^-$ and for some $d_v \geq 0$ write:

$$P(x) = c + \sum_{v=1}^{m} \left[c_v^+ \frac{1}{(1+x)^v} + d_v \frac{x}{(1+x)^v} \right]. \quad (45)$$

Let us write $P(x) = c + P^o(x)$, where $P^o(x)$ is a polynomial with non-negative coefficients. Then by Lemma 5 there is a GNN whose output neurons (O) takes the value:

$$q_O = \frac{P^o(x)}{1 + P^o(x)}.$$

Clearly, we can consider that this GNN constitutes one network with only one output neuron, and we have $y(x) = c + P^o(x) = P(x)$, completing the proof. □

The next theorem shows that a CGNN with a *single* hidden layer is also a universal approximator to continuous functions on $[0, 1]$. We omit the proof, which follows closely the approach used in the proofs of Theorems 4 and 6.

Theorem 7. *For any continuous function $f : [0,1] \mapsto R$ and any $\epsilon > 0$, there exists a GNN of three layers (only one hidden layer), one output neuron (O), and a constant c called the clamping constant, resulting in a function $y(x) = A_O + c$, which approximates f uniformly on $[0,1]$ with error less than ϵ.*

4. Approximation of Continuous Functions of s Variables

Now that the process for approximating a one-dimensional continuous function with the BGNN or the CGNN having a single hidden layer is well understood, consider the case of continuous functions of s variables, i.e.,

$f : [0,1]^s \mapsto R$. As a starting point, consider the straightforward extension of Lemma 1 to the case of s inputs such that there is a polynomial:

$$P(x) = \sum_{m_1 \geq 0, \ldots, m_s \geq 0, \sum_{v=1}^{s} m_v = m} c(m_1, \ldots, m_s) \prod_{v=1}^{s} \frac{1}{(1+x_v)^{m_v}}, \quad (46)$$

with coefficients $c(m_1, \ldots, m_s)$ which approximates f uniformly. We now extend Lemma 2 to Lemma 8 and Theorem 8, which are given below.

Lemma 8. *Consider a term of the form*

$$\frac{1}{(1+x_{z1})^{m_{z1}}} \cdots \frac{1}{(1+x_{zK})^{m_{zK}}}$$

for $0 \leq x_{zj} \leq 1$, positive integers $m_{zj} > 0$ and $j = 1, \ldots, K$. There exists a feedforward GNN with a single output neuron $(\mu+1, 1)$ and input $x \in [0,1]$ such that

$$q_{\mu+1,1} = \frac{1}{(1+x_{z1})^{m_{z1}}} \cdots \frac{1}{(1+x_{zK})^{m_{zK}}}. \quad (47)$$

Proof. Without loss of generality set $m_{z1} \leq m_{z2} \leq \cdots \leq m_{zK}$. The resulting network is a cascade connection of a set of networks. The first network is identical in structure to that of Lemma 2, and has $m_{z1} + 1$ neurons numbered $(1,1), \ldots, (1, m_{z1}+1)$. Now set:

- $\Lambda(1,1) = x_{z1}$, $\Lambda(1,2) = 1/m_{z1}$, and $\Lambda(1,j) = 0$ for $j = 3, \ldots, m_{z1}+1$;
- $\lambda(1,j) = 0$ for all $j = 1, \ldots, m_{z1}+1$, and $d(1,j) = 0$ for $j = 1, \ldots, m_{z1}$;
- $\omega^-((1,1),(1,j)) = 1/m_{z1}$, and $\omega^+((1,1),(1,j)) = 0$ for $j = 2, \ldots, m_{z1}+1$;
- $r(1,j) = \omega^+((1,j),(1,j+1)) = 1/m_{z1}$ for $j = 2, \ldots, m_{z1}+1$;
- finally the connection from the first network into the second network is made via $p^+((1, m_{z1}+1),(2,2)) = m_{z1}/m_{z2} \leq 1$, with $d(1, m_{z1}+1) = (1 - m_{z1}/m_{z2})$.

It is easy to see that $q_{1,1} = x_{z1}$, and that

$$q_{1,m_{z1}+1} = \frac{1}{(1+x_{z1})^{m_{z1}}}. \quad (48)$$

The second network has $m_{z2} + 1$ neurons numbered $(2,1), \ldots, (2, m_{z2}+1)$. Now set:

- $\Lambda(2,1) = x_{z2}$ and $\Lambda(1,j) = 0$ for $j = 2, \ldots, m_{z2}+1$;
- $\lambda(2,j) = 0$ for all $j = 1, \ldots, m_{z2}+1$, and $d(2,j) = 0$ for $j = 1, \ldots, m_{z2}$;

- $\omega^{-}((2,1),(2,j)) = 1/m_{z2}$, and $\omega^{+}((2,1),(2,j)) = 0$ for $j = 2, \ldots, m_{z2}+1$;
- $r(2,j) = \omega^{+}((2,j),(2,j+1)) = 1/m_{z2}$ for $j = 2, \ldots, m_{z2}+1$;
- the connection from the second network into the third network is made via $p^{+}((2, m_{z2}+1),(3,2)) = m_{z2}/m_{z3} \leq 1$, with $d(2, m_{z2}+1) = (1 - m_{z2}/m_{z3})$.

It is easy to see that $q_{2,1} = x_{z2}$, and that

$$q_{2,m_{z2}+1} = \frac{1}{(1+x_{z1})^{m_{z1}}} \frac{1}{(1+x_{z2})^{m_{z2}}}. \tag{49}$$

The remaining construction just pursues the same scheme. □

Theorem 8. *For any continuous function* $f : [0,1]^s \mapsto R$ *and any* $\epsilon > 0$, *there exists a BGNN with one positive output neuron* $(O,+)$, *one negative output neuron* $(O,-)$, s *input variables* $X = (x_1, \ldots, x_s)$, *and output variable* $y(X)$ *such that:*

$$y(X) = A_{O,+} + A_{O,-}, \tag{50}$$

$$A_{O,+} = \frac{q_{O,+}}{1 - q_{O,+}}, \tag{51}$$

$$A_{O,-} = \frac{-q_{O,-}}{1 - q_{O,-}}, \tag{52}$$

and $\sup_{x \in [0,1]} |f(X) - y(X)| < \epsilon$. *We will say that the BGNN's output uniformly approximates* $f(X)$.

Proof. The proof follows the proof of Theorem 3, using the polynomial of (46). Lemma 7 establishes that the terms of such a polynomial can be realized by a GNN. We then construct two polynomials, one with non-negative coefficients only, and the other with negative coefficients, and show how they are realized with the BGNN. We will not go through the steps of the proof since it is a step-by-step duplicate of the proof of Theorem 3. □

We now extend Lemma 7 to the case of s inputs.

Lemma 9. *For any continuous function* $f : [0,1]^s \mapsto R$ *and for any* $\epsilon > 0$, *there exists a function of the form*

$$P_s(x) = \sum_{i=1}^{r} \sum_{0 \leq m_1 \leq 1, \ldots, 0 \leq m_s \leq 1} b(m_1, \ldots, m_s, i) \prod_{v=1}^{s} \frac{1}{(a_{v,i} + x_v)^{m_v}}, \tag{53}$$

where $a_{v,i} > 0$, $v = 1, \ldots, s$, $i = 1, 2, \ldots$, *such that* $\sup_{x \in [0,1]} |f(x) - P_s(x)| < \epsilon$ *is satisfied.*

Proof. This is simply an extension of Lemma 7. □

As a consequence, we can now establish the following general result.

Theorem 9. *For any continuous function $f : [0,1]^s \mapsto R$ and any $\epsilon > 0$, there exists a BGNN of no more than $s + 2$ layers (s hidden layers), one positive output neuron $(O, +)$, one negative output neuron $(O, -)$, s input variables $X = (x_1, \ldots, x_s)$, and output variable $y(X)$ determined by (50) such that $\sup_{x \in [0,1]} |f(X) - y(X)| < \epsilon$.*

Proof. The proof is by construction. By Lemma 9, we only need to find an appropriate BGNN of the form as described in Theorem 9 to realize any function of the form (53). We construct a BGNN with s input neurons $(1, 1), \ldots, (1, s)$, one positive output neuron $(O, +)$, one negative output neuron $(O, -)$, and M parallel sub-networks between the input layer and the output layer, where

$$M \equiv \sum_{i=1}^{r} \sum_{0 \leq m_1 \leq 1, \ldots, 0 \leq m_s \leq 1} 1(b(m_1, \ldots, m_s, i) \neq 0), \tag{54}$$

$1(X) = 1$ when X is true otherwise $1(X) = 0$. Each sub-network is a cascade connection of no more than s neurons. The output of the last neuron of each sub-network takes the value in proportion to each term in function (53).

Without loss of generality, we consider a term of the form

$$\frac{1}{a_{z1} + x_{z1}} \cdots \frac{1}{a_{zK} + x_{zK}}, \tag{55}$$

where $a_{z1} \geq a_{z2} \geq \cdots \geq a_{zK}$. Now we want to construct a sub-network which has K neurons and of which the last neuron's output takes the value in proportion to the term. Number the K neurons as $(2, 1), (3, 1), \ldots, (K + 1, 1)$, and set:

- $\Lambda(1, i) = x_i$, $\lambda(1, i) = 0$, $r(1, i) = 1$, for $i = 1, \ldots, s$;
- $\omega^+((1, z1), (2, 1)) = 0$, $\omega^-((1, z1), (2, 1)) = 1/M$;
- $r(2, 1) = a_{z1}/M$, $\Lambda(2, 1) = a_{z1}/M$, $\lambda(2, 1) = 0$.

It is easy to see that

$$q_{2,1} = \frac{a_{z1}}{a_{z1} + x_{z1}}. \tag{56}$$

Then set:

- $p^+((k, 1), (k + 1, 1)) = a_{zK}/a_{z(K-1)}$, for $k = 2, \ldots, K$;
- $\omega^+((1, zk), (k+1, 1)) = 0$, $\omega^-((1, zk), (k+1, 1)) = 1/M$, for $k = 2, \ldots, K$;

- $r(k+1,1) = a_{zk}/M$, $\Lambda(k+1,1) = 0$, $\lambda(k+1,1) = 0$, for $k = 2,\ldots,K$.

We will find

$$q_{3,1} = \frac{a_{z1}a_{z2}}{(a_{z1}+x_{z1})(a_{z2}+x_{z2})} \tag{57}$$

$$\vdots$$

$$\frac{a_{z1}\cdots a_{zK}}{(a_{z1}+x_{z1})\cdots(a_{zK}+x_{zK})}, \tag{58}$$

which is in proportion to (55).

Next we connect all the last neurons of the sub-networks to $(O,+)$ or $(O,-)$. The parameter setting follows the steps in the proof of Theorem 4 which connect the neurons in the hidden layer to the output neurons. Since the sub-networks are parallel and each sub-network contains no more than s neurons, there are in total no more than s hidden layers in this constructed BGNN. Thus, we complete the construction. □

We can now obtain Theorems 10 and 11, which generalize Theorems 6 and 7, in a similar manner.

Theorem 10. *For any continuous function* $f : [0,1]^s \mapsto R$ *and any* $\epsilon > 0$, *there exists a GNN with one output neuron* (O), *and a constant c called the clamping constant, resulting in a function* $y(X) = A_O + c$ *which approximates f uniformly on* $[0,1]^s$ *with error less than* ϵ.

Theorem 11. *For any continuous function* $f : [0,1]^s \mapsto R$ *and any* $\epsilon > 0$, *there exists a GNN of no more than* $s+2$ *layers* (s *hidden layers*), *one output neuron* (O), *and a constant c called the clamping constant, resulting in a function* $y(X) = A_O + c$, *which approximates f uniformly on* $[0,1]^s$ *with error less than* ϵ.

5. Conclusions

The approximation of functions by neural networks is central to the learning theory of neural networks. It is also a key to many applications of neural networks such as pattern recognition, data compression, time series prediction, adaptive control, etc.

The random neural network introduced and developed in Refs. 5, 6, 9 and 17 differs significantly from standard connexionist models in that information travels between neurons in this model in the form of random spike trains, and the network state is represented by the joint probability distributions that the n neurons in the network are excited. This model has a mathematical structure which is significantly different from that of the connexionist model, the Hopfield model, or the Boltzman machine.[3] Thus the approximation capability of these networks also needs to be examined in a manner distinct from that of previous models.[4] In particular, the "Gelenbe" random neural network model[5,6,9,17] does not use sigmoid functions which are basic to the standard models' approximation capabilities.

The most basic requirement for a neural network model is that it should be a universal function approximator, i.e., to any continuous function f on a compact set, we should be able to find a specific network which implements a mapping close enough, in some precise sense to f, to a given degree of accuracy. Furthermore, among all networks which satisfy this property, we may wish to choose the one with the "smallest" size or the most simple structure.

In Ref. 16 we showed that the BGNN and the CGNN, two simple extensions of the basic "Gelenbe" Random Neural Network model, are universal approximators of continuous real-valued functions of s real variables. However, we had not previously established the specific "size" constraints for the approximating networks.

In this paper, we limit the networks to being feedforward and consider the case where the number of hidden layers does not exceed the number of input variables. With these constraints we show that the feedforward CGNN and the BGNN with s hidden layers (total of $s + 2$ layers) can uniformly approximate continuous functions of s variables. We also extend a theorem in Ref. 16 on universal approximation using the CGNN with two output neurons to the CGNN with only one output neuron.

The theoretical results we report in this paper are needed to justify the empirically observed success obtained in a variety of applications of the "Gelenbe" random neural network,[7,8,10–15] and to support further applied work in spiked stochastic neural network models. We believe that these results will lead to new developments in the design of network structures which are adapted to certain specific learning or approximation tasks.

References

1. W. E. Feller, *An Introduction to Probability Theory and Its Applications*, Vol. I (3rd Edition) and Vol. II (Wiley, 1968, 1966).
2. M. J. D. Powell, *Approximation Theory and Methods* (Cambridge University Press, 1981).
3. J. L. McClelland, D. E. Rumelhart, *et al.*, *Parallel Distributed Processing*, Vols. I and II (MIT Press, 1986).

4. K. Funahashi, On the approximate realization of continuous mapping by neural network, *Neural Networks* **2** (1989), 183–192.
5. E. Gelenbe, Random neural networks with negative and positive signals and product form solution, *Neural Computation* **1**(4) (1989), 502–511.
6. E. Gelenbe, Stability of the random neural network model, *Neural Computation* **2**(2) (1990), 239–247.
7. E. Gelenbe, A. Stafylopatis and A. Likas, Associative memory operation of the random network model, in *Proc. Int. Conf. Artificial Neural Networks*, Helsinki (1991), 307–312.
8. E. Gelenbe and F. Batty, Minimum cost graph covering with the random neural network, in *Computer Science and Operations Research* ed. O. Balci (Pergamon, New York, 1992), 139–147.
9. E. Gelenbe, Learning in the recurrent random neural network, *Neural Computation* **5**(1) (1993), 154–164.
10. E. Gelenbe, V. Koubi and F. Pekergin, Dynamical random neural network approach to the traveling salesman problem, *Proc. IEEE Symp. Syst., Man, Cybern.* (1993), 630–635.
11. A. Ghanwani, A qualitative comparison of neural network models applied to the vertex covering problem, *Elektrik* **2**(1) (1994), 11–18.
12. E. Gelenbe, C. Cramer, M. Sungur and P. Gelenbe, Traffic and video quality in adaptive neural compression, *Multimedia Systems* **4** (1996), 357–369.
13. C. Cramer, E. Gelenbe and H. Bakircioglu, Low bit rate video compression with neural networks and temporal subsampling, *Proc. IEEE* **84**(10) (1996), 1529–1543.
14. E. Gelenbe, T. Feng and K. R. R. Krishnan, Neural network methods for volumetric magnetic resonance imaging of the human brain, *Proc. IEEE* **84**(10) (1996), 1488–1496.
15. E. Gelenbe, A. Ghanwani and V. Srinivasan, Improved neural heuristics for multicast routing, *IEEE J. Selected Areas in Communications* **15**(2) (1997), 147–155.
16. E. Gelenbe, Z. H. Mao and Y. D. Li, Function approximation with the random neural network, *IEEE Trans. Neural Networks* **10**(1) (1999), 3–9.
17. E. Gelenbe and J. M. Fourneau, Random neural networks with multiple classes of signals, *Neural Computation* **11** (1999), 721–731.

Appendix: Proof of Technical Lemmas

Proof of Lemma 1. This is a direct consequence of Weierstrass' Theorem (see Ref. 2, p. 61) which states that for any continuous function $h : [a, b] \mapsto R$, and some $\epsilon > 0$, there exists a polynomial $P(u)$ such that $\sup_{u \in [a,b]} |h(u) - P(u)| < \epsilon$. Now let $u = 1/(1 + x)$, $u \in [1/2, 1]$ and select $x = (1 - u)/u$ with $h(u) = f\left(\frac{1-u}{u}\right) = f(x)$. If $f(x)$ is continuous, then so is $h(u)$, so that there exists an algebraic polynomial of the form

$$P(u) = c_0 + c_1 u + \cdots + c_m u^m, \quad 1/2 \leq u \leq 1, \tag{59}$$

such that $\sup_{u \in [1/2,1]} |h(u) - P(u)| < \epsilon$. Therefore, $P(x)$ is given by (18), and $\sup_{x \in [0,1]} |f(x) - P(x)| < \epsilon$. □

Proof of Lemma 2. Construct a feedforward GNN with $v + 1$ neurons numbered $(1, 1), \ldots, (v + 1, 1)$. Now set:

- $\Lambda(1, 1) = x$, $\Lambda(2, 1) = 1/v$, and $\Lambda(j, 1) = 0$ for $j = 3, \ldots, v + 1$;
- $\lambda(j, 1) = 0$ for all $j = 1, \ldots, v + 1$, and $d(j, 1) = 0$ for $j = 1, \ldots, v$;
- $\omega^-((1,1),(j,1)) = 1/v$, and $\omega^+((1,1),(j,1)) = 0$ for $j = 2, \ldots, v + 1$;
- $r(j, 1) = \omega^+((j, 1), (j + 1, 1)) = 1/v$ for $j = 2, \ldots, v$;
- finally $d(v + 1, 1) = 1$.

It is easy to see that $q_{1,1} = x$, and that

$$q_{j+1,1} = \left(\frac{1}{1+x}\right)^j, \tag{60}$$

for $j = 1, \ldots, v$ so the lemma follows. □

The next result exhibits a simple a construction process for algebraic expressions using the feedforward GNN.

Remark. If there exists a feedforward GNN with a single output neuron $(L, 1)$, and a function $g : [0, 1] \mapsto [0, 1]$ such that:

$$q_{L,1} = g(x), \tag{61}$$

then there exists an $L + 1$ layer feedfowrward GNN with a single output neuron (Q) such that:

$$q_O = \frac{g(x)}{1 + g(x)}. \tag{62}$$

Proof. The simple proof is by construction. We simply add an additional neuron (Q) to the original GNN, and leave all connections in the original

GNN unchanged except for the output connections of the neuron $(L, 1)$. Let the firing rate of neuron $(l, 1)$ be $r(L, 1)$. Then:

- $(L, 1)$ will now be connected to the new neuron $(L + 1, 1)$ by $\omega^+((L, 1), Q) = r(L, 1)/2$, $\omega^-((L, 1), Q) = r(L, 1)/2$;
- $r(Q) = r(L, 1)/2$.

This completes the proof. □

Proof of Lemma 3. The proof is by construction. Let C_{MAX} be the largest of the coefficients in $P^+(x)$ and write $P^*(x) = P^+(x)/C_{\text{MAX}}$. Let $c_j^* = c_j/C_{\text{MAX}} \leq 1$ so that now each term $c_j^* \frac{1}{(1+x)^j}$ in $P^*(x)$ is no greater than 1, $j = 1, \ldots, m$. We now take m networks of the form of Lemma 2 with $r(j, 1) = 1$, $j = 1, \ldots, m$ and output values

$$q_{j,1} = \left(\frac{1}{1+x}\right)^j, \qquad (63)$$

and connect them to the new output neuron (O) by setting the probabilities $p^+((j, 1), O) = c_j^*/2$, $p^-((j, 1), O) = c_j^*/2$. Furthermore, we set an external positive and negative signal arrival rate $\Lambda(O) = \lambda(O) = c_0^*/2$ and $r(O) = 1/(2C_{\text{MAX}}$ for the output neuron. We now have:

$$q_O = \frac{\frac{P^*(x)}{2}}{\frac{1}{2C_{\text{MAX}}} + \frac{P^*(x)}{2}}. \qquad (64)$$

We now multiply the numerator and the denominator on the right-hand side of the above expression by $2C_{\text{MAX}}$ to obtain

$$q_O = \frac{P^+(x)}{1 + P^+(x)}, \qquad (65)$$

which completes the proof of the lemma. □

Proof of Lemma 4. The proof is very similar to that of Lemma 2. Construct a feedforward GNN with $v+1$ neurons numbered $(1, 1), \ldots, (v+1, 1)$. Now set:

- $\Lambda(1, 1) = x$, and $\Lambda(j, 1) = 0$ for $j = 2, \ldots, v + 1$;
- $\lambda(j, 1) = 0$ for all $j = 1, \ldots, v + 1$, and $d(j, 1) = 0$ for $j = 1, \ldots, v$;
- $\omega^+((1, 1), (2, 1)) = 1/(v + 1)$, $\omega^-((1, 1), (j, 1)) = 1/(v + 1)$ for $j = 2, \ldots, v + 1$, and $\omega^+((1, 1), (j, 1)) = 0$ for $j = 3, \ldots, v + 1$;
- $r(j, 1) = \omega^+((j, 1), (j + 1, 1)) = 1/(v + 1)$ for $j = 2, \ldots, v$;
- finally, $d(v + 1, 1) = 1$.

It is easy to see that $q_{1,1} = x$, and that

$$q_{j+1,1} = \frac{x}{(1+x)^j}, \qquad (66)$$

for $j = 1, \ldots, v$ so the lemma follows. □

Finally, we state without proof another lemma, very similar to Lemma 4, but which uses terms of the form $x/(1+x)^v$ to construct polynomials. Its proof uses Lemma 5, and follows exactly the same lines as Lemma 4.

Lemma 6. *Let $P^o(x)$ be a polynomial of the form*

$$P^o(x) = c_0 + c_1 \frac{x}{1+x} + \cdots + c_m \frac{x}{(1+x)^m}, \quad 0 \leq x \leq 1, \qquad (67)$$

with non-negative coefficients, i.e., $c_v \geq 0$, $i = 1, \ldots, m$. Then there exists a feedforward GNN with a single output neuron $(O, +)$ such that:

$$q_O = \frac{P^o(x)}{1 + P^o(x)}, \qquad (68)$$

so that the average potential of the output neuron is $A_O = P^o(x)$.

CHAPTER 6

The Achilles' Heel of Computer Performance Modeling
and the Model Building Shield

Vittoria De Nitto Personè and Giuseppe Iazeolla[*]
*Department of Computer Science, Faculty of Engineering,
University of Roma, TorVergata, Italy*
*iazeolla@info.uniroma2.it

Computer performance modeling is a recognized academic discipline that, however, sometimes plays a limited role in practical system design. In many cases, system designers feel that features of system architecture, implementation languages and software aspects, determinant to system performance, are represented in the model only to a limited degree. This chapter conjectures that the limited attention to such computer-tied aspects besides wakening the confidence of system designers in performance evaluation, brings in an empirical approach to system analysis that is the Achilles' heel of performance modeling. A shield to protect the heel is foreseen in the so-called multilevel model building method the chapter introduces. The method includes in the performance model all system aspects, from the physical platform to the various software layers that exist between the platform and the user level. The approach enables the system designer to introduce performance evaluation into his best practices. It provides the model at a selected abstraction level, and gives ways to incorporate in the model both the software overhead and the application program workloads. The approach is based on models each progressively more abstract than the next, thus recalling Ken Sevcik's method of layers.

1. Introduction

The art of computer performance modeling dates back about forty years, from the times of the pioneering work by A. L. Scherr on the analysis of time-shared computer systems.[1] Since that time, many advancements have been made, as documented in books, scientific papers and conference proceedings.

Nevertheless, the designers of computer systems have only included performance analysis into their best practices to a limited extent. Many of them still consider performance analysis as an academic discipline rather than a discipline to use in design.

One reason could be that during the forty years of its life, the art of system modeling has directed its thoughts and efforts more on model evaluation methods (analytic, simulation, hybrid evaluation methods where the discipline has reached respectable levels of rigor and sophistication) than on model building methods to incorporate in the performance model aspects of the system platform and of the various software layers that exist between the platform and the user level.

One can believe the fathers of performance modeling had given an answer to the question of how to build a model and that the answer was lost in the mists of time. So, the performance modelers since then had assumed that the model was empirically given, based on intuition and experience, and that the only significant problem was model evaluation.

On the other hand, computer systems have in the meantime developed such complexity that the use of intuitive and empirical approaches to model building can be the performance modeling Achilles' heel.

In this chapter, a formal model building method is introduced. The method includes in the performance model all system aspects and enables the system designer to introduce performance evaluation into his design practices by incorporating in the model the description of both the physical platform and the various software layers up to the user level. The chapter is organized as follows. Section 2 describes the current status of the field, Sec. 3 introduces the system description to include all abstraction levels from the physical platform to the user application level, Sec. 4 gives the model building method, and Sec. 5 the comparison with existing approaches. Conclusions are given finally in Sec. 6.

2. The Current Status of Model Building

Existing approaches to performance modeling can be divided in two broad categories: the *conventional* approach and the *one-level* approach.

The *conventional* approach is documented in the majority of books of the last thirty years on performance analysis,[1-17] where the problem is substantially reported as: "assuming the following model (queueing network, or Petri net, or Markov, etc.) is the right model for the system under study, let us learn how to evaluate it (give throughputs, response times, queue lengths, etc.)." This approach is empirical and intuitive both in the model definition and in the model parameterization (see Sec. 5).

The second type of approach, the *one-level* approach, documented in journals[18–23,30,31] and conference papers,[24–29] is a substantial improvement on the former. Indeed, it obtains[15,19,22] the model definition by a formal method, but remains incomplete in model parametrization. Besides that, it defines the model at only a specific abstraction level, and only empirically considers the remaining levels (see Sec. 5). In other words, the one-level approach still does not give the expected answer to the Achilles' heel problem.

For a model building methodology to hold, a multilevel approach should be foreseen to quantitatively take into consideration all abstraction levels of the system. The approach may vary from the queueing network model case, to the Petri net one, to the Markovian model, etc. In this chapter, the queueing network (QN) case is dealt with.

The method introduced enables the system designer to include performance evaluation into his best practices. Given the study objective, the system designer may identify the abstraction level of the required performance model. While providing the model at the selected abstraction level, the method gives him the capability of incorporating in the model both the software overheads from the underlying levels and the program workload from the superior ones.

3. System Multilevel Description

Synthetically, a QN performance model can be built based on three descriptions of the system at hand:[15,32]

(i) the vertical description,
(ii) the horizontal description,
(iii) the software description.

We briefly remind ourselves of these descriptions in order to better understand the model building method of Sec. 4.

```
┌─────────────┐
│    VM₅      │ ⎫
├─────────────┤ ⎬ Logical
│    VM₄      │ ⎪ machines    ⎫
├─────────────┤ ⎭              ⎬ Performance modeling
│    VM₃      │                ⎪   machines
├─────────────┤ ⎫              ⎪
│    VM₂      │ ⎬ Physical machine ⎭
├─────────────┤ ⎭
│    VM₁      │
├─────────────┤
│    VM₀      │
└─────────────┘
```

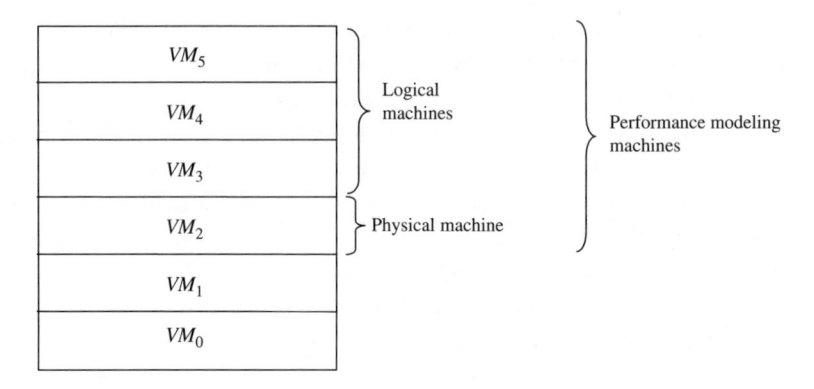

Fig. 1. System vertical description.

3.1. *The system vertical description*

In the vertical description, the system is seen as a hierarchy of virtual machines $VM_0, VM_1, VM_2, \ldots, VM_5$, where

VM_0 is the circuitry machine (electronic level),
VM_1 is the firmware machine (microprogram level),
VM_2 is the physical machine (platform level),
VM_3 is the lower level logical machine (operating-system level),
VM_4 is the middle level logical machine (application-program level),
VM_5 is the upper level logical machine (user-program level),

as shown in Fig. 1.

Computing resources of interest to performance modeling (processing units, memory units, I/O units, etc.) first become visible at the VM_2 level. At that level they are of a physical type, and of a logical type at the superior levels. Machines VM_2, VM_3, VM_4 and VM_5 are thus the only ones we consider in the model building method.

From the computational point of view, each logical machine VM_i ($i = 3, \ldots, 5$) has its own language L_i. Language L_5 is the user high-level language, L_4 the application program language, L_3 the operating system language, L_2 the base or machine language. Every operation or command of L_i ($i = 3, \ldots, 5$) is implemented (through compilation/interpretation) by a program written in the language L_{i-1} of the lower-level machine VM_{i-1}. In other words, the computational process goes as follows:

- the VM_4 programs (application programs) implement the VM_5 operations written in L_5;
- the VM_3 programs (operating system programs) implement the VM_4 operations written in L_4;

- the VM_2 programs (machine language programs) implement the VM_3 operations written in L_3.

As seen next, the vertical description plays a role in the multilevel model building method (Sec. 4), giving ways to derive the QN model *parameters* (the holding times of the QN service centers, the job classes and the routing probabilities) that incorporate in the model all overheads introduced by the various levels of the system software.

In such a way, the derivation of, for example, the response time "seen" from, say, the middle level virtual machine, VM_4, takes into consideration the work performed by machines VM_3 and VM_2. In a similar way, the response time "seen" from the upper level virtual machine, VM_5, takes into consideration the work performed by VM_4, VM_3 and VM_2.

3.2. *The system horizontal description*

Besides a language L_i, each virtual machine VM_i ($i = 2, \ldots, 5$) is characterized by a set $\mathbf{R}^i$ of resources (processing units, memory units, network link units, etc.). The way such resources are interconnected is expressed by the so-called horizontal scheme, inspired by the PMS notation (Processor-Memory-Switch),[33] as shown in Fig. 2(a), which illustrates a heterogeneous computer network consisting of a set of client hosts $A_1, \ldots, A_Z$ and a server

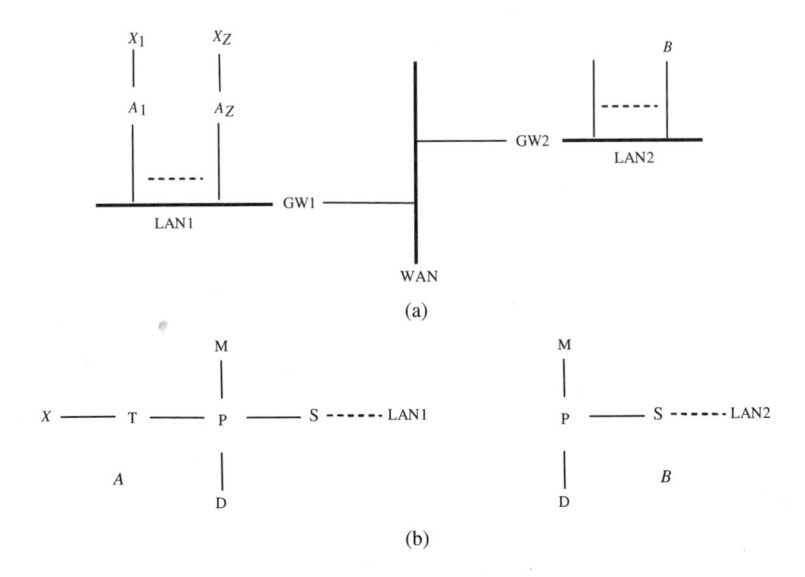

Fig. 2. System horizontal description.

host B, connected by their respective local area networks LAN1, LAN2 and by the wide area network WAN through their respective gateways GW1 and GW2. Symbols $X_1, \ldots, X_Z$ denote users sitting at client locations $A_1, \ldots, A_Z$ and interacting with B.

The inner structure of each component of Fig. 2(a) can in turn be detailed as in Fig. 2(b), which gives the inner structures of hosts A and B, with lines representing links, and symbols T, P, M, D, S representing Terminal unit, Processing unit, Memory unit, Disk unit, and Switching unit, respectively. A similar reasoning applies to the LANs, the WAN and the gateways.

Both units and links are resources, and take physical or logical meanings depending on the level of the virtual machine VM_i they belong to.

At the VM_2 level, the system units and links are physical entities (physical memory unit M, physical processing unit P, physical communication processor unit, gateway, router, physical link unit, etc.), which interpret and execute commands and operations in machine language L_2.

At the upper VM_i levels ($i = 3, 4, 5$) all such units and links are logical (instead of physical) entities that interpret and execute commands and operations in language L_i (operating system language for $i = 3$, application language for $i = 4$, user language for $i = 5$).

As seen next, the horizontal description plays a role in the definition of the performance model components and interconnections, and provides ways to derive the QN model *topology* (the set of QN service centers and their interconnections).

Let us denote by H_i the horizontal description of VM_i developed at its PMS detail.

Descriptions H_2, H_3, H_4, H_5 will be used in the multilevel QN model building method in Sec. 4.

3.3. *The system software description*

The software workload description is by use of execution graphs,[8] which consist of conventional flow graphs with associated resource demands for each block of the graph. Each block represents a segment of code, and blocks can be fine-grained depending on the level of detail of the study. Such graphs are easily derivable from software description formalisms such as UML.[15,19,24]

Let us denote by EG_i the execution graph that describes the programs in language L_i of the virtual machine VM_i. Graph EG_i describes the workload machine VM_i generates for the underlying machine VM_{i-1}.

In Fig. 3, an example is given of a set of hypothetical[a] execution graphs, EG_5, EG_4, EG_3, which are related to each other: EG_4 is the translation of EG_5's code into the language L_4 of the middle-level virtual machine, and EG_3 the translation of EG_4's code into the language L_3 of the lower-level virtual machine.

Graph EG_5 consists of a single block A for the command issued by a user in the language L_5 of machine VM_5, e.g., a web command entered by one of the hosts A in Fig. 2 for accessing a web page at host B.

Graph EG_4 is the hypothetical explosion of EG_5 and consists of various blocks for the various operations that machine VM_4 executes in language L_4 to implement command A from VM_5. Blocks in EG_4 include programs $A1$ and $A2$ that result from the translation of command A into language L_4, and the associated overhead programs $O4$ introduced by machine VM_4. In a similar way, graph EG_3 is the hypothetical explosion of EG_4 and includes programs $A11$, $A12$, $A21$, $A22$ (from the translation of $A1$ and $A2$), besides the overhead programs $O41$, $O42$ (from the translation of $O4$), and the new overhead $O3$ introduced by machine VM_3.

Graph EG_3 gives the effective workload the level-5 user command A generates for the physical machine VM_2.

According to Fig. 2, there exist many system users $(X_1, \ldots, X_Z)$ each generating a similar level-5 command and thus up to Z workloads of type EG_3 can be assumed to weigh on the physical machine VM_2 and compete for its resources.

Let QN_i denote the queueing network performance model of machine VM_i and by $\{1, 2, \ldots, h, \ldots, k, \ldots, m\}$ the service centers of QN_i.

A resource demand vector

$$d^i = \left(d_1^i, d_2^i, \ldots, d_h^i, \ldots, d_m^i\right)$$

is associated to each block of EG_i in Fig. 3 ($i = 3, 4, 5$) where d_h^i denotes the number of operations the block demands to center h of machine VM_i, and m is the number of centers.

As seen next, graph EG_{i+1} plays a role in the definition of the parameters of QN_i: in other words its service center rates μ_h, its routing probabilities p_{hk}, its job classes. Giving the technique to derive QN parameters from an EG is beyond the scope of this chapter and the reader can find them in the literature.[15,22]

---

[a]A working example of an EG_4 for a web application involving two hosts, the client host A and the server host B that interact through the LAN1-WAN-LAN2 network as in Fig. 2 can be found in Ref. 22.

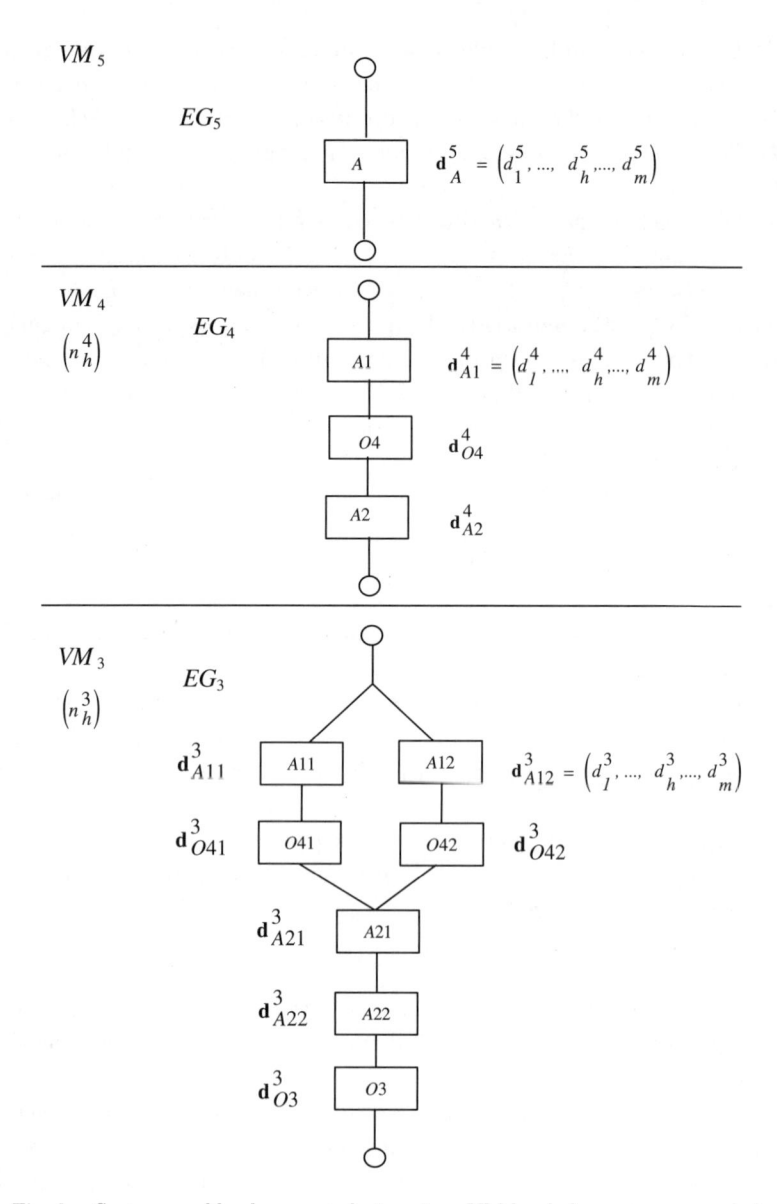

Fig. 3. System workload generated at various VM levels by user command A.

According to such techniques, job classes in the QN are derived from the EG blocks. Each block yields a job class. Depending on the desired level of detail, blocks can be compacted[6] to reduce the EG complexity, and thus the resulting number of QN classes.

As detailed in Sec. 4, the model building method obtains various models QN_i ($i = 2, 3, 4$) as follows:

(i) First the model QN_2 of VM_2 is obtained based on H_2, on the workload EG_3 from the upper logical machine, and on the manufacturer's data of the lower physical machine.
(ii) Then model QN_3 of VM_3 is obtained based on H_3, on the workload EG_4 from the upper logical machine, and on data from the evaluation of the lower model QN_2.
(iii) Finally, QN_4 of VM_4 is obtained based on H_4, on the workload EG_5 from the upper logical machine, and on data from the evaluation of the lower model QN_3.

Models QN_2, QN_3, QN_4 are each progressively more abstract than the next. The first relates to the physical machine, the second to the lower-level logical machine, and the latter to the middle-level logical machine. Model QN_2 is the most detailed one, dealing with the largest number of job classes (seven classes per user command in the Fig. 3 example but in general with thousands of them, as there are blocks in EG_3), while models QN_3 and QN_4 are progressively less detailed, the first dealing with a lower number of job classes (as there are blocks in EG_4) and the second with just one job class (the single EG_5 block) per user command.

Model QN_4 is thus less time-consuming if studies are to be carried out on the sensitiveness of the system performance to various profiles of the user command A of EG_5 (e.g., various profiles of its demand vector $\mathbf{d}^5$).

In a similar way, model QN_3 is less time-consuming to study the sensitiveness of system performance to profiles of the VM_4 software overhead $O4$ (see Fig. 3).

Model QN_2 obviously remains the most general one, since it includes job class representatives of all the existing software components ($A11$ through $O3$). It could, in principle, be used for any study but, due to the large number of classes, its use remains limited to the strictly necessary cases, e.g., to study the sensitiveness of system performance to profiles of $O3$, the VM_3 software overhead.

The complete view of the relative advantages (or disadvantages) of using either model may, however, require an analysis that is beyond the scope of this chapter.

4. The Multilevel Model Building Method

Let us denote by R_h^i resource h of machine VM_i. The set of VM_i resources is denoted $R^i = \{R_1^i, R_2^i, \ldots, R_h^i, \ldots, R_m^i\}$. Some such resources are processing units, others are memory units, link units, etc. For the sake of simplicity, we shall assume that each such resource yields a service center in network QN_i, in other words, we denote by R_h^i also the hth service center.

Let us denote by C_h^i the operating capacity of R_h^i. If resource R_h^i is a processing unit, capacity C_h^i gives its processing speed (number of language L_i operations per sec). When $i = 2$, we are at the VM_2 machine level, and capacity C_h^2 denotes R_h^2's physical capacity (machine language L_2 operations per sec) derived from the manufacturer's data sheets. When $i = 3, 4$ or 5, C_h^i denotes R_h^i's logical capacity (higher level language L_i operations per sec) and is derived by the method we introduce below.

In a similar way, if R_h^i is a link unit, capacity C_h^i gives its (physical or logical) bandwidth.

If R_h^i is a memory unit, capacity C_h^i gives its (physical or logical) capacity, and so on.

For the sake of conciseness, in the following we shall only deal with time-consuming resources (processing units, link units, etc.), in other words, resources that yield active-queue service centers[5,6] in QN_i. Memory resources give rise to passive-queue service centers that are easy to consider but are not dealt with in this chapter.

As mentioned above, each given R_h^i is a physical resource at level $i = 2$ and a logical one at levels $i = 3, 4$. For the sake of simplicity, we shall assume that, other than being physical or logical, resources remain in number m at the various levels.

4.1. *The top-down bottom-up process*

As anticipated in Sec. 3.2, the model building method starts with a *top-down* process that consists of the derivation of graph EG_4 from EG_5, and of graph EG_3 from EG_4.

Once EG_3 has been obtained, model QN_2 of the physical machine VM_2 can be defined. At this point, if the models of the logical machines VM_3 and VM_4 are also needed, a *bottom-up* process takes place, which derives

QN_3 from the evaluation of QN_2 and, if needed, obtains QN_4 from the evaluation of QN_3, as detailed below.

Let μ_h^i denote the service rate of center R_h^i and p_{hk}^i its routing probabilities ($h, k = 1, \ldots, m$). The model QN_i of VM_i ($i = 2, 3, 4$) is built by first deriving its *topology* (its service centers R_h^i and their interconnections) by use of the system horizontal description H_i, and then by deriving its parameters (μ_h^i and p_{hk}^i, and job classes for each center R_h^i) by the use of graph EG_{i+1}, as well as by the use of C_h^i coming from the evaluation of QN_{i-1} and by the use of additional data n_h^i, as illustrated in Fig. 4.

The model building method is carried out in two steps as follows:

Top-down step: Derive from the user-level graph EG_5 the application level EG_4 and from this the operating system level EG_3.

Bottom-up step: Obtain model QN_i of VM_i ($i = 2, 3, 4$) as follows:

(i) Use the horizontal description H_i to derive QN_i's topology (its service centers R_h^i and their interconnections).

(ii) Based on software knowledge, obtain n_h^i, the average number of operations in language L_i of center R_h^i necessary to implement an operation in language L_{i+1}.

(iii) Obtain from EG_{i+1}: the job classes (one class for each block); the resource demand d_h^{i+1} for each class of jobs; the routing probabilities p_{hk}^i between service centers in QN_i ($h, k = 1, \ldots, m$).

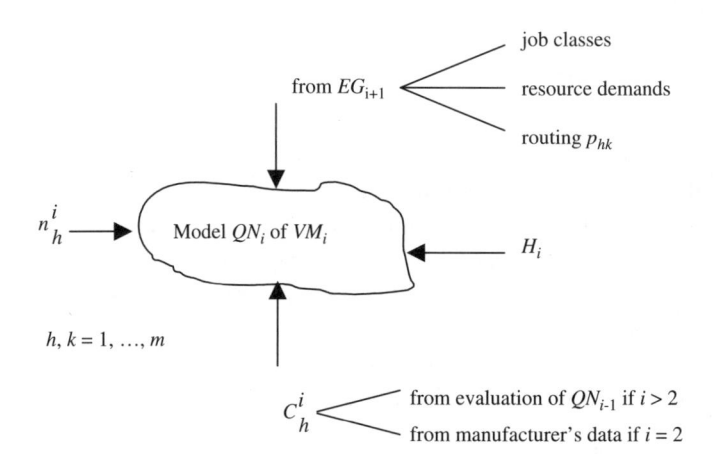

Fig. 4. Building model QN_i of machine VM_i ($i = 2, 3, 4$).

(iv) For each center R_h^i in QN_i and job class, set the center capacity C_h^i to the values:

$$C_h^i = \lambda_h^{i-1} \quad \text{for } i > 2,$$
$$C_h^i = \text{manufacturer's data} \quad \text{for } i = 2,$$

where λ_h^{i-1} is the throughput of center R_h^{i-1} in QN_{i-1} (derived from the evaluation of QN_{i-1}).

(v) Set the average service time of each center R_h^i in QN_i to the value:

$$E(t_s)_h^i = \frac{d_h^{i+1} \times n_h^i}{C_h^i},$$

from where[b] the center service rate parameter is derived:

$$\mu_h^i = \frac{1}{E(t_s)_h^i}.$$

Point (iv) of the bottom-up step incorporates in QN_i the software overheads of VM_{i-1} by giving to each center h of QN_i a capacity C_h^i that considers the extra work due to software overheads.

As specified at the beginning of Sec. 4, capacity C_h^i is physical or logical, depending on the level. Thus, for each center h, its capacities C_h^2, C_h^3, C_h^4 evaluated at point (iv) of the bottom-up step will take progressively decreasing values as the center moves from the physical, to the lower-level, to the middle-level logical machine. Indeed, such capacities progressively incorporate the effects of increasing overheads. Namely, C_h^3 incorporates the effects of the operating system overheads, and C_h^4 the effects of both the operating system and the application programs overheads.

In conclusion, the use of the method for performance studies implies that:

(a) if a study is needed at level VM_2, then QN_2 is to be obtained by application of the bottom-up step for $i = 2$;
(b) if instead a study is needed at level VM_3, then first QN_2 is to be obtained as in (a), then QN_2 itself has to be evaluated, and finally QN_3 is to be obtained by application of the bottom-up step for $i = 3$;
(c) if a study is needed at level VM_4, then first QN_3 is to be obtained as in (b), then QN_3 itself has to be evaluated, and finally QN_4 is to be obtained by application of the bottom-up step for $i = 4$.

---

[b]When center h is a CPU, the case has to be considered that service time $E(t_s)_h^i$ is spent in v number of visits[8,15] to the I/O. In that case, its value has to be divided by v.

Point (iv) of the bottom-up step shows that an evaluation of QN_{i-1} is necessary to incorporate into the capacity of QN_i service centers the effects of the software overheads. This is an aspect of model time-complexity to also consider in the analysis of the relative advantages (or disadvantages) of using one model or another, as discussed at the end of Sec. 3.3.

5. Comparison with Existing Approaches

As seen in Sec. 2, existing approaches to performance modeling can be divided into two broad categories, the *conventional* and the *one-level* approach.

In more detail, we can now say that the *conventional* approach[1-17] uses experience and intuition to define two aspects of the model: the model *topology* and the model *parameters*. Looking at points (i) through (iv) of the bottom-up step above, one can now evaluate how erroneous such an approach could be.

The second type of approach, the *one-level* approach, is a substantial improvement over the former. It obtains[15,19,22] the model *topology* by a formal method, but remains incomplete in its derivation of model *parameters*. Indeed the approach defines the model at only a specific abstraction level (say, the VM_4 level) and derives important parameters, namely the operating capacities of the logical processing units at that level, by scaling down by an empirical factor the operating capacities of the physical units.

The way in which the logical operating capacities C_h^i are derived at point (iv) of the bottom-up step now makes it evident that the second approach can also be erroneous, since it gives to each logical unit (logical processor, logical disk, link, etc. of, say, the example level 4) a static capacity; in other words, a capacity value independent of the throughputs of the remaining units. In substance, it gives to each logical unit (of the example level 4) a capacity of physical type (even though scaled down by the empirical factor), rather than a logical capacity value $C_h^4 = \lambda_h^3$ which should be obtained from the evaluation of the entire QN_3 model, so bringing in the congestion-dependent behaviors of all remaining processing and linking resources that operate at level 3 together with R_h^3.

In conclusion, with respect to this chapter's *multilevel* approach, the *conventional* approach remains doubly erroneous (in the derivation of the model topology and model parameters), while the *one-level* approach remains incomplete in the derivation of model parameters.[c]

6. Conclusions

During the forty years of its life, computer performance modeling has directed its efforts more on the model *evaluation* methods than on the model building methods, thus neglecting substantial computer-tied aspects of the systems under study, such as features of system platform, as well as implementation languages and software aspects.

Besides awakening the confidence of system designers in computer performance evaluation, this tendency has also brought in an empirical approach to system analysis that is going to be the Achilles' heel of computer performance modeling.

As a possible shield to protect the heel, a multilevel model building method has been introduced that includes all system components in the performance model, from the physical platform to the various software layers that exist between the platform and the user level.

The method enables the system designer to introduce performance evaluation into his best practices. Given the study objective, the system designer may identify the abstraction level of the required performance model. While providing the model at the selected abstraction level, the method provides the capability of incorporating in the model both the software overheads of the underlying levels and the workload of the superior ones.

Acknowledgment

Work partially supported by the FIRB research on the performance of complex systems, the University of Roman TorVergata research on performance modeling for quality verification, and the Certia Research Center.

---

[c] In the method of layers[31] by Rolia and Sevcik, a concept can be found similar to that in this chapter concept of deriving the parameters of a given QN from the evaluation of a second QN. Their method, however, deals with QN models that belong to a common abstraction level VM_i. Thus, it falls into the category of one-level approach methods, and shares their problems. Besides that, it also shares some problems of the conventional approach since, in the derivation of the model topology, a central server model is assumed for any system study.

References

1. A. L. Sherr, *An Analysis of Time Shared Computer Systems* (The M.I.T. Press, 1966).
2. L. Kleinrock, *Queueing Systems*, Vols. 1 and 2 (Wiley, 1975).
3. P. J. Courtois, *Decomposability: Queueing and Computer System Applications* (Academic Press, 1977).
4. E. Gelenbe and I. Mitrani, *Analysis and Synthesis of Computer Systems* (Academic Press, 1980).
5. S. S. Lavenberg, *Computer Performance Modelling Handbook* (Academic Press, 1983).
6. C. Sauer and G. A. MacNair, *Simulation of Computer Communication Systems* (Prentice Hall, 1983).
7. E. D. Lazowska, J. Zahorian, G. S. Graham and K. C. Sevcik, *Quantitative System Performance* (Prentice Hall, 1984).
8. C. U. Smith, *Performance Engineering of Software Systems* (Addison Wesley, 1990).
9. A. O. Allen, *Probability Statistics and Queueing Theory with Computer Applications* (Academic Press, 1990).
10. K. Kant, *Introduction to Computer System Performance Evaluation* (McGraw-Hill, 1992).
11. H. G. Perros, *Queueing Networks with Blocking* (Oxford University Press, 1994).
12. T. G. Robertazzi, *Computer Networks and Systems: Queueing Theory and Performance Evaluation* (Springer, 1994).
13. C. Lindemann, *Performance Modelling with Deterministic and Stochastic Petri Nets* (Wiley, 1998).
14. S. Balsamo, V. DeNitto Personè and R. Onvural, *Analysis of Queueing Networks with Blocking* (Kluwer, 2001).
15. C. U. Smith and L. G. Williams, *Performance Solutions: A Practical Guide to Creating Responsive Scalable Software* (Addison Wesley, 2002).
16. G. Bolch, S. Greiner, H. do Meer and K. Trivedi, *Queueing Networks and Markov Chains* (Wiley, 1998).
17. K. S. Trivedi, *Probability and Statistics with Reliability, Queueing and Computer Science Applications* 2nd edn. (Wiley, 2002).
18. M. Woodside, C. Hrischuk, B. Selic and S. Bayarov, Automated performance modeling of software generated by a design environment, *Perform. Evaluation* **45**, 2 & 3 (2001), 107–123.
19. V. Cortellessa, A. D'Ambrogio and G. Iazeolla, Automatic derivation of software performance models from CASE documents, *Perform. Evaluation* **45**, 2 & 3 (2001), 81–105.
20. U. Herzog and G. Rolia, Performance validation tools for software/hardware systems, *Performance Evaluation* **45**, 2 & 3 (2001), 125–146.
21. V. Grassi and R. Mirandola, Derivation of Markov models for effectiveness analysis of adaptable software architectures for mobile computing, *IEEE Trans. Mobile Comput.* **2**(2) (2003), 114–131.

22. A. D'Ambrogio and G. Iazeolla, Steps toward the automatic production of performance models of web applications, *Comput. Networks* **41**(1) (2003), 29–39.
23. A. D'Ambrogio, G. Iazeolla and L. Pasini, Production of simulation models of interacting paradigms for web applications, in *Simulation Practice and Theory* (Elsevier, 2004).
24. V. Cortellessa and R. Mirandola, Deriving a queueing network based performance model from UML diagrams, in *Proc. 2nd Int. Workshop on Software and Performance (WOSP2000)*, Ottawa, Canada, September, 2000.
25. G. P. Gu and D. Petriu, XSLT transformation from UML models to LQN performance models, in *Proc. 3rd Int. Workshop on Software and Performance (WOSP2002)*, Roma, Italy, July, 2002.
26. F. Andolfi, F. Aquilani, S. Balsamo and P. Inverardi, Deriving performance models of software architectures from message sequence charts, in *Proc. 2nd Int. Workshop on Software and Performance (WOSP2000)*, Ottawa, Canada, September, 2000.
27. C. Lindemann, A. Thummler, A. Klemm, M. Lohmann and O. P. Waldhorst, Quantitative system evaluation with DSPNexpress 2000, in *Proc. 2nd Int. Workshop on Software and Performance (WOSP2000)*, Ottawa, Canada, September, 2000.
28. S. Bernardi, S. Donatelli and J. Merseguer, From UML sequence diagrams and state charts to analyzable Petri Net models, in *Proc. 3rd Int. Workshop on Software and Performance (WOSP2002)*, Roma, Italy, July, 2002.
29. P. King and R. Pooley, Using UML to derive stochastic Petri Net models 2, in *Proc. 5th UK Performance Engineering Workshop*, University of Bristol, eds. N. Davies and J. Bradley, July, 1999.
30. M. Woodside, A three-view model for performance engineering of concurrent software, *IEEE Trans. Software Eng.* **21**(9) (1995), 754–767.
31. J. A. Rolia and K. C. Sevcik, The method of layers, *IEEE Trans. Software Eng.* **21**(8) (1995), 689–700.
32. G. Iazeolla, Impianti, Reti e Sistemi Informatici: Modellistica, Valutazione delle Prestazioni e Progetto con tecniche analitiche e di simulazione ("Computer Systems and Networks: Modeling, Performance Evaluation and Design by analytic and simulation techniques") (Franco Angeli, Milano, 2004).
33. D. P. Siewiorek, G. G. Bell and A. Newell, *Computer Structures, Readings and Examples* (McGrawHill, 1982).

CHAPTER 7

Wireless Network Simulation: Towards a Systematic Approach

Satish K. Tripathi

*Department of Computer Science and Engineering,
University at Buffalo, SUNY,
Buffalo, NY 14260, USA
tripathi@buffalo.edu*

J. Jobin[*] and Michalis Faloutsos[†]

*Department of Computer Science and Engineering,
University of California, Riverside, CA 92521, USA
[*]jobin@cs.ucr.edu
[†]michalis@cs.ucr.edu*

Network simulation is a widely used tool in wireless network research. However, this widespread use of simulation has also resulted in the creation of new problems. In this study, we consider two of these problems and investigate their impact on the study of network behavior.

The first problem arises due to the large number of parameters typically found in a simulation model. Simulation models abound in the wireless domain and the parameters vary from model to model. Moreover, there is no consensus on values for these parameters across models, even on common parameters. This makes the task of analyzing simulation results complex. We propose a framework to address this issue. Our framework is based on reducing the large parameter space into a smaller set of a few, essential parameters. We also propose a new metric, *steady state utilization*, to capture the inherent capacity of a network and show how this can be used in the comparison of results across models.

The second problem arises due to the assumption of homogeneity in various aspects of modeling and simulation. Homogeneity is often resorted to in order to simplify the task of implementing a simulation and interpreting the subsequent results. We show that this can often hide subtle details that affect the network performance and can result in erroneous interpretations if the analysis of results is not done properly.

1. Introduction

In this work, we present a framework to systematize the modeling and simulation of wireless networks. Typical models of wireless networks use a large number of parameters and this causes problems in interpreting results from different models. We propose a framework to reduce this parameter space into a smaller set that captures the essence of the network. Additionally, we consider the assumption of homogeneity in wireless networks. We show that homogeneity, though it can make the task of simulation and modeling easier, can also lead to flawed interpretations of results in the absence of caution.

Most simulation models have an abundance of parameters. However, there are no commonly accepted standard values for these parameters. This has resulted in researchers using arbitrary values for parameters, thus making it difficult to interpret and compare results from different studies. Clearly, we need a framework in order to reduce this complexity. Ideally, we would like to have as few parameters and metrics in the model as possible.

The issue can be understood with the help of an example. Assume that we want to compare the performance of two networks A and B. Assume that network A has an arrival rate of 50 users per second, 85% utilization, and 5% loss and that the corresponding figures for network B are of 45 users per second, 73% utilization, and 3% loss. It is clear that one cannot judge easily which system performs better. In order to compare the systems, we need to be able to compare the offered load in the two systems. However, this requires knowledge of the other parameters (and their values) that can affect the network performance. Even if we were to assume that we have a comparable setup, we still cannot determine whether higher utilization is better than lower loss. Our approach attempts to resolve these problems.

We propose the reduction of the vast parameter space into a smaller, more compact set that captures the essence of the network. In this context, we introduce the novel concept of *steady state utilization*, which tries to capture the inherent capacity of the network.

The second problem has its origin in the assumption of homogeneity. Wireless network models are inherently complex due to several reasons, one of them being the large number of parameters. A commonly used method to combat this complexity is to assume homogeneity in as many parameters as possible. This reduces the complexity in implementing the model as well as interpreting the results. However, homogeneity is not a realistic assumption; indeed, recent studies have shown heterogeneity in the form of highly skewed distributions in several aspects of networks: long range dependence, bursty phenomena, Pareto distribution, power-law distribution, etc. Our goal is to study the effects of heterogeneity in a wireless cellular network.

There have been some studies that explored aspects of heterogeneity, but we were unable to find studies that focused on the overall effects of heterogeneity. Especially in the wired networks domain, there have studies of heterogeneity such as Ref. 19 where the authors conduct a network traffic analysis by separating traffic into *alpha traffic* and *beta traffic* and show that these two types have different behavior which is not detectable when traffic is aggregated. Floyd *et al.* discuss the difficulties in simulating the Internet because of *"the network's great heterogeneity and rapid change"*.[8] They address heterogeneity in a variety of aspects of the wired Internet. We were unable to find similar work in wireless networks.

Homogeneity results in the reduction of the parameter space over which simulations are conducted. This can hide or change significant aspects of the network behavior. In this paper, we argue that heterogeneity must be considered more seriously in performance analysis studies of wireless networks.

To summarize our contributions:

- We propose a framework to systematize the modeling and simulation of wireless cellular networks.
- As part of our framework, we introduce the novel metric of steady state utilization to capture the inherent capacity of a network. We utilize this to show how we can simplify the task of analyzing simulation results.
- We show that heterogeneity has to be modeled carefully. Our results indicate that in heterogeneous classes of users, the least demanding class dominates over time. Therefore, the simulation results do not necessarily reflect the proportion of users in different classes that exist at the beginning of the simulation.

The remainder of this chapter is organized as follows. Section 2 discusses the background of the problem of the large parameter space. In Sec. 3, we describe our framework to systematize network modeling and simulation. In Sec. 4, we describe our experimental results. We describe the problems arising from the assumption of homogeneity in Sec. 5 followed by the related evaluation results in Sec. 6. Finally, we conclude in Sec. 7.

This paper is largely based on the material in Refs. 12–14.

2. Background and Model

We employ the commonly used model for wireless cellular networks where a network is made up of hexagonal cells with six neighbors each.[2] Each cell has a base-station which is responsible for managing the users and the associated tasks such as admitting users, allocating and releasing bandwidth, ejecting users, etc. A user enters a system if there is bandwidth available, otherwise it is *blocked*. The point of entry can be any cell in the network. A user, once it is in the systems, spends some time in each cell which is referred to as the *cell latency*. The user moves from one cell to another (adjacent) cell until it voluntarily ends its session or is *dropped* due to lack of requisite resources.

Most simulation models for wireless cellular networks have a large number of parameters. Moreover, the choice of values for these parameters is done in an arbitrary manner. To add to this problem, the sensitivity of the simulation results to these parameters is not well established. These issues make it difficult to analyze and compare results from different models. While this has been a problem with simulations in general, it is worse in wireless networks due to the inherent complexity of such networks.

Researchers have investigated this problem with the aim of reducing the complexity of wireless network models. Most research studies try to achieve this goal by use of a simple or standardized model that attempts to abstract lower level details. Huang *et al.*[9] discuss the idea of abstraction, where they try to reduce or eliminate unnecessary details. Fall[7] proposes decreasing the number of objects in a simulation by aggregating some of them and by coarsening the resolution of some parts of the model. A standard framework for simulation has been suggested in Ref. 3. It aims to facilitate easy comparison across models by assuming that everyone is going to use the same framework. However, from a practical point of view, this is not always easy to enforce. Thus, it is clear that we need to be able to reduce the number of parameters that deal with system specific details without losing any components that could be critical to the model.

Apart from the reduction of parameters, another area that has room for improvement is performance metrics. Not all metrics are of significant importance or have sufficient efficacy. For instance, consider network utilization. Reseach so far considers utilization and loss separately.[11,15,18] However, this can be a problem when comparing two networks as we saw in the example of networks A and B in the introduction section. Even though the two metrics were given, it was not possible to decide which network was better without having further information.

3. Description of Our Framework

We now describe our framework. First, we describe the system parameters and then the performance metrics and then we propose our approach to reduce them into a smaller set.

3.1. *System parameters*

We now describe the system parameters that we propose in order to abstract lower level details of the wireless network model.

(i) *Steady State Utilization*: This is an indicator of the the maximum load a system can support without loss. We now describe how to find the steady state utilization of a given network. We start with a fully loaded system, i.e., all cells in the network have the maximum number of users which can be supported. The system has no arrivals after this point and no scheduled departures. We then let the users move around in the system. We assume that users stay in the system forever and the only way they leave the system is when they get dropped. In the beginning, as the users move, some of them find themselves in cells that are too crowded and consequently, they get dropped. This results in a lower contention for resources among the remaining users. Therefore, we observe that, initially, the drop rate is significant but this rate slows downs gradually until we reach a point where it is practically zero. We refer to the utilization at this point the *steady state utilization* of the system.

(ii) *Steady State Arrival Rate* ($SSAR$): This is the arrival rate of users that is required to keep the system functioning at its steady state utilization. Recall that steady state utilization, as defined earlier, assumes no arrivals and no departures. However, in a system where the users have a finite lifetime, the number of users will keep decreasing with time, thereby bringing the system down from its steady state utilization level. Therefore, in order to keep the system at that level, we need to replace the exiting users with new users. Thus, there is a corresponding arrival rate of users to keep the system functioning at the steady state utilization. We define this arrival rate as the steay state arrival rate ($SSAR$):

$$SSAR = Util_{ssu} * \frac{MaxUsers}{T}. \qquad (1)$$

$Util_{ssu}$ is the steady state utilization, $MaxUsers$ is the maximum number of users that the system can support, and T is the average call duration of a user.

(iii) *Relative Arrival Rate (RAR)*: This is the ratio of the actual arrival rate (λ) over SSAR. This is for easier comparison of relative loads of different networks:

$$RAR = \frac{\lambda}{SSAR}. \qquad (2)$$

Note that when the arrival rate equals $SSAR$, RAR is equal to 1. It is useful when comparing systems: for example, two different systems with different traffic loads are being equivalently utilized if their RAR values are equal to 1.

(iv) *Cell-User Bandwidth Ratio*: This is the ratio of cell bandwidth to user bandwidth. This indicates how many users each cell can accommodate on average.

3.2. Performance metrics

We describe the metrics that we use in our framework. Some of them are novel, some are not.

(i) *Observed Utilization*: A commonly used metric for the evaluation of network performance is *observed utilization*. Observed utilization is the same as the *utilization* commonly found in the literature. It is an indicator of the bandwidth used in the system or the number of users in the system. The *observed utilization* is the percentage of the network bandwidth that is actually used. Note that this includes all users that are currently active in the system, even those that might get dropped later.

(ii) *Wasted Utilization*: This is the percentage of the network bandwidth at any given instant that is occupied by users that will eventually be dropped. Recall that the observed utilization includes all active users, even those that might get dropped. Thus, it is also incorporating the bandwidth that is wasted. The wasted utilization metric tries to distinguish this. Wasted utilization has a direct negative impact on the utilization of the system and therefore it is important to distinguish this.

(iii) *Effective utilization*: This tries to incorporate utilization and loss into one metric. We noted earlier that often a model states both the utilization and the loss of a system. However, this makes it difficult to understand the system performance on an intuitive level. For instance, it might seem that a system is being utilized at a certain level; in reality, depending upon the wasted utilization, the actual utilization (which accounts for the successfully used bandwidth only) is less than the observed utilization. We refer to this utilization as the *effective utilization*. Later, we will show that effective utilization can provide us with new insight into our performance analysis. An analogy to effective utilization is the *goodput* often found in literature.[4]

3.3. Our framework

Having described our parameters, we now use them to create an abstract model. Our model has two advantages. First, we have fewer parameters. Second, the parameters hide unnecessary details. This makes the task of analyzing and understanding results easier. Figure 1 shows the mapping of old parameters to our new parameters.

The commonly used parameters are shown on the left side of the diagram while our equivalent parameters are shown on the right side. For example, cell latency (on the right side) is the amount of time that a user spends in a cell on an average. This is determined by the diameter of the cell, the speed of the user, and the mobility pattern of the user. Thus, cell latency is abstracting these three parameters. So, if we know the cell latency for two different networks, we do not need to be concerned about the other three (lower level) parameters. Our steady state utilization concept subsumes both the cell bandwidth and the network capacity. (It also abstracts details such as the the shape of the cell and the moving direction of a user.) It indicates the inherent network capacity. From the steady state utilization, we can derive the steady state arrival rate, which in turn, helps us define the relative arrival rate. These are a measure of the load placed on the network.

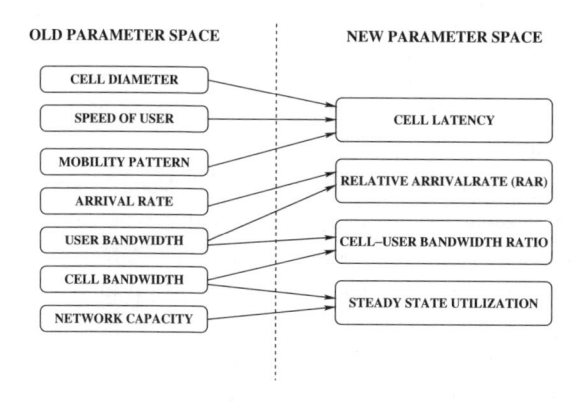

Fig. 1. Reduction of parameter space.

4. Experimental Results

For our experiments, we assume a wireless cellular network with homogeneous cells. We also assume that the users have the same bandwidth requirements and unless stated otherwise, they also have the same mean value of cell latency. This is only for ease of exposition. Steady state utilization can be determined even for heterogeneous networks. The cell capacity is in terms of the number of users that a cell can support. In order to change the cell capacity, we change the cell-user-bandwidth ratio. The simulation program was written in C using the CSIM package.

4.1. *Parameters that affect steady state utilization*

First, we conduct some experiments to study the effect of different parameters on the steady state utilization. The objective is to understand the robustness of steady state utilization to different parameters.

(i) *Cell-user-bandwidth ratio*: In Figure 2, we plot utilization versus time for three different scenarios. The lowest plot (r20) corresponds to the case where we have a single class of users and the cell-user bandwidth ratio is 20 (i.e., each cell can hold a maximum of 20 users). The steady state utilization level is about 37%. The topmost plot (r100) is for the case where this ratio is 100. Now, the steady state utilization is about 65%. The steady state utilization is more when users have smaller bandwidth requirements. This is because if a higher bandwidth user is dropped, it will affect the effective utilization more. Thus, the experiments suggest that finer granularity of user bandwidth leads to higher steady state utilization.

(ii) *Multiple classes of users*: Next, we divide the users equally into two classes with cell-user bandwidth ratio of 100 and 20. The result is seen in the middle plot (r20-100) in Fig. 2, where the steady state utilization is now about 43%. We see that the combination of two classes leads to a steady state utilization that is in between the steady state utilization of the two individual classes.

(iii) *Cell latency*: Here, we consider the effect of cell latency on the steady state utilization level. Figure 3 is for two different mean values of cell latency — 50 and 500 seconds. As seen, when the mean cell latency increases from 50 to 500 seconds, the steady state utilization increases from 64% to 70%. Intuitively, as the cell latency increases, the users move slower, there are fewer drops, and hence the steady state utilization increases.

However, it is interesting to see what happens when we plot time in terms of cell latency units. Figure 4 shows how utilization varies with time.

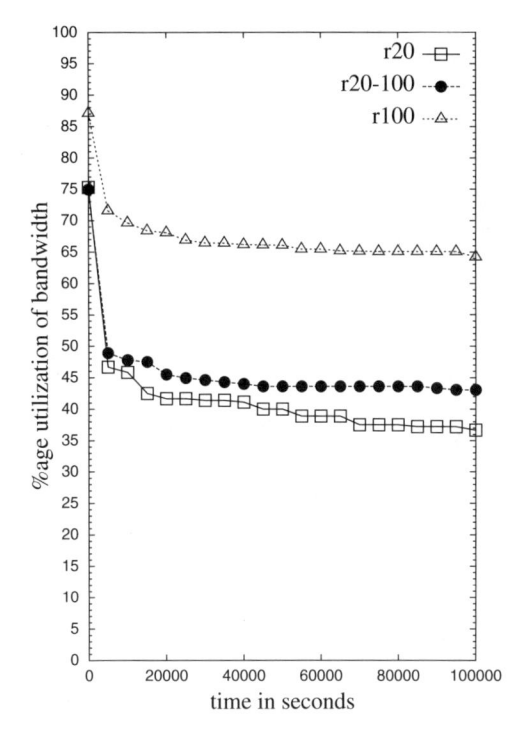

Fig. 2. Change in steady state utilization with cell-user-bandwidth ratio and the number of classes.

Time is plotted on the x-axis in terms of the mean cell latency. The graph shows seven plots corresponding to different cell latency values. Here, cell latency does not seem to affect the value of steady state utilization for a network; the range of values for the utilization is less than 1%. Indeed, steady state utilization is achieved after a certain number of time units of cell latency. Thus, it is dependent on the number of hops a user makes on an average, as opposed to the actual cell latency. This also indicates an inherent nature of the network to support a particular number of users. An implication is that we can use the steady state utilization without being concerned about the cell latency.

We also studied the effect of cell latency in both hexagon and square cell networks with three different sizes. The range of values for utilization for all cases was less than 2% except in the case of a square cell network with 16 cells where it was less than 3%.

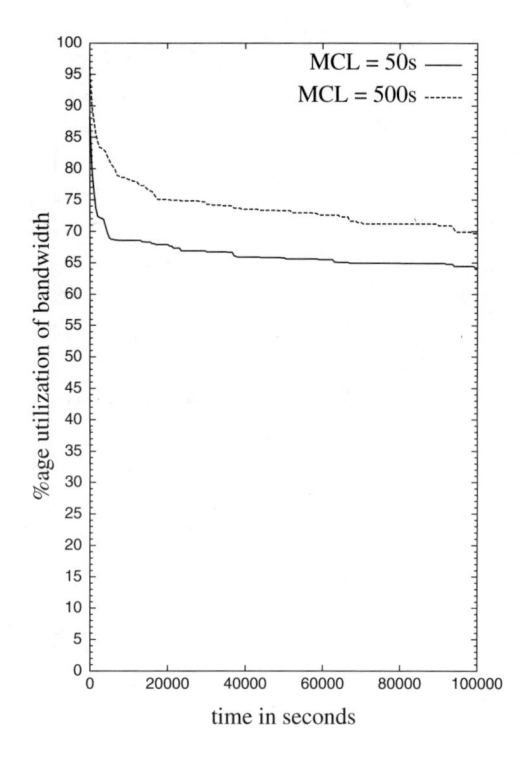

Fig. 3. Change in steady state utilization with cell latency.

(iv) *Network size*: First, we consider a hexagon cell network. Figure 5 shows that there is negligible effect of network size on the steady state utilization. The utilization in the 18 cell network is only marginally better — about 0.5%. This implies that if all other factors are constant, there is no dependence on the size.

Similar results were obtained for a square cell network. We experiment with three sizes (16, 49, and 81); the utilization seems to be unaffected by size, except that the 16 cell network is only marginally better — about 0.5%. These results indicate that size is inconsequential except when it is too small. Intuitively, we believe this is because the remainder of the parameters are the same, the users are randomly distributed uniformly throughout the cells, and the cells themselves are all the same. In a smaller network, the correlation between cells is higher and hence, there is a larger margin of error. Indeed, the 18 and 16 cell networks seem to differ a bit from the others.

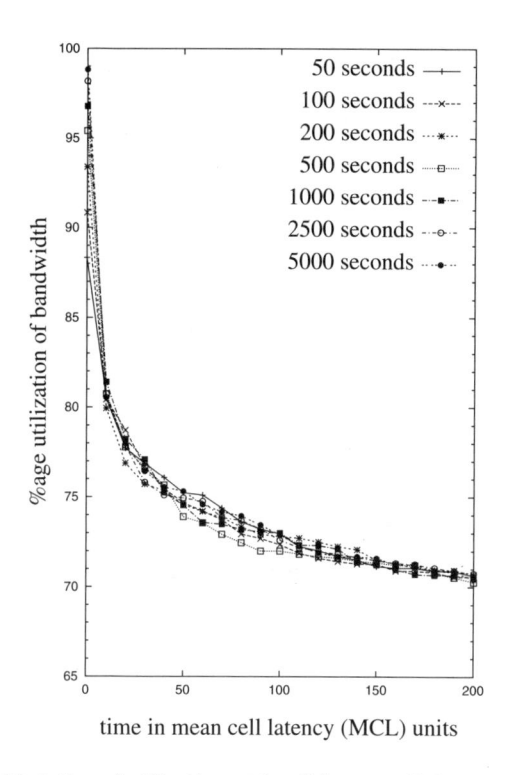

Fig. 4. Variation of utilization with cell latency: 48 hexagonal cells.

(v) *Shape of the cell*: We experiment with two kinds of cells — hexagon and square. Hexagon cells are the most commonly found cells in literature.[2,11,21] We consider three different network sizes for both types of networks. As we saw earlier, the network size does not seem to affect the steady state utilization. So, a hexagon cell network can be safely compared to a square cell network of equivalent size without being concerned about any side-effects.

As seen in Figure 6, a hexagon cell network of 18 cells has a similar utilization as a square cell network of 16 cells. This suggests that the shape of the individual cells in a network does not play an important role in the final results. We obtained similar results when we compared a 48 hexagon cell network to a 49 square cell network and an 80 hexagon cell network to an 81 square cell network.

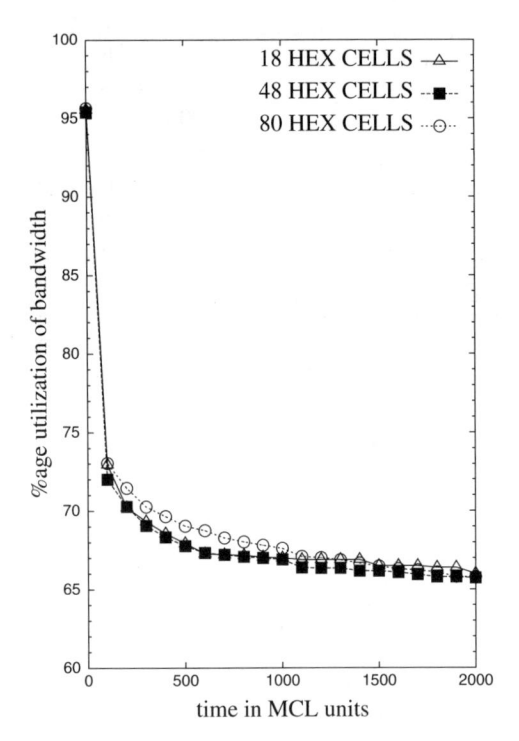

Fig. 5. Variation of utilization with network size: 18, 48, and 80 hexagonal cells (MCL = mean cell latency).

4.2. *The significance of steady state arrival rate*

As we saw earlier, given the steady state utilization and call duration, we can calculate the steady state arrival rate. Then, we can describe any arrival rate with the relative arrival rate (RAR). For $RAR = 1$, the system is at its steady state utilization. We now examine the behavior for other values of RAR. We vary the RAR, thereby subjecting the system to different loads corresponding to different values of the arrival rates.

Figure 7 shows the comparison between the observed utilization and the effective utilization when the arrival rate is varied. We see that if RAR is below 1, there is no wasted bandwidth but the system is underutilized: the effective utilization is below the steady state utilization.

We have no losses while $RAR \leq 1$ (i.e., $\lambda \leq SSAR$). For $RAR = 1$, we reach the steady state utilization. As RAR increases beyond 1, we start to see wasted bandwidth and a decrease in the effective utilization. Thus, we

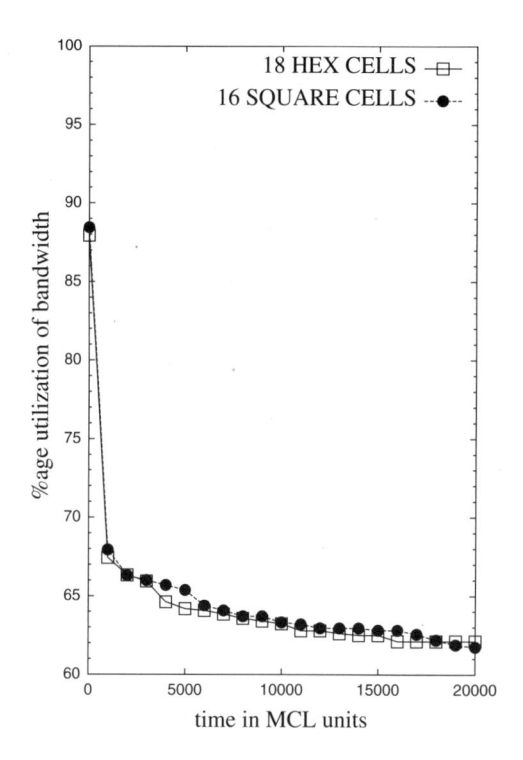

Fig. 6. Effect of shape on utilization: 18 hexagonal versus 16 square cells.

see that for $RAR = 1$, we have the maximum effective utilization without loss. Above the SSAR, effective utilization increases slightly and then starts to drop.

4.3. Discussion and applications

Our methodology can be used in the following manner: (i) Given a network and a traffic load, find the steady state utilization.[a] (ii) Find the corresponding steady state arrival rate. (iii) Plot effective utilization and observed utilization for different values of the relative arrival rate and study the plot to see if the system is near its steady state utilization.

So, given a network and its load characteristics, one can say whether it is being under-utilized or over-utilized. Moreover, one can also determine what

---

[a] Our criterion for finding the steady state utilization was a change of less than 5% in the utilization in a time duration of 500 times the mean cell latency.

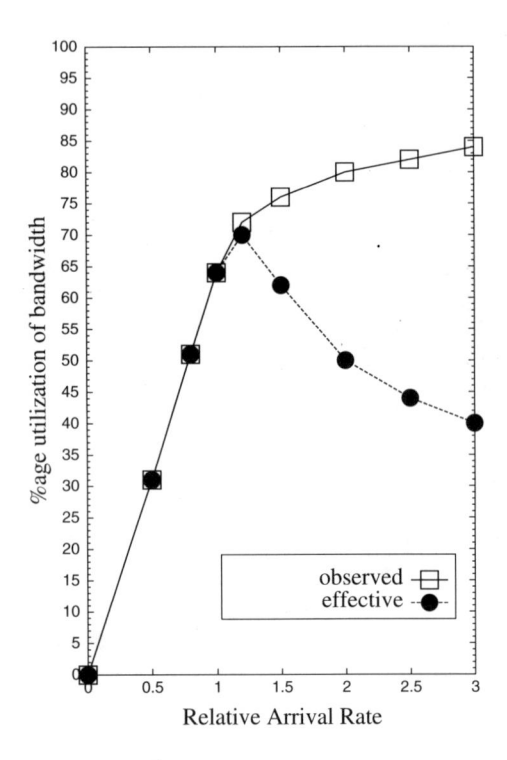

Fig. 7. Observed and effective utilization versus RAR.

the arrival rate should be in order to achieve steady state utilization. Thus, *SSAR* provides us with a reference point using which we can understand how the network is being utilized.

We apply our methodology to a specific problem — to study the benefits of advance reservations in wireless networks. Reservations have been studied as a way of improving the quality of service.[2,5,21] In brief, the idea is to make reservations in some of the neighboring cells that a user is likely to move into ahead of time. Statistical data like a mobility profile[5] can make the advance reservations more accurate. We study how reservations impact the effective utilization.

For reservations, the next cell has to be predicted in advance, before the user moves into it. We consider two cases. (1) We assume we are always able to predict correctly the next cell that the user will move into; this is the *perfect-reservation* case. Here, we need to reserve only one adjacent cell for each user. Perfect-reservation is an ideal scenario but it provides us with a good benchmark. (2) We make reservations in two cells; this is the the 2-cell reservation case. This is a more realistic scenario.

We assume a cellular mobile wireless network for the simulation. For simplicity we assume that all users have the same bandwidth requirements and the same cell latency. First, we follow the steps of our methodology and plot the utilization at different values of the relative arrival rate. Figure 8 shows a comparison between the reservation and no-reservation scenarios. The topmost plot corresponds to the no reservation case, the middle one is for the perfect reservation case, and the bottom plot is for the 2-cell reservation case. As the figure shows, under low and medium loads, no reservation is better than having reservations, even if they are perfect. Not having perfect reservations only degrades the performance further. The 2-cell reservation scheme exhibits much lower effective utilization as compared to no reservations. These results indicate that a system might actually perform better without reservation.

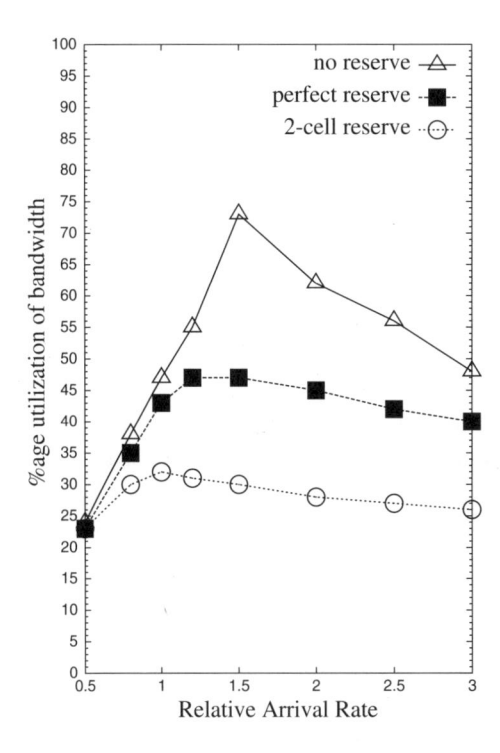

Fig. 8. Effective utilization with and without reservation.

This work addresses the issue of heterogeneity in the modeling of wireless cellular networks. Wireless network modeling is a complex task because of the large number of parameters involved and the intricate nature of wireless networks. In order to simplify network modeling, researchers often make the assumption of homogeneity; for instance, all cells in a cellular network are assumed to have the same size and capacity, all nodes have the same bandwidth requirements, etc. However, in the real world, networks do not conform to such assumptions of homogeneity; heterogeneity is more prevalent. Therefore, it is important to understand how it affects the modeling of wireless networks so that we can improve the task of network design.

In this work, we introduce heterogeneity in various modeling parameters and study its effect on the network behavior. We show that heterogeneity can hide several subtleties, which, if not properly modeled, can lead to misleading conclusions. The goal of this work is to raise the awareness of the community about the importance of heterogeneity and the attention that we need to devote to its realistic modeling.

5. Homogeneity

Homogeneity is often used in modeling wireless networks since it simplifies the task of modeling and the subsequent analysis of results. Most models assume homogeneity in several factors. We now describe some of them briefly.

Most models for wireless cellular networks typically use a network of made up of hexagonal cells. This is based on the classical cellular architecture first described by MacDonald.[17] Each cell is a hexagon with six neighbors. A base station in each cell is responsible for user management in that cell. A user enters one of these cells at random and after spending some time (cell latency) in that cell, moves to one of its neighboring cells provided there is enough bandwidth in that destination cell.

Homogeneity is assumed in several parameters while modeling. For instance, most research assumes hexagon cells[23] for their models. Most of them also assume that the network is a wrap-around network, in which the users, when they reach the edge of the network, continue on to the other side of the network instead of bouncing back into the same cell from where they came from. One can visualize the network as the surface of a soccer ball. The reason for using such a network is is to avoid edge effects, which can skew the uniformity of the cells, and the user distribution and therefore, affect the results.

Cells are usually assumed to be homogeneous in their capacity and their size (diameter/radius). The assumption of same size along with the assumption of same shape, implies that all of them have the same number of neighbors.

Users are also assumed to be homogeneous. For example, they have the same bandwidth requirements, move at the same speed (within a range), and use the same mobility model. Occasionally, there might be more than one class of users in terms of their bandwidth requirements or speed.[6,16] For instance, a network could have three types of users: low, medium, and high bandwidth users. This would correspond to users using voice, data, and video traffic. The network could have two classes of users in terms of speed: city users and highway users, with the users moving relatively faster on the highway.

5.1. *Related work*

There has been some research in addressing the issue of heterogeneity in wired networks.[8,19] However, there is a lack of similar research in the wireless networks domain.

Akl *et al.* note that there is a dearth of research in CDMA network cell design.[1] They mention that most research uses uniform cells. They show that the size of the cell can affect a CDMA network. Their explanation is that the larger cells can affect the smaller cells due to intercell interference.

Chih-Lin I *et al.* propose a two-tiered architecture to improve capacity and reduce network control.[10] The authors mention that smaller cells are more conducive to higher capacity whereas larger cells reduce network control. They aim to get the best of both factors and to this end, they introduce a two tier architecture consisting of microcells and macrocells. However, in their study, all the microcells are assumed to have the same size.

Sidi *et al.* show that the speed of a user in a cellular network can affect its blocking probability.[20] They note that this blocking probability is fundamentally different for very slow and very fast users. Additionally, they make a distinction between blocking probabilities of new users and existing users and show that these depend on the type of the user mobility.

In Ref. 14, we have considered hotspots in wireless cellular networks as a form of heterogeneity. Hotspots are due to contention for resources and we show that hotspots can arise due to different causes and that depending on their causes they affect the network behavior in different ways. However, we will not discuss hotspots in this chapter; we refer the reader to Ref. 14.

5.2. Metrics for comparison

Wireless network models use a large variety of metrics for performance evaluation, such as utilization, throughput, dropping and blocking probability, bit error rate, number of retransmissions, etc. For our evaluation, we use utilization. Recall that we noted earlier that utilization by itself is usually not a good indicator since a network could be experiencing loss. Therefore, we use the steady state utilization for evaluating performance.

6. Evaluation

To study heterogeneity and its effects on network behavior, we isolate each parameter and conduct the experiments while introducing heterogeneity in that parameter. Our experiments use a 36 cell wrap-around network, unless otherwise specified. Each cell can support 100 users. Each point in the plots that follow represents the average of ten simulation runs.

6.1. Cell shape (number of neighbors)

The shape of a cell is directly related to the number of neighbors. The typical assumption is that all cells have the same shape and size and also the same number of neighbors. Here we investigate two issues: (a) Does a shape other than a hexagon make a difference? (b) How does heterogeneity in shape impact network performance?

Traditionally, a hexagon shape has been used since it is the closest to a circle which is theoretically what the coverage area of a basestation with omnidirectional antennas would look like. However, in real life, due to the presence of objects such as buildings and poles, coverage areas are not always perfectly circular. Moreover, in real networks, cells can be of different sizes. This could happen due to several reasons, e.g., as a consequence of cell splitting to increase capacity. This means that one could have a different number of neighbors for different cells in the same network.

We experiment with networks having cells with hexagon, square, and triangle shapes. Additionally, we experiment with: (a) Two dimensional chain network. This is a set of cells that are joined at two ends, i.e., the network wraps around in only one dimension. (b) Heterogeneous networks where the number of neighbors of the cells varies from three to seven. (c) Same-shape-different-size-cell (SSDSC) network. Here the cells are all of the same shape (square, in this case) but some of them are larger than the others.

Note that these different shapes are only meant to study the effect of the cells having different numbers of neighbors. Shapes such as a triangle might

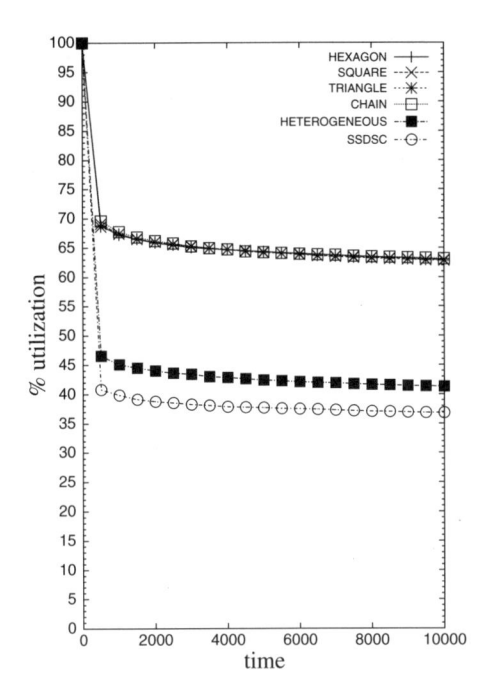

Fig. 9. Comparison of six different networks. The lower most plot is for the SSDSC network and the one above it is for the heterogeneous one.

not necessarily exist in a real network, but they help in understanding how the introduction of heterogeneity changes network behavior irrespective of the original (homogeneous) shapes.

We compare these different networks using utilization to gauge their performance. Figure 9 shows how utilization varies with the shape of the cell in six different networks. The utilization is the same as the steady state utilization mentioned earlier. In our experiments, we are not concerned about the actual steady state utilization values but, instead, we want to study how the nature of utilization is affected by heterogeneity.

The utilization curves are remarkably similar to each other except for the heterogeneous cell network and the SSDSC network which are shown by the two lower most plots in the graph. (The heterogeneous network is the upper of the two lower most plots.) Thus, as long as all cells are homogeneous in shape, and have the same size, the network exhibits similar performance. However, as soon as one introduces a heterogeneity in the shape, the behavior of the network changes and utilization drops. Intuitively, the non-uniformity of the cells leads to reduced utilization.

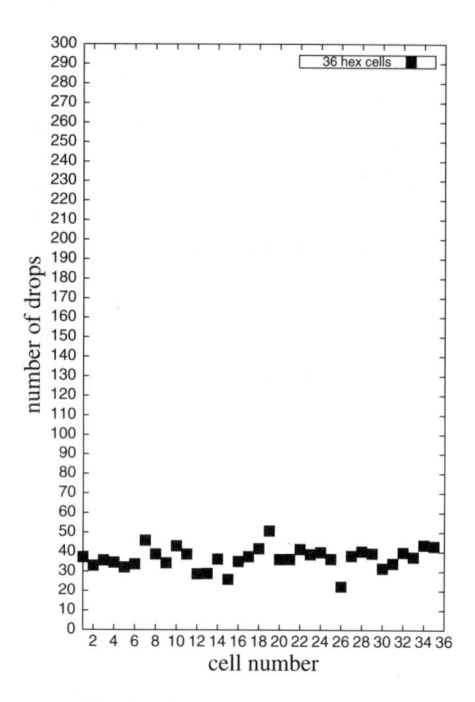

Fig. 10. With hexagon cells: the drops are uniform across the cells. The effect of heterogeneity on network utilization.

To understand why heterogeneity in the shape decreases utilization, we consider drops on a per cell basis. Consider Figure 10 that shows the number of drops in a homogeneous network. The y-axis plots the number of drops in each cell and x-axis plots the cell number which ranges from 1 to 36. The graph shows that the number of drops to be uniform across all cells. Contrast this with Figure 11 (heterogeneous network) where there is no uniformity in the number of drops across cells. We obtained similar results for the other homogeneous networks (which we do not show here due to space constraints).

Intuitively, as the number of neighbors increases, a cell is bound to experience more handoffs and is therefore more likely to drop users than a cell with fewer neighbors. Indeed, Figure 12 shows that in the case of heterogeneous networks, the number of drops increases with the number of neighbors.

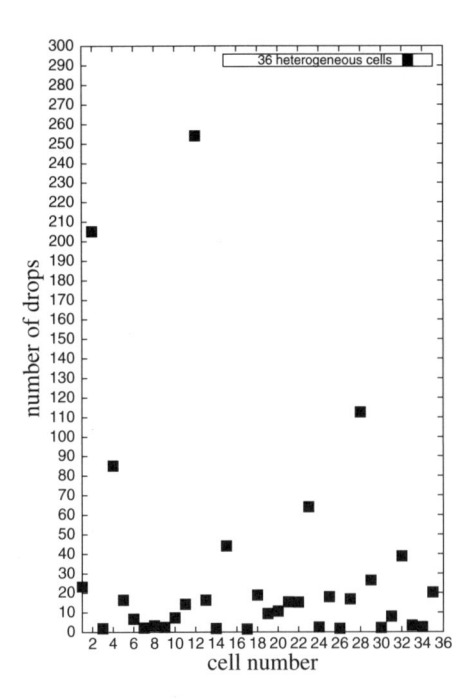

Wireless Network Simulation: Towards a Systematic Approach 95

Fig. 11. With heterogeneous cells: drops vary widely across the cells.

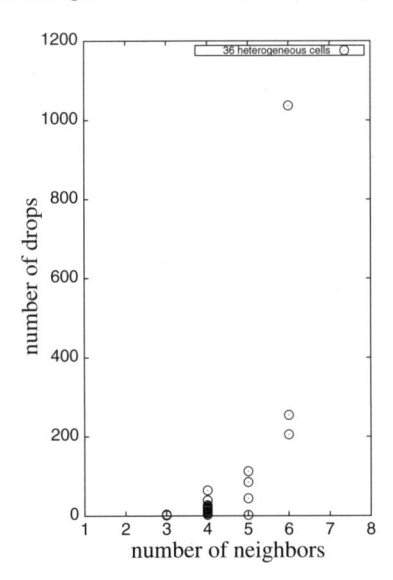

Fig. 12. Heterogeneous network: more neighbors means more drops. Heterogeneous networks — more drops.

Thus, we see that making assumptions of homogeneity can hide such subtle issues that can have a significant effect on the behavior of the network and consequently, the interpretation of results.

6.2. User speed

The speed of a user is typically assumed to be exponentially distributed or a fixed constant or a value within a fixed range such as $[V_{min}, V_{max}]$, where V_{min} is the minimum value and V_{max} is the maximum value. However, this can sometimes lead to strange behavior. As shown in Ref. 22, the speed was the factor which lead to differences in the performance of AODV and DSR protocols depending on the implementation. A common assumption is that all users belong to one homogeneous class in terms of speed.

Often, users are divided into classes based on whether they are in the city (slow speed) or on a highway (fast speed). We experiment with multiple classes of speed to study how this affects utilization.

We experiment with two classes of users: class 1 (slower) and class 2 (faster). Users are equally distributed between the two classes. One would expect that faster users would experience more handoffs and hence would be more likely to be dropped than slower users. We do not show our results here due to space constraints. Indeed, this is what happens, as Table 1 shows.

The ratio column in the table indicates the ratio of the two speeds. As the ratio increases, the number of slower users increases and the number of faster users decreases. However, even this seems to stabilize. This is because as the ratio increases, the speed of the slower users becomes very slow as

Table 1. User classes based on speed: distribution of users.

Speed ratio	Class 1	Class 2	Total
1	1135	1135	2270
2	1367	919	2286
5	1597	723	2320
20	1723	617	2340
50	1759	599	2358
100	1777	575	2352
200	1788	598	2386
500	1795	587	2382

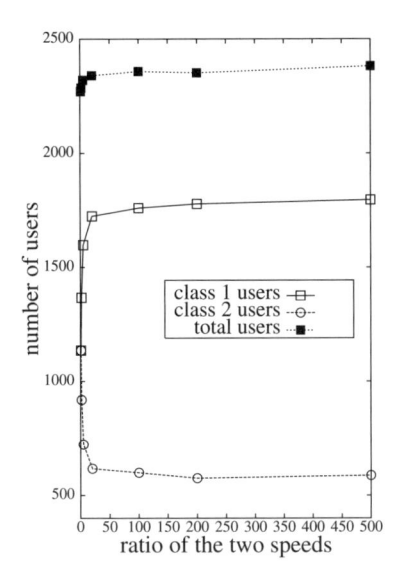

Fig. 13. The number of users as the ratio of the two speeds increases.

compared to the faster users. In the limit, one could think of the slower users being almost stationary while the faster ones move around. We also note that the overall network utilization as indicated by the total number of users does not seem to be significantly affected by the presence of these classes.

However, we note that our results indicate that lower speed users dominate faster speed users over time. Thus, a simple assumption that a user distribution is 1:1 for two classes of users at the beginning of an experiment may not hold at the end of the experiment.

6.3. User bandwidth requirement

Users are typically assumed to have the same bandwidth requirement. Often, researchers divide them into two or three different classes, e.g., classes based on data, voice, and video.

One would expect that given all other factors are similar, a lower bandwidth user has a better chance of survival in a network as congestion increases. The handoff rates remain the same regardless of a user's bandwidth requirement. However, as overall availability of bandwidth in the network decreases, a higher bandwidth user is more likely to find itself getting dropped in scenarios where a lower bandwidth user might be able

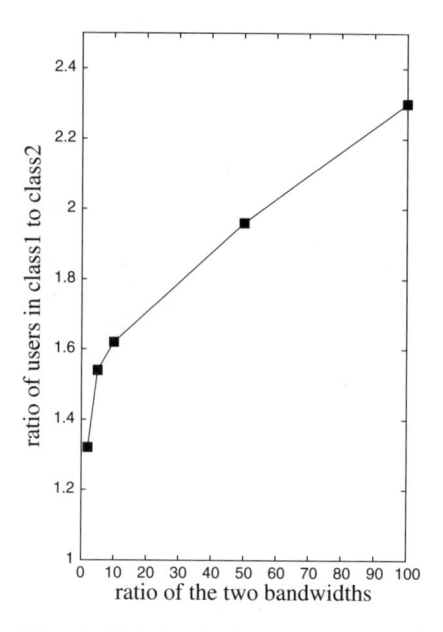

Fig. 14. Proportion of low- to high-bandwidth users increases as the ratio of the two bandwidths increases.

to obtain the needed bandwidth. Figure 14 shows how the proportion of low- and high-bandwidth users changes as we change the ratio of the two bandwidths.

Thus, an assumption that the ratio of two classes of users is 1:1 at the beginning of the experiment might not be valid at the end of the experiment. This is to be borne in mind while analyzing and interpreting results.

7. Conclusion

The goal of this paper is to increase the awareness of the research community about the importance of using heterogeneity in modeling wireless networks. We show that the same network with a seemingly small amount of heterogeneity can exhibit significantly different performance. In addition, we show that heterogeneity needs to be modeled carefully in order to avoid misinterpretations such as thinking that we have 50% high bandwidth users when we really have less.

Specifically, we considered heterogeneity in the shape of the cell, the speed of the users, and the bandwidth requirement of the users. We showed that heterogeneity has significant effect on the the performance of the network and resorting to homogeneity can hide these.

This work is a first step in addressing the issue of heterogeneity. We plan to experiment with more parameters and distributions and also explore this issue in other domains such as wireless ad hoc networks and sensor networks.

We proposed a performance evaluation methodology for wireless network simulation models. Our methodology reduces the number of parameters and introduces new metrics that facilitate the evaluation and comparison of system performance across different models.

We introduced the concept of steady state utilization which captures the inherent capacity of a network for a given workload. We defined steady state arrival rate as the arrival rate that will keep the system utilization at the maximum possible level, without losses. Moreover, we proposed *effective utilization* as a more insightful metric which combines both the utilization and the loss.

Finally, we looked at a case study to understand our methodology. As future work, we would like to study in more detail, the interdependencies of our parameters both analytically and with simulations.

References

1. R. G. Akl, M. V. Hegde, M. Naraghi-Pour and P. S. Min, Multicell CDMA network design, *IEEE Trans. Vehi. Techn.* **50**(3) (2001), 711–722.
2. A. R. Aljadhai and T. F. Znati, A framework for call admission control and QoS support in wireless environments, in *Proc. IEEE INFOCOM*, March 23–25, New York (IEEE, 1999), pp. 1019–1026.
3. S. Bajaj, L. Breslau, D. Estrin, K. Fall, S. Floyd, P. Haldar, M. Handley, A. Helmy, J. Heidemann, P. Huang, S. Kumar, S. McCanne and R. Rejaie, Improving simulation for network research, *USC Computer Science Department Technical Report*, March, 1999.
4. H. Balakrishnan, V. N. Padmanabhan, S. Seshan and R. Katz, A comparison of mechanisms for improving TCP performance over wireless links, *IEEE/ACM Trans. Networking* **5**(6) (1997), 756–769.
5. V. Bharghavan and J. P. Mysore, Profile-based next-cell prediction in indoor wireless LANs, *IEEE Int. Conf. Networking* (1997).
6. S. Choi and K. G. Shin, Comparison of connection admission-control schemes in the presence of hand-offs in cellular networks, in *Proc. ACM MOBICOM* (1998), 264–275.
7. T. C. Fall, A framework for the simulation experimentation process, *Proc. 1997 Winter Simulation Conference.*
8. S. Floyd and V. Paxson, Difficulties in simulating the Internet, *IEEE/ACM Trans. Networking* **9**(4) (2001), 392–403.

9. P. Huang, D. Estrin and J. Heidemann, Enabling large-scale simulations: Selective abstraction approach to the study of multicast protocols, in *Proc. 6th Int. Symp. Modeling, Analysis, and Simulation of Computer and Telecommunications Systems (MASCOTS '98)*, Montreal, Canada, July, 1998.
10. I. Chin-Lin, L. J. Greenstein and R. D. Gitlin, A microcell/macrocell cellular architecture for low- and high-mobility wireless users, *IEEE J. Selec. Areas Commu.* **11**(6) (1993), 885–891.
11. Y. Iraqi and R. Boutaba, A novel distributed call admission control for wireless mobile multimedia networks, in *Proc. 3rd ACM Int. Workshop Wireless Mobile Multimedia* (2000), 21–27.
12. J. Jobin, M. Faloutsos and S. K. Tripathi, Performance evaluation of mobile wireless networks: A new perspective, *Fourth ACM Int. Workshop on Modeling, Analysis, and Simulation of Wireless and Mobile Systems* (2001).
13. J. Jobin, M. Faloutsos and S. K. Tripathi, Simplifying the analysis of wireless cellular network simulation, *Int. Symp. Performance Evaluation of Computer and Telecommunication Systems* (2002).
14. J. Jobin, M. Faloutsos, S. K.Tripathi and S. V. Krishnamurthy, Understanding the effects of hotspots in wireless cellular networks, *IEEE INFOCOM 2004*, Hong Kong, March, 2004.
15. B. Li, C. Lin and S. T. Chanson, Analysis of a hybrid cutoff priority scheme for multiple classes of traffic in multimedia wireless networks, *Wireless Networks* **4** (1998), 279–290.
16. D. A. Levine, I. F. Akyildiz and M. Naghshineh, A resource estimation and call admission algorithm for wireless multimedia networks using the shadow cluster concept, *IEEE/ACM Trans. Networking* **5**(1) (1997), 1–12.
17. V. H. MacDonald, The cellular concept, *Bell Systems Technical J.* **58**(1) (1979), 15–43.
18. J. R. Moorman, J. W. Lockwood and S.-M. Kang, Real-time prioritized call admission control in a base station scheduler, in *Proc. 3rd ACM Int. Workshop on Wireless Mobile Multimedia* (2000), 28–37.
19. S. Sarvotham, R. Riedi and R. Baraniuk, Connection-level analysis and modeling of network traffic, in *Proc. 1st ACM SIGCOMM Internet Measurement Workshop*, November, 2001, 99–103.
20. M. Sidi and D. Starobinski, New call blocking versus handoff blocking in cellular networks, *Wireless Networks* **5** (1997), 15–27.
21. S. Singh, Quality of service guarantees in mobile computing, *J. Comput. Commun.* **19** (1996), 359–371.
22. J. Yoon, M. Liu and B. Noble, Random waypoint considered harmful, IEEE INFOCOM, 2003.
23. F. Yu and V. C. M. Leung, Mobility-based predictive call admission control and bandwidth reservation in wireless cellular networks, IEEE INFOCOM, 2001.

CHAPTER 8

Location- and Power-Aware Protocols for Wireless Networks with Asymmetric Links

Guoqiang Wang[*], Yongchang Ji[†] and Dan C. Marinescu[‡]

*School of Computer Science,
University of Central Florida,
Orlando, FL 32816-2450, USA*
[*]*gwang@cs.ucf.edu*
[†]*yji@cs.ucf.edu*
[‡]*dcm@cs.ucf.edu*

Damla Turgut[§] and Ladislau Bölöni[¶]

*Department of Electrical and Computer Engineering,
University of Central Florida,
Orlando, FL 32816-2450, USA*
[§]*turgut@cpe.ucf.edu*
[¶]*lboloni@cpe.ucf.edu*

Asymmetric links are common in wireless networks for a variety of physical, logical, operational, and legal considerations. An asymmetric link supports unidirectional communication between a pair of mobile stations and requires a set of relay stations for the transmission of packets in the other direction. We evaluate m-limited forwarding, a technique to disseminate information in location- and power-aware networks with symmetric and/or asymmetric links. Then we introduce a network and a MAC layer protocol for wireless networks with asymmetric links. The network layer protocol takes advantage of the location information to reduce the number of retransmissions and thus reduces the power consumption via the m-limited forwarding technique. The MAC layer protocol requires fewer nodes to maintain silence during a transmission than the protocols proposed in Refs. 1 and 2. We present a set of metrics characterizing the ability of a medium access control protocol to silence nodes which can cause collisions.

1. Introduction and Motivation

In a wireless environment, at any given time, an asymmetric link supports unidirectional communication between a pair of mobile stations and requires a set of relay stations for the transmission of packets in the other direction. Throughout this chapter, the term "asymmetric" is related to the transmission range of a node at time t and a communication channel linking two nodes. Two nodes linked by an asymmetric link at time t may find themselves in close proximity, or may be able to increase their transmission range and to reach each other at time $t + \tau$ and thus be connected by a bi-directional link. Thus we feel compelled to make a distinction between unidirectional and asymmetric links in wireless networks. We shall drop this distinction whenever the context allows us to. Several scenarios contribute to the asymmetry of communication links in a wireless environment:

(a) *Transmission range limited by the node hardware.* The hardware properties of the node (for instance, the antenna or the radio circuits) determine the maximum transmission range. This can be different for different nodes, leading to asymmetric links, which cannot be avoided except by physically changing the nodes hardware components, for instance, by installing a different antenna.

(b) *Power limitation.* Two nodes have different power constraints, e.g., A has sufficient power reserves and a transmission range enabling it to reach B; however, B has limited power, and either (i) cannot reach A, or (ii) may choose not to reach A to save power. The two scenarios lead to different protocol design. In the second scenario, B is capable to reach A and we could exploit this capability for short transmissions when necessary, e.g., during a network setup phase and thus avoid setting up a bidirectional overlay.[a]

(c) *Interference.* A can reach B and B can reach A, but if B were to transmit at a power level sufficient to reach A, it would interfere with C who might be a licensed user of the spectrum. This scenario is critical for transmitters which attempt to opportunistically exploit unused parts of the licensed spectrum (such as unused television channels). Even if operating in the un-licensed bands, dynamic spectrum management arrangements might have given the priority to node C; thus B needs to refrain from sending at a power level above a given threshold.

(d) *Stealth considerations.* A and B attempt to communicate and wish to hide the existence or the exact location of B from O. One way to achieve

---

[a]Some approaches use network layer tunneling to enable the transmission of ACK packets at the MAC layer. However, a working network layer requires a working MAC layer.

this is to restrict the transmission power of node B to the minimum and/or transmit on frequencies which make location detection more difficult (low probability of detection (LPD) systems). This is especially important in military/battlefield applications.[3,4]

(e) *Unidirectional links required by dynamic spectrum management.* In the emerging field of software defined radios, the nodes can transmit in virtually any band across the spectrum, but they need to share the spectrum with devices belonging to licensed operators as well as devices with limited flexibility. Once any of the reasons discussed previously force a link to be unidirectional additional constraints, e.g., the need for a reverse path between some pairs of nodes may cause other links to change their status and operate in a unidirectional mode even when there is no explicit reason for unidirectionality.

We discuss briefly two potential applications of the network and MAC layer protocols for location- and power-aware networks with asymmetric links discussed in this chapter: software radios and *ad hoc* grids.

Software radios can sense their RF environment and modify their frequency, power, and/or modulation, allowing for real-time spectrum management. A software radio has distinctive advantages: (a) it covers a wide operational frequency spanning multiple bands of the spectrum, (b) it can support multiple networking protocols, (c) a single hardware unit can be programmed to work with multiple waveforms, and (d) a software radio can be updated to work with new protocols, designed after the radio hardware.

An *ad hoc grid* consists of a hierarchy of mobile systems with different hardware, software, and communication capabilities.[6] The processor speed, amount of main memory, secondary storage, speed of communication devices, and sophistication of the software support increase as we move from one class to another in this hierarchy. Informally, we call the four classes of systems: disposable or C4, wearable or C3, portable or C2, and back-end or C1. There are many potential applications of *ad hoc* grids for sporting events, discovery expeditions, natural resource exploration, disaster management, and battlefield management.[6]

The contributions of this chapter are: an evaluation of m-limited forwarding, a technique to disseminate information in location- and power-aware networks with symmetric and/or asymmetric links. We also introduce a routing and a MAC layer protocol for wireless networks with asymmetric links. The network layer protocol exploits the location information to reduce the number of retransmissions and thus reduces the power consumption. The MAC layer protocol requires fewer nodes to maintain silence during a transmission than the protocols proposed in Refs. 1 and 2. We introduce a set of metrics characterizing the ability of a medium access control protocol to silence nodes which can cause collisions.

2. Related Work

Ad hoc routing protocols are: (i) *table-driven*, or *proactive*, such as DSDV,[8] CGSR,[9] DREAM,[10] and OLSR[11]; (ii) *on-demand*, *reactive*, or *source-initiated*, such as DSR,[12] AODV,[13] LAR,[14] and TORA.[15] In the case of proactive routing protocols, nodes periodically propagate routing update advertisements with their neighbors in order to maintain up-to-date routing information. Routes are immediately available upon a node's request. In reactive routing protocols, a route is found on demand when the source needs to send a packet to a destination. Routes are valid only for a limited period, after which routes are considered to be obsolete. No periodical route information propagation is required. Reactive protocols require less bandwidth and power than proactive ones, but discovering routes on demand leads to higher latency. *Hybrid protocols*, such as Zone Routing Protocol (ZRP)[16] combine the features of proactive and reactive protocols. In a hybrid protocol, routes for a subset of nodes are maintained in a routing table proactively while routes for the remaining nodes are discovered when needed. *Location-aware protocols* use location information provided by an attached GPS to improve the performance. LAR[14] and DREAM[10] are examples of such protocols.

Reducing power consumption is critical for wireless communication protocols.[17,18] *Power-aware* routing protocols take into account power consumption when determining a route.[19,20]

MAC-layer protocols specify the rules for contending users to access a shared wireless medium in a fair, stable and efficient way. A MAC-layer protocol for wireless *ad hoc* networks should take into account additional considerations: (i) *mobility* — the connection between nodes can become unstable because of the independent movement of the nodes; (ii) *quality of channel* — a wireless channel has a higher *Bit Error Rate* (BER) than a wired network; (iii) *collisions* — wireless transceivers work in a half-duplex mode; nodes do not "listen" when "talking" and do not "talk" when "listening." The sender is unable to detect the collision and the receiver is unable to notify the sender of the collision during the transmission of a packet. *Collision avoidance* is almost mandatory.

In Carrier Sensing Multiple Access (CSMA)[26] every node senses the carrier before transmitting its data; it defers transmission if it detects the medium is busy. CSMA reduces the possibility of collisions in the vicinity of the sender. Multiple Access Collision Avoidance (MACA)[27] and its variant MACAW[28] are alternative medium access schemes for wireless *ad hoc* networks that aim to solve the hidden node problem by reducing the possibility of collisions in the vicinity of the receiver. The Floor Acquisition Multiple Access (FAMA)[29] protocol consists of both carrier sensing and a collision avoidance handshake between sender and receiver of a packet. Once the control of the channel is assigned to one node, all other nodes in the network should become silent. Carrier Sensing Multiple Access based on Collision Avoidance (CSMA/CA), the combination of CSMA and MACA, is considered a variant of FAMA protocols. The IEEE 802.11 Standard[30] is the best-known instance of CSMA/CA.

In a wireless network with symmetric links only, a *hidden node* is generally defined as *a node out of the range of the sender and in the range of the receiver*.[31] According to this definition such a node is hidden from the sender but exposed from the receiver (see Fig. 1(a)). The hidden node problem can be solved by a RTS-CTS handshake mechanism proposed by MACA[27] (RTS stands for *Request to Send* and CTS for *Clear to Send*).

However, in a heterogeneous wireless *ad hoc* network, a *hidden node* should be defined as *a node out of the range of the sender and whose range covers the receiver* (see Fig. 1(b)). According to this definition, a hidden node is hidden from the sender and possibly hidden from the receiver as

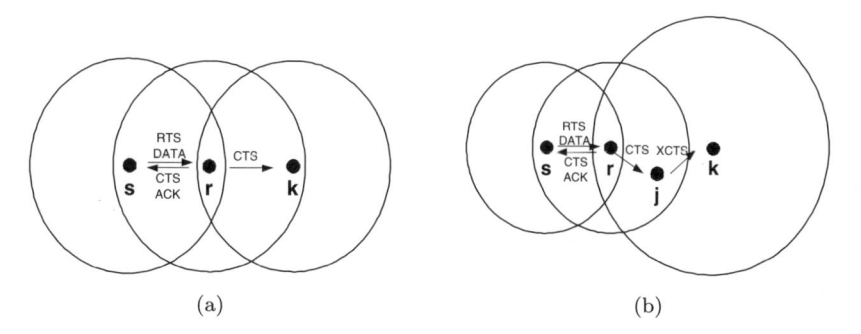

Fig. 1. (a) Hidden node problem in a "classical" wireless network with mobile nodes. All links are assumed to be bidirectional. A hidden node is a node out of the range of the source and in the range of the receiver node. k is a hidden node for a transmission from node s to node r. (b) Hidden node problem in a heterogeneous wireless network with mobile nodes. A hidden node is a node out of the range of the sender and whose range covers the receiver. k is a hidden node as for a transmission from node s to node r.

well. The RTS-CTS handshake mechanism is not a solution for such networks since a CTS packet may not be able to reach hidden nodes.

Several solutions to the hidden node problem in a heterogeneous wireless *ad hoc* network exist. The authors of Ref. 1 propose that a node rebroadcasts a CTS packet if it is received from a low-power node. To decrease the probability of collisions, each node waits a random number $(1,\ldots,6)$ of SIFS (Short Inter-Frame Spacing) periods before transmitting a CTS packet. The authors of Ref. 2 made several improvements relative to Ref. 1: (i) not only CTS but also RTS packets are rebroadcasted; (ii) nodes with a CTS packet to rebroadcast, first sense the medium and transmit only if the medium is not busy; and (iii) only high-power nodes rebroadcast RTS or CTS packets. The solutions proposed by Refs. 1 and 2 can lead to inefficient use of the channel if nodes are *misclassified* as hidden nodes. In such situations, nodes that could have been active are silenced due to misclassification, severely degrading the channel utilization. References 1 and 2 routinely assume routing over symmetric links so that the sender is able to receive both CTS and ACK packets. In the presence of asymmetric links, however, the sender might not receive the CTS or ACK packets; thus the sender cannot trigger the transmission of DATA packets, and does not know whether a transmission was successful or not. The MAC protocol to be presented in Sec. 6 is designed to handle these situations as well.

The Sub Routing Layer (SRL) project[32,33] adds an intermediary layer between the MAC and network layers. This layer partially isolates the routing protocol from the MAC layer, although it still allows the routing protocol to directly contact the MAC layer. For unidirectional links, reverse paths are computed using the Reverse Distributed Bellman-Ford algorithm. Another approach is to tunnel packets by encapsulating them at higher level protocols, thus creating virtual reverse links.[34] Although the details of implementation differ, both approaches create a virtual reverse link by substituting it with a reverse path. Even though a bidirectional abstraction is created, the reverse link has a significantly higher latency, and possibly, lower bandwidth.

3. The Model of the System

Let $\mathcal{N}$ be the set of nodes. We assume that:

(a) The number of nodes is relatively small, say $|\mathcal{N}| \leq 10^4$.
(b) The mobility of individual nodes is limited and differs from one node to the other.

(c) Nodes are able to adjust their transmitting power according to their residual power so that their lifetime is extended.

Every node $i \in \mathcal{N}$ is characterized by a minimal set of attributes:

(i) *Id*, Id_i; unique string used for node identification.
(ii) *Class*, C_i; the nodes of a heterogeneous mobile network are classified in several classes based on the hardware and software resources. Throughout this chapter we assume a four level hierarchy.
(iii) *Location* at time t, $L_i(t)$; the geographical coordinates of the position of node i at time t, and
(iv) *Residual power* at time t, $P_i^{res}(t)$; the amount of power available at time t.

Other attributes can be derived from the ones in the minimal set.

(v) *Transmission range* at time t, $R_i(t)$; a function of the residual power and possibly other factors including the configuration of the terrain, atmospheric conditions, and so on.

The *distance* between two nodes $i, j \in \mathcal{N}$ at time t, $d_{ij}(t)$ is a function of the position of the two nodes:

$$d_{ij}(t) = d_{ji}(t) = f(L_i(t), L_j(t)).$$

(vi) *Average velocity* over an interval $\Delta t = t_2 - t_1 > 0$, $v_i^{\Delta t}$; $v_i^{\Delta t} = f(L_i(t_2), L_i(t_1))/\Delta t$.
(vii) *Mobility region* over an interval $\Delta t = t_2 - t_1 > 0$, $M_i^{\Delta t}$; a circle of radius $v_i^{\Delta t} \times \Delta t$, centered at $L_i(t_1)$.

The Boolean *reachability function* $\mathcal{R}_{ij}(t)$ is defined as

$$\mathcal{R}_{ij}(t) = \text{true} \Leftrightarrow R_i(t) \geq d_{ij}(t);$$
$$\mathcal{R}_{ij}(t) = \text{false} \Leftrightarrow R_i(t) < d_{ij}(t).$$

Definition 1. Two nodes $i, j \in \mathcal{N}$ are in *neighbor* relationship at time t if there is a direct communication link between them. We recognize several types of neighbors:

(i) *Out-bound neighbor*: j is the out-bound neighbor of i, if i can reach j but j cannot reach i. In this case the link L_{ij} between the two nodes is unidirectional:

$$\mathcal{R}_{ij}(t) = \text{true} \quad \text{and} \quad \mathcal{R}_{ji}(t) = \text{false}.$$

Call $Out_i(t) \subset \mathcal{N}$ the set of Out-bound neighbors of i at time t.

(ii) *In-bound neighbor*: j is the In-bound neighbor of i, if j can reach i but i cannot reach j. In this case the link L_{ji} between the two nodes is unidirectional:

$$\mathcal{R}_{ij}(t) = \text{false} \quad \text{and} \quad \mathcal{R}_{ji}(t) = \text{true}.$$

Call $In_i(t) \subset \mathcal{N}$ the set of In-bound neighbors of i at time t.

(iii) *In/Out-bound neighbor*: j is the In/Out-bound neighbor of i, if i and j can reach each other. In this case the link L_{ij} between the two nodes is bidirectional:

$$\mathcal{R}_{ij}(t) = \text{true} \quad \text{and} \quad \mathcal{R}_{ji}(t) = \text{true}.$$

Call $InOut_i(t) \subset \mathcal{N}$ the set of In/Out-bound neighbors of i at time t.

Definition 2. If node i is an Out-bound neighbor of node j, we call i the *high-range node* (*H*-node) and j the *low-range node* (*L*-node) of the asymmetric link L_{ij}.

Definition 3. A set of m nodes $i_1, i_2, \ldots, i_m \in \mathcal{N}$ are in an *m-party proxy set* if each node can reach the other $m-1$ nodes either directly or through a subset of the other $m-2$ members.

Proposition 1. *At least one of the links of an m-party proxy set must be bidirectional.*

Proof. Suppose Proposition 1 is false, that is, there exists an m-party proxy set with no bidirectional link. Let the m nodes in the m-party proxy relationship be $i_1, i_2, \ldots, i_m \in \mathcal{N}$ and arbitrarily pick up an asymmetric link (i_u, i_v) where $1 \leq u, v \leq m, u \neq v$. Thus, node i_u can reach node i_v directly, but the reciprocal is not true, $\mathcal{R}_{i_u i_v}(t) = true$ and $\mathcal{R}_{i_v i_u}(t) = false$, which is equivalent to

$$R_{i_u}(t) \geq d_{i_u i_v}(t) > R_{i_v}(t).$$

By the definition of m-party proxy set, there exists at least a path for node i_v to reach node i_u. Let us choose the shortest path from node i_v to node i_u. There are no duplicate nodes on this path, otherwise a shorter path can be obtained by removing the sub-path consisting of all the nodes connecting the two duplicate nodes. Call the set of nodes on the shortest path $(i_v, i_{N_1}, i_{N_2}, \ldots, i_{N_p}, \ldots, i_{N_k}, i_u)$, where $N_p \neq N_q, N_p \neq u, N_p \neq v, 1 \leq p,$

$q \leq k \leq m-2, p \neq q$. Similarly, we have

$$R_{i_v}(t) \geq d_{i_v i_{N_1}}(t) > R_{i_{N_1}}(t)$$
$$\geq d_{i_{N_1} i_{N_2}}(t) > R_{i_{N_2}}(t)$$
$$\geq \cdots > R_{i_{N_p}} \geq d_{i_{N_p} i_{N_{p+1}}}(t) > R_{i_{N_{p+1}}}(t)$$
$$\geq \cdots > R_{i_{N_k}} \geq d_{i_{N_k} i_u}(t) > R_{i_u}(t).$$

The above inequalities are contradictory, thus Proposition 1 must be true. □

Figures 2(a) and (b) show two possible configurations of a three-party proxy set with unidirectional links only. The configuration in Fig. 2(a) is infeasible according to Proposition 1, while the configuration in Fig. 2(b) is infeasible because k cannot reach either i or j.

Proposition 2. *For m ($m > 2$) nodes, an m-party proxy set with one and only one bidirectional link can always be found by adjusting their transmission ranges and geographical locations.*

The configuration in Fig. 2(c) and any configuration obtained by a permutation of the nodes in the set has one bidirectional link. In this configuration i can reach j and k directly, j can reach k directly and i via k, and

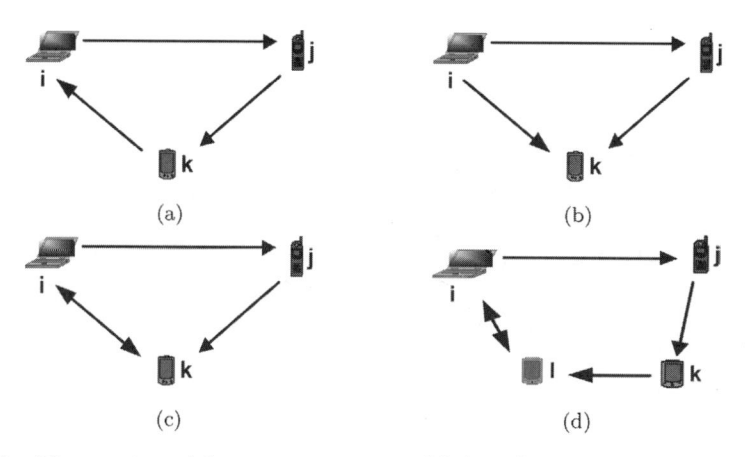

Fig. 2. Three-party and four-party proxy sets. (a) An infeasible scenario for a three-party proxy set involving three unidirectional links. (b) A second infeasible scenario for a three-party proxy set involving three unidirectional links. (c) A feasible scenario for a three-party proxy set with one bidirectional link. (d) A feasible scenario for a four-party proxy set with one bidirectional link.

finally k can reach i directly and j via i. The ranges and distances among the nodes of the configuration in Fig. 2(c) are

$$R_j < d_{ij} \leq R_i, \quad R_k < d_{jk} \leq R_j; \qquad d_{ik} \leq R_i, \quad d_{ki} \leq R_k.$$

To show that there is at least one configuration of four-party proxy set with one bidirectional link, we consider the configuration in Fig. 2(d). Since there is a loop $i \to j \to k \to l \to i$, every node can reach the other nodes in the set.

The ranges and distances among the nodes of the configuration in Fig. 2(d) must satisfy the following constraints:

$$\begin{cases} R_j < d_{ij} \leq R_i, \quad R_k < d_{jk} \leq R_j, \quad R_l < d_{kl} \leq R_k; \quad d_{li} \leq R_i, \quad d_{li} \leq R_l; \\ d_{ik} > R_i, \quad d_{jl} > R_j, \quad d_{ki} > R_k, \quad d_{lj} > R_l. \end{cases}$$

In the general case of an m-party proxy set, consider the nodes $i_1, i_2, \ldots, i_m \in \mathcal{N}$ connected as follows: nodes i_k and i_{k+1} ($1 \leq k \leq m-2$) are connected by unidirectional links from node i_k to node i_{k+1}, and nodes i_1 and i_m are connected by a bidirectional link. The ranges and distances among nodes must satisfy the following constraints

$$\begin{cases} R_{k+1} < d_{k,k+1} \leq R_k, \quad 1 \leq k \leq m-2; \quad d_{1m} \leq R_1, \quad d_{m1} \leq R_m; \\ d_{k,(k+j) \bmod m} > R_k, \quad 2 \leq j \leq m-1, \quad 1 \leq k \leq m. \end{cases}$$

Definition 4. Define the *average number of neighbors* for a bidirectional *ad hoc* network given a mobility area S, at time t, $\omega(S, \mathcal{N}, t)$, as $\Sigma_{i \in \mathcal{N}}(\omega_i(t))/|\mathcal{N}|$, where $\omega_i(t)$ is the number of neighbors of node i at time t.

Proposition 3. *Assume (i) the set of nodes $\mathcal{N}$ is uniformly distributed throughout the area S and (ii) all the nodes have the same transmission range R. Let S be a rectangle with length X and width Y, $X, Y \geq 2R$. We can approximate the average number of neighbors of a node as:*

$$\omega(S, \mathcal{N}, t) \approx |\mathcal{N}| \left[\frac{R^4}{(XY)^2} - \frac{3}{4}\left(\frac{1}{X^2 Y} + \frac{1}{XY^2}\right) R^3 + \frac{\pi R^2}{XY} \right] - 1.$$

Corollary 1. *If $X = Y$, $\omega(S, \mathcal{N}, t) \approx |\mathcal{N}|\left[\left(\frac{R}{X}\right)^4 - 1.5\left(\frac{R}{X}\right)^3 + \pi\left(\frac{R}{X}\right)^2\right] - 1.$*

Corollary 2. *If $X = Y = mR$, $m \geq 2$, $\omega(S, \mathcal{N}, t) \approx |\mathcal{N}|\left(\frac{1}{m^4} - \frac{1.5}{m^3} + \frac{\pi}{m^2}\right) - 1.$*

4. m-Limited Forwarding

m-limited forwarding is a technique to reduce the cost of disseminating information in a power-constrained environment by limiting the cardinality of the subset of nodes which will retransmit a packet. In case of flooding in an *ad hoc* network, when node j transmits a packet at time t the nodes in the set $H_j(t)$, the set of all neighbors within the transmission range of node j, retransmit the packet. There are $n_j(t) = |H_j(t)|$ nodes in this set. We wish to limit the size of the subset of nodes which forward the packet to at most $m < n_j(t)$. The nodes in this subset, called *m-forwarding subset*, $F_j(t) \subset H_j(t)$ should be the ones optimally positioned vis-a-vis the packet destination and with the most favorable balance of power. The parameter m should be chosen to satisfy a subset of sometimes contradictory requirements, e.g., minimize the power consumption, ensure some stability of the routes when the nodes move within a certain area, minimize error rates, minimize retransmission, and so on.

Informally, in the method discussed in this chapter, the sender of a packet, node j provides a "hint," we call this value a *forwarding cutoff*, $\kappa_j(t)$, and sends it to all its neighbors together with the original information. Each node $i \in H_j(t)$ determines if it belongs to the selected subset, $i \in F_j(t)$, by evaluating a function, the *forwarding priority* function, $\varphi_i(t)$, and then compares the value of this function with the *forward cutoff*. Node i forwards the packet if and only if $\varphi_i(t) \geq \kappa_j(t)$. Obviously, the destination recognizes its own `nodeID` and does not further forward the packet. If the location of the destination is not known, the sender sets $\kappa_j(t) = -1$ and all nodes in H_j retransmit the packet. If $|F_j(t)| < m$ then $\kappa_j(t) = 0$ and in this case individual nodes in H_j make their own decision whether to forward or not.

Note that information regarding the position and the residual power of each node in the set $H_j(t)$ may, or may not, be very accurate, due to node mobility and to node activity which affects the residual power. As a result, $\kappa_j(t)$ may allow fewer than m nodes to forward, if some have moved away from their location known to node j, or may have further depleted their power reserves. The actual number of nodes forwarding the packet may be larger than m if new nodes have moved into the optimal forwarding area, or recharged their batteries.

A forwarding fitness function measures the fitness of a node as the next hop. Different heuristics can be used when designing a forwarding fitness function.

One example of a forwarding fitness function is

$$\tau_k(i,j) = \frac{1}{d_{ik} + c}, \tag{1}$$

where j is the sender, i is the destination, k is the next hop candidate, d_{ik} is the distance between node i and node k, and c is a positive constant.

Another instance of a forwarding fitness function is proposed in Ref. 35:

$$\eta_k(i,j) = \begin{cases} 0 & \text{if } R_k \le d_{ik} - r_{ij}, \\ \pi \cdot r_{ij}^2 & \text{if } R_k \ge d_{ki} + r_{ij}, \\ \frac{1}{2}[r_{ij}^2(\varphi - \sin\varphi) + R_k^2(\theta - \sin\theta)] & \text{otherwise,} \end{cases} \quad (2)$$

where $r_{ij} = d_{ij} - R_j$, $\theta = 2\arccos\frac{R_k^2 + d_{ik}^2 - r_{ij}^2}{2 \cdot R_k \cdot d_{ki}}$, and $\varphi = 2\arccos\frac{r_{ij}^2 + d_{ik}^2 - R_k^2}{2 \cdot r_{ij} \cdot d_{ik}}$.

If we assume that the number of nodes in a given area is proportional to the size of the area, this fitness function based upon geometric considerations favors nodes which have more neighbors who could possibly either reach the destination, or reach other nodes best positioned to reach the destination.

4.1. Simulation study

m-limited forwarding can be used for wireless networks with symmetric/bidirectional links as well as wireless networks with asymmetric/unidirectional links. We choose to study the first type of networks because we wanted to clearly distinguish the advantages and the drawbacks of the algorithm in a traditional setting, without the additional effects due to asymmetric links.

We use NS-2,[36,37] an object-oriented, event-driven simulator developed at the Lawrence Berkeley National Laboratory as part of the VINT project, with the CMU wireless extensions.[38] To describe the movement of nodes in the system we use the "random waypoint" model.[12,39] In our simulations we use traffic patterns generated by *constant bit rate* (CBR) sources sending UDP packets. We are concerned with the impact of network load, node mobility, and network density upon power consumption, packet loss ratio, and latency. We run several simulation experiments and vary the number of nodes, the speed in the "random waypoint" model, and the number of CBR sources. Table 1 illustrates the default settings and the range of the parameters for our simulation experiments. To construct 95% confidence intervals, we repeat each experiment ten times for a pair of scenario and traffic pattern, the two elements affecting the results of a performance study.

The Effect of the Network Load. We expect the network load to affect differently the power consumption, the packet loss ratio, as well as the average packet delay of the five routing schemes, flooding, and two- and three-limited forwarding with $\tau_k(i,j)$ and $\eta_k(i,j)$ fitness functions. Figure 3(a)

Table 1. The default values and the range of the parameters for our simulation studies.

Field	Value	Range
Simulation area	500 × 500 (m^2)	
Number of nodes	80	30–100
Transmission range	100 (m)	
Average number of neighbors	8.22	2.46–10.53
Speed	1 (m/s)	2–20 (m/s)
Pause time	15 (s)	
Simulation time	800 (s)	
Number of CBR sources	30	5–40
CBR packet size	64 (bytes)	
CBR sending rate	512 (bps)	

illustrates average power consumption versus network load. As expected, flooding needs more power than routing with m-limited forwarding schemes.

Figure 3(b) illustrates packet loss ratio versus network load. Packet loss could be due to several factors: (i) the forwarding set calculated by the forwarding fitness function excludes nodes on the critical path from source to destination; (ii) packets are dropped due to collisions or excessive retransmission failures at MAC layer; (iii) nodes move fast and the routing tables become outdated frequently. When the traffic load is light, the major cause of packet loss is exclusion of nodes on the path from source to destination, while for heavy traffic, the collisions become the major source of traffic loss. Node movement is a minor factor affecting the packet loss as the node speed is relatively low in this experiment.

As a general rule flooding causes more collisions than m-limited forwarding. When network load is relatively heavy, routing schemes using m-limited forwarding outperform flooding as collisions become a major concern.

Figure 3(c) illustrates average latency versus network load. The average latency is calculated based solely on delivered packets. Higher latency is due to heavy traffic and/or paths with a large number of hops. To avoid collisions, the binary exponential backoff algorithm of the MAC layer protocol requires that packets are retransmitted after timeouts lasting increasingly longer after subsequent collisions.

Not surprisingly, the average latency of flooding is lower than that of routing with m-limited forwarding using $\eta_k(i,j)$. Flooding tends to find routes with the shortest latency while routing with m-limited forwarding scheme using $\eta_k(i,j)$ may exclude nodes on the shortest path. However,

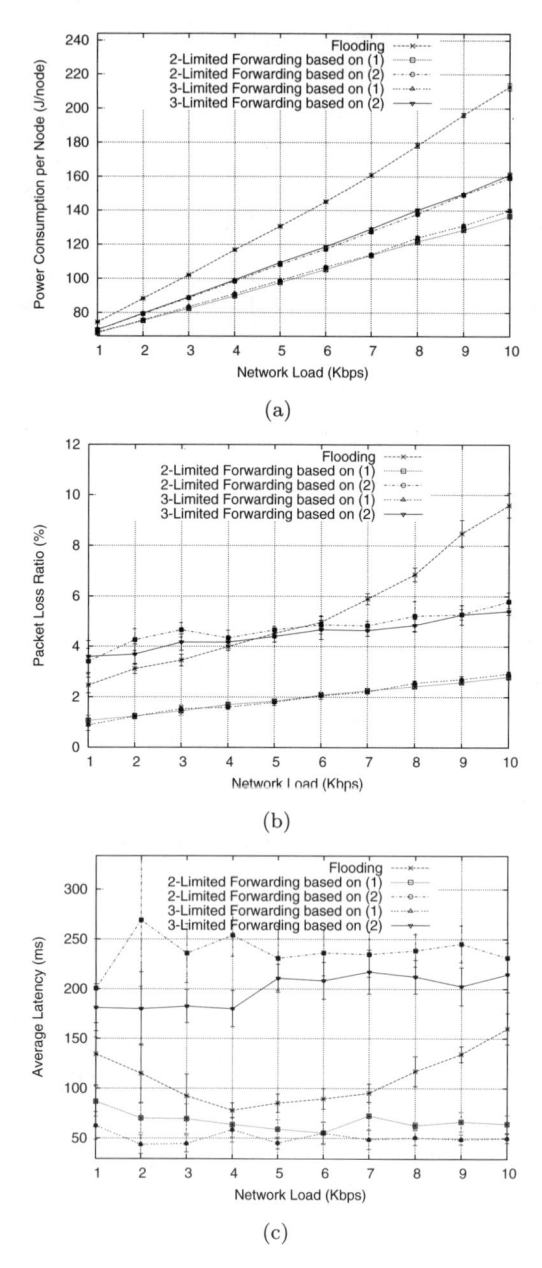

Fig. 3. The impact of network load on power consumption, packet loss ratio, and latency. (a) Average power consumption versus network load. (b) Packet loss ratio versus network load. (c) Average latency versus network load.

when the network load is high, flooding may experience higher average latency than routing with m-limited forwarding using $\tau_k(i,j)$.

The Effect of Node Mobility. Node mobility is measured by the speed of the node movement. Figure 4(a) illustrates the average power consumption versus node mobility. When node mobility is high, the routing table becomes outdated quickly and the average power consumption of all routing schemes increases, as additional power is dissipated to find new routes. As expected, m-limited forwarding requires less power than flooding. For example, the power consumption of two-limited forwarding using $\tau_k(i,j)$ is 20.55% at 2 m/s and 10.01% at 20 m/s less than flooding.

Figure 4(b) presents packet loss ratio versus node mobility. In all routing schemes packet loss ratio increases sharply when node mobility increases due to outdated routing tables. All routing schemes are very sensitive to node mobility, for example, for flooding the packet loss ratio increases from 6.07% at 2 m/s to 26.56% at 20 m/s.

Figure 4(c) illustrates average latency versus node mobility. When the node speed increases, the routing table becomes outdated more often and the path discovery process, which is very demanding in terms of network bandwidth, is initiated more often. For all routing schemes the average latency increases with the node mobility due to congestion caused by frequent retransmissions and the need to discover new routes.

The Effect of Network Density. We expect node density to affect network performance and study its effects on power consumption, packet loss ratio, and average delay. In Fig. 5(a), as the network density increases, the power consumption of routing based upon m-limited forwarding increases nearly linearly, while for flooding the increase is nearly exponential. The two-limited forwarding using $\tau_k(i,j)$ is more efficient than flooding; the savings in power consumption range from 19.50% for 30 nodes (average number of neighbors is 2.46) to 46.08% for 100 nodes (average number of neighbors is 10.53).

Figure 5(b) illustrates packet loss ratio versus network density. The packet loss ratio of all routing schemes is relatively low when network density is small. When the number of nodes is larger than 70, the packet loss ratio for flooding increases sharply due to excessive congestion and the collisions. The packet loss ratio of flooding increases from 1.96% for 30 nodes to 32.67% for 100 nodes.

Figure 5(c) illustrates average latency versus network density. The average latency of all routing schemes is relatively low when the number of nodes

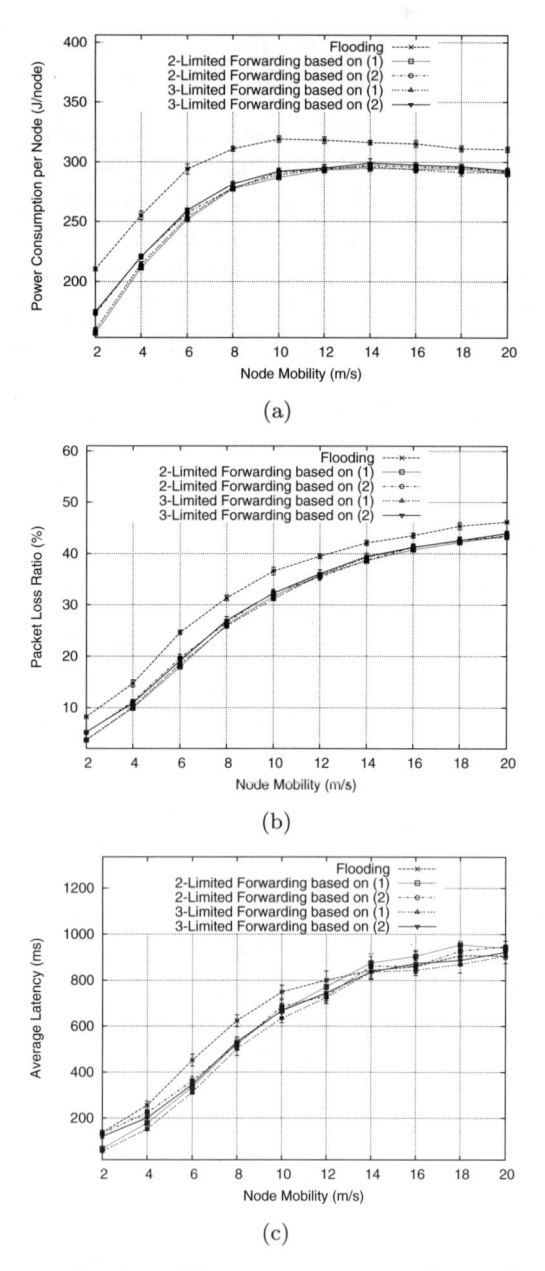

Fig. 4. The impact of node mobility on power consumption, packet loss ratio, and latency. (a) Average power consumption versus node mobility. (b) Packet loss ratio versus node mobility. (c) Average latency versus node mobility.

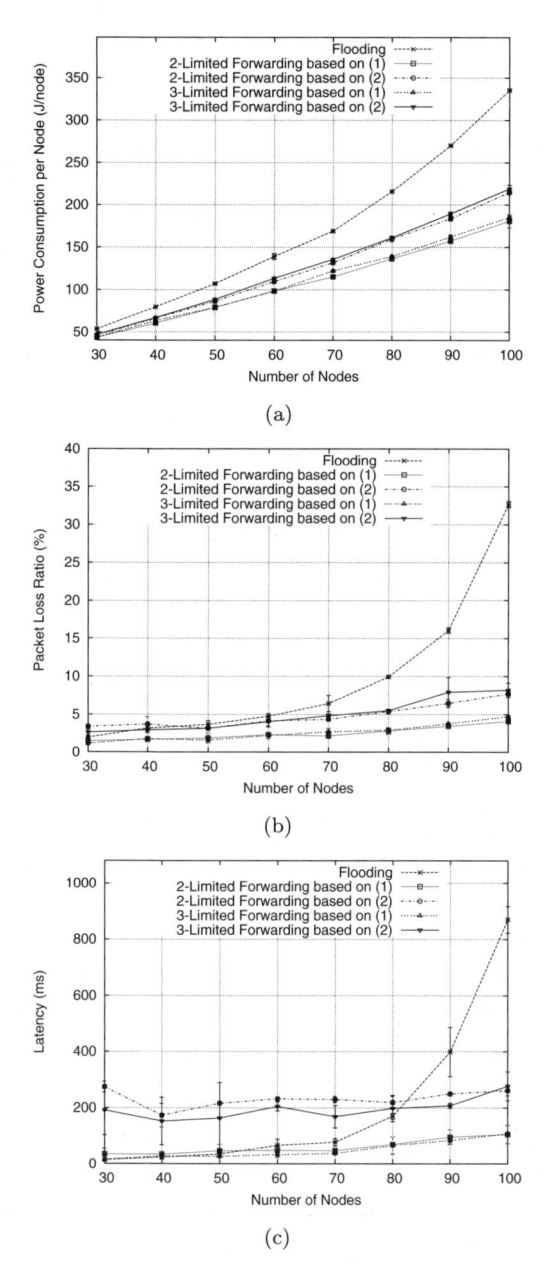

Fig. 5. The impact of network density on power consumption, packet loss ratio, and latency. (a) Average power consumption versus network density. (b) Packet loss ratio versus network density. (c) Average latency versus network density.

is relatively small. When the number of nodes is larger than 70, the average latency for flooding increases sharply due to excessive collisions.

In terms of power dissipation, m-limited forwarding outperforms flooding when network load, node mobility, and node density increase. Among the four m-limited forwarding schemes, the two-limited forwarding with $\tau_k(i,j)$ performs the best. When network load increases, the power dissipation of flooding increases faster than that of m-limited forwarding schemes. The power consumption increases almost linearly with the node density for m-limited forwarding while the increase is faster for flooding.

The packet loss ratio is another aspect of network performance where m-limited forwarding is on par if not better than flooding. For a light network load flooding performs slightly better than m-limited forwarding using $\eta_k(i,j)$ but worse than m-limited forwarding using $\tau_k(i,j)$. All routing schemes are very sensitive to node mobility and the packet loss ratio increases sharply when node mobility increases. Flooding is only slightly worse than m-limited forwarding. In terms of node density m-limited forwarding fares better than flooding. The packet loss ratio for flooding at high node density increases exponentially due to excessive collisions.

Finally, the packet delay increases due to heavy traffic and/or paths with a large number of hops. Flooding is slightly better than routing with m-limited forwarding at light network load using $\eta_k(i,j)$ but worse than m-limited forwarding using $\tau_k(i,j)$ at heavy network load. For all routing schemes the average latency increases with the node mobility due to congestion caused by frequent retransmissions and the need to discover new routes. The average latency for flooding increases sharply due to excessive collisions when the network density increases.

It is possible that the ongoing evaluation of m-limited forwarding for heterogeneous wireless *ad hoc* networks with asymmetric links will lead to slightly different conclusions, e.g., it is likely that $\eta_k(i,j)$- may prove to be better than $\tau_k(i,j)$-based policies.

5. Routing Protocol

The A^4LP protocol[35] consists of an initialization phase when each node discovers its In-, In/Out-, and Out-bound neighbors, a path discovery phase using m-limited forwarding, and a path maintenance phase.

Information Maintained by a Node and Packet Types. A node $i \in \mathcal{N}$ maintains several data structures, a routing table (see Table 2), a path request

Table 2. The fields of a routing table.

Field	Description
dstId	Destination node id
dstLoc	Destination location information
dstClass	Destination class
dstPower	Destination residual power
dstRange	Destination transmission range
dstSeq	Destination sequence number
dstNeighborType	Neighbor type of destination
nextHop	Next hop to forward a packet
expTime	Expiration time

sequence number and a node sequence number.

(i) *Routing Table at Node j* (RT_j): caches information for all neighbors and for most recently used destination (Table 2). The field *dstNeighborType* takes one of the following values: In-bound, Out-bound, In/Out-bound, or Not-neighbor. *expTime* records the expiration time for an entry after which it is no longer valid.

(ii) *Request Sequence Number* (reqSeq): a counter, uniquely identifies a path request packet sent by the the node with nodeId. The reqSeq is incremented every time a route request is sent.

(iii) *Node Sequence Number* (seq): a counter revealing the freshness of a node, incremented when the node detects the change of location, residual power, transmission range, routing table, and so on.

5.1. Neighbor discovery

In-bound Neighbor Discovery. In-bound neighbor discovery (which, incidentally, leads also to the discovery of neighbors which will later turn out to be In/Out-bound) is initiated when a node joins the network. Each node broadcasts periodically a Hello packet to inform all the neighbors in its range of its current location, residual power, and transmission range. The time between two such transmissions is called a *hello interval.*

Upon receiving a Hello packet, a node either updates an existing entry in its routing table or creates a new one. Acknowledgments are not required (actually not possible for In-bound neighbors). A node deletes the entries of Out- and In/Out-bound neighbors if it does not receive their Hello packets for several hello intervals. A Hello packet is a broadcast packet with a life time of one hop. The `Hello` packet provides the location, the class, the residual power, and the range of the sender.

Out-bound Neighbor Discovery. Due to the nature of asymmetric links, Out-bound neighbors are not detected directly as their signals cannot be heard. For example, in the three-party proxy set in Fig. 2(c), the `Hello` packet from node j cannot reach node i; thus node i cannot know that node j is an Out-bound neighbor. However, node k, which is an In/Out-bound neighbor of node i and an Out-bound neighbor of node j, is aware that link L_{ij} is asymmetric with i as the H-node and j as the L-node. Thus, node k sends a `Convey` packet to node i with the information of node j, and, at the same time, records node i as the next hop to reach node j.

In the Out-bound neighbor discovery, a node periodically checks the link relationship between its neighbors, sets up the route to its In-bound neighbor if a three-party proxy set is detected, and informs the H-node of an asymmetric link, when it detects one. The time between two Out-bound neighbor discovery is called a *convey interval*. The `Convey` packet contains the Id of the sender and of the destination (the H-node of the asymmetric link), the Id, the location, the class, the residual power, the range, and the sequence number of the L-node of the asymmetric link.

5.2. *Location and power update*

Dissemination of the approximate node location as well as its residual power are critical for any location-aware and power-aware routing scheme, yet it is not the focus of this chapter. It can be achieved by (i) gossiping algorithms, (ii) a broadcast scheme, in which updates are sent infrequently and locally, (iii) a hierarchical scheme: nodes form clusters around *head of a cluster*, which covers a relatively large area and is able to exchange information collected from members of the cluster, or some other scheme.

In A^4LP a node sends location and power updates only when (i) it joins the network, (ii) it has moved significantly since the last reported location, and (iii) its residual power goes below *low water mark*.

5.3. *Route discovery*

When the sender does not have a route to the destination, it initiates *route discovery*. Traditional reactive *ad hoc* protocols consider only symmetric links; thus, the *forward/reverse route* from source/destination to destination/source consists of the same set of nodes, but in reverse order.

In A^4LP, the forward and reverse route will not be the same when asymmetric links are involved. The source initiates a route request packet, and uses *m-limited forwarding* to send this packet toward the destination. A forward route is found when the route request packet arrives at the destination. For each sender-receiver pair, if the link is symmetric, the reverse route is in the reverse order; otherwise, as we assume an asymmetric link can be used only if a three proxy set relationship exists among the sender, the receiver and a proxy node, the reverse route from the sender to the destination can be known by neighbor discovery protocol. Thus, once a forward route is established, the reverse route is also established. The destination unicasts a route reply packet to the source to (i) notify each intermediate nodes to establish the routes for the source and the destination, and (ii) trigger the source to start sending data packets.

5.4. *Route maintenance*

Movement of nodes lying along an active route may cause a route to become invalid. In case a route becomes invalid, at least one of the links on the route fails. A link $(L_{i,j})$ failure could be detected, if all attempts to forward a packet from node i to the next hop j fails. All packets at a failed link will be discarded. The link failure has to be reported to the source to avoid massive retransmissions.

If the source detects the link from it to the next hop becoming unreachable, it disables the routing entry to the destination, and recover the route to the destination by the route discovery protocol. If the link failure happens at an intermediate node, it reports to the source who recovers the route to the destination by the route discovery protocol.

6. MAC Protocol

6.1. *Topological considerations*

The handling of the hidden nodes is an essential problem for wireless MAC protocols operating in the presence of asymmetric links. In the following, we introduce a series of topological concepts and attempt to classify hidden nodes. The following definitions are necessary to introduce the MAC layer protocol.

We call the proxy node through which an *L*-Node can reach an *H*-node a *P-node*. A *tunnel* is defined as the *reverse route* from an *L*-Node to an *H*-through a *P*-node. Call T_{sr} a transmission from sender s to receiver r.

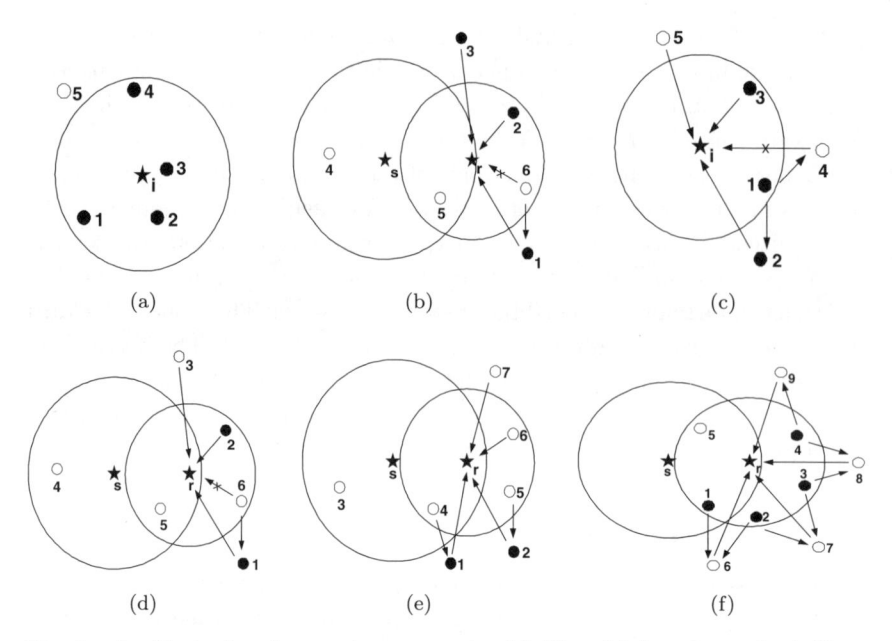

Fig. 6. An illustration for topology concepts. (a) The vicinity of a node i, $V_i = \{1, 2, 3, 4\}$. (b) The set of hidden nodes for the transmission from s to r: $H_{sr} = \{1, 2, 3\}$. (c) Example of the three-party proxy set coverage of node i: $P3_i = \{1, 2, 3\}$. (d) The $H3_{sr}$ set for a transmission T_{sr}: $H3_{sr} = \{1, 2\}$. (e) The extended hidden nodes set $XH3_{sr}$: $XH3_{sr} = \{1, 2\}$. (f) The extended hidden nodes relay set $XHR3_{sr}$ for a transmission T_{sr}. In the illustrated scenario, $XHR3_{sr} = \{1, 2, 3, 4\}$, $mXHR3_{sr} = \{2, 4\}$ or $\{1, 3, 4\}$, $MXHR3_{sr} = \{2, 4\}$.

Definition 5. Call V_i the *vicinity* of node i. V_i includes all nodes that could be reached from node i (see Fig. 6(a)):

$$V_i = \{j | \mathcal{R}(i, j)\}.$$

Definition 6. Call H_{sr} the set of *hidden nodes of a transmission* T_{sr}. H_{sr} includes nodes that are out of the range of the sender and whose range covers the receiver (see Fig. 6(b)):

$$H_{sr} = \{k | \neg \mathcal{R}(s, k) \wedge \mathcal{R}(k, r)\}.$$

Note that H_{sr} are the hidden nodes for the transmission of the DATA packets, while H_{rs} are the hidden nodes for the transmission of ACK packets.

Definition 7. Call $P3_i$ the *three-party proxy set coverage* of node i. $P3_i$ is the set of nodes nodes reachable either by node i directly, or participate in a three-party proxy set with node i and a third node (see Fig. 6(c)):

$$P3_i = \{k | \mathcal{R}(i,k) \vee \exists_j \; (\mathcal{R}(i,j) \wedge \mathcal{R}(j,k) \wedge \mathcal{R}(k,i))\}.$$

Definition 8. Call $H3_{sr}$ the *hidden nodes* of a transmission T_{sr} in the three-party proxy set coverage of node r. The set $H3_{sr}$ includes hidden nodes covered by $P3_r$ (see Fig. 6(d)):

$$H3_{sr} = H_{sr} \cap P3_r.$$

Definition 9. Call $XH3_{sr}$ the *extended hidden nodes* of a transmission T_{sr} in three-party proxy set coverage of node r. The set $XH3_{sr}$ includes nodes in $H3_{sr}$ covered by V_r (see Fig. 6(e)):

$$XH3_{sr} = H3_{sr} - V_r.$$

Definition 10. Call $XHR3_{sr}$ the *extended hidden nodes relay set* of a transmission T_{sr} in three-party proxy set coverage of node r. $XHR3_{sr}$ includes *all* nodes in $P3_r$ that could relay traffic from node r to nodes belonging to $XH3_{sr}$ (see Fig. 6(f)):

$$XHR3_{sr} = \{j \mid j \in V_r \wedge \exists_{k \in XH3_{sr}} (\mathcal{R}(j,k))\}.$$

Definition 11. Call $mXHR3_{sr}$ the *minimal extended hidden nodes relay set* of a transmission T_{sr} in three-party proxy set coverage of node r. $mXHR3_{sr}$ includes a set of nodes in $XHR3_r$ ($mXHR3_r \subseteq XHR3_r$) such that (i) the node r can relay traffic to any node in $XH3_{sr}$ through some nodes from $mXHR3_{sr}$; (ii) the removal of any nodes in $mXHR3_{sr}$ makes some nodes in $XH3_{sr}$ unreacheable from node r (see Fig. 6(f)):

$$\forall_{k \in XH3_{sr}} \exists_{j \in mXHR3_{sr}} (\mathcal{R}(j,k))$$

and

$$\forall_{j' \in mXHR3_{sr}} \exists_{k \in XH3_{sr}} \not\exists_{j \in mXHR3_{sr} - \{j'\}} (\mathcal{R}(j,k)).$$

Note that $mXHR3_{sr}$ may not be unique, and different minimal extended hidden nodes relay sets could contain a different number of nodes.

Definition 12. Call $MXHR3_{sr}$ the *minimum extended hidden nodes relay set* of a transmission T_{sr} in three-party proxy set coverage of node r. $MXHR3_{sr}$ is the subset of $mXHR3_{sr}$ with the smallest number of nodes (see Fig. 6(f)):

$$MXHR3_{sr} \in mXHR_{sr}$$

and

$$\forall r \in mXHR3_{sr} \; (|MXHR3_{sr}| \leq |r|).$$

Finally, we introduce a set of metrics characterizing the ability of a MAC protocol to silence nodes which can cause collisions.

Definition 13. Let $\mathcal{F}$ be an algorithm of a MAC protocol that silences proper nodes during a transmission. Call the set of nodes silenced by $\mathcal{F}$ during a transmission T_{sr}, $\mathcal{S}_{sr}(\mathcal{F})$. Ideally, an algorithm should silence all nodes that have the potential to be hidden nodes, as well as nodes that could potentially be affected by the transmission T_{sr}. Assume there exists an algorithm $\mathcal{I}$ which classifies all the nodes that should be silenced during a transmission T_{sr}. Thus,

$$\mathcal{S}_{sr}(\mathcal{I}) = H_{sr} \cup H_{rs} \cup V_s \cup V_r.$$

Definition 14. Call $Misc_{sr}(\mathcal{F})$ the *misclassification ratio* of an algorithm $\mathcal{F}$ for a transmission T_{sr}. $Misc_{sr}(\mathcal{F})$ measures the ratio of nodes that are incorrectly silenced by $\mathcal{F}$:

$$Misc_{sr}(\mathcal{F}) = \frac{|\mathcal{S}_{sr}(\mathcal{F}) - \mathcal{S}_{sr}(\mathcal{I})|}{|\mathcal{S}_{sr}(\mathcal{I})|}.$$

Definition 15. Call $Miss_{sr}(\mathcal{F})$ the *miss ratio* of an algorithm $\mathcal{F}$ for a transmission T_{sr}. $Miss_{sr}(\mathcal{F})$ measures the ratio of nodes which are not silenced by the algorithm $\mathcal{F}$, although they should be:

$$Miss_{sr}(\mathcal{F}) = \frac{|\mathcal{S}_{sr}(\mathcal{I}) - \mathcal{S}_{sr}(\mathcal{F})|}{|\mathcal{S}_{sr}(\mathcal{I})|}.$$

Definition 16. Let $\overline{Misc(\mathcal{F})}$ and $\overline{Miss(\mathcal{F})}$ be the *average misclassification ratio* and *average miss ratio* of an algorithm $\mathcal{F}$, respectively. The averages are computed over a network $\mathcal{N}$:

$$\overline{Misc(\mathcal{F})} = \frac{\sum_{\forall s, r \in \mathcal{N}} \mathcal{R}(s,r) |\mathcal{S}_{sr}(\mathcal{F}) - \mathcal{S}_{sr}(\mathcal{I})|}{\sum_{\forall s, r \in \mathcal{N}} \mathcal{R}(s,r) |\mathcal{S}_{sr}(\mathcal{I})|}$$

and

$$\overline{Miss(\mathcal{F})} = \frac{\sum_{\forall s, r \in \mathcal{N}} \mathcal{R}(s,r) |\mathcal{S}_{sr}(\mathcal{I}) - \mathcal{S}_{sr}(\mathcal{F})|}{\sum_{\forall s, r \in \mathcal{N}} \mathcal{R}(s,r) |\mathcal{S}_{sr}(\mathcal{I})|}.$$

6.2. A solution to the hidden node problem

A heterogeneous wireless *ad hoc* network of mobile devices is composed of devices with different computation and communication capabilities.

Asymmetric links dominate routing in such a network[35] and the sender may not be able to receive the CTS or ACK packets from the receiver. In such a case, a DATA packet, or the next frame, cannot be sent. The IEEE 802.11 protocol assumes that all the connections are symmetric. Our protocol relaxes this assumption, asymmetric links can be used provided that they are part of a *three-party proxy set*.[35]

Our protocol retains the use of RTS, CTS, DATA and ACK frames defined in the IEEE 802.11 standard. In addition to these, we have four additional frames: XRTS (Extended RTS), XCTS (Extended CTS), TCTS (Tunneled CTS), and TACK (Tunneled ACK).

An ideal MAC layer protocol should be based upon a scheme which delivers the RTS and CTS packets to all hidden nodes in H_{rs} and H_{sr}, respectively. Such a scheme, however, can be impractical because (i) a node may not have knowledge of all its In-bound neighbors; (ii) the number of hops needed to reach an In-bound neighbor might be large; thus the time penalty and the power consumption required for the RTS/CTS diffusion phase might outweigh the benefits of a reduced probability of collision.

Our solution is to send RTS and CTS packets to the nodes in $H3_{rs}$ and $H3_{sr}$, respectively. In this way, a considerable number of nodes that are misclassified as "hidden" nodes by Ref. 1, referred to as protocol A, and Ref. 2, referred to as protocol B, are allowed to transmit (see Fig. 7). Note

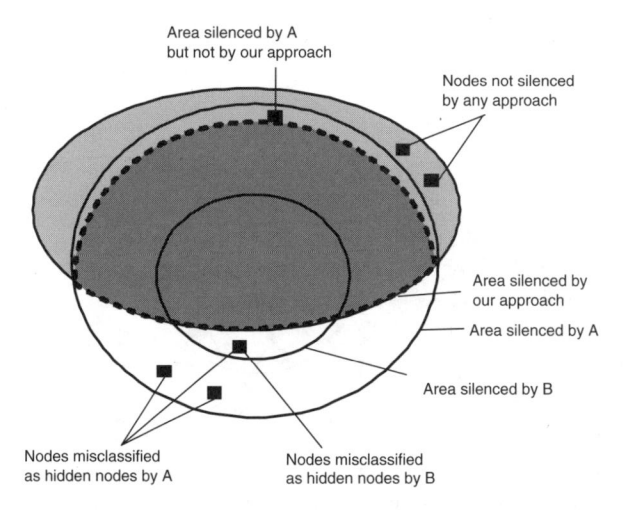

Fig. 7. The ability of three MAC layer protocols, A, B, and the one introduced in this chapter, to correctly classify "hidden" nodes. A protocol may incorrectly require nodes to be silent ("missclassify" them) and miss nodes which should be silent.

that our approach does not identify all hidden nodes, but neither methods A or B are able to identify all hidden nodes.

6.3. Node status

In IEEE 802.11, when a node overhears an RTS or a CTS packet, it becomes *silent* and cannot send any packet from then on until its NAV expires. In this way, nodes in the relay set cannot send XRTS/XCTS as they should be in a *silent* state after overhearing the RTS/CTS packet. To resolve this dilemma, we replace the *silent* state with a *quasi silent* state, in which a node is allowed to send control packets, except RTS and CTS.

In the medium access model proposed in this chapter, a node is either in an *idle* state, *active* state, *quasi silent* state, or *silent* state. When a node is in an *idle* state, it is able to send or receive any type of packets. When a node is in *active* state, the node is either sending or receiving a packet. When a node is in *quasi silent* state, the node can either receive packets or send any packet type except RTS, CTS, or DATA packet. When a node is in *silent* state, the node can receive packets but cannot send any packet.

6.4. Medium access model

The medium access model of our protocol is an extended four-way handshake (see Fig. 8). For short data frames, there is no need to initiate an

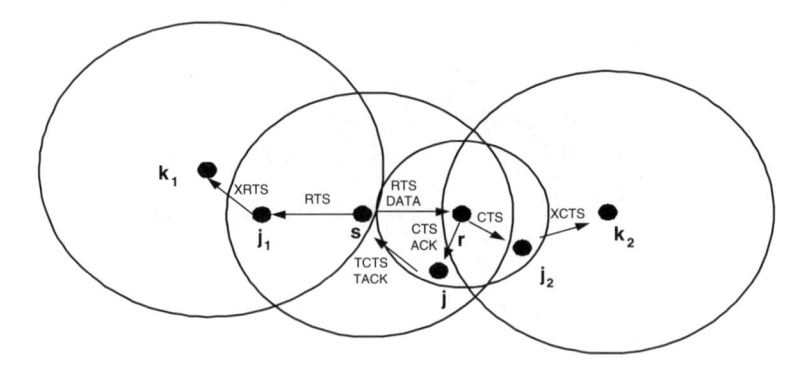

Fig. 8. Routing over asymmetric links in a heterogeneous wireless *ad hoc* network. Node s is the sender, r is the receiver, the link from node s to r is asymmetric, and node j is the proxy node that can relay traffic to s for r. Nodes k_1 and k_2 are hidden nodes for transmissions T_{rs} and T_{sr}, respectively. Nodes j_1 and j_2 are the proxy nodes that can relay traffic from s to k_1 and from r to k_2, respectively.

RTS-CTS handshake. For long data frames we recognize several phases:

(i) *Sensing phase.* The sender s senses the medium. If it does not detect any traffic for a DIFS period, the sender starts the contention phase; otherwise, it backs off for a random time before it senses again.
(ii) *Contention phase.* The sender s generates a random number $\gamma \in [0,$ contention window] slot time. The sender s starts a transmission if it does not detect any traffic for γ slot time.
(iii) RTS *transmission phase.* The sender s sends an RTS packet to the receiver r. The RTS packet specifies the NAV(RTS), *link type* of L_{sr} and $MXHR3_{rs}$. The *link type* field is used to determine whether symmetric or asymmetric medium access model is used.
(iv) CTS *transmission phase.* The receiver r checks whether the link is symmetric or not. If link L_{sr} is symmetric, node r sends a CTS packet back to node s; otherwise, node r sends a TCTS packet to node s. A TCTS packet specifies both the proxy node and the receiver s. The proxy node forwards the TCTS packet to the original sender s after receiving it. A CTS/TCTS packet can be sent only after sensing a free SIFS period. Instead of $MXHR3_{sr}$, $MXHR3_{rs} - MXHR3_{sr}$ is specified in the CTS/TCTS packet so that every extended hidden node relay is included only once; thus the duration of XCTS/XRTS diffusion phase can be reduced.
(v) XRTS/XCTS *diffusion phase.* All nodes that overhear a RTS/CTS/TCTS packet enter a *quasi silent* state. After the CTS transmission phase, all extended hidden node relays that are either specified in RTS or CTS/TCTS start contention for broadcasting XRTS/XCTS to its neighbors. When a node captures the medium, all other nodes back off for a random number of $(1,4)$ SIFS period, and continue the contention until the XRTS/XCTS diffusion phase finishes. An XRTS/XCTS diffusion phase lasts for δ SIFS periods, after which all nodes except the proxy node becomes *silent*.
(vi) *Data transmission phase.* When the XRTS/XCTS diffusion phase finishes, the sender s starts sending DATA packets to the receiver r after sensing a free SIFS period.
(vii) *Acknowledgment phase.* Once the receiver r successfully received the DATA packet from the sender s, it replies with an ACK if link L_{sr} is symmetric, or a TACK packet if link L_{sr} is asymmetric. An ACK/TACK packet can be sent only after sensing a free SIFS period. When the sender s receives an ACK/TACK packet, it starts contending the medium

for the next frame. Meanwhile, the NAVs that are reserved for this transmission should expire.

6.5. *A simulation study*

To evaluate the performance of the MAC layer protocols which support asymmetric links, we conducted a simulation study. We compared the protocols in Refs. 1 and 2, and that presented in this chapter. We assume that the nodes are immobile and wish to study the number of nodes which are silenced by the RTS-CTS protocol as well as nodes which should be silenced but are not. In this experiment we do not consider other characteristics of devices, such as power reserve. We plan to expand these studies for the case when the nodes are mobile and assume that the nodes in the same class have a slight variation in their power reserve.

A node is *misclassified* as a hidden node and it is silenced by an algorithm while it should not have been. A node is *missed* if it should be considered a hidden node and silenced by an algorithm but it is not. We measure the average misclassification and the average miss ratio of the protocols under several scenarios and construct 95% confidence intervals for these averages. The scenario involves a rectangular simulation area of 500×500 meters. The transmission range for the four class of nodes,[6,35] $C1$, $C2$, $C3$, and $C4$ are random variables normally distributed with the mean $25, 50, 75$, and 100 meters, respectively; the standard deviation for each class is 5 meters. The simulation scenario is created using a set of 40 to 100 nodes, which belong to one of the four classes. The initial positions of the nodes are uniformly distributed in the area, while the number of nodes in each class is equal.

For each generated scenario, we repeat the experiment 100 times. For each replica of the experiment, the nodes are in slightly different positions. The displacement is normally distributed around an initial position and the standard deviation is 20% of its transmission range.

Figure 9(a) illustrates the average misclassification ratio of protocols A[1] and B[2] as a function of the number of nodes. A and B perform similarly; the average misclassification ratio ranges from 34.10% to 70.42%, and increases with the number of nodes. As an artifact of node immobility, in our simulation the algorithm introduced in this chapter has a zero average misclassification ratio.

Figure 9(b) illustrates the average miss ratio of protocols A, B, and the one introduced in this chapter as a function of the number of nodes. The protocols perform similarly; the average miss ratio ranging from 5.55% to

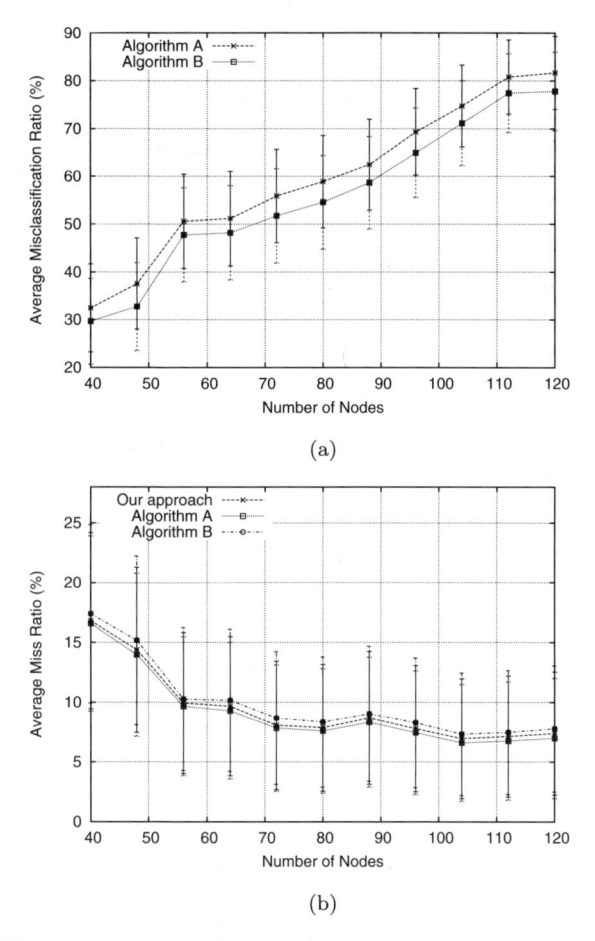

Fig. 9. (a) The average misclassification ratio of protocols A and B as a function of the number of nodes. As an artifact of node immobility in our simulation study, the protocol introduced in this chapter has a zero average misclassification ratio. A node is misclassified if it is required to be silent unnecessarily. (b) The average miss ratio of protocols A, B, and our approach, as a function of the number of nodes. Missed nodes should be required to be silent but are not.

16.36%. The average miss ratio for our approach is slightly larger than that of protocol A but smaller than the average miss ratio of protocol B. The average miss ratio decreases as the number of nodes increases. Protocol A achieves a slightly better performance but requires more power consumption and generates additional collisions, compared to protocol B and our approach.

7. Cross-Layer Architecture

There is a growing consensus that cross-layer communication is necessary to fully exploit the possibilities offered by wireless networks. The complex nature of heterogeneous wireless networks with asymmetric links requires information flow across several layers of the protocol stack. For example, software radio requires dynamic spectrum management. The goal of dynamic spectrum management is to determine the rights of nodes to transmit on a certain channel, at a specific power, time interval and geographic location. There is a strong interdependency between the spectrum management and the MAC and routing protocols. The spectrum allocation determines the possible topologies which can be achieved by the MAC and network layers. Conversely, we want the minimum spectrum allocation which makes a given topology feasible. The ability of the MAC and routing protocols to handle asymmetric links allows spectrum management to determine the transmission rights of the nodes independently; the pairing requirements, inevitable for bidirectional links, are not applicable. This allows for a more efficient spectrum allocation.

One of the consequences of operating in the context of a MANET with asymmetric links is that the information of three-party proxy sets needs to be maintained both at the MAC and the network layer. With the knowledge of three-party proxy sets, reverse routes (for upper routing protocol) or tunnels (for underlying MAC protocol) for an asymmetric link can be computed.

In our approach, the required information is maintained by the MAC layer protocol `TPSDM` (Three-party Proxy Set Discovery and Maintenance). `TPSDM` stores information of three-party proxy sets at a shared module, which could be fetched by the routing module of network layer.

In `TPSDM`, each node maintains a *neighbor table* that contains six fields: node id, location, transmission range, neighbor type, P-node list, and timestamp list. Each node periodically broadcasts a 1-hop limited *Hello* message which encloses the node id, location and transmission range of its neighbors along with its own. When a node receives a *Hello* message, it applies a `TPSDM` Algorithm on the incoming *Hello* message and its own neighbor table. The algorithm first identifies the neighbors of the current node for each entry of the incoming *Hello* message and stores them into the neighbor table along with the neighbor type. For each entry of the incoming message, a three-party proxy set is found if a directed circle is formed by the links connecting the current node, the node of the incoming *Hello* message, and the node of an entry. If a node detects a three-party proxy set in which it plays the role of L-node or H-node of an asymmetric link, the proxy node and the current time are appended onto the *P-node list* and the *timestamp list* of H-node entry in the neighbor table, respectively. In case the current node is an L-node, the P-node is the node through which the current node can reach the H-node, thus one or more tunnels to the H-node is established; in case the current node is the H-node, the *Hello* message of the P-node carries the information of the L-node, which notifies or renews the information of the L-node at the current node.

The maintenance of three-party proxy sets is achieved by periodically checking the *timestamp list* field. When TPSDM detects the expiration of a timestamp, the associated P-node is purged; when the *P-node list* becomes empty, the entry of the node is purged from the neighbor table in the case that it is an Out-bound neighbor.

8. Work in Progress

We have implemented the network and MAC layer protocols in NS-2 and we are conducting experiments to assess their advantages over protocols based upon IEEE 802.11 and their performance. We discuss briefly an example when the A^4LP protocol uses asymmetric links to route messages from node 0 to node 4 while protocols for symmetric links fail to find a route. In our simulation we use FTP as the transport layer protocol.

The initial position of nodes is depicted in Fig. 10, which shows also the transmission range and the distance between the nodes. The nodes do not move during the simulation. The forward and reverse routes are found and

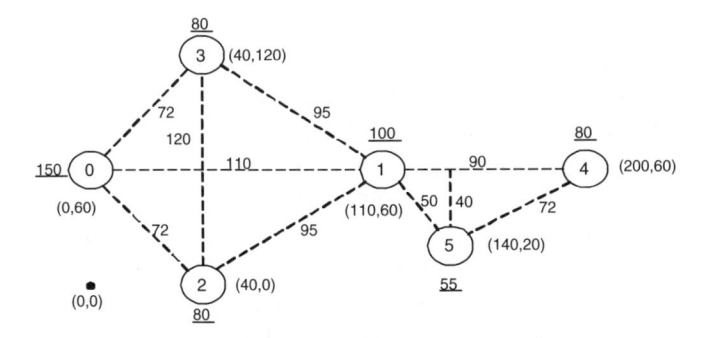

Fig. 10. The topology of a network when the A^4LP protocol routes messages from node 0 to node 4 over asymmetric links, while protocols for symmetric links fail to find a route. The initial position, range, and distance between nodes are shown.

established by A^4LP, and MAC layer acknowledgments are assured by our MAC protocol. For instance, node 5 is a proxy node that forwards CTS and ACK packets for a unidirectional transmission from node 1 to node 4 at MAC layer. The packets are successfully delivered and acknowledged.

9. Summary

In this chapter, we argue that asymmetry of the transmission range in wireless networks is a reality and should be treated as such. This asymmetry makes reliable communication more difficult and complicates medium access control as well as network layer protocols. In some instances, e.g., in the case of software radio, we should be able to take advantage of this asymmetry.

The models of traditional multiple access networks assume that all nodes share a single communication channel and have access to the feedback (success, idle slot, collision) from any transmission. In this case splitting algorithms allow sharing of the communication channel in a cooperative environment with reasonable efficiency and fairness. This is no longer the case for wireless networks with symmetric or bidirectional links, where the sender and the receiver do not share the feedback channel and hidden nodes may interfere with a transmission. In the case of networks with asymmetric links, hidden nodes are out of the reach of the sender and the receiver, but their transmissions may interfere with the reception of a packet by the intended destination. The problem of hidden nodes is further complicated in this case because the feedback from the receiver in an RTS–CTS exchange may have to pass through several relay stations before reaching all the nodes which are supposed to be silent. Some of the solutions proposed in the literature reduce the probability of a collision by requiring a larger than necessary set of nodes to be silent. In turn, this has negative effects upon the communication latency and the overall network throughput. We propose a MAC layer protocol which reduces the number of nodes that have to be silent but, as all the other schemes proposed, may miss some of the nodes which should have been classified as "hidden."

MAC layer and routing protocols are further complicated by the need to minimize the number of retransmissions to reduce power consumption and collisions. We propose a technique to address this concern: m-limited forwarding was conceived to reduce the cost of disseminating information in a power-constrained environment by limiting the cardinality of the subset of nodes which retransmit a packet.

While further studies are necessary to confirm our results that m-limited forwarding with $\tau_k(i,j)$ fitness function and $m = 2$ is a serious contender to flooding for disseminating control information in a power-constrained, location-aware *ad hoc* network with bidirectional links. Ongoing evaluation of m-limited forwarding for wireless networks with asymmetric links may lead to slightly different conclusions, e.g., it is likely that $\eta_k(i,j)$- may prove to be better than $\tau_k(i,j)$-based policies.

There is a growing consensus that cross-layer communications are necessary to fully exploit the possibilities offered by wireless networks. The complex nature of heterogeneous wireless networks with asymmetric links requires information flow across several layers of the protocol stack. In this chapter, we sketch a possible architecture which allows information about network status to flow across layers.

Our future work is dedicated to the applications of m-limited forwarding to MAC and network layer protocols for heterogeneous *ad hoc* networks with asymmetric links. We have reported only on partial results; further simulation and possibly analytical studies are needed to provide conclusive proof that the protocols presented in this chapter offer a viable alternative and perform better than existing solutions.

Acknowledgments

The research reported in this work was partially supported by National Science Foundation Grant Nos. MCB9527131, DBI0296035, ACI0296035, and EIA0296179.

References

1. N. Poojary, S. V. Krishnamurthy and S. Dao, Medium access control in a network of ad hoc mobile nodes with heterogeneous power capabilities, in *Proc. IEEE ICC 2001*, Vol. 3, 2001, pp. 872–877.
2. T. Fujii, M. Takahashi, M. Bandai, T. Udagawa and I. Sasase, An efficient MAC protocol in wireless ad-hoc networks with heterogeneous power nodes, in *5th Int. Symp. Wireless Personal Multimedia Communications (WPMC '2002)*, Hawaii, Vol. 2, 2002, pp. 776–780.
3. DARPA Advanced Technology Office — FCS Communications Program, http://www.darpa.mil/ato/programs/fcs_comm.htm.
4. Joint Tactical Radio System (JTRS), http://jtrs.army.mil.
5. Federal Communications Commission Notice of Inquiry FCC 03-289 regarding the interference temperature model, http://hraunfoss.fcc.gov/docs_public/attachmatch/FCC-03-289A1.pdf.

6. D. C. Marinescu, G. M. Marinescu, Y. Ji, L. Bölöni and H. Siegel, Ad hoc grids: Communication and computing in a power constrained environment, in *Proc. Workshop on Energy-Efficient Wireless Communications and Networks (EWCN)*, 2003, pp. 113–122.
7. Y. Afek and E. Gafni, Distributed algorithms for unidirectional networks, *SIAM Journal on Computing* **23**(6) (1994), 1152–1178 [Online: citeseer.ist.psu.edu/afek93distributed.html].
8. C. Perkins and P. Bhagwat, Highly dynamic destination-sequenced distance-vector routing (DSDV) for mobile computers, in *ACM SIGCOMM '94*, 1994, pp. 234–244.
9. C.-C. Chiang, H.-K. Wu, W. Liu and M. Gerla, Routing in clustered multi-hop, mobile wireless networks with fading channel, in *Proc. IEEE SICON'97*, 1997, pp. 197–211.
10. S. Basagni, I. Chlamtac, V. R. Syrotiuk and B. A. Woodward, A distance routing effect algorithm for mobility (DREAM), in *Proc. ACM MOBICOM '98*, 1998, pp. 76–84.
11. T. Clausen, P. Jacquet, A. Laouiti, P. Muhlethaler, A. Qayyum and L. Viennot, Optimized link state routing protocol for ad hoc networks, in *Proc. IEEE INMIC*, December, 2001, pp. 62–68.
12. D. B. Johnson and D. A. Maltz, Dynamic source routing in ad hoc wireless networks, in *Mobile Computing*, eds. Imielinski and Korth (Kluwer Academic Publishers, 1996), Ch. 5, pp. 153–181.
13. C. Perkins and E. Royer, ad hoc on-demand distance vector routing, in *Proc. 2nd IEEE Workshop on Mobile Computing Systems and Applications*, 1999, pp. 99–100.
14. Y. Ko and N. Vaidya, Location-Aided Routing (LAR) in mobile ad hoc networks, in *Proc. 4th Annual ACM Int. Conf. on Mobile Computing and Networking (MobiCom 1998)*, 1998, pp. 66–75.
15. V. Park and M. Corson, A highly adaptive distributed routing algorithm for mobile wireless networks, in *Proc. INFOCOM '97*, Vol. 3, 1997, pp. 1405–1413.
16. Z. Haas and M. Pearlman, The zone routing protocol (ZRP) for ad hoc networks, in *Internet Draft*, 1998.
17. C. E. Jones, K. Sivalingam, P. Agrawal and J. C. Chen, A survey of energy efficient network protocols for wireless networks, *Wireless Networks* **7** (2001), 343–358.
18. M. Maleki, K. Dantu and M. Pedram, Power-aware source routing protocol for mobile ad hoc networks, in *Proc. 2002 Int. Symp. Low Power Electronics and Design*, 2002, pp. 72–75.
19. S. Singh, M. Woo and C. Raghavendra, Power-aware routing in mobile ad hoc networks, in *Proc. 4th Annual ACM/IEEE Int. Conf. Mobile Computing and Networking (MOBICOM '98)*, 1998, pp. 181–190.
20. J. H. Y. Xu and D. Estrin, Geography-informed energy conservation for ad hoc routing, in *Proc. 7th Annual Int. Conf. Mobile Computing and Networking (Mobicom '01)*, 2001, pp. 70–84.

21. D. B. Johnson, D. A. Maltz and J. Broch, DSR: The dynamic source routing protocol for multi-hop wireless ad hoc networks, in *Ad Hoc Networking*, ed. C. E. Perkins (Addison-Wesley, 2001), ch. 5, pp. 139–172.
22. Z. Haas, M. Pearlman and P. Samar, The intrazone routing protocol (IARP), in *Internet Draft, draft-ietf-manet-zone-iarp-02.txt*, 2002.
23. Z. Haas, M. Pearlman and P. Samar, The interzone routing protocol (IERP), in *Internet Draft, draft-ietf-manet-zone-ierp-02.txt*, 2002.
24. P. Sinha, S. Krishnamurthy and S. Dao, Scalable unidirectional routing using ZRP extensions for wireless ad-hoc networks, in *Proc. IEEE WCNC 2000*, September, 2000, pp. 1329–1339.
25. S. Corson, S. Papademetriou, P. Papadopoulos, V. Park and A. Qayyum, An Internet MANET Encapsulation Protocol (IMEP), IETF, Internet Draft, August, 1999.
26. L. Kleinrock and F. Tobagi, Packet switching in radio channels: Part I — carrier sense multiple-access modes and their throughput-delay characteristics, *IEEE Trans. Commun.* **COM-23**(12) (1975), 1400–1416.
27. P. Karn, Maca — A new channel access method for packet radio, in *Proc. 9th ARRL Computer Networking Conference*, 1990, pp. 134–140.
28. V. Bharghavan, A. Demers, S. Shenker and L. Zhang, MACAW: A media access protocol for wireless LAN's, in *Proc. ACM SIGCOMM '94*, 1994, pp. 221–225.
29. C. Fullmer and J. J. Garcia-Luna-Aceves, Floor Acquisition Multiple Access (FAMA) for packet-radio networks, in *Proc. ACM SIGCOMM '95*, 1995, pp. 262–273.
30. IEEE std 802.11b-1999. Part 11: Wireless LAN Medium Access Control (MAC) and Physical Layer (PHY) Specifications, Tech. Report, August, 1999.
31. V. Bharghavan, A New Protocol for Medium Access in Wireless Packet Networks, Urbana, IL: Timely Group, Tech. Report, 1997.
32. V. Ramasubramanian and D. Moss, Statistical analysis of connectivity in unidirectional ad hoc networks, in *Proc. Int. Workshop on Ad Hoc Networking 2002*, Vancouver, 2002, pp. 109–115.
33. V. Ramasubramanian, R. Chandra and D. Mosse, Providing a bidirectional abstraction for unidirectional ad-hoc networks, in *Proc. INFOCOM 2002*, Vol. 3, 2002, pp. 1258–1267.
34. S. Nesargi and R. Prakash, A tunneling approach to routing with unidirectional links in mobile ad-hoc networks, in *Proc. 9th Int. Conf. Computer Communications and Networks*, 2000, pp. 522–527.
35. G. Wang, Y. Ji, D. C. Marinescu and D. Turgut, A routing protocol for power constrained networks with asymmetric links, in *Proc. ACM Workshop on Performance Evaluation of Wireless Ad Hoc, Sensor, and Ubiquitous Networks (PE-WASUN)*, 2004, pp. 69–76.
36. L. Breslau, D. Estrin, K. Fall, S. Floyd, J. Heidemann, A. Helmy, P. Huang, S. McCanne, K. Varadhan, Y. Xu and H. Yu, Advances in network simulation, *IEEE Computer* **33**(5) (2000), 59–67.

37. VINT project. the ucb/lbnl/vint network simulator-ns (version 2), http://www.isi.edu/nsnam/ns.
38. CMU Monarch extensions to ns, http://www.monarch.cs.cmu.edu.
39. J. Broch, D. A. Maltz, D. B. Johnson, Y. Hu and J. Jetcheva, A performance comparison of multi-hop wireless ad hoc network routing protocols, in *Proc. Mobile Computing and Networking*, 1998, pp. 85–97.
40. V. Kawadia and P. Kumar, A cautionary perspective on cross layer design, University of Illinois, Tech. Report, June, 2003.

CHAPTER 9

Multi-Threaded Servers with High Service Time Variation for Layered Queueing Networks

Greg Franks[*] and Murray Woodside[†]

Department of Systems and Computer Engineering, Carleton University, Ottawa, ON K1S 5B6, Canada
[*]*greg@sce.carleton.ca*
[†]*cmw@sce.carleton.ca*

Jerry Rolia

*Internet Systems and Storage Lab,
Hewlett Packard Laboratories, Palo Alto, CA, 94301, USA
jerry.rolia@hp.com*

Distributed application systems are often implemented as layers of software services. The services provide functions, which we refer to as service entries, that can have significantly different demands on resources such as CPUs and on requests for service from other service entries. Significantly different demands within service entries lead to high service time variation for a service. Such services are typically deployed within application server containers each having some bound on its level of concurrency refered to as its maximum threading level. We have modeled such systems using a layered queueing network approach. Each queue represents a first-come-first-served multi-threaded server with multiple entries that may have high service time variation. This chapter describes a simple and intuitive residence time expression for such queues. Simulation results show that the technique is both fast and accurate when compared with other techniques from the literature.

1. Introduction

Layered queueing networks (LQN) have been proposed as a performance modeling framework for distributed application systems.[11,24,31] They can be used to support software performance engineering exercises[29] and performance management for these complex systems. LQNs are based on mean value analysis methods with residence time expressions that represent features common to distributed application systems. This chapter describes a residence time expression for multi-threaded servers with high service time variation.

Layered queueing networks are extended queueing networks that have a nested queueing structure. Within these networks requests arrive at server queues. When a server thread is available, it accepts a request. Once in service the request may use resources such as CPUs and disks, but it may also make requests for service at other queues. The original server thread is not released until the demands of the request are satisfied. If a server does not have sufficient threads, then requests may incur significant queueing delays. Limits on concurrency and high service time variation can have a significant impact on request response times and system throughput.

The performance of a layered queueing network is predicted by decomposing the network into a series of queuing network submodels that are solved iteratively. Predictions from one submodel affect the input parameters of other models.

Multi-threaded queues with high service time variation are similar to FCFS service centers with service demands that vary by request chain. Queueing networks with these characteristics do not have a product form solution.[3,18] Fortunately, solutions have been proposed that provide estimates for queueing delays at such queues.

This chapter describes our work on a residence time expression for these queues. The approach is a mean value analysis approach most closely related to the method of Reiser and Lavenburg.[22] The technique is a generalization of work by Rolia and Sevick that appears in Rolia's Ph.D. dissertation.[25] We compare the technique with other residence time expressions from the literature[2,7,22,26,27] and find that it provides quick and accurate results.

Section 2 presents notation the various residence time expressions. Section 3 compares the solution speed and accuracy of the techniques. Examples of case studies that have relied on these methods are given in Sec. 4. A summary and concluding remarks are offered in Sec. 5

2. Residence Time Expressions

This section describes seven residence time expressions for our queue under study. These expressions were chosen because they can be used in a mean value approximation (MVA). Table 1 gives notation for the expressions for a system with population vector **N**, with one customer component per chain.

Table 1. Nomenclature.

j, k	Server index ($j = 1, \ldots$) and customer class index ($k = 1, \ldots, K$).
$\mathbf{n}$	A population vector $(n_1, \ldots, n_K)$ by customer class (i.e., by service entry) at a server.
$\mathbf{e}_k$	A unit vector i in the kth direction in a K-dimensional space.
M_j	The number of server threads at server j.
V_{kj}	The mean number of visits of class k customers at server j.
S_{kj}	The mean service time per visit of a class k customers at server j.
μ_{kj}	The mean service rate, $\mu_{kj} = S_{kj}^{-1}$.
$\alpha_j(i)$,	The service rate multiplier for i customers in total, or population vector $\mathbf{n}$, at server j.
$\alpha_j(\mathbf{n})$	
$P_j(i, \mathbf{N})$	The probability that server j has i customers in total.
$P_j(\mathbf{n}, \mathbf{N})$	The probability that server j has the population $\mathbf{n}$.
$PB_j(\mathbf{N})$	The probability that all M_j server threads are busy at server j.
	$PB_j(\mathbf{N}) = 1 - \sum_{i=1}^{M_j} P_j(i, \mathbf{N})$
$L_{kj}(\mathbf{N})$	The mean number of class k customers at server j including those in service.
$Q_{kj}(\mathbf{N})$	The mean number of class k customers at server j excluding those in service.
	$Q_{kj}(\mathbf{N}) = L_{kj}(\mathbf{N}) - U_{kj}(\mathbf{N})$
$W_{kj}(\mathbf{N})$	The mean residence time for a single visit of a class k customer at server j.
$U_{kj}(\mathbf{N})$	The utilization of class k customers at server j.
$U_{kj}^{(1)}(\mathbf{N})$	The utilization of one class k customer at queue j.

Appendix A lists the expressions used to calculate the marginal probabilities. Without loss of generality, we assume each class of customers visits only one entry at any server.

2.1. MVA waiting time expressions

Reiser and Lavenberg[22] gave the exact MVA expression for a multiserver based on special product-form networks with multiclass multiservers:

$$W_{kj}(\mathbf{N}) = S_{kj} + \frac{S_{kj}}{M_j} \left[\sum_{c=1}^{K} Q_{cj}(\mathbf{N} - \mathbf{e}_k) + PB_j(\mathbf{N} - \mathbf{e}_k) \right], \quad (1)$$

where the first term is the customer's own service, the second term is the time the customer spends in the queue waiting for service and the third term is the busy probability. For FCFS scheduling, the service time terms

S_{kj} must be equal for each class. Equation (1) is often expressed as

$$W_{kj}(\mathbf{N}) = \frac{S_{kj}}{M_j}\left[1 + \sum_{c=1}^{K} L_{cj}(\mathbf{N} - \mathbf{e}_k) + \sum_{i=0}^{M_j-2}(M_j - 1 - i)P_j(i, \mathbf{N} - \mathbf{e}_k)\right]. \tag{2}$$

Ruth[26] evaluated a version of (2) where each of the individual terms is multiplied by the service time. The class dependent service times are used for the customers in queue (the first summation) and the overall mean service time $\overline{S_j}$ is used for the customers in service (the second summation).

$$W_{kj}(\mathbf{N}) = \frac{1}{M_j}\left[S_{kj} + \sum_{c=1}^{K} S_{cj} L_{cj}(\mathbf{N} - \mathbf{e}_k)\right.$$
$$\left. + \overline{S_j} \sum_{i=0}^{M_j-2}(M_j - 1 - i)P_j(i, \mathbf{N} - \mathbf{e}_k)\right]. \tag{3}$$

De Souza e Silva and Muntz[7] incorporated class-dependent FCFS scheduling into multiservers by applying the approximation by Reiser for load-independent servers[23] to (1). This approximation was incorporated into Linearizer approximate MVA by Conway with good results.[6] The complete waiting time expression, describing the terms xe and xr, is given in Appendix B.

$$W_{kj}(\mathbf{N}) = S_{kj} + \sum_{c=1}^{K} xe_{kcj}(\mathbf{N})Q_{cj}(\mathbf{N} - \mathbf{e}_k) + PB_j(\mathbf{N} - \mathbf{e}_k)xr_{kj}(\mathbf{N}). \tag{4}$$

Bruell, Baldo and Afshari[2] list several well-known expressions used for mixed, multiple class BCMP networks with load dependent service stations, including

$$W_{kj}(\mathbf{N}) = \sum_{\mathbf{n} \leq \mathbf{N}} \frac{|\mathbf{n}|S_{kj}}{\alpha_j(\mathbf{n})} P_j(\mathbf{n} - \mathbf{e}_k, \mathbf{N} - \mathbf{e}_k), \tag{5}$$

which has class-dependent service times. Restrictions exist on the rate multiplier terms, α. Further, the queueing discipline, called *composite queuing*, is not FCFS. The marginal probabilities are computed for every feasible customer population $\mathbf{n}$. Schmidt[27] also uses the marginal probabilities based on customer population but approximates FCFS queueing:

$$W_{kj}(\mathbf{N}) = \sum_{\mathbf{n} \in \mathbf{N}} \left[S_{kj} + \frac{\max(0, |\mathbf{n}| - M_j)}{M_j(|\mathbf{n}| - 1)} \left(\sum_{c=1}^{K} \frac{n_c V_{cj} S_{cj} - V_{kj} S_{kj}}{V_{kj}} \right) \right]$$
$$\times P_j(\mathbf{n} - \mathbf{e}_k, \mathbf{N} - \mathbf{e}_k). \qquad (6)$$

Rolia and Sevcik[24,25] developed a multiserver residence time expression for the Method of Layers that does not require computation of marginal probabilities at all. However, it had only been described as a multi-threaded server for queues with single entries:

$$W_{kj}(\mathbf{N}) = S_{kj} \left[1 + \frac{U_j^{(1)}(\mathbf{N} - \mathbf{e}_k)^{M_j}}{M_j} \sum_{c=1}^{K} L_{cj}(\mathbf{N} - \mathbf{e}_k) \right]. \qquad (7)$$

Franks[14] generalized Eq. (7) to support multiple entries by multiplying the chain-dependent service times by the chain queue lengths, which better represents the delays due to each chain:

$$W_{kj}(\mathbf{N}) = S_{kj} + \frac{U_j^{(1)}(\mathbf{N} - \mathbf{e}_k)^{M_j}}{M_j} \sum_{c=1}^{K} S_{cj} L_{cj}(\mathbf{N} - \mathbf{e}_k). \qquad (8)$$

Equations (2) through (6) all use marginal probabilities, either for the total number of customers at the server, $P_j(i, \mathbf{N} - \mathbf{e}_k)$, or for each population vector, $P_j(\mathbf{n} - \mathbf{e}_k, \mathbf{N} - \mathbf{e}_k)$. When using exact MVA to solve a queueing network, these terms are all computed recursively starting with zero customers, and with $P_j(0, \mathbf{0}) = 1$ and $P_j(\mathbf{0}, \mathbf{0}) = 1$. When using approximate MVA, the usual backwards MVA approximation step to find the value of $P_j(i, \mathbf{N} - \mathbf{e}_k)$ is to simply let $P_j(i, \mathbf{N} - \mathbf{e}_k) = P_j(i, \mathbf{N})$. This assignment often leads to infeasible marginal probabilities. Better approximations, given by Krzesinski and Greyling[17] for $P_j(i, \mathbf{N} - \mathbf{e}_k)$, and by Schmidt[27] for $P_j(\mathbf{n} - \mathbf{e}_k, \mathbf{N} - \mathbf{e}_k)$ have been used in this work. The exact and approximate expressions are shown in Appendix A.

3. Accuracy and Computation-Time Comparisons

The accuracy and computation times of the layered queueing solution using these residence time expressions was evaluated using models based on the LQN shown in Fig. 1. Customers in the queueing network are represented by the icons labeled "Class1" through "Class4"; the number of customers in each class is shown within "{}". The servers in the queueing network are represented be the icons labelled "S1" through "S6". Stacked icons

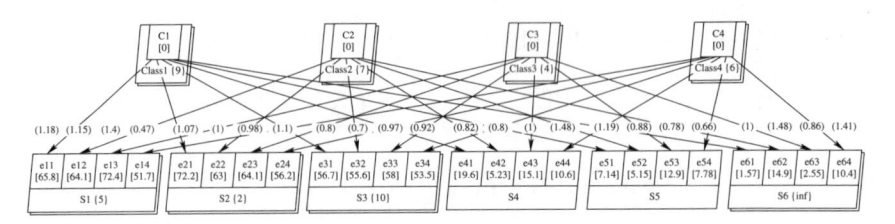

Fig. 1. Layered Queueing Network adapted from Conway.[5]

represent multiservers, or in the case of S6, a delay (or infinite) server. The queueing submodels were solved using the waiting time expressions within the Linearizer approximation MVA.[4]

The structure of the test model is based on the model by Conway.[5] Each server has a distinct service entry for each of the four classes of user, represented by the small parallograms in the figure. Service time demands are shown using "[ ]" and request rates are shown using "( )". Two hundred cases were created with random model parameters, with demands at each of the lower-level servers chosen from the range (1.57, 72.39) and the number of visits to each of the servers by each class of customer in (0.35, 2.30). For each case, the expressions were compared to simulation results with an accuracy of ±1% (their 95% confidence interval).

Table 2 shows

- the percent Mean Relative Error (MRE) in throughput at the clients, MRE = $\frac{apprx-sim}{sim} \times 100$, and the standard deviation in MRE,

Table 2. Accuracy and computation-time comparisons.

Expression	MRE	σ	ARE	Run time (min:sec)
Simulation				42:37.9
(2)	11.18	0.41	13.91	0:02.0
(3)	−1.68	0.01	3.52	0:02.2
(4)	−0.59	0.00	1.55	1:25.9
(5)	11.27	0.42	15.07	2:55.4
(6)	−3.64	0.07	8.51	4:38.5
(7)	11.99	0.38	14.16	0:02.1
New (8)	0.48	0.01	2.91	0:02.3

Note: Mean Relative Error and mean Absolute Relative Error of client throughput when compared to simulation. All of the simulations have 95% confidence intervals of ± 1%.

- the percent mean Absolute Relative Error (ARE) in throughput at the clients, $\text{ARE} = \frac{|\text{apprx}-\text{sim}|}{\text{sim}} \times 100$, and
- the average run time for the test cases as *min:sec*.

Equations (2), (5) and (7) all give large errors because they do not represent the chain-dependent service times. Based on the MRE metric, (8) performs the best, and based on ARE, (4) performs the best. The MRE error for (4) is slightly larger because it gives a slight bias, underestimating the throughput. Of these two, Eq. (8) is superior in run time because it does not need to compute marginal probabilities nor does it have multiple product terms like those used by the de Souza e Silva and Muntz approximation. Equation (8) is thus a good compromise of accuracy and runtime.

4. Example Case Studies

This section describes two applications of layered queueing networks that have relied on the multi-threaded multiple-entry queue with high service time variation. The first describes performance management of a Web server system. The second describes a software performance engineering exercise for an electronic bookstore.

4.1. *Systems management example*

Figure 2 illustrates a layered queueing network for a Web server that provides access to certain scripts via CGI, HTML forms and images.[8] Client requests traverse the Internet and are accepted by a listener process that forwards the requests to a pool of server threads. In layered queueing models, a forwarding call acts as a series of requests with a single reply. The first request is to the listener, the second to the pool of server threads. The reply is from the pool. The pool has three service entries that correspond to the CGI, HTML, and image requests. Detailed measurements were obtained to discover the percentage of requests to each of the service entries and the per-entry CPU and resulting network transfer times. Per-entry disk demands could not be measured directly so they had to be estimated. Because of caching, disk demands were quite small, so the final conclusions were unlikely to be affected by the estimates.

In the model, the Internet is a delay centre, the listener thread is an FCFS server, and the pool of server threads is a multi-threaded server with multiple entries. CPU demands were significantly different per entry. The network transfer time for results dominated and were also significantly

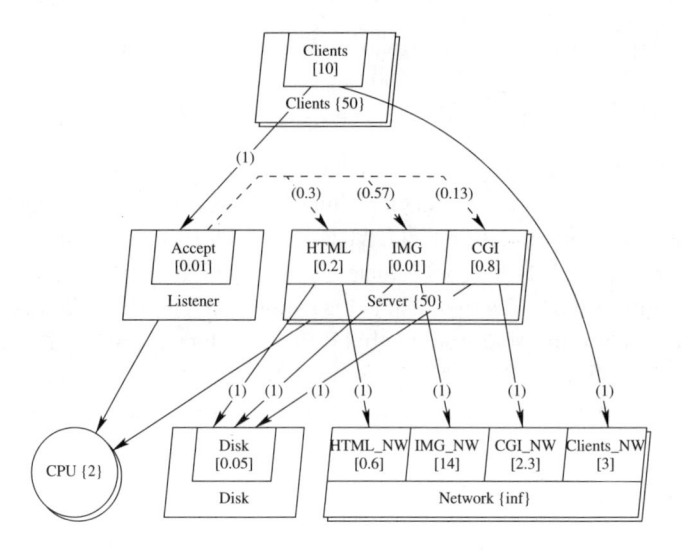

Fig. 2. Web server from Dilley.[8] Forwarded requests are shown using the dashed arcs.

different per entry. The demand values for (CPU, network) for the cgi, html, and image entries of the server pool were (800, 2300), (200, 600), and (10, 14000) ms, respectively.

The study helped to explain an anomaly with respect to response time measurements for the system. Other analysts had observed that mean client response times were higher at night even though the traffic loads were lower. This followed from the fact that clients from different geographic regions were accessing the site at different times of day. Each region had its own transmission latency and hence network demand value. Clients from distant regions with higher network latencies tended to use the system when it was nighttime at the server.

The layered queueing network was used to show the impact of user geography, thread pool size, request mix, and number of server CPUs on client response times. The results were used to recommend appropriate thread pool sizes.

High service time variation is common in distributed application systems. Others have reported service entry CPU demands that differed by as much as a factor of five hundred.[16]

4.2. Electronic bookstore example

In a paper by Petriu and Woodside,[20] an electronic bookstore system with multiple application servers was studied as part of its requirements analysis.

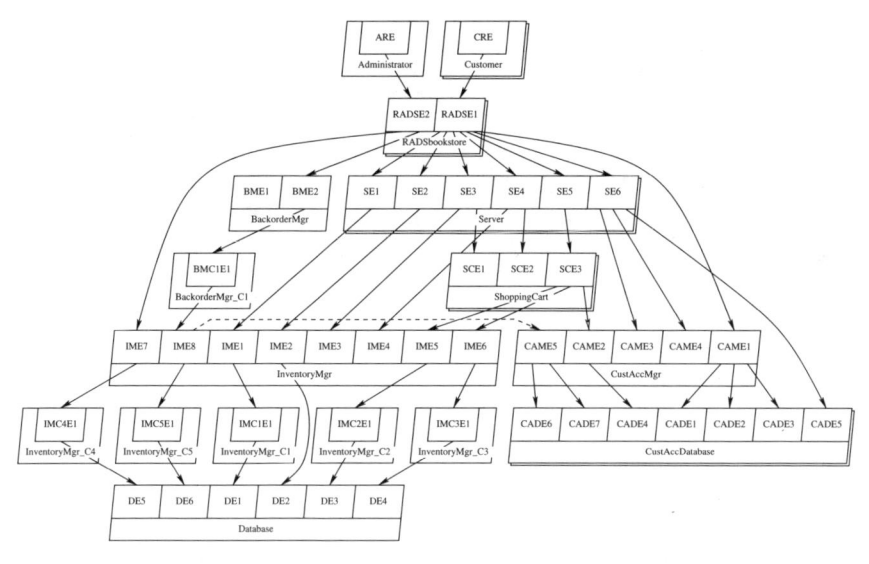

Fig. 3. Web bookstore example. The request from IME8 to CAME5 is forwarded. The request from SCE3 to CAME2 is asynchronous — no reply is generated. CustAccDatabase and Database run on a common "Database" processor. Administrator and Customer represent customers. All other servers share the "Bookstore" processor.

The motivation was to explore potential performance problems in executing Use Cases which were stated as scenarios (Use Case Maps) over a set of distributed software components. The layered model of the system is shown in Fig. 3, suppressing entry-level detail of the tasks but indicating the components and their layered interactions. There are up to 150 Customers active at one time, and one Administrator accessing the RADSbookstore interface, which could be a Web server. The Customers execute a shopping scenario which randomly combines subscenarios which access various functions of Server (to browse, add to a shopping cart, check out, etc.), while the Administrator accesses the InventoryMgr directly to query the system status. The model was derived automatically from the Use Case Maps specification.[19,21] The performance model parameters were taken from assumed values provided during the analysis.[19]

The application task called Server was initially given five threads, and for up to 50 Customers the system had good response time for them, but a rapidly degrading response time to the Administrator. The service times to these classes are very different (for Administrator it is much longer). Simulation results from the original work[20] are shown in Fig. 4 giving the response times and throughouts of the two classes. Customers have

(a) Response Time

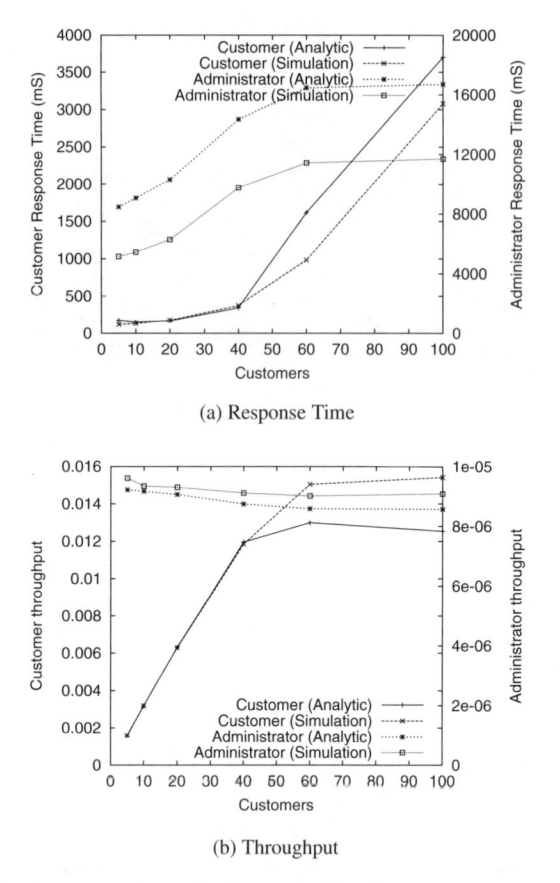

(b) Throughput

Fig. 4. The e-bookstore results in the base case. Simulation results have 95% confidence intervals of ± 2%. Analytic results were generated using (8) with Linearizer.

a three-second thinking time between requests, and a response time which gradually degrades, while the Administrator has a 100-second thinking time and a response time which levels off at about 12 seconds.

The model was solved by simulation and by two of the analytic approximations described here, given by the expressions (4) (Conway) and (8) (Franks) using both Linearizer and Bard–Schweitzer[1,28] approximate MVA. The results in Table 3, show that a typical simulation took about 15 minutes on a 2 GHz Pentium to give delay results accurate to one or two percent. Solving the same model analytically using (4) and (8) with Linearizer took approximately 40 seconds on average using (8), and less than 1 second using

Table 3. Bookstore accuracy and computation-time comparisons.

Expression	MRE	σ	ARE	Run time (min:sec)
Simulation				14:17.84
(4) Linearizer	−5.15	9.35	5.40	0:25.50
(4) Bard–Schweitzer	−4.78	7.04	4.78	0:00.67
(8) Linearizer	−4.34	6.95	4.75	0:38.00
(8) Bard–Schweitzer	−3.90	5.02	4.05	0:00.67

Note: Mean Relative Error and mean Absolute Relative Error of client throughput when compared to simulation. All of the simulations have 95% confidence intervals of ±2%.

Bard–Schweitzer. The error columns in the table show the relative throughput error for the Administrator and Customer. The errors of less than 5% appear to be acceptable for rapid preliminary evaluation. It is interesting to note that for this example the errors with respect to (8) are slightly lower than for (4) but that the Linearizer based solution time is higher. However, Eq. (4) scales poorly with larger numbers of customer classes and customers.

The errors in throughput are mostly small but for heavy loads they approach 15%. The errors in response time are small for the large group up to moderate loads, but they approach 30% at heavy loads and for the Administrator at all loads. These delay errors are large but still useful for rapid screening of preliminary models, as in this case study.

The study went on to consider other configurations. Fifty Server threads gave even worse performance to the Administrator, as the real bottleneck is in the InventoryMgr task. The Administrator effectively is flooded with competitors at that level, when threads are increased. Figure 5 shows the new results. An alternative structure was then modeled, with a read-only Catalogue data base for browsing the inventory, so the Customers only access InventoryMgr when they perform add-to-cart. This gave good performance to both classes of users, as indicated in Fig. 6.

This example illustrates several aspects of modeling with layered queueing networks with multi-threaded servers. Multiple threads are an intrinsic part of the application and have multiple entries with highly variable service times. A considerable range of experiments with different configurations and model structures may be required to explore useful possibilities. Fast

(a) Response time.

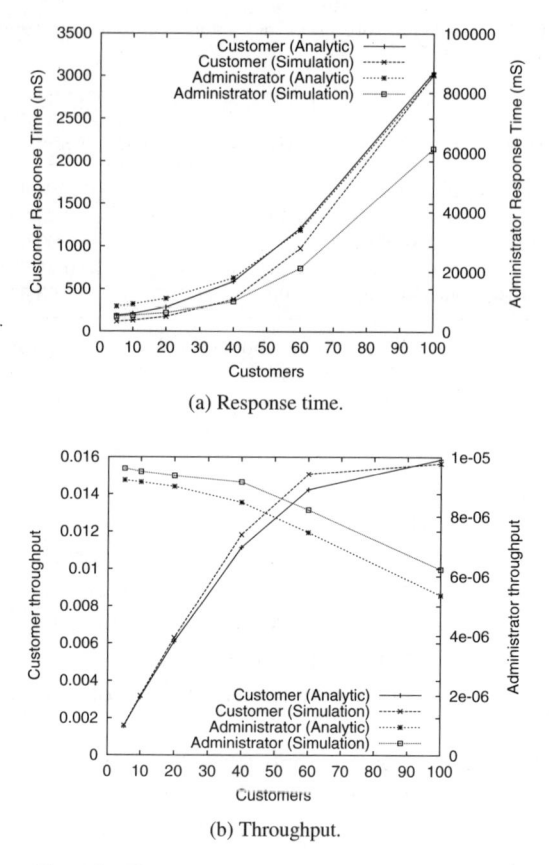

(b) Throughput.

Fig. 5. 50 Server Threads. The customer response time is comparable with the results in Fig. 4. The administrator response time is roughly five times worse.

analytic methods are much faster than simulation, by two orders of magnitude, but slow ones are entirely impractical (and worse than simulation) with large but reasonable-sized populations of users.

5. Conclusions

Fast, accurate approximations have been identified here for first-come-first-served multi-threaded servers with multiple entries. This is the first careful comparison we know of for all the different residence time expressions that have been given for these multiservers. The expressions were evaluated in the context of layered queueing network models, in terms of accuracy and runtime performance. Of the expressions, four explicitly take into

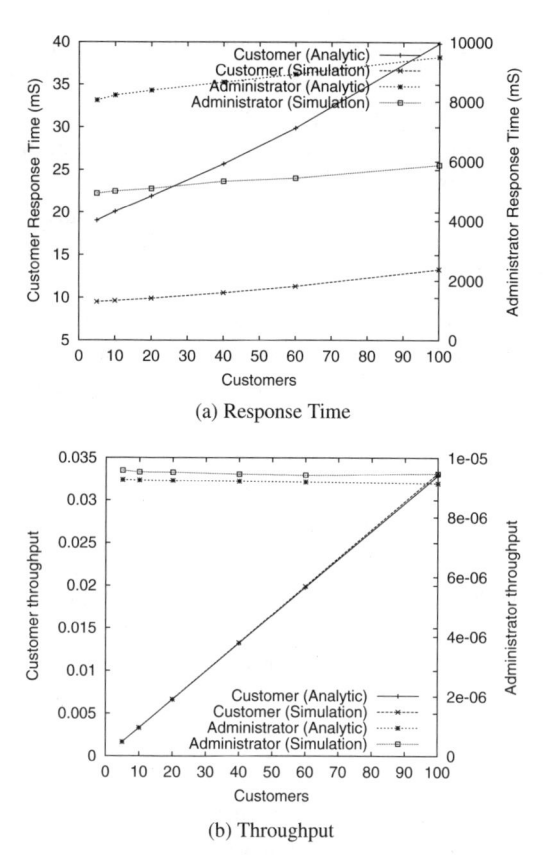

Fig. 6. A successful reorganization with 50 Server Threads and a Read-only catalogue database for browsing. The Customer response time is two orders of magnitude better than the results in Fig. 4. The Administrator response time is halved.

consideration class-dependent service times: Eqs. (3), (4), (6) and (8). These expressions are more accurate for solving systems with customer dependent services times; in some cases, by an order of magnitude. When run-time efficiency is also considered, the proposed waiting time expression (8) is best because it is both accurate and fast. This expression (and Rolia and Sevcik's approximation (7), which it is based on) scale exceptionally well because it does not rely on the marginal probabilities.

The results from Tables 2 and 3 suggest that there are two serious candidates for multi-server queues with class-dependent service times, expressions (4) and (8). It may be more accurate to use (4) if the expression solves in a reasonable length of time, otherwise (8) is the best choice.

The results presented here were studied in layered queueing networks because this type of queueing network is a convenient way of analyzing the performance of distributed application systems. However, layered queueing networks are solved using conventional queueing networks, so the new residence time expressions can also be used to solve a conventional queueing network. Finally, residence time expressions have been developed to reflect many features of distributed applications in layered queueing networks.[10,12,13,30]

The resulting LQNs have sufficient accuracy to support design and management exercises. However, the manual nature of model building has been a major challenge to applying these techniques on a wide scale. We have explored techniques for automating the model building process[9,15] but they typically require detailed instrumentation or estimates for large numbers of parameters by software designers.[19] Fortunately, best practices for software system design and systems management are evolving towards model based methods as a way to deal with complexity. We plan to leverage information captured in such models so that layered queueing network models can become a more commonly used tool for software performance engineering and systems performance management exercises for distributed application systems.

Acknowledgments

This research was supported by the Natural Sciences and Engineering Research Council of Canada and by Communications and Information Technology Ontario (CITO).

Appendix A. Marginal Probabilities

The following equations are the marginal probabilities of finding i customers (of any class) at a server j for a customer population $\mathbf{N}$. They are found recursively from an initial condition of zero customers in the network:

$$P_j(i, \mathbf{N}) = \frac{1}{i} \sum_{k=1}^{K} U_{kj}(\mathbf{N}) P_j(i-1, \mathbf{N} - \mathbf{e}_k), \qquad 0 < i < M_j,$$

$$PB_j(\mathbf{N}) = \frac{1}{M_j} \sum_{k=1}^{K} U_{kj}(\mathbf{N})[PB_j(\mathbf{N} - \mathbf{e}_k) + P_j(M_j - 1, \mathbf{N} - \mathbf{e}_k)], \quad \text{(A.1)}$$

$$P_j(0, \mathbf{N}) = 1 - \sum_{i=1}^{M_j - 1} P_j(i, \mathbf{N}) - PB_j(\mathbf{N}).$$

The following equations are the marginal probabilities of finding **n** customers at a server j for a customer population **N**. They are found recursively from an initial condition of zero customers in the network:

$$P_j(\mathbf{n}, \mathbf{N}) = \sum_{k=1}^{K} \frac{U_{kj}(\mathbf{N})}{\alpha_{kj}(\mathbf{n})} P_j(\mathbf{n} - \mathbf{e}_k, \mathbf{N} - \mathbf{e}_k), \qquad \forall \mathbf{n}, \mathbf{0} < \mathbf{n} \leq \mathbf{N},$$

$$P_j(\mathbf{0}, \mathbf{N}) = 1 - \sum_{\mathbf{0} < \mathbf{n} \leq \mathbf{N}} P_j(\mathbf{n}, \mathbf{N}).$$

(A.2)

When using approximate MVA, the marginal probabilities at a customer population $\mathbf{N} - \mathbf{e}_k$ are found by assigning $P_j(i, \mathbf{N} - \mathbf{e}_k) = P_j(i, \mathbf{N})$. This assignment often leads to infeasible probabilities if (A.1) or (A.2) is used.

Krzesinski and Greyling[17] developed the following set of equations to find the marginal probabilities of finding i customers at a server when using Linearizer approximate MVA. $P_j(0, \mathbf{N})$ is set to 1, then used in (A.1) to find pseudo-probabilities $P_j(i, \mathbf{N})$ and $PB_j(\mathbf{N})$. The sum of these expressions is then used to re-normalize the probabilities, yielding:

$$P_j(0, \mathbf{N}) = \left(1 + \sum_{i=1}^{M_j - 1} P_j(i, \mathbf{N}) + PB_j(\mathbf{N}) \right)^{-1},$$

$$P_j(i, \mathbf{N}) = \frac{U_j^i(\mathbf{N})}{\prod_{l=1}^{i} \alpha_j(l)}, \qquad 0 < i < M_j, \qquad (A.3)$$

$$PB_j(\mathbf{N}) = \frac{U_j^{M_j}(\mathbf{N})}{\prod_{l=1}^{M_j} \alpha_j(l)} \cdot \frac{U_j(\mathbf{N})}{M_j - U_j(\mathbf{N})}.$$

Schmidt also found that (A.2) frequently needed renormalization.[27] He assumed that customers were distributed binomially within a queue at a multiclass FCFS multiserver:

$$P_j(\mathbf{n}, \mathbf{N}) = \prod_{k=1}^{K} \binom{N_k}{n_k} \left(\frac{L_{kj}(\mathbf{n})}{N_k} \right)^{n_k} \left(1 - \frac{L_{kj}(\mathbf{n})}{N_k} \right)^{N_k - n_k},$$

$$\forall \mathbf{n}, \mathbf{0} \leq \mathbf{n} \leq \mathbf{N}. \quad (A.4)$$

This equation is perfectly suited for approximate MVA because the marginal probabilities with one customer from chain k removed are not needed at all.

Appendix B. de Souza e Silva and Muntz Approximation

The following equations are the basis of the de Souza e Silva and Muntz approximation for multiclass multiservers with first-come first-served queueing.[7] These equations were also used by Conway with Linearizer approximate MVA with good results[6]:

$$W_{kj}(\mathbf{N}) = D_{kj} + \sum_{c=1}^{K} xe_{kcj}(\mathbf{N})Q_{cj}(\mathbf{N} - \mathbf{e}_k) + PB_j(\mathbf{N} - \mathbf{e}_k)xr_{kj}(\mathbf{N}),$$

$$xe_{kcj}(\mathbf{N}) = \sum_{\mathbf{n} \in \mathbf{A}_{ck}} \frac{PS_{jk}(\mathbf{n}, c, \mathbf{N})}{\sum_{i=1}^{K} n_k \mu_{ji}},$$

$$xr_{kj}(\mathbf{N}) = \sum_{\mathbf{n} \in \mathbf{B}_k} \frac{PS_{jk}(\mathbf{n}, \mathbf{N})}{\sum_{i=1}^{K} n_k \mu_{ji}},$$

$$PS_{jk}(\mathbf{n}, \mathbf{N}) = \frac{A_j(\mathbf{n}, \mathbf{N} - \mathbf{e}_k)}{C_j(\mathbf{N} - \mathbf{e}_k)},$$

$$PS_{jk}(\mathbf{n}, c, \mathbf{N}) = \frac{A_j(\mathbf{n}, \mathbf{N} - \mathbf{e}_k)}{C_{jc}(\mathbf{N} - \mathbf{e}_k)},$$

$$A_j(\mathbf{n}, \mathbf{N} - \mathbf{e}_k) = M_j! \prod_{i=1}^{K} \frac{F_{ij}^{n_i}(\mathbf{N} - \mathbf{e}_k)}{n_i!},$$

$$C_{jc}(\mathbf{N} - \mathbf{e}_k) = \sum_{\mathbf{n} \in \mathbf{A}_{ck}} A_j(\mathbf{n}, \mathbf{N} - \mathbf{e}_k),$$

$$C_j(\mathbf{N} - \mathbf{e}_k) = \sum_{\mathbf{n} \in \mathbf{B}_k} A_j(\mathbf{n}, \mathbf{N} - \mathbf{e}_k),$$

$$F_{ij}(\mathbf{N} - \mathbf{e}_k) = \frac{U_{ij}(\mathbf{N} - \mathbf{e}_i)}{\sum_{c=1}^{K} U_{cj}(\mathbf{N} - \mathbf{e}_i)},$$

$$\mathbf{A}_{ck} = \left\{ \mathbf{n} \left| \sum_{i=1}^{K} n_i = M_j, \, \mathbf{n} \leq \mathbf{N} - \mathbf{e}_k, n_c > 0 \right. \right\},$$

$$\mathbf{B}_k = \left\{ \mathbf{n} \left| \sum_{i=1}^{K} n_i = M_j, \, \mathbf{n} \leq \mathbf{N} - \mathbf{e}_k \right. \right\}.$$

References

1. Y. Bard, Some extensions to multiclass queueing network analysis, in *Performance of Computer Systems*, eds. M. Arato, A. Butrimenko and E. Gelenbe (North Holland, Amsterdam, 1979).

2. S. C. Bruell, G. Balbo and P. V. Afshari, Mean value analysis of mixed, multiple class BCMP networks with load dependent service centers, *Perform. Evaluation* **4** (1984), 241–260.
3. K. Mani Chandy, J. H. Howard, Jr and D. Towsley, Product form and local balance in queueing networks, *J. ACM* **24**(2) (1977), 250–263.
4. K. Mani Chandy and D. Neuse, Linearizer: A heuristic algorithm for queueing network models of computing systems, *Commun. ACM* **25**(2) (1982), 126–134.
5. A. E. Conway and D. O'Brien, Validataion of an approximation technique for queueing network models with chain-dependent FCFS queues, *Comput. Syst. Sci. Eng.* **6**(2) (1991), 117–121.
6. A. E. Conway, Fast approximate solution of queueing networks with multi-server chain-dependent FCFS queues, in *Modeling Techniques and Tools for Computer Performance Evaluation*, eds. R. Puigjaner and D. Potier (Plenum, New York, 1989), pp. 385–396.
7. E. de Souza e Silva and R. R. Muntz, Approximate solutions for a class of non-product form queueing network models, *Perform. Evaluation* **7** (1987), 221–242.
8. J. Dilley, R. Friedrich, T. Jin and J. Rolia, Web server performance measurement and modeling techniques, *Performance Evaluation* **33**(1) (1998), 5–26.
9. F. ElRayes, J. Rolia and R. Friedrich, The performance impact of workload characterization for distributed applications using ARM, in *24th Int. Computer Measurement Group Conference*, Anaheim, CA, USA, December, 1998, Computer Measurement Group, pp. 821–830.
10. G. Franks, Traffic dependencies in client-server systems and their effect on performance prediction, in *IEEE Int. Computer Performance and Dependability Symposium*, Erlangen, Germany, April, 1995, pp. 24–33.
11. G. Franks, A. Hubbard, S. Majumdar, D. Petriu, J. Rolia and M. Woodside, A toolset for performance engineering and software design of client-server systems, *Perform. Evaluation* **24**(1&2) (1995), 117–135.
12. G. Franks and M. Woodside, Performance of multi-level client-server systems with parallel service operations, in *Proc. 1st Int. Workshop on Software and Performance (WOSP '98)*, Santa Fe, NM, October, 1998, pp. 120–130.
13. G. Franks and M. Woodside, Effectiveness of early replies in client-server systems, *Performance Evaluation* **36&37** (1999), 165–184.
14. R. G. Franks, *Performance Analysis of Distributed Server Systems*, Ph.D. Thesis, Department of Systems and Computer Engineering, Carleton University, Ottawa, Ontario, Canada, December, 1999.
15. C. E. Hrischuk, C. M. Woodside and J. A. Rolia, Trace-based load characterization for generating software performance models, *IEEE Trans. Software Eng.* **25**(1) (1999), 122–135.
16. M. Arlitt, D. Krishnamurthy and J. Rolia, Characterizing the scalability of a large web-based shopping system, *ACM Trans. Internet Tech.* **1**(1) (2001), 44–69.
17. A. Krzesinski and J. Greyling, Improved linearizer methods for queueing networks with queue dependent service centers, in *Proc. Performance '84*

and *1984 ACM SIGMETRICS on Measurement and Modeling of Computer Systems*, Cambridge, MA, August, 1984.
18. R. D. Nelson, The mathematics of product form queuing networks, *ACM Comput. Surveys* **25**(3) (1993), 339–369.
19. D. B. Petriu, D. Amyot and C. M. Woodside, Scenario-based performance engineering with UCMNav, in *11th SDL Forum (SDL'03)*, in Lecture Notes in Computer Science, Vol. 2708 (Springer-Verlag, Stuttgart, Germany, 2003), pp. 117–136.
20. D. Petriu and M. Woodside, Analysing software requirements specifications for performance, in *Proc. 3rd Int. Workshop on Software and Performance (WOSP '02)*, Rome, Italy, July 24–26, 2002, pp. 1–9.
21. D. Petriu and M. Woodside, Software performance models from system scenarios in use case maps, in *Computer Performance Evaluation: Modelling Techniques and Tools — 12th International Conference, TOOLS 2002*, ed. Anthony J. Field, April 14–17, 2002, Lecture Notes in Computer Science, Vol. 2324 (Springer-Verlag, London, UK), pp. 141–158.
22. M. Reiser and S. S. Lavenberg, Mean value analysis of closed multichain queueing networks, *J. ACM* **27**(2) (1980), 313–322.
23. M. Reiser, A queueing network analysis of computer communication networks with window flow control, *IEEE Trans. Commun.* **COM-27**(8) (1979), 1199–1209.
24. J. A. Rolia and K. A. Sevcik, The method of layers, *IEEE Trans. Software Eng.* **21**(8) (1995), 689–700.
25. J. A. Rolia, *Predicting the Performance of Software Systems*, Ph.D. Thesis, Univerisity of Toronto, Toronto, Ontario, Canada, January, 1992.
26. A. Rüth, Entwicklung, Implementierung und Validierung neuer Approximationsverfahren für die Mittelwertanalyse (MWA) zur Leistungsberechnung von Rechnersystemen, Diplomarbeit am IMMD der Friedrich-Alexander-Universität Erlangen-Nürnberg, 1987.
27. R. Schmidt, An approximate MVA algorithm for exponential, class-dependent multiple servers, *Perform. Evaluation* **29** (1997), 245–254.
28. P. Schweitzer, Approximate analysis of multiclass closed networks of queues, in *Proc. Int. Conf. on Stochastic Control and Optimization*, Amsterdam, 1979.
29. C. U. Smith and L. G. Williams, *Performance Solutions: A Practical Guide to Creating Responsive, Scalable Software*, Object Technology Series (Addison Wesley, 2002).
30. J. A. Rolia and U. Herzog, Performance validation tools for software/hardware systems, *Perform. Evaluation* **45**(2&3) (2001), 125–146.
31. C. Murray Woodside, J. E. Neilson, D. C. Petriu and S. Majumdar, The stochastic rendezvous network model for performance of synchronous client-server-like distributed software, *IEEE Trans. Comput.* **44**(8) (1995), 20–34.

CHAPTER 10

Quantiles of Sojourn Times

Peter G. Harrison[*] and William J. Knottenbelt[†]

*Department of Computing, Imperial College London,
South Kensington Campus, London SW7 2AZ, UK*
[*]pgh@doc.ic.ac.uk
[†]wjk@doc.ic.ac.uk

Fast response times and the satisfaction of response time quantile targets are important performance criteria for almost all transaction processing, computer-communication and other operational systems. However, response time quantiles tend to be difficult to obtain in stochastic models, even when the mean value of the response time has a relatively simple mathematical expression. Expressions have been obtained for the Laplace transform of the probability density function of sojourn times in many queueing models, including some complex single queues and networks of simple queues. These can sometimes be inverted analytically, giving an explicit expression for the density as a function of time, but more often numerical inversion is necessary. More generally, interesting sojourn times can be expressed in terms of passage times between states in continuous time Markov and semi-Markov chains. Quantiles for these can be computed in principle but can require extensive computational resources, both in terms of processing time and memory. Consequently, until recently, only trivial problems could be solved by this direct method. With recent technological advances, including the widespread use of clusters of workstations and limited availability of parallel supercomputers, very large Markov and semi-Markov chains can be solved directly for passage time densities, allowing many realistic systems to be investigated. This chapter reviews the various approaches taken to compute sojourn time quantiles in systems ranging from simple queues to arbitrary semi-Markov chains, by the authors and others, over the past twenty years and more.

1. Introduction

The probability distribution of many response, or sojourn, times constitutes a vital quality of service (QoS) metric in many operational systems such as computer networks, logistical systems and emergency services. For example in the United Kingdom, ambulances must arrive at the scene of a life-threatening emergency within eight minutes at least 75% of the time. For on-line transaction processing (OLTP) and other real-time systems, quantiles are often specified in Service Level Agreement contracts and industry standard benchmarks such as TPC-C, which specifies the 90th percentile of response time.[41]

The mean values of such time delays provide a good overall description of performance and are readily obtained by conventional techniques, but means alone are often insufficient. For example, we may wish to predict the variability of response time in a multi-access system or various reliability measures, such as the probability that a message transmission time exceeds a given value. The importance of obtaining quantiles of distributions — i.e., time intervals that are not exceeded with a specified probability — has therefore acquired increased recognition.

This chapter is a review of various techniques used to compute quantiles numerically over the past quarter of a century and more. It is a mainly personal viewpoint and it should be remembered that there have been many excellent (and often mathematically more sophisticated) contributions by other researchers in the field, for example, Onno Boxma and Hans Daduna.[4]

Queueing network models which compute queue length distributions in a steady state network are well established; from the mean queue lengths, mean passage-time along a given path can be determined directly through Little's result.[34] Mathematically, the simplest type of network to analyze is open, acyclic and Markovian, i.e., has external arrivals from independent Poisson processes and exponentially distributed service times at the queueing nodes. The arrival process at every server is then independent and Poisson. Unfortunately, even these assumptions are too weak to allow the distribution of the sojourn time along an arbitrary path to be obtained in a simple form. For paths on which a task cannot be overtaken, we can consider sojourn time as the sum of waiting times at independent single-server (M/M/1) queues and obtain a simple solution. If any of these assumptions is violated (e.g., for any closed network of servers, independence is lost) the above approach fails. However, a more complex result can be derived for overtake-free paths in Markovian closed networks. Some analytical solutions have been found for sojourn-time distributions in small networks of more general structure, but these are complex and often numerically intractable; see, for example, Refs. 26 and 36. To derive sojourn-time distributions in more general networks usually requires either direct analysis of the underlying Markov chain, where numerically feasible, or else approximate methods.

Rather than the distributions themselves, it is often easier to work with their Laplace transforms, especially when a sojourn time is the sum of an independent set of smaller time delays. To obtain quantiles, of course, it is necessary to be able to invert the Laplace transform of the passage-time probability density function so as to recover the distribution itself. In general, inversion is by numerical methods which may be difficult to implement accurately over the whole time domain of interest — especially at the important high quantiles, i.e., in the tail of a distribution, although this is becoming less of a problem as increasingly sophisticated inverters become available and as computing technology advances. Furthermore, analytical inversion is possible in many of the solvable networks referred to above, including some complex, Markov modulated G-queues[a] with batches of customers and open and closed, overtake-free, Markovian networks. Where an analytical solution based on the inherent structure of the system under consideration is not possible, analysis of passage times between states in the underlying Markov chain solves the problem exactly when the state space is not excessively large — representing significant models of over 10 million states with the computing power available today.

In the next section we consider the sojourn-time distribution for a single-server queue, showing the remarkable effect of different queueing disciplines, which typically do not influence resource-oriented quantities like the queue length at equilibrium. Surprisingly, a Markov modulated queue with batch processing and negative customers[27] does have a tractable solution for the sojourn-time distribution in the time domain, provided customers are removed from the *front* of the queue by negative arrivals. This queue is considered in Sec. 3. Next, we look at sojourn-time distributions on paths in open, overtake-free or tree-like networks of Markovian queues in Sec. 4.1. The Laplace transform of the sojourn-time distribution on overtake-free paths in closed Markovian networks, together with its analytical inversion, is considered in Sec. 4.2. Section 5 reviews recent results on passage times in Markov chains, in particular, techniques developed for the parallel computation of quantiles. These include the application of the uniformization technique in very large unstructured Markov models, using hypergraph

---

[a] "Gelenbe queues" which have negative customers.[14,15]

partitioning to minimize interprocessor communication while maintaining a good load balance. We demonstrate this approach by calculating passage time densities and quantiles in a 10.8 million state Markov chain derived from a closed tree-like queueing network, for which we also have an analytical solution. Section 6 considers a technique for extracting passage times for large unstructured semi-Markov models using numerical Laplace transform inversion. Finally, in Sec. 7, we conclude, sketching out some current research in progress.

2. Time Delays in the Single Server Queue

In this section we first consider the waiting (response) and queueing times of a customer in an M/G/1 queue with FCFS discipline and then the *busy period* of the server, i.e., the interval between successive idle periods. Busy time analysis — a special case of delay-cycle analysis[40] — leads to the waiting time distribution of an M/G/1 queue with LCFS queueing discipline. The processor sharing (PS) queueing discipline is also considered, but only for M/M/1 queues where we can use the memoryless property at all times to exploit an analysis of infinitesimal intervals. In fact, we will see that this method can also be used for other queueing disciplines — even in the MM CPP/GE/c G-queue, with batches of customers and Markov modulation.

2.1. *Waiting time distribution in the M/G/1 queue*

The waiting time distribution for the FCFS discipline is traditionally obtained from the following observation. For $n \geq 1$, the queue, of length X_n, existing on the departure of the nth customer, C_n, comprises precisely the customers that arrived during that customer's waiting time. The distribution of the queue length at a departure instant, which is known to be the same as that at a random instant, is therefore equal to the distribution of the number of arrivals in a waiting time.

Hence, if, at equilibrium, we denote the waiting time random variable by W and the queue length random variable by X, then the generating function of the queue length may be expressed as

$$\Pi(z) = E[E[z^X \mid W]] = E[e^{-\lambda W(1-z)}] = W^*(\lambda(1-z)),$$

where $W^*(s)$ is the Laplace–Stieltjes transform of $W(t)$, the probability distribution function of the waiting time (we use the same naming convention for all random variables). This is because X, conditional on W, has a Poisson distribution with parameter λW. Writing $s = \lambda(1-z)$ so that $z = (\lambda - s)/\lambda$, we now have

$$W^*(s) = \Pi((\lambda - s)/\lambda) = \frac{(1-\rho)sB^*(s)}{s - \lambda[1 - B^*(s)]},$$

using the Pollacek–Khintchine formula for Π, where B is the service time random variable and the load $\rho = -\lambda B^{*\prime}(0)$. We can now easily demonstrate Little's result for the M/G/1 queue since $-W^{*\prime}(0) = -\lambda^{-1}\Pi'(1)$. Notice too that we get the required exponential distribution in the case of an M/M/1 queue where Π is the generating function of the geometric random variable with parameter ρ.

2.2. Busy periods

To investigate the busy period, we first observe that its distribution is the same for all queueing disciplines that are work-conserving and for which the server is never idle when the queue is non-empty. Suppose that, at equilibrium, whilst an initial customer C_1 is being served, customers $C_2, \ldots, C_{Z+1}$ arrive, where the random variable Z, conditional on service time B for C_1, is Poisson with mean λB. Without loss of generality, we assume a LCFS queueing discipline with no preemption so that, if $Z \neq 0$, the second customer to be served is C_{Z+1}. Any other customers that arrive while C_{Z+1} is being served will also be served before C_Z. Now let N be the random variable for the number of customers served during a busy period and let N_i be the number of customers served between the instants at which C_{i+1} commences service and C_i commences service ($1 \leq i \leq Z$). Then $N_1, \ldots, N_Z$ are independent and identically distributed as N. This is because the sets of customers counted by $N_Z, N_{Z-1}, \ldots, N_1$ are disjoint and (excluding $C_{Z+1}, C_Z, \ldots, C_2$ respectively) arrive consecutively after C_{Z+1}. Thus,

$$N \sim \begin{cases} 1 + N_Z + N_{Z-1} + \cdots + N_1 & \text{if } Z \geq 1, \\ 1 & \text{if } Z = 0. \end{cases}$$

(The symbol $\sim$ denotes "equal in distribution.") Now, denoting the busy time random variable by H, we have

$$H \sim \begin{cases} B + H_Z + H_{Z-1} + \cdots + H_1 & \text{if } Z \geq 1, \\ B & \text{if } Z = 0, \end{cases}$$

where H_i is the length of the interval between the instants at which C_{i+1} and C_i commence service, $1 \leq i \leq Z$. Moreover, the H_i are independent random variables, each distributed as H, and also independent of B. This is because the customers that arrive and complete service during the intervals H_i are disjoint. Thus

$$\begin{aligned} H^*(s) &= E[E[E[e^{-sH} \mid Z, B] \mid B]] \\ &= E[E[E[e^{-s(B+H_1+\cdots+H_Z)} \mid Z, B] \mid B]] \\ &= E[E[e^{-sB} E[e^{-sH}]^Z \mid B]] \\ &= E[e^{-sB} E[H^*(s)^Z \mid B]] \\ &= E[e^{-sB} e^{-\lambda B(1-H^*(s))}], \end{aligned}$$

since Z (conditioned on B) is Poisson with mean λB. Thus we obtain

$$H^*(s) = B^*(s + \lambda(1 - H^*(s))).$$

Although this equation cannot be solved in general for $H^*(s)$, we can obtain the moments of busy time by differentiating at $s = 0$. For example, the mean busy period b is given by $b = -H^{*\prime}(0) = -B^{*\prime}(0)[1 + \lambda(-H^{*\prime}(0))] = (1 + \lambda b)\mu^{-1}$ since $H^*(0) = 1$, and so $b = (\mu - \lambda)^{-1}$, yielding the M/M/1 queue result (where μ is the reciprocal of mean service time). The above technique, in which a time delay is defined in terms of independent, identically distributed time delays, is often called "delay cycle analysis" and is due to Takacs.[40]

2.3. Waiting times in LCFS queues

Now consider waiting times under LCFS disciplines. For the preemptive-resume variant, we note that a task's waiting time is independent of the queue length it faces on arrival, since the whole of the queue already there is suspended until after this task completes service. Thus, without loss of generality, we may assume that the task arrives at an idle server. Waiting time then becomes identical to the busy period. We therefore conclude that the waiting time distribution in a LCFS-PR M/G/1 queue has Laplace–Stieltjes transform $H^*(s)$. For LCFS without preemption we can modify the busy period analysis. First, if a task arrives at an empty queue, its waiting time is the same as a service time. Otherwise, its queueing time Q is the sum of the residual service time R of the customer in service and the service times of all other tasks that arrive before it commences service. This definition is almost the same as that of a busy period given above. The only differences are that the time spent in service by the initial customer C_1' (C_1 above) is not a service time but a residual service time and the random variable Z' (Z above) is the number of customers that arrive whilst C_1' is in residual service. Proceeding as before, we obtain

$$Q \sim \begin{cases} R + H_{Z'} + H_{Z'-1} + \cdots + H_1 & \text{if } Z' \geq 1, \\ R & \text{if } Z' = 0. \end{cases}$$

We therefore derive

$$Q^*(s) = R^*(s + \lambda(1 - H^*(s))).$$

But since R is a forward recurrence time,[24] $R^*(s) = \mu[1 - B^*(s)]/s$. Thus,

$$Q^*(s) = \frac{\mu(1 - H^*(s))}{s + \lambda(1 - H^*(s))}.$$

Finally, since a customer arrives at an empty queue with probability $1 - \rho$ at equilibrium, we obtain

$$W^*(s) = (1 - \rho)B^*(s) + \rho B^*(s)Q^*(s)$$
$$= B^*(s)\left(1 - \rho + \frac{\lambda(1 - H^*(s))}{s + \lambda(1 - H^*(s))}\right),$$

since waiting time is the sum of the independent queueing time and service time random variables.

To illustrate, compare the response time variability in an M/G/1 queue, under FCFS and non-preemptive LCFS queueing disciplines. We can do this to a great extent by comparing the first two moments, which are obtained by differentiating the respective formulae for $W^*(s)$ at $s = 0$. We obtain the same result for the mean waiting time, as expected from Little's result since the mean queue lengths are the same under each discipline.[b] However, it turns out that the second moment of waiting time for FCFS discipline is $(1 - \rho)$ times that for LCFS. Thus, LCFS discipline suffers a much greater variability as ρ approaches 1, i.e., as the queue begins to saturate.

---

[b]Notice that LCFS-PR gives a different mean waiting time in general. This is reasonable because we cannot expect the mean queue length (and hence, using Little's result, the mean waiting time) to be the same since the preemption invalidates the argument used to derive the queue length distribution. Intuitively, the average amount of work left to do in the queue should be the same, but since the queue will, in general, contain partially served customers, its expected length should be different. In fact, as we saw above, mean waiting time is the same as for the case of an M/M/1 queue. This is a consequence of the memoryless property of the exponential distribution: a partially served customer is stochastically identical to one that has received no service.

2.4. Waiting times with Processor-Sharing discipline

The problem with the PS discipline is that the rate at which a customer receives service during his sojourn at a server varies as the queue length changes due to new arrivals and other departures. Thus, we begin by analyzing the waiting time of a customer with a given service time requirement in a PS M/M/1 queue.

Proposition 1. *In a PS M/M/1 queue with fixed arrival rate λ and fixed service rate μ, the Laplace transform of the waiting time probability density function, conditional on a customer's service time being x, is*

$$W^*(s \mid x) \frac{(1-\rho)(1-\rho r^2)e^{-[(1-r)\lambda+s]x}}{(1-\rho r)^2 - \rho(1-r)^2 e^{-[\mu/r - \lambda r]x}},$$

where r is the smaller root of the equation $\lambda r^2 - (\lambda + \mu + s)r + \mu = 0$ and $\rho = \lambda/\mu$.

This result, proved in Ref. 24, was first derived in Ref. 10. We can now obtain the Laplace transform of the unconditional waiting time density as

$$W^*(s) = \int_0^\infty W^*(s \mid x) \mu e^{-\mu x} dx.$$

The essential technique used in the proof of Proposition 1 splits the waiting time in an M/M/1 queue into an infinitesimal initial interval and the remaining waiting time. In fact, the technique is quite general, applying to more disciplines than PS. In particular, it can be used to find the Laplace transform of the waiting time density in an M/M/1 queue with "random" discipline, FCFS discipline with certain queue-length-dependent service rates and in M/M/1 G-queues (with negative customers).[22,25] We outline the method in the following section, with a more general, recent application.

3. MM CPP/GE/c G-Queues: Semi-Numerical Laplace Transform Inversion

The infinitesimal initial interval (III) approach to finding passage time densities in Markov processes is well illustrated in a recent result that determines the waiting time density in the MM CPP/GE/c G-queue, abbreviated to MBG (modulated, batched G-queue).[21,27] The queue is Markovian, has c servers, FCFS queueing discipline and RCH "killing strategy" whereby the customer at the head of the queue (i.e., in service), if any, is removed by a negative arrival.[c] The queue's parameters are modulated by an N-phase Markov process with generator matrix Q. In phase k, the arrival rate of positive (respectively negative) customers is λ_k (respectively κ_k) and the parameters of their geometric batch sizes are θ_k (respectively ρ_k), $1 \leq k \leq N$. Similarly, the service time is generalized exponential with parameter μ_k and batch size parameter ϕ_k in phase k. The following diagonal matrices are defined:

- Λ: the positive arrival rate matrix, $\Lambda_{kk} \equiv \lambda_k$;
- Θ: the positive batch size geometric distribution parameter matrix, $\Theta_{kk} \equiv \theta_k$;
- M: the service rate matrix, $M_{kk} \equiv \mu_k$;
- Φ: the (truncated) service completion batch size geometric distribution parameter matrix, $\Phi_{kk} \equiv \phi_k$;
- K: the negative arrival rate matrix, $K_{kk} \equiv \kappa_k$;
- R: the negative batch size geometric distribution parameter matrix, $R_{kk} \equiv \rho_k$.

The equilibrium state probability for state (j,k), representing queue length $j \geq 0$ and phase k is denoted $[\mathbf{v}_j]_k$, i.e., the kth component of the state probability vector $\mathbf{v}_j$. The solution for $\{\mathbf{v}_j \,|\, j \geq 0\}$ is assumed to have been determined by the method of spectral analysis,[37] which yields a solution for $j \geq c$ of the form:

$$\mathbf{v}_j = \sum_{k=1}^{N} a_k \xi_k^j \psi_k,$$

where (ξ_k, ψ_k) is the kth eigenvalue-eigenvector pair of the method and the a_k are scalar constants — see Ref. 9.

The III method yields the following solution for the Laplace transform of the sojourn-time density, after simplification.

Proposition 2. *The sojourn-time density in the above MBG-queue has Laplace transform:*

$$L(s) = \left(\sum_{j=0}^{c-1} \left(\sum_{q=0}^{j} \mathbf{v}_q \Theta^{-q} \right) \Theta^j \right) (I - \Theta)(\Lambda/\lambda^*) \mathbf{L}_0(s)$$
$$+ \sum_{k=1}^{N} a_k \xi_k \psi_k (\xi_k I - \Theta)^{-1} (I - \Theta)(\Lambda/\lambda^*) \mathbf{D}(\xi_k, s)$$

for certain vector-functions of s given in Ref. 21.

---
[c]Other killing strategies are also considered in Ref. 21.

The proof idea is the following. Consider the passage of a special "tagged" customer through the queue. Ultimately, this customer will either be served or killed by a negative customer; we require the probability distribution function of the sojourn time of customers that are not killed, i.e., the time elapsed between the arrival instant and the completion of service. Let the random variables $I(x)$ and $A(x)$ denote respectively the phase of the modulating Markov chain and the number of customers ahead of the tagged customer at time x, and let T denote the time remaining, without loss of generality at time 0, up to the departure of the tagged customer. For $j \geq 0$, we define the probability distributions $\mathbf{F}_j(t) = (F_{1j}(t), \ldots, F_{Nj}(t))$ where, for $1 \leq k \leq N$,

$$F_{kj}(t) = P(T \leq t \mid I(0) = k, A(0) = j).$$

Now, when the state is (j, k), we consider an initial small interval of length h and derive an expression for $\mathbf{F}_j(t+h)$ in terms of $\{\mathbf{F}_a(t) \mid a \geq 0\}$. By the Markov property and stationarity, we can write, for $j \geq c$:

$$\begin{aligned}
\mathbf{F}_j(t+h) &= (I + Qh - Kh - cMh)\mathbf{F}_j(t) \\
&+ h \sum_{s=1}^{j-c+1} K(I-R)R^{s-1}\mathbf{F}_{j-s}(t) \\
&+ hKR^{j-c+1}\mathbf{0} \\
&+ h \sum_{s=1}^{j-c+1} cM(I-\Phi)\Phi^{s-1}\mathbf{F}_{j-s}(t) \\
&+ hcM\Phi^{j-c+1}\mathbf{e} + o(h),
\end{aligned} \qquad (1)$$

where $\mathbf{0}$ and $\mathbf{e}$ are the zero-vector and $(1, \ldots, 1)$ of length N respectively. The details appear in Ref. 21, but to clarify, consider the special case of the Markov modulated M/M/1 G-queue with no batches, obtained by setting $c = 1, \Theta = \Phi = R = 0$. This gives the much simpler equation

$$\begin{aligned}
\mathbf{F}_j(t+h) &= (I + Qh - Kh - Mh)\mathbf{F}_j(t) \\
&+ hK\mathbf{F}_{j-1}(t) + h\delta_{j0}K\mathbf{0} + hM\mathbf{F}_{j-1}(t) + h\delta_{j0}M\mathbf{e} + o(h).
\end{aligned}$$

Returning to the general case, taking the term $I\mathbf{F}_j(t)$ to the left-hand side in Eq. (1) and dividing by h now yields the vector differential-difference equation:

$$\frac{d\mathbf{F}_j(t)}{dt} = (Q - K - cM)\mathbf{F}_j(t)$$

$$+ K(I - R) \sum_{s=1}^{j-c+1} R^{s-1}\mathbf{F}_{j-s}(t)$$

$$+ cM(I - \Phi) \sum_{s=1}^{j-c+1} \Phi^{s-1}\mathbf{F}_{j-s}(t)$$

$$+ cM\Phi^{j-c+1}\mathbf{e}. \qquad (2)$$

For $j < c$, the tagged customer is in service and so his progress is influenced solely by the negative arrivals and the service completion time at his particular server. Thus, $\mathbf{F}_j(t) = \mathbf{F}_0(t)$ for $0 \leq j < c$ and we have:

$$\mathbf{F}_0(t+h) = (I + Qh - Mh - (K/c)h)\mathbf{F}_0(t) + hM\mathbf{e} + h(K/c)\mathbf{0} + o(h).$$

This yields the vector differential equation

$$\frac{d\mathbf{F}_0(t)}{dt} = (Q - M - K/c)\mathbf{F}_0(t) + M\mathbf{e}, \qquad (3)$$

which has solution

$$\mathbf{F}_0(t) = (1 - e^{-(M+K/c-Q)t})(M + K/c - Q)^{-1}M\mathbf{e}.$$

We can now derive recurrence formulas for the Laplace transforms $\mathbf{L}_j(s)$ of the $\mathbf{F}_j(t)$, which we solve using the generating function method — the vector $\mathbf{D}$ is defined by: $\mathbf{D}(z,s) = \sum_{j=c}^{\infty} \mathbf{L}_j(s) z^j$.

The surprising result obtained for this complex queue is that the Laplace transform can be inverted analytically for any given numerical parameterization.

Proposition 3. *The Laplace transform $L(s)$ is analytically invertible and gives an unconditional sojourn-time density function which is a mixture of exponential and Erlang densities as well as those of the types $e^{at}\cos(bt)$ and $e^{at}\sin(bt)$, for real numbers $a \leq 0$ and $b > 0$.*

Proof. The expression of Proposition 2 for $L(s)$ is a sum of terms, each of which depends on s through either the function $\mathbf{L}_0(s)$ or $\mathbf{D}(z,s)$, for some particular value of z which is an eigenvalue in the spectral analysis solution. These eigenvalues are either real or occur in complex conjugate pairs. It is shown in Ref. 27 that both of these functions are sums of rational functions of the form $u/(sv)$, where u and v are polynomials in s with real coefficients. Consequently, v has real roots, $\{x_1, \ldots, x_k\}$ say, and roots that form complex conjugate pairs, $\{y_1 \pm iz_1, \ldots, y_l \pm iz_l\}$, where all $x_i, y_j < 0$ for $1 \leq i \leq k$ and $1 \leq j \leq l$. The polynomial v is of higher order than u and it is therefore possible to re-write each term using partial fractions. Further routine analysis yields the stated result. □

This is a semi-numerical inversion in that the parameters of the resulting mixtures of exponential and Erlang densities must be computed numerically, but subsequently a solution can be found directly as a function of time. There is no need to invert the Laplace transform numerically.

4. Time Delays in Networks of Queues

The analysis of networks of queues is entirely different to that of a single server queue — even a stationary Markovian network. This is because, although we may know the distribution of the queue lengths at the time of arrival of a given (tagged) customer at the first queue in his path (by the Random Observer Property or the Job Observer Property), we cannot assume this stationary distribution exists upon arrival at subsequent queues. The reason is that the arrival times at the subsequent queues are only finitely later than the arrival time at the first queue. Hence, the state existing at the subsequent arrival times must be conditioned on the state that existed at the time of arrival at the first queue. Effectively, a new time origin is set at the first arrival instant, with known initial joint queue length probability distribution — usually a stationary distribution. Even in open networks with no feedback, where it is easy to see that all arrival processes are Poisson, this conditioning cannot be overlooked and we cannot assume all queues on a path are independent and in an equilibrium state at the arrival times of the tagged customer. This is in contrast to Jackson's Theorem because we are not considering the queues at the same time instant. However, things are not quite as hopeless as they seem. First, we can prove that the FCFS queues in an *overtake-free* path in a Markovian open network behave as if they were independent and in equilibrium when observed at the successive arrival times of a tagged customer. By an overtake-free path, or a path with *no overtaking*, we mean that a customer following this path will depart from its last queue before any other customer that joins any queue in that path after the said customer. Surprisingly, a similar result holds for overtake-free paths in closed networks, e.g., all paths in networks with a tree-like structure — see Fig. 3. In the next two subsections, we consider respectively those open and closed networks for which a solution for the time delay density along a given path can be derived.

4.1. Open networks

The simplest open network structure we can consider is a series of tandem queues. In this case, the distribution of the time delay of a customer passing through them is the convolution of the stationary waiting time distributions at each queue in the series considered in isolation. This follows from the following stronger result.

Proposition 4. *In a tandem series of stationary M/M/1 queues with fixed-rate servers and FCFS discipline, the waiting times of a given customer in each queue are independent.*

Proof. First we claim that the waiting time of a tagged customer, C say, in a stationary M/M/1 queue is independent of the departure process before the departure of C. This is a direct consequence of the reversibility of the M/M/1 queue.

To complete the proof, let A_i and T_i denote C's time of arrival and waiting time respectively at queue i in a series of m queues ($1 \leq i \leq m$). Certainly, by our claim, T_1 is independent of the arrival process at queue 2 before A_2 and so of the queue length faced by C on arrival at queue 2. Thus, T_2 is independent of T_1. Now, we can ignore customers that leave queue 1 after C since they cannot arrive at (nor influence the rate of) any queue in the series before C, again because all queues have single servers and FCFS discipline. Thus, T_1 is independent of the arrival process at queue i before A_i and so of T_i for $2 \leq i \leq m$. Similarly, T_j is independent of T_k for $2 \leq j < k \leq m$. □

Observe that if service rates varied with queue length, we could not ignore customers behind a given tagged customer, even though they could not overtake, because they would influence the service rate received by the tagged customer.

From the proposition above it follows that, since the waiting time probability density at the stationary queue i with service rate μ_i (considered in isolation) has Laplace transform $(\mu_i - \lambda)/(s + \mu_i - \lambda)$ when the external arrival rate is λ, the probability density of the time to pass through the whole series of m queues is the convolution of these densities, with Laplace transform $\prod_{i=1}^{m}(\mu_i - \lambda)/(s + \mu_i - \lambda)$. There is one obvious generalization

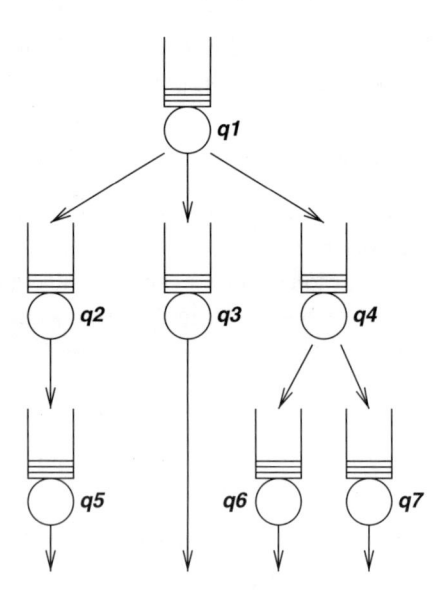

Fig. 1. An open tree-like network of queues.

of this result: the final queue in the series need not be M/M/1 since we are not concerned with its output. Also, the same result holds, by the same reasoning, when the final queue is M/G/c for $c > 1$. Moreover, Proposition 4 generalizes to *tree-like networks* which are defined as follows and illustrated in Fig. 1. A tree-like network consists of:

- a linear *trunk segment* containing one or more queues in tandem, the first being called the *root* queue;
- a number (greater than or equal to zero) of disjoint *subtrees*, i.e., tree-like subnetworks, such that customers can pass to the roots of the subtrees from the last queue in the trunk segment or else leave the network with specified routing probabilities.

The *leaf* queues (or just *leaves*) are those from which customers leave the network.

The proof of Proposition 4, extended to tree-like networks, carries through unchanged since every path in the network is overtake-free. Hence we can ignore the customers that leave any queue on the path after the tagged customer. Indeed, we can generalize further to overtake-free paths in any Markovian open network for the same reason. Conditional on the choice of path of queues numbered, without loss of generality, $1, \ldots, m$, the Laplace transform of the passage time density is the same as for the tandem

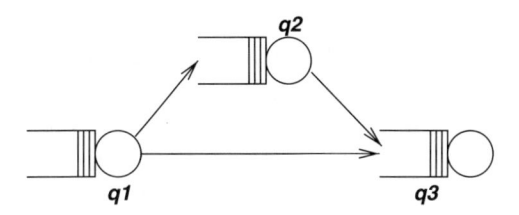

Fig. 2. A three-node network with overtaking.

queue of m servers considered above, but with each arrival rate λ_i at the ith queue adjusted to the actual traffic rate.

To generalize the network structure further leads to serious problems and solutions have been obtained only for special cases. The simplest case of a network with overtaking is the network of Fig. 2.

In this network the path of queues numbered $\{q1, q3\}$ is overtake-free and so the passage time density can be obtained as described above. However, overtaking is possible on the path $\{q1, q2, q3\}$ since when the tagged customer C is at queue 2, any customers departing queue 1 (after C) can reach queue 3 first. The arrival processes to every queue in this network are independent Poisson, by Burke's theorem together with the decomposition and superposition properties of Poisson processes. However, this is not sufficient for the passage time distribution to be the convolution of the stationary sojourn-time distributions at each queue on a path with overtaking: and so the proof of Proposition 4 breaks down. This particular problem has been solved by considering the state of the system at the departure instant of the tagged customer from server 1 and using complex variable methods in an III analysis.[36] A similar analysis is required — for similar reasons — to analyze a tandem pair of queues with negative customers.[26] In this case, negative arrivals at the second queue allow the first queue to influence the sojourn time of a tagged customer in the second; departures from the first queue offer a degree of "protection." Although these networks are solved problems, their results are almost numerically intractable; more general networks appear mathematically intractable as well.

4.2. *Closed networks*

As for the case of open networks, we begin with the simplest case, a cyclic network that comprises a tandem network with departures from its last queue fed back into the first queue. There are no external arrivals and hence a constant population. Again, all service disciplines are FCFS and all service rates are constant.

We solve for the Laplace transform of the cycle time probability density function by considering a dual network, viz. the tandem, open network consisting of the same servers $1, \ldots, m$ with no external arrivals. Eventually, therefore, the dual network has no customers, i.e., its state is $\mathbf{0} = (0, \ldots, 0)$, the empty state, with probability 1. All other states with one or more customers are transient. Now, given that the state immediately after the arrival of the tagged customer at queue 1 is u, the ensuing cycle time in the closed network is the same as the time interval between the dual network entering states u and $\mathbf{0}$ — the (first) passage time from u to $\mathbf{0}$. This is so because there is no overtaking and service rates are constant. Thus the progress of the tagged customer in its cycle cannot be influenced by any customer behind it. We only need consider customers ahead of the tagged customer and can ignore those recycling after leaving the last queue. We therefore seek the density of the passage time from state u to $\mathbf{0}$ in the dual network, $f(t \mid u)$, where i is a state of the form $(i_1, \ldots, i_m)$ with $i_1 > 0$, corresponding to the tagged customer having just arrived at server 1. We know the probability distribution of the state seen by the tagged customer on arrival at the first queue by the Job Observer Property[24] and so can calculate the cycle time density by deconditioning f.

Given a cyclic network of population n, let the state space of the dual network be $S_n = \{(u_1, \ldots, u_m) \mid 0 \le u_i \le n,\ 1 \le i \le m;\ \sum_{i=1}^m u_i \le n\}$ and define, for $u \in S_n$,

$$\lambda_u = \sum_{i=1}^m \mu_i \epsilon(u_i),$$

where μ_i is the service rate of server i, $\epsilon(n) = 1$ if $n > 0$ and $\epsilon(0) = 0$. Thus, λ_u is the total service rate in state u, i.e., the total instantaneous rate out of state u in the Markov process defining the dual network. The holding time in state u is an exponential random variable with parameter λ_u and so has a density with Laplace transform $\lambda_u/(s + \lambda_u)$. Given that the network next enters state v after u, the passage time from u to $\mathbf{0}$ is the sum of the holding time in state u and the passage time from v to $\mathbf{0}$. Thus the density of the passage time from u to $\mathbf{0}$ has Laplace transform $L(s \mid u)$ given by the equations

$$L(s \mid u) = \sum_{v \in S_n} q_{uv} \frac{\lambda_u}{s + \lambda_u} L(s \mid v), \quad (u \ne \mathbf{0}),$$

$$L(s \mid \mathbf{0}) = 1,$$

where q_{uv} is the one-step transition probability from state u to v. Now let $\mu(u,v)$ be the rate of the server from which a departure causes the state transition $u \to v$. Then $q_{uv} = \mu(u,v)/\lambda_u$ and, writing $q^*_{uv} = \mu(u,v)/(s+\lambda_u)$, we have the matrix-vector equation

$$\mathbf{L} = Q^*\mathbf{L} + \mathbf{1}_0,$$

where $\mathbf{L} = (L(s\,|\,u)\,|\,u \in S_n)$, $Q^* = (q^*_{uv}\,|\,u,v \in S_n)$ and $\mathbf{1}_w$ is the unit vector with component corresponding to state w equal to 1, the rest 0. Using this equation and deconditioning on the initial state u, we obtain a product-form for the Laplace transform of cycle time density.

This approach extends directly to cycle times in closed tree-like queueing networks. Such networks are defined in the same way as open tree-like networks except that customers departing from leaf-queues next visit the root queue. Clearly such networks have the no-overtaking property and if paths are restricted to start at one given server (here the root), they define the most general class for which it holds. Consider a closed tree-like network with M nodes and population N, in which node i has service rate μ_i and visitation rate (proportional to) v_i, $1 \leq i \leq M$, defined by $v_i = \sum_{j=1}^{M} v_j\,p_{ji}$ where p_{ji} is the probability that a customer leaving node j next visits node i. Let G be the network's normalizing constant function for the joint equilibrium state probabilities, i.e., at population k,

$$G(k) = \sum_{\substack{\sum_{i=1}^{M} n_i = k \\ n_i \geq 0}} \prod_{i=1}^{M} x_i^{n_i},$$

where $x_i = v_i/\mu_i$. Without loss of generality, the root node is numbered 1 and we define the cycle time random variable to be the elapsed time between a customer's successive arrival instants at node 1. Then we have the following result.[13,18,29]

Proposition 5. *For the above closed tree-like network, the Laplace transform of the cycle time density function, conditional on choice of path* $\mathbf{z} = (z_1, z_2, \ldots, z_m)$ *(*$m \leq M$, $z_1 = 1$*) is*

$$L(s\,|\,\mathbf{z}) = \frac{1}{G(n-1)} \sum_{\substack{\sum_{i=1}^{M} u_i = n-1 \\ u_i \geq 0}} \prod_{i=1}^{M} x_i^{u_i} \prod_{j=1}^{m} \left(\frac{\mu_{z_j}}{s+\mu_{z_j}}\right)^{u_{z_j}+1},$$

where $z_1 = 1$, z_m *is a leaf node and* $p_{z_i z_{i+1}} > 0$ *for* $1 \leq i \leq m-1$.

Without loss of generality, we take $z_i = i$ for $1 \leq i \leq m$, i.e., we consider the path $1, \ldots, m$. First, we can simplify the summation giving $L(s \,|\, \mathbf{z})$ by partitioning it over the state space according to the total number of customers c at servers in the overtake-free path $1, 2, \ldots, m$. This gives

$$L(s \,|\, \mathbf{z}) = \frac{1}{G(n-1)} \sum_{c=0}^{n-1} G_m(n-c-1) \sum_{\substack{\sum_{i=1}^{m} n_i = c \\ n_i \geq 0}} \prod_{i=1}^{m} x_i^{n_i} \prod_{j=1}^{m} \left(\frac{\mu_j}{s + \mu_j}\right)^{n_j + 1},$$

where $G_m(k)$ is the normalizing constant of the whole network with servers $1, \ldots, m$ removed and population $k \geq 0$, i.e.,

$$G_m(k) = \sum_{\substack{\sum_{i=m+1}^{M} n_i = k \\ n_i \geq 0}} \prod_{i=m+1}^{M} x_i^{n_i}.$$

Now, the Laplace transforms in the inner sum are products of the Laplace transforms of Erlang densities. Moreover, their coefficients are geometric. Such transforms can be inverted analytically. In the simplest case, all the servers on the overtake-free path are identical, i.e., have the same rate, and the inversion can be done by inspection, as in Sec. 4.2.2 and Ref. 24. In the case that the μ_i are all distinct ($1 \leq i \leq m$), the density function is given by the following proposition, derived in Ref. 19; in Ref. 20, the question of degenerate μ_i (when not all are equal) is considered.[d]

Proposition 6. *If the servers in an overtake-free path $(1, 2, \ldots, m)$ have distinct service rates $\mu_1, \mu_2, \ldots, \mu_m$, the passage time density function, conditional on the choice of path, is*

$$\frac{\prod_{i=1}^{m} \mu_i}{G(n-1)} \sum_{c=0}^{n-1} G_m(n-c-1) \sum_{j=1}^{m} \frac{e^{-\mu_j t}}{\prod_{1 \leq i \neq j \leq m} (\mu_i - \mu_j)} \sum_{i=0}^{c} \frac{(v_j t)^{c-i}}{(c-i)!} K^m(j, i),$$

where $K^m(j, \cdot)$ is the normalizing constant function for the subnetwork comprising only nodes in the set $\{1, \ldots, m\} \backslash \{j\}$ with the ratio $x_k = v_k / \mu_k$

---

[d]Essentially, we start with the case of distinct rates and successively combine any two servers with equal rates. The combination involves manipulation of the summations and reduces the problem to two similar problems on networks with one less node in the overtake-free path. Thus, in each step, one degenerate server is removed until all the remaining problems are on paths with distinct rates.

replaced by $\frac{v_k - v_j}{\mu_k - \mu_j}$ for $1 \leq k \neq j \leq m$, i.e.,

$$K^m(j,l) = \sum_{\substack{\sum_{i=1}^m n_i = l \\ n_i \geq 0; n_j = 0}} \prod_{\substack{k=1 \\ k \neq j}}^m \left(\frac{v_k - v_j}{\mu_k - \mu_j}\right)^{n_k}.$$

$K^m(j,l)$ is just a normalizing constant that may be computed efficiently, along with $G_m(n - c - 1)$ and $G(n - 1)$, by Buzen's algorithm.[7] Thus we define the recursive function k, for real vector $\mathbf{y} = (y_1, \ldots, y_a)$ and integers a, b ($0 \leq a \leq M$, $0 \leq b \leq N - 1$) by

$$k(\mathbf{y}, a, b) = k(\mathbf{y}, a - 1, b) + y_a k(\mathbf{y}, a, b - 1), \quad (a, b > 0),$$
$$k(\mathbf{y}, a, 0) = 1, \quad (a > 0),$$
$$k(\mathbf{y}, 0, b) = 0, \quad (b \geq 0).$$

Then we have

$$G_m(l) = k(\mathbf{x}_m, M - m, l), \quad (0 \leq l \leq n - 1),$$
$$G(n-1) \equiv G_0(n-1) = k(\mathbf{x}, M, n - 1),$$
$$K^m(j,l) = k(\mathbf{w}_j, m - 1, l),$$

where $\mathbf{x} = (x_1, \ldots, x_M)$, $\mathbf{x}_m = (x_{m+1}, \ldots, x_M)$ and, for $1 \leq j \leq m$,

$$(\mathbf{w}_j)_k = \begin{cases} (v_k - v_j)/(\mu_k - \mu_j) & \text{if } 1 \leq k < j, \\ (v_{k+1} - v_j)/(\mu_{k+1} - \mu_j) & \text{if } j \leq k < m. \end{cases}$$

In fact Propositions 5 and 6 hold for any overtake-free path in a closed Jackson queueing network — recall the preceding discussion.

4.2.1. *Cyclic networks*

For a cyclic network of M exponential servers with distinct rates $\mu_1, \ldots, \mu_M$ and population N, the cycle time distribution is

$$\frac{\left(\prod_{i=1}^M \mu_i\right) t^{N-1}}{(N-1)! G(N)} \sum_{j=1}^M \frac{e^{-\mu_j t}}{\prod_{i \neq j}(\mu_i - \mu_j)}.$$

This follows by setting $v_1 = \cdots = v_M = 1$ in Proposition 6, so that all the terms $K^m(j,i)$ are zero except when $n_k = 0$ for all k, i.e., when $i = 0$. Finally, note there is only one partition of the state space, namely the one with all $N-1$ customers at the servers $1, \ldots, M$. Thus we have $G_M(n) = 1$ if $n = 0$ and $G_M(n) = 0$ if $n > 0$, so that only terms with $c = N - 1$ give a non-zero contribution.

4.2.2. *Paths with service rates all equal*

When all the service rates in the path are the same, equal to μ say, the Laplace transform of passage time is a mixed sum of Erlang densities of the form $[\mu/(s+\mu)]^{c+m}$. Each term can therefore be inverted by inspection and we get:

Proposition 7. *If the servers in overtake-free path $1,\ldots,m$ in the network of Proposition 5 all have service rate μ, the path's time delay density function is*

$$\frac{\mu^m e^{-\mu t}}{G(n-1)} \sum_{c=0}^{n-1} G_m(n-c-1) G^m(c) \mu^c \frac{t^{c+m-1}}{(c+m-1)!},$$

where $G^m(k)$ is the normalizing constant for the subnetwork comprising servers $1,\ldots,m$ only, with population $k \geq 0$.

From this result we can immediately obtain formulas for moments higher than the mean of a customer's transmission time.

Corollary 1. *For a path of equal rate servers, message transmission time has kth moment equal to*

$$\frac{1}{\mu^k G(n-1)} \sum_{c=0}^{n-1} G_m(n-c-1) G^m(c) (c+m) \cdots (c+m-k+1).$$

5. Passage Times in Continuous Time Markov Chains

In this section we consider the analysis of passage times in arbitrary finite continuous time Markov chains (CTMCs). While such chains can be specified manually, it is more usual for them to be generated automatically from one of several high-level modeling formalisms, such as queueing networks, stochastic Petri nets, or stochastic process algebras. Since the memory and processing power of a single workstation is easily overwhelmed by realistic models (which may typically contain tens of millions of states or more), our approach is a parallel uniformization-based algorithm that uses hypergraph partitioning to minimize interprocessor communication.[12]

5.1. *First passage times in CTMCs*

Consider a finite, irreducible, continuous time Markov Chain (CTMC) with n states $\{1, 2, \ldots, n\}$ and $n \times n$ generator matrix Q. If $X(t)$ denotes the state of the CTMC at time $t \geq 0$, then the first passage time from a source state i into a non-empty set of target states $\vec{j}$ is

$$T_{i\vec{j}}(t) = \inf\{u > 0 : X(t+u) \in \vec{j} \mid X(t) = i\}, \quad (\forall t \geq 0).$$

For a stationary, time-homogeneous CTMC, $T_{i\vec{j}}(t)$ is independent of t, so

$$T_{i\vec{j}} = \inf\{u > 0 : X(u) \in \vec{j} \mid X(0) = i\}.$$

$T_{i\vec{j}}$ is a random variable with an associated probability density function $f_{i\vec{j}}(t)$. To determine $f_{i\vec{j}}(t)$ we must convolve the exponentially distributed state holding times over all possible paths (including cycles) from state i into any of the states in the set $\vec{j}$. As shown in the next subsection, the problem can also be readily extended to multiple initial states by weighting first passage time densities.

5.2. *Uniformization*

Uniformization[16,39] transforms a CTMC into one in which all states have the same mean holding time $1/q$, by allowing "invisible" transitions from a state to itself. This is equivalent to a discrete-time Markov chain (DTMC), after normalization of the rows, together with an associated Poisson process of rate q. The one-step DTMC transition matrix P is given by

$$P = Q/q + I,$$

where $q > \max_i |q_{ii}|$ (to ensure that the DTMC is aperiodic). The number of transitions in the DTMC that occur in a given time interval is given by a Poisson process with rate q.

While uniformization is normally used for transient analysis, it can also be employed for the calculation of response time densities.[35,38] We add an extra, absorbing state to our uniformized chain, which is the sole successor state for all target states (thus ensuring we calculate the *first* passage time density). We denote by P' the one-step transition matrix of the modified, uniformized chain. Recalling that the time taken to traverse a path with n hops in this chain will have an Erlang distribution with parameters n and q, the density of the time taken to pass from a set of source states $\vec{i}$ into a set of target states $\vec{j}$ is given by

$$f_{\vec{i}\vec{j}}(t) = \sum_{n=1}^{\infty} \frac{q^n t^{n-1} e^{-qt}}{(n-1)!} \sum_{k \in \vec{j}} \pi_k^{(n)}, \qquad (4)$$

where

$$\pi^{(n+1)} = \pi^{(n)} P' \quad \text{for } n \geq 0,$$

with

$$\pi_k^{(0)} = \begin{cases} 0 & \text{for } k \notin \vec{i}, \\ \pi_k / \sum_{j \in \vec{i}} \pi_j & \text{for } k \in \vec{i}, \end{cases} \quad (5)$$

and in which π is any non-zero solution to $\pi = \pi P$. The corresponding passage time cumulative distribution function is given by

$$F_{\vec{i}\vec{j}}(t) = \sum_{n=1}^{\infty} \left\{ \left(1 - e^{-qt} \sum_{k=0}^{n-1} \frac{(qt)^k}{k!} \right) \sum_{k \in \vec{j}} \pi_k^{(n)} \right\}. \quad (6)$$

Truncation is employed to approximate the infinite sums in Eqs. (4) and (6), terminating the calculation when the Erlang term drops below a specified threshold value. Concurrently, when the convergence criterion,

$$\frac{\|\pi^{(n+1)} - \pi^{(n)}\|_\infty}{\|\pi^{(n)}\|_\infty} < \epsilon, \quad (7)$$

is met,[e] for given tolerance ϵ, the steady state probabilities of P' are considered to have been obtained with sufficient accuracy and no further multiplications with P' are performed.

5.3. *Hypergraph partitioning*

The key opportunity for parallelism in the uniformization algorithm is the sparse matrix-vector product $\pi^{(n+1)} = \pi^{(n)} P'$ (or equivalently $\pi^{(n+1)T} = P'^T \pi^{(n)T}$, where the superscript T denotes the transpose operator). To perform these operations efficiently it is necessary to map the non-zero elements of P' onto processors such that the computational load is balanced and communication between processors is minimized. To achieve this, we use hypergraph-based partitioning techniques to assign matrix rows and corresponding vector elements to processors in a row-striped decomposition.

Hypergraphs are extensions of graph data structures that, until recently, were primarily applied in VLSI circuit design. Formally, a hypergraph $\mathcal{H} = (\mathcal{V}, \mathcal{N})$ is defined by a set of vertices $\mathcal{V}$ and a set of nets (or hyperedges) $\mathcal{N}$, where each net is a subset of the vertex set $\mathcal{V}$.[8] In the context of a row-wise decomposition of a sparse matrix, matrix row i $(1 \leq i \leq n)$ is represented by a vertex $v_i \in \mathcal{V}$ while column j $(1 \leq j \leq n)$ is represented by net $N_j \in \mathcal{N}$. The vertices contained within net N_j correspond to the row numbers of the non-zero elements within column j, i.e., for matrix A,

---

[e]$\|\pi\|_\infty = \max_i |\pi_i|$.

$v_i \in N_j$ if and only if $a_{ij} \neq 0$. The weight of vertex i is given by the number of non-zero elements in row i, while the weight of a net is its contribution to the hyperedge cut, defined as one less than the number of different partitions (in the row-wise decomposition) spanned by that net.

The overall objective of a hypergraph sparse matrix partitioning is to minimize the total hyperedge cut while maintaining a load balancing criterion. Like graph partitioning, hypergraph partitioning is NP-complete. However, there are a small number of hypergraph partitioning tools which implement fast heuristic algorithms, for example, PaToH[8] and hMeTiS.[28]

5.4. *Parallel algorithm and tool implementation*

The process of calculating a response time density begins with a high-level model, which we specify in an enhanced form of the DNAmaca Markov Chain Analyser interface language.[30,31] This language supports the specification of queueing networks, stochastic Petri nets, stochastic process algebras and other models that can be mapped onto Markov chains. Next, a probabilistic, hash-based state generator[33] uses the high-level model description to produce the generator matrix Q of the model's underlying Markov chain as well as a list of the initial and target states. Normalized weights for the initial states are then determined from Eq. (5), which requires us to solve $\pi Q = 0$. This is readily done using any of a variety of steady-state solution techniques (e.g. Refs. 11 and 32). From Q, P'^T is constructed by uniformizing and transposing the underlying Markov chain and by adding the extra, terminal state that becomes the sole successor state of all target states. Having been converted into an appropriate input format, P'^T is then partitioned using a hypergraph or graph-based partitioning tool.

The pipeline is completed by our distributed response time density calculator, which is implemented in C++ using the Message Passing Interface (MPI)[17] standard. This means that it is portable to a wide variety of parallel computers and workstation clusters.

Initially each processor tabulates the Erlang terms for each t-point required (cf. Eq. (4)). Computation of these terms terminates when they fall below a specified threshold value. In fact, this is safe to use as a truncation condition for the entire passage time density expression because the Erlang term is multiplied by a summation which is a probability. The terminating condition also determines the maximum number of hops m used to calculate the right-hand factor, a sum which is independent of t.

Each processor reads in the rows of the matrix P'^T that correspond to its allocated partition into two types of sparse matrix data structure and also computes the corresponding elements of the vector $\pi^{(0)}$. *Local* non-zero elements (i.e., those elements in the diagonal matrix blocks that will be multiplied with vector elements stored locally) are stored in a conventional compressed sparse row format. *Remote* non-zero elements (i.e., those elements in off-diagonal matrix blocks that must be multiplied with vector elements received from other processors) are stored in an ultrasparse matrix data structure — one for each remote processor — using a coordinate format. Each processor then determines which vector elements need to be received from and sent to every other processor on each iteration, adjusting the column indices in the ultrasparse matrices so that they index into a vector of received elements. This ensures that a minimum amount of communication takes place and makes multiplication of off-diagonal blocks with received vector elements very efficient.

The vector $\pi^{(n)}$ is then calculated for $n = 1, 2, 3, \ldots, m$ by repeated sparse matrix-vector multiplications of form $\pi^{(n+1)T} = P'^T \pi^{(n)T}$. Actually, fewer than m multiplications may take place since a test for steady state convergence is made after every iteration (cf. Eq. (7)); if the convergence criterion is satisfied, the matrix-vector multiplication is not performed and we set $\pi^{(n+1)T} = \pi^{(n)T}$ in subsequent iterations.

For each matrix-vector multiplication, each processor begins by using non-blocking communication primitives to send and receive remote vector elements, while calculating the product of local matrix elements with locally stored vector elements. The use of non-blocking operations allows computation and communication to proceed concurrently on parallel machines where dedicated network hardware supports this effectively. The processor then waits for the completion of non-blocking operations (if they have not already completed) before multiplying received remote vector elements with the relevant ultrasparse matrices and adding their contributions to the local matrix-vector product cumulatively.

From the resulting local matrix-vector products each processor calculates and stores its contribution to the sum $\sum_{k \in \vec{j}} \pi_k^{(n)}$. After m iterations have completed, these sums are accumulated onto an arbitrary master processor where they are multiplied with the tabulated Erlang terms for each t-point required for the passage time density. The resulting points are written to a disk file and are displayed using the GNUplot graph plotting utility.

5.5. Numerical example

As an example we consider the cycle time in the closed tree-like queueing network of Fig. 3. This network has six servers with rates $\mu_1, \ldots, \mu_6$ and non-zero routing probabilities as shown. Thus the visitation rates $v_1, \ldots, v_6$ for servers 1 to 6 are respectively proportional to: 1, p_{12}, p_{13}, p_{14}, p_{12}, p_{14}. Here we set $\{\mu_1, \mu_2, \mu_3, \mu_4, \mu_5, \mu_6\} = \{3, 5, 4, 6, 2, 1\}$ and $\{p_{12}, p_{13}, p_{14}\} = \{0.2, 0.5, 0.3\}$. As described in Sec. 4.2, analytical results for the cycle time density in this type of overtake-free tree-like queueing network with M servers and population n are known, and can be rapidly computed.

To compute the cycle time density in this network in terms of its underlying Markov Chain using the uniformization technique described in this paper requires the state vector to be augmented by three extra components so that a "tagged" customer can be followed through the system. The extra components are: the queue containing the tagged customer l, the position of the tagged customer in that queue k, and the cycle sequence number c (an alternating bit, flipped whenever the tagged customer joins $q1$). For this augmented system with n customers, the underlying Markov chain has

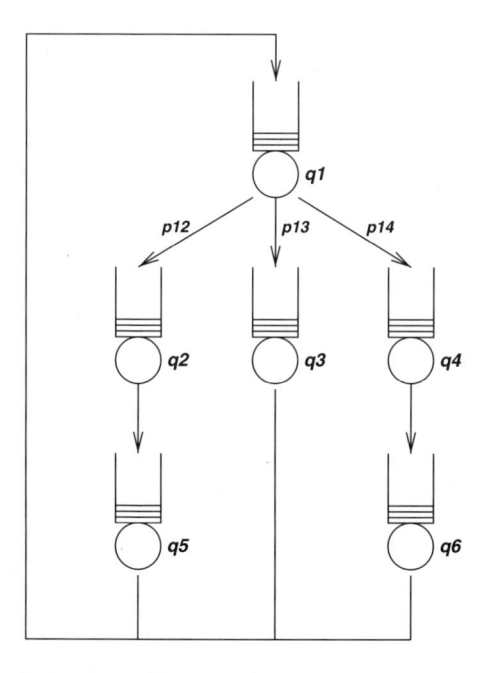

Fig. 3. A closed tree-like network and its routing probabilities.

$12\binom{n+5}{6}$ states. Source states are those in which $l = 1$, $k = n_1 - 1$ and $c = 0$ while target states are those in which $l = 1$, $k = n_1 - 1$ and $c = 1$.

For a small six customer system with 5,544 states, Fig. 4 shows the resulting transposed P' matrix and associated hypergraph decomposition produced by hMeTiS. Statistics about the per-iteration communication associated with this decomposition are presented in Table 1. Around 90% of the non-zero elements allocated to each processor are local, i.e., they are

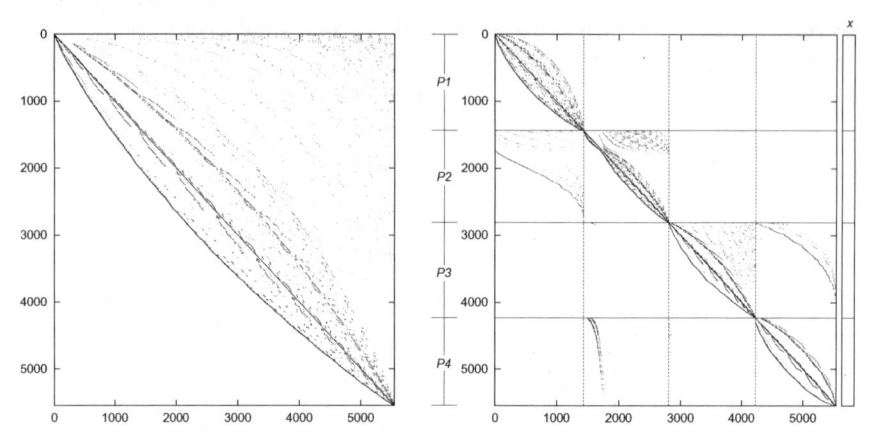

Fig. 4. Transposed P' matrix (left) and hypergraph-partitioned matrix (right) for the tree-like queueing network with six customers (5,544 states).

Table 1. Communication overhead in the queueing network model with six customers (top) and interprocessor communication matrix (bottom).

Processor	Non-zeros	Local %	Remote %	Reused %
1	7,022	99.96	0.04	0
2	7,304	91.41	8.59	34.93
3	6,802	88.44	11.56	42.11
4	6,967	89.01	10.99	74.28

	1	2	3	4
1	—	407	—	4
2	3	—	16	181
3	—	—	—	12
4	—	1	439	—

multiplied with vector elements that are stored locally. The remote non-zero elements are multiplied with vector elements that are sent from other processors. However, because the hypergraph decomposition tends to align remote non-zero elements in columns (well illustrated in the second block belonging to processor 4), reuse of received vector elements is good (up to 74%) with correspondingly lower communication overhead. The communication matrix on the right in Table 1 shows the number of vector elements sent between each pair of processors during each iteration (e.g., 181 vector elements are sent from processor 2 to processor 4).

Moving to a more sizeable model, the queueing network with 27 customers has an underlying Markov Chain with 10,874,304 states and 82,883,682 transitions. This model is too large to partition using a hypergraph partitioner on a single machine (even one with 2 GB RAM), and there are currently no parallel hypergraph partitioning tools available. Consequently a lesser quality graph-based decomposition produced by the parallel graph partitioner ParMeTiS (running on the PC cluster) was chosen. It must be noted that this decomposition still offers a great reduction in communication costs over other methods available: a 16-way partition has an average of 95.8% local non-zero elements allocated to each processor and a reused received non-zero element average of 30.4%. Table 2 shows the per-iteration communication overhead for randomized (i.e., random assignment of rows to partitions), linear (i.e., simple in-order allocation of rows to processors such that the number of non-zeros assigned to each processor is the same) and graph-based allocations. The graph-based method is clearly superior, both in terms of number of messages sent and (especially) communication volume.

Figure 5 compares the numerical and analytical cycle time densities (computed by Proposition 6) for the queueing network with 27 customers. Agreement is excellent and the results agree to an accuracy of 0.00001% over

Table 2. Per-iteration communication overhead for various partitioning methods for the queueing network model with 27 customers on 16 processors.

Partitioning method	Communication overhead	
	Messages	Volume (MB)
Randomised	240	450.2
Linear	134	78.6
Graph-based	110	19.7

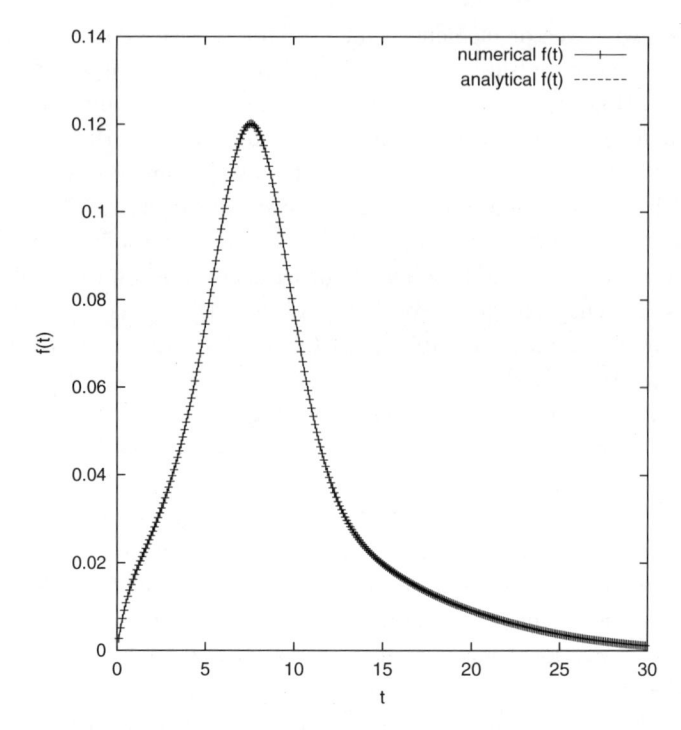

Fig. 5. Numerical and analytical cycle time densities for the tree-like queueing network of Fig. 3 with 27 customers (10,874,304 states).

the time range plotted. The numerical density is computed in 968 seconds (16 minutes 8 seconds) for 875 iterations using 16 PCs. The memory used on each PC is just 84 MB. It was not possible to compute the density on a single PC (with 512 MB RAM) but the same computation on a dual-processor server machine (with 2 GB RAM) required 5,580 seconds (93 minutes).

6. Passage Times in Continuous Time Semi-Markov Processes

Semi-Markov processes (SMPs) are a generalization of Markov processes that allow for arbitrarily distributed state sojourn times, so that more realistic models can be described while still maintaining some of the analytical tractability associated with Markov models. This section summarizes an iterative technique for passage time analysis of large, structurally unrestricted semi-Markov processes.[5,6,23] Our method is based on the calculation and subsequent numerical inversion of Laplace transforms and is amenable to a highly scalable distributed implementation. One of the biggest problems involved in working with semi-Markov processes is how to store the Laplace transform of state sojourn times in an effective way, such that accuracy is maintained but representation explosion does not occur. We address this issue with a constant-space representation of a general distribution function based on the evaluation demands of the numerical inversion algorithm employed. Results for a distributed voting system model with up to 1.1 million states are presented and compared against simulation.

6.1. *First passage times in SMPs*

Consider a Markov renewal process $\{(X_n, T_n) : n \geq 0\}$, where T_n is the time of the nth transition ($T_0 = 0$) and $X_n \in \mathcal{S}$ is the state at (just after) the nth transition. Let the kernel of this process be

$$R(n, i, j, t) = \mathbb{P}(X_{n+1} = j, T_{n+1} - T_n \leq t \,|\, X_n = i)$$

for $i, j \in \mathcal{S}$. The continuous time semi-Markov process (SMP), $\{Z(t), t \geq 0\}$, defined by the kernel R, is related to the Markov renewal process by

$$Z(t) = X_{N(t)},$$

where $N(t) = \max\{n : T_n \leq t\}$, i.e., the number of state transitions that have taken place by time t. Thus $Z(t)$ represents the state of the system at time t. We consider time-homogeneous SMPs, in which $R(n, i, j, t)$ is independent of n:

$$\begin{aligned} R(i, j, t) &= \mathbb{P}(X_{n+1} = j, T_{n+1} - T_n \leq t \,|\, X_n = i) \\ &= p_{ij} H_{ij}(t), \end{aligned}$$

where $p_{ij} = \mathbb{P}(X_{n+1} = j \,|\, X_n = i)$ is the state transition probability between states i and j and $H_{ij}(t) = \mathbb{P}(T_{n+1} - T_n \leq t \,|\, X_{n+1} = j, X_n = i)$, is the sojourn-time distribution in state i when the next state is j.

Consider a finite, irreducible, continuous-time semi-Markov process with N states $\{1, 2, \ldots, N\}$. Recalling that $Z(t)$ denotes the state of the SMP at time t ($t \geq 0$), the first passage time from a source state i at time t into a non-empty set of target states $\vec{j}$ is

$$P_{i\vec{j}}(t) = \inf\{u > 0 : Z(t+u) \in \vec{j} \,|\, Z(t) = i\}.$$

For a stationary time-homogeneous SMP, $P_{i\vec{j}}(t)$ is independent of t and we have:

$$P_{i\vec{j}} = \inf\{u > 0 : Z(u) \in \vec{j} \,|\, Z(0) = i\}. \tag{8}$$

$P_{i\vec{j}}$ is a random variable with an associated probability density function $f_{i\vec{j}}(t)$. In general, the Laplace transform of $f_{i\vec{j}}$, $L_{i\vec{j}}(s)$, can be computed by solving a set of N linear equations:

$$L_{i\vec{j}}(s) = \sum_{k \notin \vec{j}} r^*_{ik}(s) L_{k\vec{j}}(s) + \sum_{k \in \vec{j}} r^*_{ik}(s) \quad \text{for } 1 \leq i \leq N, \tag{9}$$

where $r^*_{ik}(s)$ is the Laplace–Stieltjes transform (LST) of $R(i, k, t)$ and is defined by

$$r^*_{ik}(s) = \int_0^\infty e^{-st} dR(i, k, t).$$

Equation (9) has a matrix-vector form, $A\tilde{x} = \tilde{b}$, where the elements of A are arbitrary complex functions; care needs to be taken when storing such functions for eventual numerical inversion (see Sec. 6.3). For example, when $\vec{j} = \{1\}$, Eq. (9) yields

$$\begin{pmatrix} 1 & -r^*_{12}(s) & \cdots & -r^*_{1N}(s) \\ 0 & 1 - r^*_{22}(s) & \cdots & -r^*_{2N}(s) \\ 0 & -r^*_{32}(s) & \cdots & -r^*_{3N}(s) \\ \vdots & \vdots & \ddots & \vdots \\ 0 & -r^*_{N2}(s) & \cdots & 1 - r^*_{NN}(s) \end{pmatrix} \tilde{x} = \begin{pmatrix} r^*_{11}(s) \\ r^*_{21}(s) \\ r^*_{31}(s) \\ \vdots \\ r^*_{N1}(s) \end{pmatrix}, \tag{10}$$

where $\tilde{x} = (L_{1\vec{j}}(s), L_{2\vec{j}}(s), \ldots, L_{N\vec{j}}(s))^T$. When there are multiple source states, denoted by the vector $\vec{i}$, the Laplace transform of the passage time distribution at steady-state is

$$L_{\vec{i}\vec{j}}(s) = \sum_{k \in \vec{i}} \alpha_k L_{k\vec{j}}(s), \tag{11}$$

where the weight α_k is the probability at equilibrium that the system is in state $k \in \vec{i}$ at the starting instant of the passage. If $\tilde{\pi}$ denotes the steady-state vector of the embedded discrete-time Markov chain (DTMC) with one-step transition probability matrix $P = [p_{ij} \,|\, 1 \leq i, j \leq N]$, then α_k is given by

$$\alpha_k = \begin{cases} \pi_k / \sum_{j \in \vec{i}} \pi_j & \text{if } k \in \vec{i}, \\ 0 & \text{otherwise.} \end{cases} \tag{12}$$

The row vector with components α_k is denoted by $\tilde{\alpha}$.

6.2. Iterative passage time algorithm

Recall the semi-Markov process, $Z(t)$, of Sec. 6.1, where $N(t)$ is the number of state transitions that have taken place by time t. We define the rth transition first passage time to be

$$P_{i\vec{j}}^{(r)} = \inf\{u > 0 : Z(u) \in \vec{j} \mid N(u) \leq r, Z(0) = i\}, \qquad (13)$$

which is the time taken to enter a state in $\vec{j}$ for the first time having started in state i at time 0 and having undergone up to r state transitions. $P_{i\vec{j}}^{(r)}$ is a random variable with associated probability density function, $f_{i\vec{j}}^{(r)}(t)$, which has Laplace transform $L_{i\vec{j}}^{(r)}(s)$.

$L_{i\vec{j}}^{(r)}(s)$ is, in turn, the ith component of the vector

$$\tilde{L}_{\vec{j}}^{(r)}(s) = \left(L_{1\vec{j}}^{(r)}(s), L_{2\vec{j}}^{(r)}(s), \ldots, L_{N\vec{j}}^{(r)}(s)\right),$$

which may be computed as

$$\tilde{L}_{\vec{j}}^{(r)}(s) = U(I + U' + U'^2 + \cdots + U'^{(r-1)})\tilde{e}. \qquad (14)$$

Here U is a matrix with elements $u_{pq} = r_{pq}^*(s)$ and U' is a modified version of U with elements $u'_{pq} = I_{p \notin \vec{j}} u_{pq}$, where states in $\vec{j}$ have been made absorbing (I is the indicator function). The column vector $\tilde{e}$ has entries $\tilde{e}_k = I_{k \in \vec{j}}$.

We include the initial U term in Eq. (14) so as to generate cycle times for cases such as $L_{ii}^{(r)}(s)$ which would otherwise register as 0, if U' were used instead.

From Eqs. (8) and (13):

$$P_{i\vec{j}} = P_{i\vec{j}}^{(\infty)} \quad \text{and thus} \quad L_{i\vec{j}}(s) = L_{i\vec{j}}^{(\infty)}(s).$$

Now, $L_{i\vec{j}}^{(r)}(s)$ can be generalized to multiple source states $\vec{i}$ using the normalized steady-state vector $\tilde{\alpha}$ of Eq. (12):

$$\begin{aligned} L_{\vec{i}\vec{j}}^{(r)}(s) &= \tilde{\alpha}\tilde{L}_{\vec{j}}^{(r)}(s) \\ &= (\tilde{\alpha}U + \tilde{\alpha}UU' + \tilde{\alpha}UU'^2 + \cdots \\ &\quad \cdots + \tilde{\alpha}UU'^{(r-2)} + \tilde{\alpha}UU'^{(r-1)})\tilde{e}. \end{aligned} \qquad (15)$$

The sum of Eq. (15) can be computed efficiently using sparse matrix-vector multiplications with a vector accumulator. At each step, the accumulator (initialized to αU) is post-multiplied by U' and αU is added. The worst-case time complexity for this sum is $O(N^2 r)$ versus the $O(N^3)$ of typical matrix inversion techniques.

Convergence of the sum in Eq. (15) is said to have occurred at a particular r, if for a given s-point:

$$\left|\text{Re}\left(L_{\vec{i}\vec{j}}^{(r+1)}(s) - L_{\vec{i}\vec{j}}^{(r)}(s)\right)\right| < \epsilon$$

and

$$\left|\text{Im}\left(L_{\vec{i}\vec{j}}^{(r+1)}(s) - L_{\vec{i}\vec{j}}^{(r)}(s)\right)\right| < \epsilon, \tag{16}$$

where ϵ is chosen to be a suitably small value (e.g., 10^{-8}).

6.3. *Laplace transform inversion*

The key to practical analysis of semi-Markov processes lies in the efficient representation of their generally distributed functions. Without care the structural complexity of the SMP can be recreated within the representation of the distribution functions.

Many techniques have been used for representing arbitrary distributions — two of the most popular being *phase-type distributions* and *vector-of-moments* methods. These methods suffer from, respectively, exploding representation size under composition and containing insufficient information to produce accurate answers after large amounts of composition.

As all our distribution manipulations take place in Laplace space, we link our distribution representation to the Laplace inversion technique that we ultimately use. Our implementation supports two Laplace transform inversion algorithms: the Euler technique[2] and the Laguerre method[1] with modifications summarized in Ref. 21.

Both algorithms work on the same general principle of sampling the transform function $L(s)$ at n points, $s_1, s_2, \ldots, s_n$ and generating values of $f(t)$ at m user-specified t-points $t_1, t_2, \ldots, t_m$. In the Euler inversion case $n = km$, where k typically varies between 15 and 50, depending on the accuracy of the inversion required. In the modified Laguerre case, $n = 400$ and, crucially, is independent of m.

The choice of inversion algorithm depends on the characteristics of the density function $f(t)$. If the function is continuous, and has continuous derivatives (i.e., it is "smooth") then the Laguerre method can be used. If, however, the density function or its derivatives contain discontinuities — for example, if the system exclusively contains transitions with deterministic or uniform holding-time distributions — then the Euler method must be employed.

6.4. Implementation

Whichever inversion algorithm is used, it is important to note that calculating $s_i, 1 \leq i \leq n$, and storing all the distribution transform functions, sampled at these points, will be sufficient to provide a complete inversion. Storing our distribution functions in this way has three main advantages. Firstly, the function has constant storage space, independent of the distribution-type. Secondly, each distribution has, therefore, the same constant storage even after composition with other distributions. Finally, the function has sufficient information about a distribution to determine the required passage time or transient density (and no more).

Our implementation employs a distributed master-slave architecture similar to that of the Markovian passage time calculation tool of Ref. 21. The master processor computes in advance the values of s at which it will need to know the value of $L_{\vec{i}\vec{j}}(s)$ in order to perform the inversion. The s-values are then placed in a global work-queue to which the slave processors make requests. On making a request, slave processors are assigned the next available s-value and use this to construct the matrices U and U'. The iterative algorithm is then applied to calculate the truncated sum of Eq. (15) for that s-value. The result is returned to the master and cached (both in memory and on disk so that all computation is checkpointed), and once all values have been computed and returned, the final Laplace inversion calculations are made by the master. The resulting t-points can then be plotted on a graph. As inter-slave communication is not required, the algorithm exhibits excellent scalability.

6.5. Numerical example

We demonstrate the SMP analysis techniques of the previous sections with a semi-Markov Petri net model of a distributed voting system. Semi-Markov stochastic Petri nets are extensions of GSPNs,[3] which can handle arbitrary state-dependent holding-time distributions and which generate an underlying semi-Markov process rather than a Markov process.

The semi-Markov stochastic Petri net of a distributed voting system is shown in Fig. 6. Voting agents vote asynchronously, moving from place p_1 to p_2 as they do so. A restricted number of polling units which receive their votes transit t_1 from place p_3 to place p_4. At t_2, the vote is registered with as many central voting units as are currently operational in p_5.

The system is considered to be in a failure mode if either all the polling units have failed and are in p_7 or all the central voting units have failed and are in p_6. If either of these complete failures occur, then a high priority repair is performed, which resets the failed units to a fully operational state. If some but not all the polling or voting units fail, they attempt self-recovery. The system will continue to function as long as at least one polling unit and one voting unit remain operational.

For the voting system described in Fig. 6, Table 3 shows how the size of the underlying SMP varies according to the configuration of the variables CC, MM, and NN, which are the number of voters, polling units and central voting units, respectively.

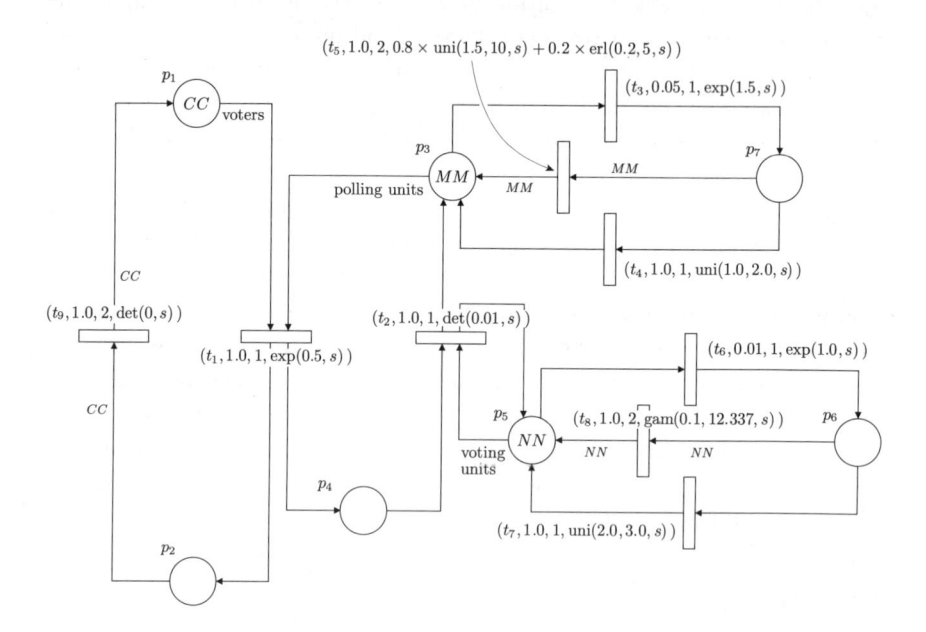

Fig. 6. A semi-Markov stochastic Petri net of a voting system.

Table 3. Different configurations of the voting system as used to present results.

System	CC	MM	NN	States
0	18	6	3	2,061
1	60	25	4	106,540
2	100	30	4	249,760
3	125	40	4	541,280
4	150	40	5	778,850
5	175	45	5	1,140,050

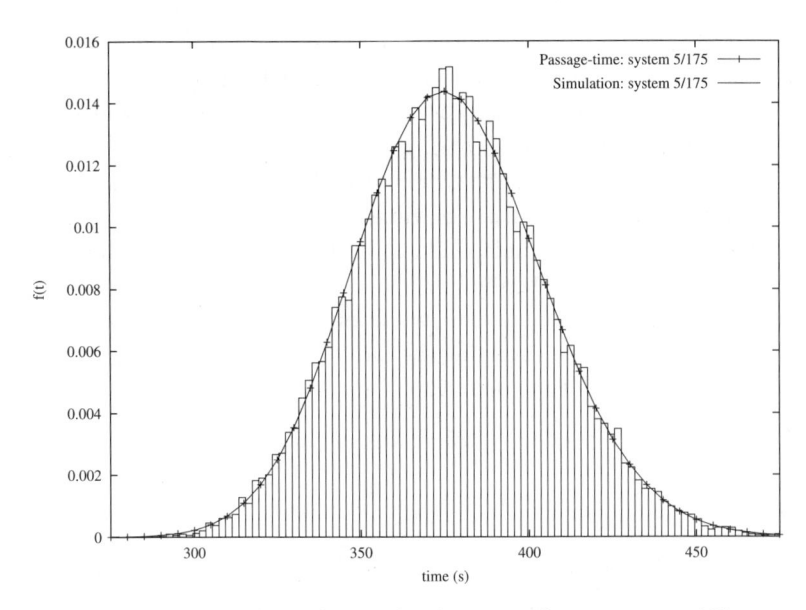

Fig. 7. Analytic and simulated density for the time taken to process 175 voters in system 5 (1.1 million states).

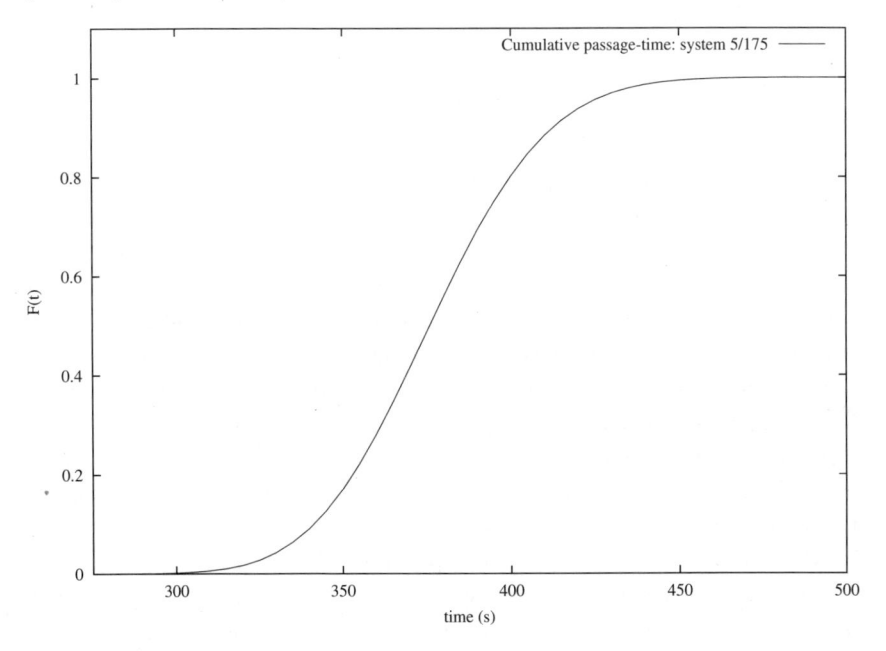

Fig. 8. Cumulative distribution function for the time taken to process 175 voters in system 5 (1.1 million states).

Figure 7 shows the density of the time taken for the passage of 175 voters from place p_1 to p_2 in system 5 as computed by both our (truncated) iterative technique and by simulation. The close agreement provides mutual validation of the analytical method, with its numerical approximation, and the simulation. It is interesting that, qualitatively, the density appears close to normal. Certainly, the passage time random variable is a (weighted) sum of a large number of independent random variables, but these are, in general, not identically distributed.

Figure 8 shows a cumulative distribution for the same passage as Fig. 7. This is easily obtained by inverting the Laplace transform $L_{\vec{i}\vec{j}}(s)/s$; it allows us to extract response time quantiles, for instance:

$$\mathbb{P}(\text{system 5 processes 175 voters in under 440s}) = 0.9858.$$

7. Conclusion

We have seen that finding time delay densities is a hard problem, often with complex and computationally expensive solutions when they can be solved at all. Consequently, in most practical applications, the performance engineer requires approximate methods. There is no single established methodology for such approximation and most of the techniques used are *ad hoc*.

The computation of quantiles of sojourn times in the performance engineering of diverse operational systems, such as internet communication, has been recognized for many years and is increasing with present day benchmarks. We have presented a personal perspective on this subject, revealing the increasing difficulties in computing the probability distribution functions of times delays — and hence quantiles — as models become more complex. From the single FCFS M/G/1 queue, through queues with more complex queueing disciplines and negative customers, to tree-like open and closed queueing networks of Markovian queues, it was shown how analytical solutions for response time distributions could be found in the time domain. More sophisticated cases, not considered here, can compute Laplace transforms of response time probability densities, but these require numerical inversion to get distribution functions, using methods such as Euler and Laguerre as discussed, in Sec. 6.3.

For many years, other problems, perhaps with no particular structure, could only be solved approximately by analytical methods, the approach of direct analysis of the Markov chain being numerically infeasible. However, in recent years, this direct approach has become viable for small-to-medium sized problems by exploiting parallel computation and the availability of very large storage systems at all levels form cache to disk file stores. We explained how the resulting matrix analytic problems can be structured to take advantage of these technological advances, in particular using hypergraph partitioning of matrices and a fixed storage representation of probability distribution functions (or rather their Laplace–Stieltjes transforms).

Quantiles can indeed now be generated numerically, exactly or nearly exactly, for many problems but even quite moderately sized ones are still intractable. The future will require approximate and asymptotic methods, e.g., for tail probabilities; this is a growing research area.

References

1. J. Abate, G. L. Choudhury and W. Whitt, On the Laguerre method for numerically inverting Laplace transforms, *INFORMS J. Comput.* **8**(4) (1996), 413–427.
2. J. Abate and W. Whitt, Numerical inversion of Laplace transforms of probability distributions, *ORSA J. Comput.* **7**(1) (1995), 36–43.
3. M. Ajmone-Marsan, G. Conte and G. Balbo, A class of Generalised Stochastic Petri Nets for the performance evaluation of multiprocessor systems, *ACM Trans. Comput. Syst.* **2** (1984), 93–122.
4. O. J. Boxma and H. Daduna, Sojourn times in queueing networks, in *Stochastic Analysis of Computer and Communication Systems*, ed. H. Takagi (North Holland, 1990), pp. 401–450.
5. J. T. Bradley, N. J. Dingle, P. G. Harrison and W. J. Knottenbelt, Distributed computation of passage time quantiles and transient state distributions in large semi-Markov models, in *Proc. Int. Workshop of Performance Modeling, Evaluation and Optimization of Parallel and Distributed Systems (PMEO-PDS 2003)*, Nice, France, April, 2003, p. 281.
6. J. T. Bradley, N. J. Dingle, W. J. Knottenbelt and H. J. Wilson, Hypergraph-based parallel computation of passage time densities in large semi-Markov models, in *Proc. 4th Int. Meeting on the Numerical Solution of Markov Chains (NSMC 2003)*, Chicago, USA, September, 2003, pp. 99–120.
7. J. P. Buzen, Computational algorithms for closed queueing networks with exponential servers; *Commun. ACM* **16** (1973), 527–531.
8. U. V. Catalyürek and C. Aykanat, Hypergraph-partitioning-based decomposition for parallel sparse-matrix vector multiplication, *IEEE Trans. Parall. Distrib. Syst.* **10**(7) (1999), 673–693.
9. R. Chakka and P. G. Harrison, A Markov modulated multi-server queue with negative customers — the MM CPP/GE/c/L G-queue, *Acta Informatica* **37**(11&12) (2001), 881–919.
10. E. G. Coffman Jr, R. R. Muntz and H. Trotter, Waiting time distribution for processor-sharing systems, *J ACM* **17** (1970), 123–130.
11. D. D. Deavours and W. H. Sanders, An efficient disk-based tool for solving large Markov models, *Perform. Evaluation* **33**(1) (1998), 67–84.

12. N. J. Dingle, P. G. Harrison and W. J. Knottenbelt, HYDRA: HYpergraph-based distributed response-time analyser, in *Proc. Int. Conf. on Parallel and Distributed Processing Techniques and Applications (PDPTA 2003)*, Las Vegas, Nevada, USA, June, 2003, pp. 215–219.
13. H. Duduna, Passage times for overtake-free paths in Gordon–Newell networks, *Adv. Applied Prob.* **14** (1982), 672–686.
14. E. Gelenbe, Queueing networks with negative and positive customers, *J. Appl. Probab.* **28** (1991), 656–663.
15. E. Gelenbe (ed.), Feature issue on G-networks, *Euro. J. Operations Research* **126** (2000), 331–339.
16. W. Grassman, Means and variances of time averages in Markovian environments, *Euro. J. Operational Research* **31**(1) (1987), 132–139.
17. W. Gropp, E. Lusk and A. Skjellum, *Using MPI: Portable Parallel Programming with the Message Passing Interface* (MIT Press, Cambridge, Massachussetts, 1994).
18. P. G. Harrison, The distribution of cycle times in tree-like networks of queues, *Comput. J.* **27**(1) (1984), 27–36.
19. P. G. Harrison, Laplace transform inversion and passage-time distributions in Markov processes, *J. Appl. Probab.* **27** (1990), 74–87.
20. P. G. Harrison, On non-uniform packet switched delta networks and the hot-spot effect, *IEE Proc. E* **138**(3) (1991), 123–130.
21. P. G. Harrison, The MM CPP/GE/c/L G-queue: Sojourn time distribution, *Queueing Syst.* **41** (2002), 271–298.
22. P. G. Harrison and A. J. Field, Sojourn times in a random queue with and without preemption, *Euro. J. Oper. Res.* **112** (1999), 646–653.
23. P. G. Harrison and W. J. Knottenbelt, Passage time distributions in large Markov chains, in *Proc. ACM SIGMETRICS 2002*, Marina Del Rey, California, June, 2002.
24. P. G. Harrison and N. M. Patel, *Performance Modelling of Communication Networks and Computer Architectures*, International Computer Science Series (Addison Wesley, 1993).
25. P. G. Harrison and E. Pitel, Sojourn times in single server queues with negative customers, *J. Appl. Probab.* **30** (1993), 943–963.
26. P. G. Harrison and E. Pitel, Response time distributions in tandem G-networks, *J. Appl. Probab.* **32** (1995), 224–246.
27. P. G. Harrison and H. Zatschler, Sojourn time distributions in modulated G-queues with batch processing, in *Proc. 1st Quantitative Evaluation of Systems Conference (QEST '04)*, Twente, the Netherlands, September, 2004.
28. G. Karypis and V. Kumar, Multilevel k-way hypergraph parititioning, Tech. Report #98-036, University of Minnesota, 1998.
29. F. P. Kelly and P. K. Pollett, Sojourn times in closed queueing networks, *Adv. Appl. Probab.* **15** (1983), 638–656.
30. W. J. Knottenbelt, Generalised Markovian analysis of timed transition systems, Master's thesis, University of Cape Town, Cape Town, South Africa, July, 1996.

31. W. J. Knottenbelt, *Parallel Performance Analysis of Large Markov Models*, Ph.D. thesis, Imperial College, London, United Kingdom, February, 2000.
32. W. J. Knottenbelt and P. G. Harrison, Distributed disk-based solution techniques for large Markov models, in *Proc. 3rd Int. Meeting on the Numerical Solution of Markov Chains (NSMC '99)*, Zaragoza, Spain, September, 1999, pp. 58–75.
33. W. J. Knottenbelt, P. G. Harrison, M. A. Mestern and P. S. Kritzinger, A probabilistic dynamic technique for the distributed generation of very large state spaces, *Perform. Evaluation* **39**(1–4) (2000), 127–148.
34. J. D. C. Little, A proof of the queueing formula $L = \lambda * W$, *Oper. Res.* **9** (1961), 383–387.
35. B. Melamed and M. Yadin, Randomization procedures in the computation of cumulative-time distributions over discrete state Markov processes, *Oper. Res.* **32**(4) (1984), 926–944.
36. I. Mitrani, Response time problems in communication networks, *J. Royal Stat. Soc. B* **47**(3) (1985), 396–406.
37. I. Mitrani, *Probabilistic Modelling* (Cambridge University Press, 1998).
38. J. K. Muppala and K. S. Trivedi, Numerical transient analysis of finite Markovian queueing systems, in *Queueing and Related Models*, eds. U. N. Bhat and I. V. Basawa (Oxford University Press, 1992), pp. 262–284.
39. A. Reibman and K. S. Trivedi, Numerical transient analysis of Markov models, *Comput. Oper. Res.* **15**(1) (1988), 19–36.
40. L. Takacs, *Introduction to the Theory of Queues* (Oxford University Press, 1962).
41. Transaction Processing Performance Council, TPC benchmark C: Standard specification revision 5.2. 2003.

CHAPTER 11

Asymptotic Solutions for Two Non-Stationary Problems in Internet Reliability

Yaakov Kogan[*] and Gagan Choudhury[†]

AT&T Labs, 200 Laurel Avenue, Middletown, NJ 07748, USA
[*]*yaakovkogan@ems.att.com*
[†]*gchoudhury@ems.att.com*

1. Introduction

This chapter is motivated by two problems related to Internet reliability, where, similar to Ref. 1, transient rather than traditional steady-state analysis is required. First, we consider a set of N routers with two route processors. The primary processor is in active mode while the secondary processor is in standby mode. When the primary processor fails, a switch-over occurs to the secondary processor with probability p and with probability $q = 1 - p$ switch-over fails, which implies outage of the entire router. We assume that only one processor is replaced even if both processors fail. The problem is to find probability distribution $p(k, t)$ for the number of failed routers k during a given time interval $[0, t]$. We model the described failure and repair process by a closed queueing network with infinite-server stations.[2,3] We prove that the distribution $p(k, t)$ is approximately Poisson and explicitly calculate its parameter if $N \gg 1$. The key step in the proof is establishing that the fraction of customers at each station converges to a constant in the steady state with probability one as $N \to \infty$.

The second problem is related to reliability of a nationwide IP backbone. An outage in the backbone triggers OSPF shortest path changes that result in increased utilization of operational links caused by traffic reallocation from a failed router or link. A situation where operational links do not have enough spare capacity to carry additional traffic during the outage time is referred to as *bandwidth loss*. We consider only one unidirectional backbone link L1 that carries unidirectional traffic and evaluate bandwidth loss caused by increased traffic offered to link L1 during a relatively short time t when some other backbone link(s) become non-operational. A link may become non-operational either due to a physical outage of the link itself or router failure (line-card or entire router) on one end of the link.

We define lost bandwidth in the context of a transient generalized Erlang or Engset loss model[6] with K types of requests to a shared resource consisting of N units. A type k request requires b_k resource units. If the requested number b_k of resource units is available then the request will hold them for the holding period with a finite mean. Otherwise, the request will be blocked and lost.

In the context of IP networks, a request corresponds to a flow initiated by an end user. Flows of different types may have different bandwidth needs. Even though the arrival process of individual packets is usually strongly non-Poisson, the arrival process of flows may usually be well approximated by a Poisson process or arrivals from a finite-source model with exponential idle period for each idle source. In many instances, the duration of a flow has been observed to have a heavy-tailed distribution. For the sake of tractability, we assume the flow duration distribution to be exponential. However, in many cases the underlying model is insensitive or only mildly sensitive to the holding time distribution (except through the mean) and so the exponential holding time assumption would be quite reasonable.

Denote by $A_k(t)$ the number of blocked attempts for a type k request during time interval $[0, t]$. The random process

$$B(t) = \sum_{k=1}^{K} b_k A_k(t)$$

is referred to as lost bandwidth. We derive asymptotic approximations for the expected loss bandwidth in the framework of generalized Erlang and Engset models when N and request arrival rates are proportionally large. Note that the process of blocked attempts $A(t)$ in loss networks has not been studied in the literature.[4] Our main result is asymptotic decomposition of the non-stationary probability distribution $Pr\{A_k(t) = l\}$ into a product of the blocking probability and a Poisson distribution. The non-stationary blocking probability is approximated by its steady value.[8] The parameter of the Poisson distribution coincides with that of the arrival process for the generalized Erlang model, while for the generalized Engset model the parameter is found by solving a minimization problem with constraints.

Note that in this chapter, we study each backbone link in isolation. The joint blocking behavior at multiple backbone links is a topic for future research.

2. Poisson Approximation for the Number of Failed Routers

We model transitions between three different router states by the following closed queueing network consisting of three infinite-server (IS) stations (cf. Ref. 2). The number of customers in the network N corresponds to the number of routers. A busy server at station 1 corresponds to a router with active primary processor. A busy server at station 2 corresponds to a router with active secondary processor and primary processor waiting for replacement. A busy server at station 3 corresponds to a failed router where both processors are not operational. (This reflects the fact that failure of the secondary processor cannot be registered before the switch-over attempt.) Assume that at time 0 all N customers are at station 1. The mean service time at station 1 is denoted by $1/\lambda$ and it is referred to as mean time between failures (MTBF). After service completion at station 1 (failure of active processor), a customer may go to station 2 (successful switch-over) with probability p or to station 3 (failed switch-over) with probability $q = 1 - p$. At station 2, a customer occupies a server until the failed active processor is replaced or the only remaining active processor fails. The customer comes back to station 1 or joins station 3 in the first and second case, respectively. At station 3 a customer occupies a server until the failed active processor is replaced. The customer joins station 2 after service completion at station 3. The mean replacement (repair) time is denoted by $1/\mu$. Let $\rho = \lambda/\mu$.

Note that such a network is not a traditional queueing network (cf. Ref. 5) as routing probabilities at station 2 depend on the type of service (failure of the only remaining processor or replacement of the failed processor).

Denote by $C_i(t)$ the number of customers at station $i = 1, 2, 3$.

Proposition 1. *Assume that time between processor failures and their replacement time are independent random variables with general non-lattice distributions $F(x)$ and $G(x)$ with finite means $1/\lambda$ and $1/\mu$, respectively. Then*

$$\lim_{N \to \infty} \lim_{t \to \infty} \frac{C_2(t)}{N} = \alpha \rho p, \tag{1}$$

$$\lim_{N \to \infty} \lim_{t \to \infty} \frac{C_2(t)}{N} = \alpha \rho^2 p, \tag{2}$$

where $\alpha = (1 + \rho p + \rho^2 p)^{-1}$.

Proof. First, we assume that distributions $F(x)$ and $G(x)$ are exponential. Define associated with our closed queueing network two-dimensional birth-and-death process $\{Y_1(t), Y_2(t)\}$ by the following conditional probabilities:

$$Pr\{Y_1(t+\Delta t) - Y_1(t) = 1 | C_2(t) = n_2, C_3(t) = n_3\}$$
$$= \lambda p(N - n_2 - n_3)\Delta t + o(\Delta t),$$
$$Pr\{Y_1(t+\Delta t) - Y_1(t) = -1 | C_2(t) = n_2, C_3(t) = n_3\}$$
$$= \mu n_2 \Delta t + o(\Delta t),$$

and

$$Pr\{Y_2(t+\Delta t) - Y_2(t) = 1 | C_2(t) = n_2, C_3(t) = n_3\} = \lambda n_3 \Delta t + o(\Delta t),$$
$$Pr\{Y_1(t+\Delta t) - Y_1(t) = -1 | C_2(t) = n_1, C_3(t) = n_3\} = \mu n_3 \Delta t + o(\Delta t).$$

The first component $Y_1(t)$ describes interactions between stations 1 and 2 while the second component $Y_2(t)$ describes interactions between stations 2 and 3. Similar to Ref. 7, processes $Y_1(t)$ and $Y_2(t)$ have the following semimartingale decompositions (drift + martingale):

$$Y_1(t) = \int_0^t \{\lambda p[N - C_2(s) - C_3(s)] - \mu C_2(s)\} ds + M_1(t)$$

and

$$Y_2(t) = \int_0^t [\lambda C_2(s) - \mu C_3(s)] ds + M_2(t),$$

where $M_1(t)$ and $M_2(t)$ are local square integrable martingales. Since jumps of $C_2(t)$ and $C_3(t)$ are disjoint, the predictable quadratic characteristics of $M_1(t)$ and $M_2(t)$ are

$$\langle M_1(t) \rangle = \int_0^t \{\lambda p[N - C_2(s) - C_3(s)] + \mu C_2(s)\} ds$$

and

$$\langle M_1(t) \rangle = \int_0^t [\lambda C_2(s) + \mu C_3(s)] ds,$$

respectively. Let $c_j^N(t) = C_j(t)/N$, $j = 1, 2, 3$ and $y_i^N(t) = Y_i(t)/N$, $i = 1, 2$. Then

$$y_1^N(t) = \int_0^t \{\lambda p[1 - c_2^N(s) - c_3^N(s)] - \mu c_2^N(s)\} ds + M_1(t)/N,$$

$$y_2^N(t) = \int_0^t \{\lambda c_2^N(s) - \mu c_3^N(s)\} ds + M_2(t)/N.$$

Similar to Ref. 7 one can prove that $M_i(t)/N \to 0$, $i = 1, 2$ with probability 1 as $N \to \infty$. This implies convergence of $y_i^N(t)$, $i = 1, 2$ as well as $c_j^N(t)$, $j = 2, 3$ to deterministic processes satisfying the following differential equations:

$$\frac{dy_1(t)}{dt} = \lambda p[1 - c_2(t) - c_3(t)] - \mu c_2(t),$$

$$\frac{dy_2(t)}{dt} = \lambda c_2(t) - \mu c_3(t).$$

As $t \to \infty$ the derivatives on the left-hand side of these equations tend to zero while $c_2(s)$ and $c_3(s)$ tend to their steady state values c_2 and c_3, respectively, satisfying the following system of linear equations:

$$\lambda p(1 - c_2 - c_3) - \mu c_2 = 0,$$

$$\lambda c_2 - \mu c_3 = 0,$$

whose solution is

$$c_2 = \alpha \rho p, \quad c_3 = \alpha \rho^2 p. \tag{3}$$

Using (3) we can obtain an explicit expression for the steady state probability distribution, which has the following form[3]:

$$P(n_2, n_3) = Pr\{C_2 = n_2, C_3 = n_3\} \tag{4}$$

$$= \frac{N! \pi_1^N}{n_2! n_3! (N - n_2 - n_3)!} \left(\frac{\pi_2}{\pi_1}\right)^{n_2} \left(\frac{\pi_3}{\pi_1}\right)^{n_3}.$$

Here $\pi_j = \nu_j/\nu$, $j = 1, 2, 3$, where ν is the expected amount of time between consecutive customer returns to station 1, and ν_j represents the expected amount of time spent at station j between regenerations at station 1 with $\nu = \nu_1 + \nu_2 + \nu_3$. Using the fact $E(C_j) = Nc_j$, where c_j, $j = 2, 3$ are given in (3), we get

$$\frac{\pi_2}{\pi_1} = \rho p, \quad \frac{\pi_3}{\pi_1} = \rho^2 p.$$

The product form solution (4) has the following asymptotic representation[9] for $N \gg 1$:

$$P(n_2, n_3) = c \exp\{-NU(x_2, x_3) + O(\ln N)\}, \tag{5}$$

where c is a constant and

$$U(x_2, x_3) = \sum_{j=2}^{j=3} [x_j \ln x_j - x_j(1 + \ln(\pi_j/\pi_1))]$$

$$+ (x_2 + x_3) + (1 - x_2 - x_3) \ln(1 - x_2 - x_3),$$

Table 1. Comparison of the Poisson approximation with simulation.

	Mean		Second moment	
T	Poisson	Simulation	Poisson	Simulation
1 month	0.5701	0.576 ± 0.01	0.8951	0.904 ± 0.03
1 year	6.9363	6.938 ± 0.01	55.049	55.064 ± 0.20
4 years	27.745	27.760 ± 0.03	797.54	798.37 ± 1.74

where $x_j = n_j/N$, $j = 2, 3$. The minimum of $U(x_2, x_3)$ is at

$$x_2^* = \alpha \rho p, \quad x_3^* = \alpha \rho^2 p,$$

which implies that

$$\lim_{N \to \infty} \frac{C_2}{N} = \alpha \rho p, \quad \lim_{N \to \infty} \frac{C_3}{N} = \alpha \rho^2 p.$$

This completes the proof. □

Corollary 1. *Assume $N \gg 1, T \gg 1$ while $\rho = O(1)$. Then the distribution $p(k, T)$ is approximately Poisson with parameter $\Lambda = \lambda \alpha N(q + \rho p)$, where $\alpha = (1 + \rho p + \rho^2 p)^{-1}$.*

Table 1 demonstrates very good accuracy of the Poisson approximation. The results in Table 1 are obtained for $N = 500, p = 0.95, \lambda^{-1} = 32000$ hours, $\mu^{-1} = 24$ hours and Simulation includes 99% confidence intervals.

3. Asymptotics of Lost Bandwidth

In the generalized Erlang or Engset models type $k, k = 1, \ldots, K$ requests are respectively generated by its own Poisson arrival stream or finite source of size N_k; they require b_k resource units and hold them for the holding period with mean $1/\mu_k$. If a type k request does not find b_k free resource units then it is lost. For the generalized Erlang model, let $\nu_k = \lambda_k/\mu_k$, where λ_k is arrival rate of request k. For the generalized Engset model, a new request from source k will be generated after an exponentially distributed idle period with the mean $1/\beta_k$. The idle period starts either at completion of service if the previous request was served, or at the time of blocking if the previous request was blocked.

Proposition 2. Consider the generalized Erlang model with $\nu_k = N\gamma_k$, where $\gamma_k, k = 1, \ldots, K$ are constant, while $N \gg 1$. Let a be the single positive solution of equation $\phi'(t) = 0$, where

$$\phi(t) = \sum_{k=1}^{K} \gamma_k t^{b_k} - \ln t,$$

and assume $a < 1$ (overloaded regime). Then

$$Pr\{A_k(t) = l\} \approx (1 - a^{b_k}) p_k(l, t; \lambda_k), \tag{6}$$

where

$$p_k(l, t; \lambda_k) = \frac{(\lambda_k t)^l}{l!} e^{-\lambda_k t}$$

is the Poisson distribution with parameter λ_k.

Corollary 2. Under the conditions of Proposition 2, the expected lost bandwidth

$$E[B(t)] \approx \sum_{k=1}^{K} \lambda_k (1 - a^{b_k}) t.$$

Proof. Let $m(t)$ be the total number of busy resource units at time t. Define $Z_N(t) = m_t/N$ and the blocking probabilities

$$E_k(t) = Pr\{Z_N(t) \geq 1 - (b_k - 1)/N | Z_N(0) = 0\}, \quad k = 1, \ldots, K.$$

First, we prove Eq. (6) for the Erlang model, where $K = 1$ and $b_1 = 1$. It is easy to see that the conditional probability

$$Pr\{A(t) = l | Z_N(t) = 1\} = \frac{(\lambda t)^l}{l!} e^{-\lambda t} \tag{7}$$

has the Poisson distribution $p(l, t; \lambda)$. Then

$$Pr\{B(t) = l | m_0 = 0\} = Pr\{A(t) = l\} = \int_0^t E(s) dp(l, s; \lambda)$$
$$= E(t) p(l, t; \lambda) - \int_0^t p(l, s; \lambda) dE(s), \quad l \geq 1. \tag{8}$$

The approximation for $Pr\{A(t) = l\}$ is given by the first term on the right-hand side of Eq. (8). Finally (see Ref. 8), we approximate $E(t)$ by the steady state blocking probability $E \approx 1 - a$, where $a = 1/\gamma$, $\gamma > 1$.

One can easily see that Eq. (7) and representation (8) for the process $A(t)$ are directly generalized for the process $A_k(t)$ with replacement of λ by

Table 2. Comparison of the approximation with simulation results for $t = 10$ with $\gamma = 2$ for the Erlang model, and $\gamma = \nu = 1$ for the generalized Erlang model. (Simulation results show 99% confidence intervals.)

	Mean lost bandwidth			
	Erlang model		Generalized Erlang	
N	Approximation	Simulation	Approximation	Simulation
50	500	475 ± 1	1,000	970 ± 3
200	2,000	$1,870 \pm 3$	4,000	$3,851 \pm 5$

λ_k and $E(t)$ by $E_k(t)$. Finally, $E_k(t)$ is approximated by the steady state loss probability for type k request $E_k \approx 1 - a^{b_k}$.

An explicit expression for the mean lost bandwidth can be also derived for the generalized Erlang model with two types of requests. In particular, for

$$\lambda_1 = N\gamma, \quad \lambda_2 = N\nu; \quad \mu_1 = \mu_2 = 1; \quad b_1 = 1, \quad b_2 = 2,$$

we have

$$E[B(t)] \approx Nt(1-a)[\gamma + 2\nu(1+a)],$$

where a is the only positive root of equation $2\nu x^2 + \gamma x - 1 = 0$. □

Table 2 demonstrates quite reasonable accuracy of the approximation. The accuracy increases for larger t and load defined by parameters γ and ν.

Proposition 3. *Consider the generalized Engset model with $\rho_k = \beta_k/\mu_k$ and $N_k = N\alpha_k$, where ρ_k and α_k, $k = 1, \ldots, K$ are constant, while $N \gg 1$. Let d be the single positive solution of equation $\psi'(t) = 0$, where*

$$\psi(t) = \sum_{k=1}^{K} \alpha_k \ln(1 + \rho_k t^{b_k}) - \ln t,$$

and assume $d < 1$ (overloaded regime). Then

$$Pr\{A_k(t) = l\} \approx (1 - d^{b_k})p_k(l, t; \lambda_k^*),$$

where

$$p_k(l, t; \lambda_k) = \frac{(\lambda_k^* t)^l}{l!} e^{-\lambda_k^* t}$$

is the Poisson distribution with parameter $\lambda_k^* = N_k \beta_k (1 - x_k^*)$, where $\mathbf{x}^* = (x_1^*, \ldots, x_K^*)$ is the solution of the following minimization problem for function:

$$U(\mathbf{x}) = \sum_{k=1}^{K}[\alpha_k x_k \ln(\alpha_k x_k) - \alpha_k x_k \ln \rho_k + \alpha_k(1-x_k)\ln(\alpha_k(1-x_k))]. \quad (9)$$

Find

$$\min U(\mathbf{x})$$

subject to

$$\sum_{k=1}^{K} \alpha_k b_k x_k = 1 \quad (10)$$

and $x_k > 0, k = 1, \ldots, K$.

Corollary 3. *Under conditions of Proposition 3, the expected lost bandwidth*

$$E[B(t)] \approx \sum_{k=1}^{K} N_k \beta_k (1-x_k^*)(1-d^{b_k})t.$$

Proof. For the generalized Engset model the state of the system is described by vector $\mathbf{n} = (n_1, \ldots, n_K)$, where n_k is number of type k requests being served. The state space is given by $\Omega = \{\mathbf{n} : 0 \leq (\mathbf{n}, \mathbf{b}) \leq N\}$, where $\mathbf{b} = (b_1, \ldots, b_K)$ and $(\mathbf{n}, \mathbf{b})$ is a scalar product. The stationary probability that $\mathbf{n}$ circuits are busy is given by

$$\pi(\mathbf{n}) = \frac{1}{G(N_1, \ldots, N_K; N)} \prod_{k=1}^{K} \binom{N_k}{n_k} \rho_k^{n_k},$$

where $G(N_1, \ldots, N_K; N)$ is the normalization constant.

The proof follows the steps of that for Proposition 2 with the following key difference. The probability distribution $Pr\{A_k(t) = l | Z_N(t) \geq 1 - (b_k - 1)/N\}$ is Poisson asymptotically for $N \gg 1$ rather than exactly as it was in the generalized Erlang model. The parameter of the asymptotic Poisson distribution is derived by finding the most likely state $\mathbf{n}^*$ of the system under the blocking condition. This problem is reduced to the minimization of function (9) subject to constraint (10) as similar to (5):

$$\pi(\mathbf{n}) = c \exp\{-NU(\mathbf{x}) + O(\ln N)\}, \quad N \gg 1,$$

where $\mathbf{x} = \mathbf{n}/N$.

As before, $E_k(t)$ is approximated by the steady state loss probability $E_k \approx 1 - d^{b_k}$.

Table 3. Comparison of the approximation with simulation results for $t = 10$ with $\beta = 2$, $\mu = 1$, $\alpha = 2$ for the Engset model, and $\mu_1 = \mu_2 = 1$, $\alpha_1 = \alpha_2 = 1$, $b_1 = b_2 = 1$, $\beta_1 = 1$, $\beta_2 = 4$ for the generalized Engset model. (Simulation results show 99% confidence intervals.)

	Mean lost bandwidth			
	Engset model		Generalized Engset	
N	Approximation	Simulation	Approximation	Simulation
50	500	503 ± 0.5	500	503 ± 1
200	2,000	$1,931 \pm 0.8$	2,000	$1,931 \pm 4$

Table 3 demonstrates the very good accuracy of our approximations.

References

1. N. G. Duffield and W. Whitt, Network design and control using on-off and multi-level source traffic models with long-tailed distributions, in *Self-Similar Network Traffic and Performance Evaluation*, eds. K. Park and W. Willinger (Wiley, New York, 2000), pp. 421–445.
2. D. P. Gaver and J. P. Lehoczky, A diffusion approximation solution for a repairman problem with two types of failure, *Management Sci.* **24** (1977), 71–81.
3. J. M. Harrison and A. J. Lemoine, A note on networks of infinite-server queues, *J. Appl. Prob.* **18** (1981), 561–567.
4. F. P. Kelly, Loss networks, *Annals Appl. Prob.* **1** (1993), 319–378.
5. H. Kobayashi, *Modeling and Analysis: An Introduction to System Performance Evaluation Methodology* (Addison-Wesley, Reading, MA, 1978).
6. Y. Kogan, Asymptotic expansions for large closed and loss networks, *Math. Problems in Eng.* **8**, (2002), 323–348.
7. Y. Kogan, R. Liptser and M. Shefild, State-dependent Benes buffer model with fast loading and output rates, *Annals Appl. Prob.* **5** (1995), 97–120.
8. D. Mitra and A. Weiss, The transient behavior in Erlang's model for large trunk groups and various traffic conditions, *Proc. 12th Int. Teletraffic Congress*, Torino (1988), 5.1B4.1–5.1B4.8.
9. B. Pittel, Closed exponential networks of queues with saturation: The Jackson-type stationary distribution and its asymptotic analysis, *Math. Oper. Res.* **4** (1979), 357–378.

CHAPTER 12

Burst Loss Probabilities in an OBS Network with Dynamic Simultaneous Link Possession

Tzvetelina Battestilli[*] and Harry Perros[†]

Department of Computer Science,
North Carolina State University,
Raleigh, NC 27695, USA
[*]tbdimitr@ncsu.edu
[†]hp@ncsu.edu

In an Optical Burst Switched (OBS) network, depending on the maximum burst size, the minimum link lengths and the data rate, bursts may span two, three and even more links *simultaneously* as they travel from their source to their destination. Bursts *dynamically* move from occupying one set of links to the next by releasing a wavelength on one link and occupying a wavelength on the next link along their route. This behavior greatly differs from the widely studied packet-switched and circuit-switched networks and thus it requires the development of new performance models. In this chapter, we consider bursts, which are assumed to be long enough to occupy wavelengths on two successive links simultaneously but our analysis can be extended for bursts that hold any number of links. The burst arrival process is modeled by a two-state Markov process, called IDLE/ON, which accurately captures the burst transmission at the edge of the OBS network. We present a new queueing model which captures the *dynamic simultaneous link possession* and allows us to evaluate the burst loss probabilities of a path in an OBS network. Decomposition and state-dependent arrivals are used in order to analyze the queueing network. The approximate results were verified by simulation for a variety of input parameters and the approximation algorithm was found to have a good accuracy.

1. Introduction

OBS is a viable solution for the next generation all-optical networks. It is characterized by a strong separation between the data and the control planes. The user data and its corresponding control information are transmitted separately in time and space through the network. The control information is transmitted prior to the user data and it is electronically processed at each node along the route. On the other hand, the user data itself travels transparently as an optical signal from the source to the destination. This is advantageous because the OBS nodes just switch the optical signals without having to know any specific information about the format or the transmission rate of the user data.

In an OBS network, the data plane consists of the upper layer traffic collected by the edge OBS users. This traffic is collected, sorted based on its destination address, and assembled into variable size data units, called *bursts*. For each burst, the OBS users construct a *control packet*, which is transmitted an *offset* time prior to the transmission of the burst. The control packet travels along the route and it reserves bandwidth resources for its corresponding burst at each OBS node. Upon receipt of the control packet, the OBS node assigns a free wavelength on the desired output port and configures its switching fabric to transparently switch the upcoming burst. After the *offset* time, the burst itself is transmitted without a positive acknowledgment that the control packet has successfully reserved the required bandwidth resources at all the nodes along the route.

Because of the predicted high data rates, most OBS architectures reported in the literature support a one-way reservation scheme in order to decrease the end-to-end transmission delay. A one-way reservation leads to the possibility of burst loss within the OBS network. In other words, without a positive acknowledgment from the destination that the optical path has been set up, a burst may be dropped if it arrives at an OBS node, where the control packet was unsuccessful at reserving a wavelength on its desired output port. Therefore the calculation of the burst loss probability is an important measure of the performance of an OBS network.

Many performance evaluation studies of OBS have been reported in the literature. For example, the JET-based OBS protocol by Qiao and Yoo[1] has been studied by focusing on a single output port of an OBS node and assuming Poisson arrivals and full wavelength conversion (see Refs. 2–4). A single output port of an OBS node is modeled as an $M/G/W$ loss system, where W is the number of wavelengths per fiber. The burst loss probability is calculated using the well-known Erlang's B formula. In these papers, the authors also studied the performance of a multi-class JET, where the bursts priority is offset-based.

Other OBS studies consider the JET protocol in an OBS node with fiber delay lines (FDLs). The reason is that an FDL can buffer the optical signals for a small amount of time in the case of contention at an output port and thus reduce the probability of burst loss. Yoo et al.[3] derived a lower bound for the blocking probability by approximating an OBS output port as an $M/M/W/D$, where W is the number of wavelengths per fiber, $D = W + W * N$, and N is the number of FDLs. More recently, Lu and Mark[5] proposed a Markovian model for an OBS port with FDLs, which captures the bounded delay and the balking properties of FDL buffers.

Deflection routing has also been proposed as a strategy for contention resolution in a JET-based OBS network. Hsu et al.[6] proposed a two-stage Markovian model that approximates the behavior of deflection routing in an OBS node with a single output port. Chen et al.[7] also proposed Markovian models for deflection routing, but theirs are more general and could be applied to an OBS node with any number of output ports.

The optical composite burst switching (OCBS)[8] is another OBS architecture. In OCBS, in the case of contention only the initial part of the burst is dropped until a free wavelength becomes available. Therefore, in OCBS the loss probability is calculated in terms of the upper layer packets rather than the OBS bursts. Detti et al.[8] developed an analytical model for OCBS with an ON-OFF arrival process. Neuts et al.[9] also analyzed OCBS but they assumed a Poisson-distributed traffic arrivals which allowed them to use an $M/G/\infty$ model.

The JIT OBS signaling protocol[10] was analyzed by Xu et al.[11] using a closed queueing network model for an edge OBS node where the arrival process was a three-state Markovian model, which allowed for short and long bursts. Xu et al.[12] also analyzed the same queueing network assuming a large number of wavelengths.

Note that all of the previously cited analytical models focus on a single OBS node. These models provide a limited insight about the overall performance of an OBS network. To our knowledge, the only published analytical model of an OBS network is that by Rosberg et al.[13] Their approach is based on the reduced load fixed point approximation, where the load to each link is approximated by considering only the reduced load caused by the blocking at the previous links along the route. They consider a Poisson-distributed arrival process and assume that each burst occupies a single wavelength from each link along its route until it is lost or until it departs from the network.

Unlike the analysis by Roseberg et al.,[13] in this chapter we study an OBS network where a burst occupies *simultaneously* more than one link along its route from its source to its destination. In addition, the arrival process of bursts is modeled by a two-stage Markov process, which captures the specific operation of the burst transmission at the edge of the OBS network.

The remainder of this chapter is organized as follows. In Sec. 2, we describe the OBS network under study and in Sec. 3, we present a queueing network model of it and we describe the burst arrival process. In Sec. 4, we present a decomposition algorithm for analyzing this queueing network, and in Sec. 5 we validate our algorithm against simulation and discuss the results. We conclude in Sec. 6.

2. Problem Description

In this chapter, we calculate analytically the end-to-end burst loss probabilities of N users transmitting over a particular path in an OBS network. Each core node of the network is an optical crossconnect (OXC), which is a non-blocking optical switch such as a micro-electro-mechanical system (MEMS) or a semiconductor optical amplifier (SOA). These devices can optically switch a burst on an incoming wavelength w_1 of an input port i to the same wavelength w_1 of any output port j. We assume that each output port has a full wavelength conversion capability. That is, in the above example, if wavelength w_1 of the output port j is busy then the burst will be converted into the frequency of any other free wavelength. The burst will be dropped if all wavelengths of the output port j are busy.

The considered OBS path consists of OXCs, connected in tandem, as shown in Fig. 1. Two adjacent OXCs are linked by a single WDM fiber. Each fiber has W transmission wavelengths. There are N OBS users, which are connected to the first OXC via N separate links, each referred to as link 1. These users collect upper layer traffic, sort it based on a destination address, and assemble it into variable-size bursts. Similarly, there are N

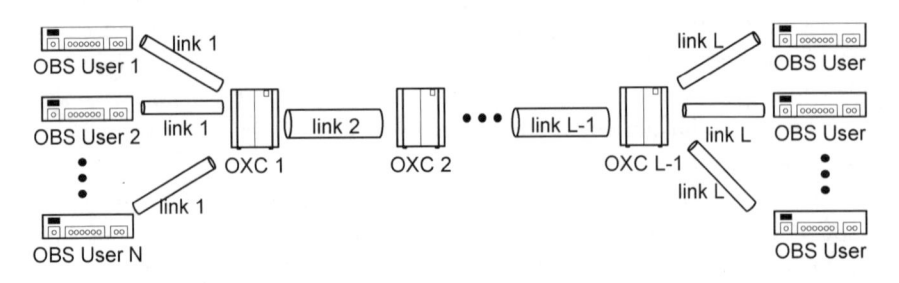

Fig. 1. Tandem OBS network.

OBS *destination* users, which are connected via N separate links to OXC $L-1$, each referred to as link L.

The size of the transmitted bursts can greatly vary and also the distance between two adjacent OXCs will vary depending on the network's topology. In view of this, it is unknown how many links each burst will occupy as it travels through the network. Short bursts will probably occupy a single link at a time but it is possible that large bursts can *simultaneously* occupy two or more links. This behavior differs from the widely studied packet-switched or circuit-switched networks. In packet-switching, a packet typically occupies a small fraction of a link in a wide-area network, due to to the high-speed of the links and the relatively small size of a packet. In contrast, in a circuit-switched network, such as a telephone network, a call simultaneously occupies one time slot on each link of the path between the source and the destination. Therefore, new techniques have to be developed in order to investigate the performance of OBS networks, where a burst may occupy more than one link, but not all the links along the path between its source and its destination.

In this chapter, we focus on large bursts which occupy two consecutive links at a time as they travel through the network. Such bursts are possible, for instance, in a WDM Metro Core network with an average link span of 250 kilometers and a transmission rate of 2.5 Gbps. Any burst larger than 390 Kb will occupy wavelengths on two consecutive links simultaneously. In the example in Fig. 1, a burst launched by a user will first occupy a wavelength on link 1 and a wavelength on link 2 simultaneously, then it will move to occupy the same wavelength on link 2 and a wavelength on link 3 simultaneously, and so on until it departs from the network.

Based on the OBS architectures reported in the literature, we assume that there are no buffers and no optical-to-electrical-to-optical conversion in the considered network. As mentioned previously, if a burst arrives at an OXC at a moment when all the outgoing wavelengths on its output port are occupied then the burst will be dropped. Therefore, the burst loss probability is an important performance measure of the operation of the considered OBS path.

3. A Queueing Network Model for an OBS Path

In order to calculate the end-to-end burst loss probabilities, we develop a queueing network model which we analyze approximately. In this section, we describe this queueing model, which is shown in Fig. 2.

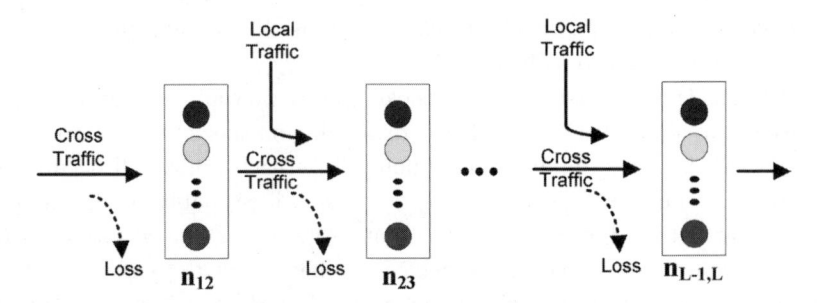

Fig. 2. The queueing network model.

Since in OBS there is no buffering, in the queueing network model there are *no* queues and burst loss is possible at each link. The queueing network consists of a number of *Erlang loss* nodes linked in tandem. Each node consists of W servers, where W is the number of wavelengths on each link. Each loss node of the queueing network represents two adjacent links of the OBS path. That is, node 12 represents links 1 and 2, node 23 represents links 2 and 3, and so on. The number of bursts $n_{i-1,i}$ in loss node $(i-1,i)$ represents the number of bursts currently occupying links $(i-1)$ and link i. For example, if $n_{12} = 2$ and $n_{23} = 1$ then there are two bursts currently being transmitted over link 1 and link 2 and one burst on link 2 and link 3 (see Fig. 3). All three bursts are currently occupying a wavelength on link 2. Note that a burst frees up a wavelength on a link as soon as its tail departs an OXC. For instance, despite the fact that the tail of burst 3 in Fig. 3 is still in link 1, a new burst can enter link 1 at the same wavelength. Similarly, as soon as the head of a burst enters a link then its assigned wavelength will be occupied for the duration of the burst. We note that a customer in our queueing network represents a burst, which always occupies a wavelength on two adjacent links at the same time. As the burst propagates through the network, the corresponding customer simply moves from one loss node of the queueing network to the next. Due to the assumption that each OBS

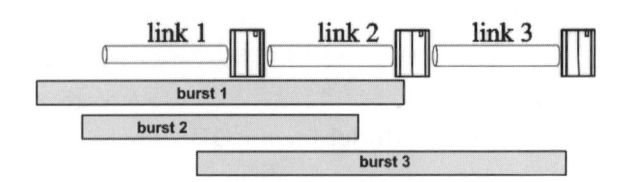

Fig. 3. Burst occupation of links.

node has a full wavelength conversion capability, a burst may occupy one wavelength on link $(i-1)$ and the same or different wavelength on link i.

The maximum capacity of each queueing node is W, which means that no more than W bursts can be transmitted over the same link at the same time. Therefore, the following constraint is true:

$$n_{ij} \leq W \quad \text{for } 1 \leq i, \ j \leq L. \tag{1}$$

Furthermore, each link of the network, with the exception of the first and the last, is represented in two consecutive nodes of the queueing network. For example, node $(i-1, i)$ and node $(i, i+1)$ both contain link i, which cannot transmit more than W bursts at one time. Therefore, the following constraint is also imposed:

$$n_{i-1,i} + n_{i,i+1} \leq W \quad \text{for } 1 < i < L. \tag{2}$$

The burst length is exponentially distributed with a mean of $1/\mu$. It is possible to model the burst length with a Coxian distribution, but this will increase the dimensionality of the queueing network.

3.1. *The arrival process*

We calculate the burst loss probability of the *cross* traffic generated by the N users, linked to OXC 1. Each user is equipped with a single tunable transmitter, which can transmit on any of the W wavelengths of link 1. The total burst arrival process is determined by the behavior of the N OBS users. If an OBS user is currently transmitting a burst then it has to wait until the current transmission is completely finished before it can start the transmission of the next burst. Therefore, the interarrival time between bursts transmitted by the same user is dependent on the time it takes to transmit a burst. We model this burst arrival process with an IDLE-ON process, which is the two-state Markov process shown in Fig. 4. An OBS user is in the ON state when it is transmitting a burst. It remains in this state for the duration of the burst, which is exponentially distributed with a mean of $1/\mu$. If the OBS user is not transmitting a burst then it is in the IDLE state which is also exponentially distributed with a mean of $1/\alpha$. Note that the IDLE-ON process differs from the popular ON-OFF process (see Ref. 14), used to model the arrival of packets. In IDLE-ON, the source transmits only *one* burst in the ON state and then it moves to the IDLE state.

The total traffic due to the N users, referred to as the *cross* traffic, is a multiplexed stream of the burst arrivals from all N OBS users. That

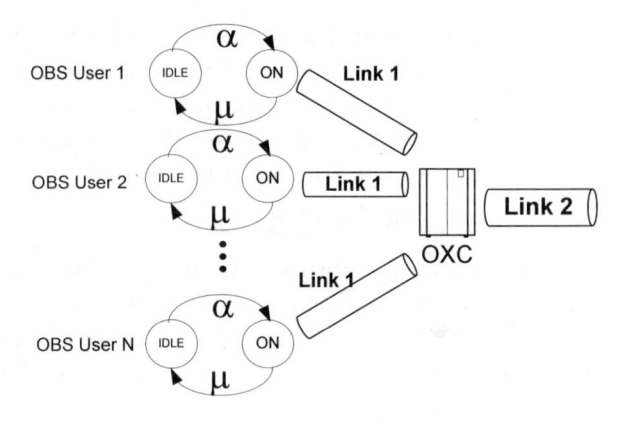

Fig. 4. Multiplexed IDLE-ON sources.

is, there are N IDLE-ON traffic sources, which generate traffic as shown in Fig. 4. We assume that all N users are modeled with an identical IDLE-ON process, i.e., each user has the same μ and α parameters. As mentioned previously, the bursts, generated by these sources, will occupy two links at once. Therefore, immediately upon entering the network, a burst will request a wavelength on link 2 and if no free wavelength is available then it will be dropped. Furthermore, only W OBS users can transmit simultaneously because even though the users own the entire bandwidth on their individual link 1, they all share the capacity of link 2. Recall that n_{12} indicates the number of bursts currently being transmitted over link 1 and 2. That is, n_{12} OBS users are in the ON state and the remaining $(N - n_{12})$ users are in the IDLE state. In view of this, the arrival rate is

$$\lambda_1(n_{12}) = (N - n_{12})\alpha, \quad 0 \leq n_{12} \leq W. \tag{3}$$

The arrival rate of the multiplexed arrival stream from the N OBS users is dependent on the current state of links 1 and 2.

In addition to the *cross* traffic, we also consider Poisson-distributed *local* traffic which loads the OBS path with extra bursts. This traffic arrives at each link, except the first one, and it subsequently becomes part of the *cross* traffic. That is, a *local* traffic burst enters the OBS path at an intermediate link and it is destined for any of the N OBS users.

Finally, we note that in the queueing model, we can also consider the case where each user is equipped with W transmitters. That is, each user can transmit simultaneously W bursts, one per wavelength. This case can easily be modeled by simply considering $N * W$ users rather than N users.

4. The Decomposition Algorithm

The queueing network, described in Sec. 3, is an *open loss queueing network*, which does not have a product form solution. However, this network possesses the Markovian property because both the duration of the bursts and their interarrival times are exponentially distributed. The underlying Markov process of this queueing network can be completely described by the tuple $(n_{12}, n_{23}, \ldots, n_{L-1,L})$, where n_{ij} is the number of customers in node ij and L is the total number of links. Depending on the size of the OBS path, however, the state space of this Markov process can become quite large. For example, an OBS path of nine links, where each link's capacity is 16 wavelengths, will result in a Markov process with 140,930,306 states. For this reason, we analyze the network approximately, by decomposing it into small sub-systems. Each sub-system is a Markov process and it is analyzed numerically. In order to analyze each sub-system, we need information from its adjacent sub-systems. This leads to a scheme where the sub-systems are analyzed iteratively. Below, we illustrate our decomposition algorithm through an example, and in Sec. 4.2 we give the general algorithm.

4.1. *An example*

We consider an OBS path, consisting of six WDM links connected in tandem. Each fiber has two wavelengths per fiber, i.e., $W = 2$. The traffic load $\lambda_1(n_{12})$ to the OBS path is generated by $N = 5$ OBS users, modeled by the multiplexed IDLE-ON process described in Sec. 3.1. Therefore, the arrival rate to link 1 is $\lambda_1(n_{12}) = (5 - n_{12})\alpha$, $0 \leq n_{12} \leq 2$. In addition, the Poisson-distributed *local traffic* at each link of the network has an average arrival rate γ.

This OBS path is modeled by the five-node tandem queueing network, shown in Fig. 5. The queueing network is decomposed into two sub-systems each containing three nodes. Sub-system 1 consists of nodes 12, 23 and 34 while sub-system 2 consists of nodes 34, 45 and 56. We note that the two sub-systems overlap with node 34 belonging to both of them.

4.1.1. *Analysis of sub-system 1*

The state of sub-system 1 can be described by a 3-tuple vector:

$$\underline{n} = (n_{12}, n_{23}, n_{34}), \tag{4}$$

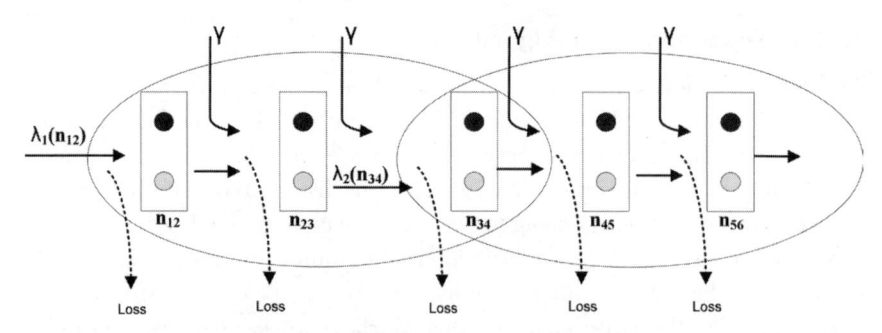

Fig. 5. Queueing network for an OBS path of six fibers with two wavelengths per fiber.

where n_{ij} represents the number of customers in node ij, $0 \leq n_{i,j} \leq W$. The state space is subject to the constraints (1) and (2) and it consists of the following states: (000), (001), (002), (010), (011), (020), (100), (101), (102), (110), (111), (200), (201), (202).

The rate matrix Q_1 for sub-system 1 is given by (5), where each diagonal element, indicated by $\star$, is the negative sum of all the non-zero transition rates on the same row:

$$Q_1 = \begin{bmatrix} \star & \gamma & 0 & \gamma & 0 & 0 & \lambda_1(0) & 0 & 0 & 0 & 0 & 0 & 0 & 0 \\ \mu & \star & \gamma & 0 & \gamma & 0 & 0 & \lambda_1(0) & 0 & 0 & 0 & 0 & 0 & 0 \\ 0 & 2\mu & \star & 0 & 0 & 0 & 0 & 0 & \lambda_1(0) & 0 & 0 & 0 & 0 & 0 \\ \mu q & \mu p & 0 & \star & \gamma & \gamma & 0 & 0 & 0 & \lambda_1(0) & 0 & 0 & 0 & 0 \\ 0 & \mu q & \mu p & \mu & \star & 0 & 0 & 0 & 0 & 0 & \lambda_1(0) & 0 & 0 & 0 \\ 0 & 0 & 0 & 2\mu q & 2\mu p & \star & 0 & 0 & 0 & 0 & 0 & 0 & 0 & 0 \\ 0 & 0 & 0 & \mu & 0 & 0 & \star & \gamma & 0 & \gamma & 0 & \lambda_1(1) & 0 & 0 \\ 0 & 0 & 0 & 0 & \mu & 0 & \mu & \star & \gamma & 0 & \gamma & 0 & \lambda_1(1) & 0 \\ 0 & 0 & \mu & 0 & 0 & 0 & 0 & 2\mu & \star & 0 & 0 & 0 & 0 & \lambda_1(1) \\ 0 & 0 & 0 & 0 & 0 & \mu & \mu q & \mu p & 0 & \star & \gamma & 0 & 0 & 0 \\ 0 & 0 & 0 & 0 & 0 & 0 & \mu & 0 & 0 & \mu q & \mu p & \mu & \star & 0 & 0 \\ 0 & 0 & 0 & 0 & 0 & 0 & 0 & 0 & 2\mu & 0 & \star & \gamma & 0 \\ 0 & 0 & 0 & 0 & 0 & 0 & 0 & 0 & 0 & 2\mu & \mu & \star & \gamma \\ 0 & 0 & 0 & 0 & 0 & 0 & 0 & 2\mu & 0 & 0 & 0 & 2\mu & \star \end{bmatrix}.$$

(5)

Note that in sub-system 1, the number of bursts at links 1, 2 or 3 can easily be calculated. The number of bursts at link 1 is simply n_{12}. Link 2 is contained in both nodes 12 and 23. Therefore, the number of bursts at link 2 is computed by adding up the number of bursts at nodes 12 and 23, i.e., $n_{12} + n_{23}$. Similarly, the number of bursts at link 3 is obtained by $n_{23} + n_{34}$.

However, in sub-system 1 we do not have enough information to determine the exact state of link 4 because we do not know the value of n_{45}.

It is necessary to know the number of bursts at link 4 in order to find out whether a burst will be dropped or not. A burst transition from node 23 to node 34 is only possible if link 4 is not completely utilized. We address this problem by conditioning some of the state transitions in sub-system 1 on sub-system 2.

Suppose that a burst is about to depart links 2 and 3 and move into links 3 and 4 and the state of sub-system 1 is currently $(1,1,1)$. There are two possibilities for that burst: it could move on successfully or it could be dropped. If the burst is successfully transmitted then the network will move into state $(1,0,2)$, and if it is lost it, will move into state $(1,0,1)$. The transition rate out of the current state is computed by using information from sub-system 2. Specifically, we find the conditional probability that link 4 is not full given that there are n_{34} bursts currently occupying links 3 and 4. Note that, node 34 is included in both sub-systems 1 and 2 and thus it must have the same value in both sub-systems. Therefore, the conditional probability p of successful burst transition from links 2 and 3 to links 3 and 4 is

$$p = Prob\{n_{45} < W - n_{34} | n_{34}\}. \qquad (6)$$

The rate of successful burst transition becomes μp. The probability that the burst is lost is $q = 1 - p$, and thus the loss transition rate is μq. Note that the probabilities in (6) come from sub-system 2. These are the values for p and q used in Q_1.

Our goal is to find the steady-state probability of each sub-system, which we denote by $\underline{\pi}_i$, $i = 1$ or 2. The steady-state probability vector $\underline{\pi}_i$ is obtained by solving the following linear equations in matrix form:

$$\underline{\pi}_1 \underline{Q}_1 = \mathbf{0}, \qquad (7)$$

$$\underline{\pi}_1 \underline{e}_1 = \mathbf{1}, \qquad (8)$$

where (8) is the normalization condition and $\underline{e}_1 = (1, 1, \ldots, 1)^T$. This system of linear equations is solved using the well-known Gauss–Seidel method (see Ref. 15).

4.1.2. *Analysis of sub-system 2*

Sub-system 2 is analyzed in the same way as sub-system 1. To this effect, we need to determine the arrival process to sub-system 2, which consists of the cross traffic which departs from links 2 and 3 and attempts to enter links 3 and 4 in addition to the Poisson-distributed local traffic γ at link 3.

Note that the departure rate of the cross traffic from node 23 is

$$\lambda_2(n_{23}) = n_{23}\mu, \quad 0 \leq n_{23} \leq W \tag{9}$$

Unfortunately, we cannot use Eq. (9) in sub-system 2 since we do not know the value of n_{23}. Instead, we express this departure rate as a function of n_{34}:

$$\lambda_2(n_{34}) = \sum_{j=0}^{W} Prob\{n_{23} = j | n_{34}\} j\mu \quad \text{for } 0 \leq n_{34} \leq W, \tag{10}$$

where the conditional probabilities $Prob\{n_{23} = j|n_{34}\}$ are calculated utilizing $\underline{\pi}_1$. With the addition of the local traffic, the total arrival rate to sub-system 2 becomes $\lambda_2^{tot}(n_{34}) = \lambda_2(n_{34}) + \gamma$. Note, that this arrival rate is *state-dependent*.

Having calculated $\lambda_2^{tot}(n_{34})$, we can analyze sub-system 2 following the same procedure as subsystem 1. The transition rate matrix for sub-system 2, is the same as (5) with the exceptions that $p = 1$, $q = 0$ and $\lambda_1(n_{12})$ is replaced by $\lambda_2^{tot}(n_{34})$. Once again, each diagonal element, indicated by $\star$, is the negative sum of the all the other non-zero elements on the same row. The rate matrix for sub-system 2 is given by

$$Q_2 = \begin{bmatrix} \star & \gamma & 0 & \gamma & 0 & 0 & \lambda_2^{tot}(0) & 0 & 0 & 0 & 0 & 0 & 0 & 0 \\ \mu & \star & \gamma & 0 & \gamma & 0 & 0 & \lambda_2^{tot}(0) & 0 & 0 & 0 & 0 & 0 & 0 \\ 0 & 2\mu & \star & 0 & 0 & 0 & 0 & 0 & \lambda_2^{tot}(0) & 0 & 0 & 0 & 0 & 0 \\ 0 & \mu & 0 & \star & \gamma & \gamma & 0 & 0 & 0 & \lambda_2^{tot}(0) & 0 & 0 & 0 & 0 \\ 0 & 0 & \mu & \mu & \star & 0 & 0 & 0 & 0 & 0 & \lambda_2^{tot}(0) & 0 & 0 & 0 \\ 0 & 0 & 0 & 0 & 2\mu & \star & 0 & 0 & 0 & 0 & 0 & 0 & 0 & 0 \\ 0 & 0 & 0 & \mu & 0 & 0 & \star & \gamma & 0 & \gamma & 0 & \lambda_2^{tot}(1) & 0 & 0 \\ 0 & 0 & 0 & 0 & \mu & 0 & \mu & \star & \gamma & 0 & \gamma & 0 & \lambda_2^{tot}(1) & 0 \\ 0 & 0 & \mu & 0 & 0 & 0 & 0 & 2\mu & \star & 0 & 0 & 0 & 0 & \lambda_2^{tot}(1) \\ 0 & 0 & 0 & 0 & 0 & \mu & 0 & \mu & 0 & \star & \gamma & 0 & 0 & 0 \\ 0 & 0 & 0 & 0 & \mu & 0 & 0 & \mu & \mu & \mu & \star & 0 & 0 & 0 \\ 0 & 0 & 0 & 0 & 0 & 0 & 0 & 0 & 0 & 2\mu & 0 & \star & \gamma & 0 \\ 0 & 0 & 0 & 0 & 0 & 0 & 0 & 0 & 0 & 0 & 2\mu & \mu & \star & \gamma \\ 0 & 0 & 0 & 0 & 0 & 0 & 0 & 0 & 2\mu & 0 & 0 & 0 & 2\mu & \star \end{bmatrix}.$$

(11)

Once Q_2 is generated, we can find $\underline{\pi}_2$ by solving the linear equations $\underline{\pi}_2 \underline{Q}_2 = 0$ using the Gauss–Seidel method and applying the normalization condition $\underline{\pi}_2 \underline{e}_2 = 1$, where $\underline{e}_2 = (1, 1, \ldots, 1)^T$.

4.1.3. *The iterative procedure*

After we have solved for the steady-state probabilities of the two subsystems, we execute the steps of the algorithm once again. First, we solve for a new $\underline{\pi}_1$, using p and q calculated based on the current known value for $\underline{\pi}_2$. Then, we calculate a new state-dependent arrival rate to sub-system 2 and solve for a new value for $\underline{\pi}_2$. We repeat these steps iteratively until the solution for $\underline{\pi}_1$ and $\underline{\pi}_2$ converges.

4.2. The decomposition algorithm

In this section, we outline the generalized decomposition algorithm, applicable to an OBS path with any number of links. We note that the superscript refers to the iteration number.

(i) The queueing network is decomposed into sub-systems, where each sub-system consists of three or two nodes and two consecutive sub-systems overlap by a single node. Let the number of sub-systems be denoted by s.

Iteration 1:

(ii) For the first sub-system:
- Generate $Q_1^{(1)}$ by using $\lambda_1^{(1)}(n_{12})$ as in Eq. (3) and setting $p^{(1)} = 1$ and $q^{(1)} = 0$. Solve for $\underline{\pi}_1^{(1)}$.

(iii) For sub-system j, where $2 \leq j \leq s$:
- Calculate the state-dependent arrival rate $\lambda_j^{(1)}(n_{j,j+1})$ to this sub-system by using $\underline{\pi}_{j-1}^{(1)}$ and Eq. (10).
- Generate $Q_j^{(1)}$ by using $\lambda_j^{(1)}(n_{j,j+1})$ and setting $p^{(1)} = 1$ and $q^{(1)} = 0$. Solve for $\underline{\pi}_j^{(1)}$.

Iteration i:

(iv) For the first sub-system:
- Generate $Q_1^{(i)}$ by using $\lambda_1^{(i)}(n_{12})$ and calculating $p^{(i)}$ and $q^{(i)}$ with Eq. (6) based on $\underline{\pi}_2^{(i-1)}$. Solve for $\underline{\pi}_1^{(i)}$.

(v) For sub-system j, $2 \leq j \leq (s-1)$:
- Calculate the state-dependent arrival $\lambda_j^{(i)}(n_{j,j+1})$ to this sub-system by using $\underline{\pi}_{j-1}^{(i)}$ and Eq. (10).
- Generate $Q_j^{(i)}$ by using $\lambda_j^{(i)}(n_{j,j+1})$ and calculating $p^{(i)}$ and $q^{(i)}$ with Eq. (6) based on $\underline{\pi}_{j+1}^{(i-1)}$. Solve for $\underline{\pi}_j^{(i)}$.

(vi) For the last sub-system:

- Calculate the state-dependent arrival $\lambda_s^{(i)}(n_{s,s+1})$ to this sub-system by using $\underline{\pi}_{s-1}^{(i)}$ and Eq. (10).
- Generate $Q_s^{(i)}$ by using $\lambda_s^{(i)}(n_{s,s+1})$ and setting $p^{(i)} = 1$ and $q^{(i)} = 0$. Solve for $\underline{\pi}_s^{(i)}$.

(vii) Repeat from Step (iv) until the steady-state probabilities $\underline{\pi}_j$ converge:

$$|\underline{\pi}_j^{(i)} - \underline{\pi}_j^{(i-1)}| < \epsilon, \quad 1 \le j \le s, \quad \epsilon = 10^{-6}.$$

Note that if the number of nodes in the queueing network is even, then the last sub-system will contain only two nodes. The analysis of a two-node sub-system is identical to a three-node sub-system. In fact, a sub-system with two nodes results in a smaller state space, which is faster to analyze.

The previously described decomposition of three nodes per sub-system with *single node overlap* results in a small number of sub-systems while keeping the state space of the sub-system manageable. We also considered a decomposition of three nodes per sub-system with *double node overlap*, i.e., two consecutive sub-systems overlap by two nodes. This type of decomposition had a slightly higher accuracy but increased the execution time because the total number of sub-systems increased. The number of states for a sub-system with three nodes is in the order of $O(W^3)$ and it is given by

$$(W+1)^2 + \frac{W(2W+1)(W+1)}{6}. \tag{12}$$

An alternative decomposition strategy is to use two nodes per sub-system with *single node overlap*. Using two nodes per sub-system, we can greatly increase the number of wavelengths per fiber and still have a manageable state space. The number of states for a sub-system of two nodes is in the order of $O(W^2)$ and therefore OBS networks with much greater number of wavelengths can be analyzed. The number of states for a two-node per subsystem decomposition is given by

$$\frac{(W+1)(W+2)}{2}. \tag{13}$$

The accuracy of this two-node decomposition was not tested, but it is expected to be less than that of the three-node decomposition. That is due to the fact that in general, the larger the sub-system, the better the accuracy of the decomposition algorithm.

4.3. Calculation of the burst loss probability

A burst is lost if it arrives at a moment when there are no free wavelengths available at its required links. That is, the burst loss probability is the probability that there are no free wavelengths and there is a burst arrival. Let us denote with b_i the cross traffic burst loss probability at link i. For presentation purposes, we use the example in Fig. 5 to show how the burst loss probabilities b_i are calculated. We note that there is no cross traffic loss on link 1 or link 6, since each of these links is dedicated to a user.

Burst Loss Probability b_2 at link 2:

The burst loss probability of the cross traffic at link 2 is given by

$$b_2 = Prob\{Link\ 2\ is\ full\ |\ Arrival\ to\ node\ 12\}$$
$$= \sum_{i=0}^{W} Prob\{n_{23} = W - i, n_{12} = i\} \frac{(N-i)\alpha}{\lambda_{12}^{(avg)}}, \quad (14)$$

where all the probabilities are obtained from $\underline{\pi}_1$, and $\lambda_{12}^{(avg)}$ is the average arrival rate to node 12 and it is given by

$$\lambda_{12}^{(avg)} = \sum_{i=0}^{W} Prob\{n_{12} = i\}(N-i)\alpha. \quad (15)$$

Burst Loss Probability b_3 at link 3:

The burst loss probability of the cross traffic at link 3 is given by

$$b_3 = Prob\{Link\ 3\ is\ full\ |\ Departure\ from\ node\ 12\}$$
$$= \sum_{i=0}^{W} Prob\{n_{23} + n_{34} = W, n_{12} = i\} \frac{i\mu}{\lambda_{23}^{(avg)}}. \quad (16)$$

All the probabilities in the above expression come from $\underline{\pi}_1$ and $\lambda_{23}^{(avg)}$ is the average cross traffic arrival rate to node 23, which is obtained by

$$\lambda_{23}^{(avg)} = \sum_{i=0}^{W} Prob\{n_{12} = i\}i\mu. \quad (17)$$

Burst Loss Probability b_4 at link 4:

The cross traffic burst loss probability at link 4 is given by

$$b_4 = Prob\{Link\ 4\ is\ full\ |\ Departure\ from\ node\ 23\}$$
$$= \sum_{i=0}^{W} Prob\{n_{45} = W - i, n_{34} = i\} \frac{\lambda_2(i)}{\lambda_{34}^{(avg)}}, \tag{18}$$

where the probabilities come from $\underline{\pi}_2$, $\lambda_2(i)$ is the state-dependent cross traffic arrival rate to sub-system 2, and $\lambda_{34}^{(avg)}$ is its average, given by

$$\lambda_{34}^{(avg)} = \sum_{i=0}^{W} Prob\{n_{34} = i\}\lambda_2(i). \tag{19}$$

Burst Loss Probability b_5 at link 5:

The burst loss probability at link 5 is calculated the exact same way as for link 3 but all the information comes from $\underline{\pi}_2$.

5. Numerical Results

We now present numerical results for the *cross* traffic burst loss probability at each link of an OBS path by utilizing our decomposition algorithm. We verify our analytical results by comparing them to simulation results, obtained with our self-developed discrete, event-driven simulator. For all the simulation results, we run each scenario 30 times and for all the performance measures we find their 95% confidence intervals. Note that the simulation results are plotted along with their 95% confidence intervals but the confidence intervals are quite small and hardly visible on the plots.

We consider an OBS path of eight links, i.e., $L = 8$, which we model as a tandem queueing network of seven Erlang loss nodes. Each link has $W = 16$ wavelengths and there are 32, i.e., $N = 32$, OBS users each modeled by an IDLE-ON source. The intensity of the cross traffic is varied based on the time spent in the IDLE state, i.e., based on the value of α. The local arrivals are Poisson-distributed and their average rate is the same at each point of the OBS path, i.e., $\gamma = 0.5$. The analytical results are obtained by decomposing the queueing network into three sub-systems each containing three nodes and overlapping by a single node.

In Fig. 6, we plot the burst loss probability b_i at each link i, where $i = 2, 3, \ldots, 7$ for various values of α. The plot verifies that our analytical results match quite closely the results obtained through simulation. The absolute errors of the burst loss probabilities at each link are given in

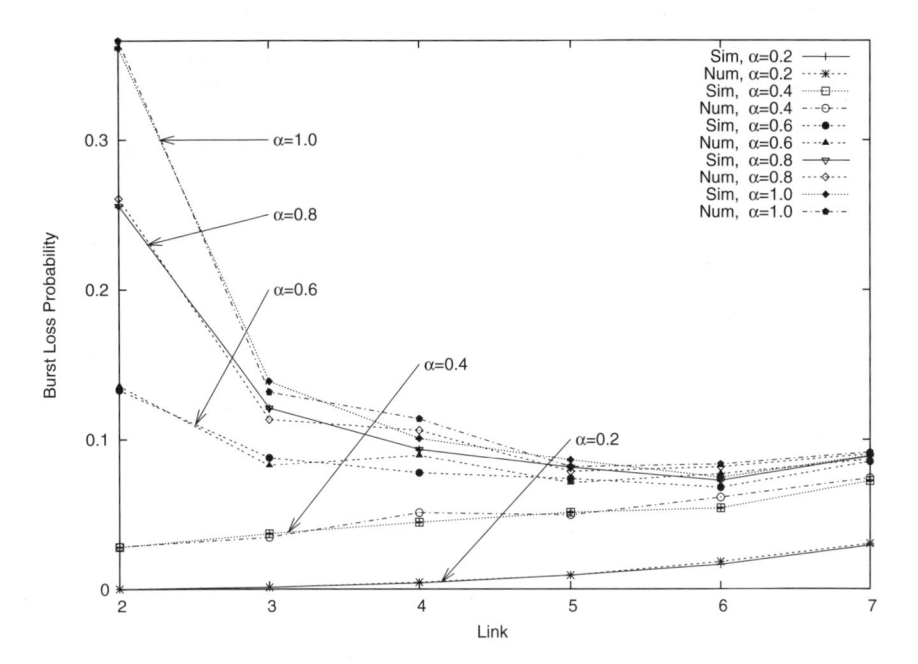

Fig. 6. Burst loss probability for $W = 16, N = 32, \gamma = 0.5$.

Table 1. Absolute errors of burst loss probabilities at each link.

Link	Max error	Min error	Average error
2	0.00487	0.00002	0.00254
3	0.00763	0.00006	0.00450
4	0.01307	0.00043	0.00891
5	0.00457	0.00009	0.00235
6	0.00907	0.00193	0.00720
7	0.00235	0.00109	0.00169

Table 1. There is a slightly higher error at links 4 and 6, whose burst loss probabilities are calculated at the overlap nodes between the three subsystems as described in Sec. 4.3. The slightly higher error is due to the approximation used in calculating the state-dependent arrivals.

We observe a *filtering effect* of the burst loss probabilities. That is, as we increase the load at the front of the OBS path, the burst loss probability at link 2 rapidly increases but that phenomenon does not carry over to the other links in the path. Each link acts as a filter because it drops some of its incoming bursts and thus the load to the following link is reduced.

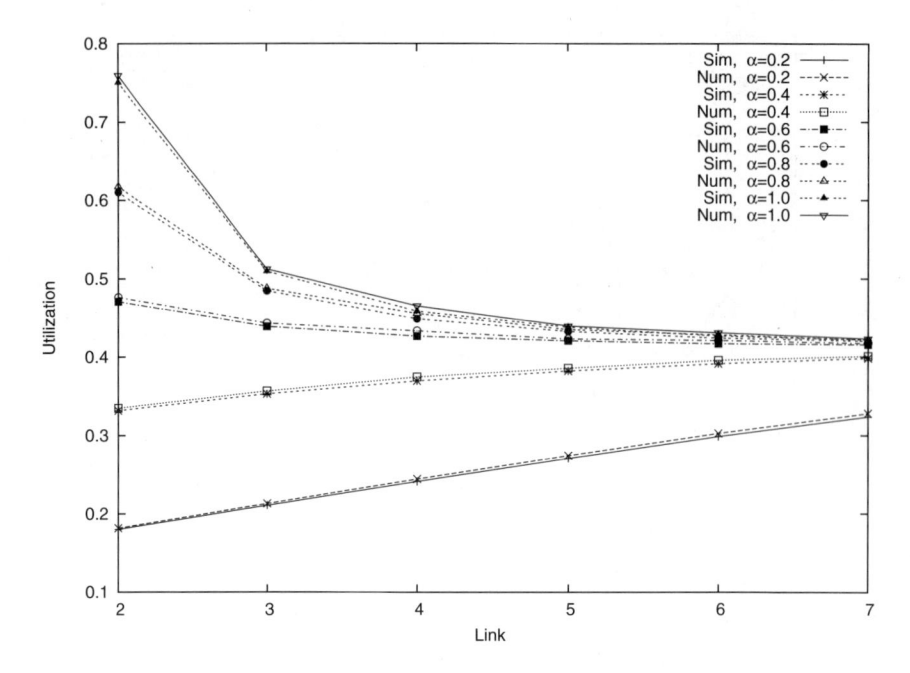

Fig. 7. Utilization $\lambda/(\mu W)$ for $W = 16, N = 32, \gamma = 0.5$.

In addition, there is a tendency for the burst loss probability to slightly increase from link 2 to link 7, which is caused by local arrivals at each link. The reason is that any local traffic burst that is not lost at the link where it arrives is carried on as part of the cross traffic to the following link. We do not plot the cross traffic burst loss at links 1 and 8 because it is zero.

We also plot the utilization $\lambda/(\mu W)$ of each link in Fig. 7. We observe that at the lower traffic intensity the link utilization increases from link 2 to link 7 because of the added local arrivals. However, as we increase the cross traffic intensity, the utilization of links 5, 6 and 7 converges. Once again, that is explained by the previously noted filtering effect.

We also investigate the effects of increasing the number of OBS users N, by setting the idle rate to a constant and removing the local arrivals, i.e., $\alpha = 0.2$ and $\gamma = 0$. The results are given in Fig. 8. We observe that increasing the number of OBS users increases the burst loss probability. In addition, for a particular value of N, the lack of local arrivals leads to burst loss probability that gradually decreases from link 2 to link 7.

Finally, in Fig. 9 we compare the simulation results for the burst loss probability in the case where bursts hold only a wavelength on a single link

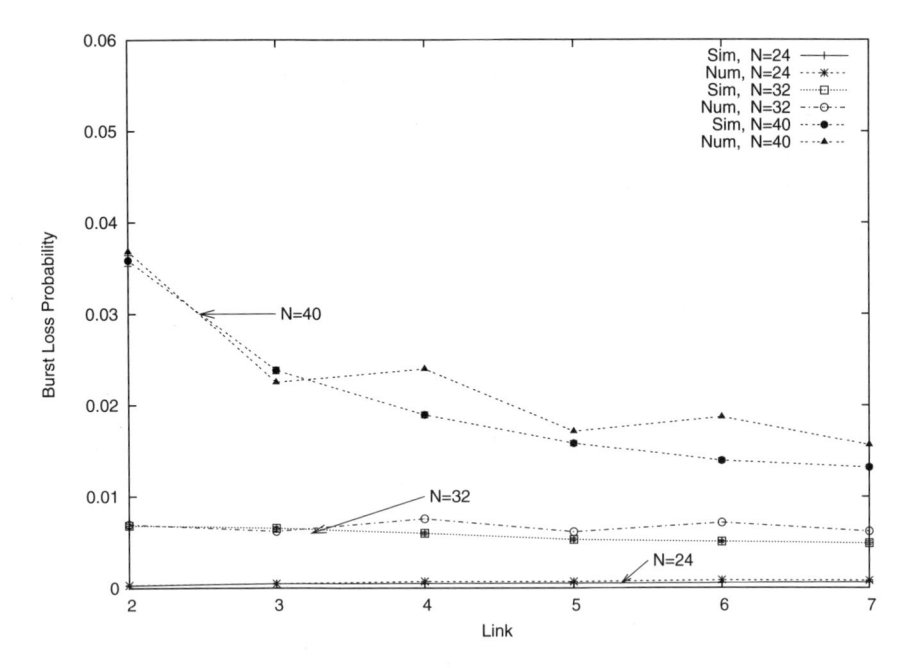

Fig. 8. Burst loss probability for $W = 16, \alpha = 0.2, \gamma = 0$.

at a time to the case where bursts require a wavelength on two consecutive links. We keep all the other input parameters constant. We observe that the OBS path with bursts which occupy two wavelengths on two consecutive links has a considerably higher burst loss probability because each burst requires more network resources. Therefore, in order to correctly evaluate the performance of an OBS network, it is necessary to determine whether or not bursts will span multiple links.

6. Conclusions

We have developed an analytical model of a path in an OBS network with dynamic simultaneous resource possession. We focused on bursts that simultaneously possess wavelengths on two consecutive links, but our analysis can be extended to solve networks where bursts span more than two links at a time. In a real OBS network, there will be a mix of bursts that span one, two or even three links simultaneously. This chapter is the first step toward our goal of analyzing an OBS network with a mix of bursts that span different numbers of links. We analytically analyzed this OBS path by constructing an open queueing network with IDLE-ON arrival process. We developed a

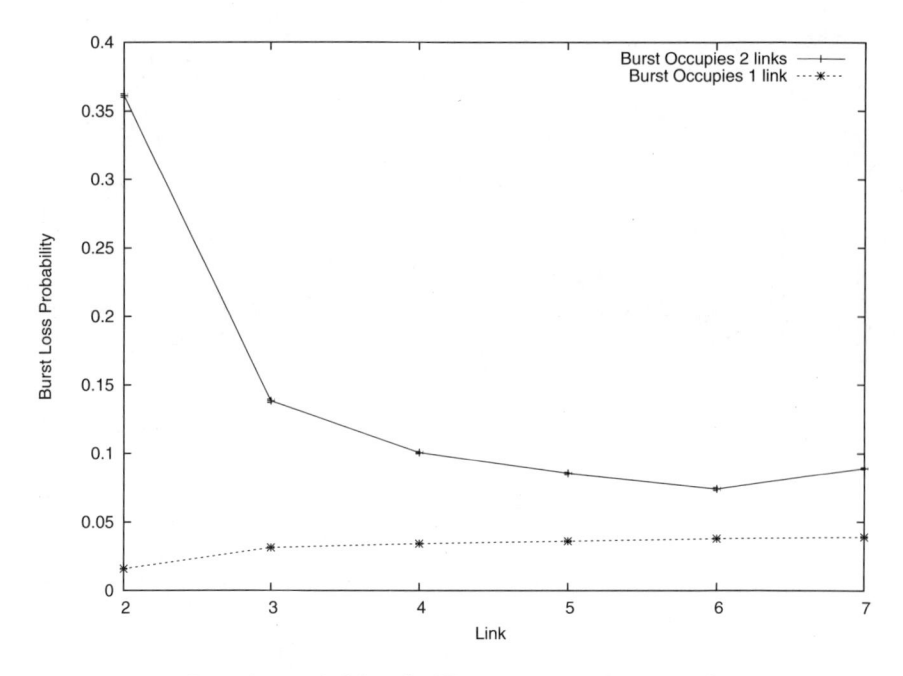

Fig. 9. Burst loss probability for $W = 16, \gamma = 0.5, N = 32$ and $\alpha = 0.5$.

decomposition algorithm and we calculated the end-to-end burst loss probabilities at each link of the OBS path. The accuracy of our algorithm was verified by simulation. We found a *filtering effect* on the traffic due to the burst losses at each link, which cannot be accurately captured in studies of a single OBS node. In addition, we found that the burst loss probability is much higher in the case where bursts occupy two links at a time compared to the case where each burst possesses a wavelength on single link.

References

1. C. Qiao and M. Yoo, Optical burst switching (OBS) — A new paradigm for an optical Internet, *J. High Speed Networks* **8**(1) (January 1999), 69–84.
2. K. Dolzer, C. Gauger, J. Spath and S. Bodamer, Evaluation of reservation mechanisms for optical burst switching, *AEU Int. J. Electronics and Communications* **55**(1) (January 2001), 18–26.
3. M. Yoo, C. Qiao and S. Dixit, QoS performance of optical burst switching in IP-over-WDM networks selected areas in communications, *IEEE J. on Areas in Communications* **18**(10) (October 2000), 2062–2071.
4. H. Le Vu and M. Zukerman, Blocking probability for priority classes in optical burst switching networks, *IEEE Communications Letters* **6**(5) (May 2002), 214–216.

5. X. Lu and B. L. Mark, A new performance model of optical burst switching with fiber delay lines, in *Proc. IEEE Int. Conf. Communications (2003. ICC '03)*, Vol. 2 (May 2003), pp. 1365–1369.
6. C.-F. Hsu, T.-L. Liu and N.-F. Huang, On the deflection routing in QoS supported optical burst-switched networks, *IEEE Int. Conf. Communications* **5** (2002), 2786–2790.
7. Y. Chen, H. Wu, D. Xu and C. Qiao, Performance analysis of optical burst switched node with deflection routing, in *Proc. IEEE Int. Conf. Communications (2003. ICC '03)*, Vol. 2 (May 2003), pp. 1355–1359.
8. A. Detti, V. Eramo and M. Listanti. Performance evaluation of a new technique for IP support in a WDM optical network: Optical composite burst switching (OCBS), *IEEE J. Lightwave Technology* **20**(2) (February 2002), 154–165.
9. M. Neuts, Z. Rosberg, H. Le Vu, J. White and M. Zukerman, Performance analysis of optical composite burst switching, *IEEE Communications Letters* **6**(8) (August 2002), 346–348.
10. J. Wei and R. McFarland, Just-in-time signaling for WDM optical burst switching networks, *J. Lightwave Technology* **18**(12) (December 2000), 2019–2037.
11. L. Xu, H. G. Perros and G. N. Rouskas, A queueing network model of an edge optical burst switching node, in *Proc. IEEE Infocom 2003*, San Francisco, CA (April 2003), pp. 2019–2029.
12. L. Xu, H. G. Perros and G. N. Rouskas, Performance analysis of an edge optical burst switching node with a large number of wavelengths, in *Proc. 18th Int. Teletraffic Congress (ITC-18)*, Berlin, Germany, August 31–September 5 (2003), pp. 891–900.
13. Z. Rosberg, H. Le Vu, M. Zukerman and J. White, Performance analyses of optical burst-switching networks, *IEEE J. Selected Areas in Communications* **21**(7) (September 2003), 1187–1197.
14. V. S. Frost and B. Melamed, Traffic modeling for telecommunications networks, *IEEE Communications Magazine* **32**(3) (March 1994), 70–81.
15. W. J. Stewart, *Introduction to the Numerical Solution of Markov Chains* (Princeton University Press, 1994).

CHAPTER 13

Stochastic Analysis of Resource Allocation in Parallel Processing Systems

Mark S. Squillante

Mathematical Sciences Department,
IBM Thomas J. Watson Research Center,
Yorktown Heights, NY 10598, USA
mss@watson.ibm.com

We derive an exact matrix-analytic analysis of a general stochastic model of parallel processing systems under dynamic spacesharing, which yields a closed-form solution for certain model instances. An analysis of a general nearly completely decomposable model of parallel program memory reference behavior is also derived, which provides measures of the distribution of the memory overhead incurred by a parallel program as a function of its server allocation. These theoretical results can be exploited to investigate the design and performance space of parallel processing systems with respect to fundamental tradeoffs related to the server and memory allocation strategies and their interactions.

1. Introduction

Stochastic modeling and related queueing-theoretic results have played a fundamental role in the design of scheduling strategies of both theoretical and practical interest. This has especially been the case in single-server queues; refer to Refs. 16, 20, 39, 46 and 59 and the references cited therein. Some important principles have also been derived for parallel-server queues, but these results have been restricted to certain parallel processing systems, such as those with customers having serial service demands (e.g., Refs. 4, 5, 41, 52 and 58) or parallel fork-join service demands (e.g., Refs. 24, 25, 29, 45, 53).

With the significant advances of computer and communication technology and the considerable development of parallel scientific and engineering applications, several classes of scheduling strategies have emerged over time each differing in the way the parallel servers are shared among the parallel jobs submitted for execution. Our present study seeks to derive stochastic modeling and related queueing-theoretic results for some of these classes of scheduling strategies. Of particular theoretical and practical interest, and the focus of this chapter, is the class of spacesharing strategies that share the parallel servers in space by partitioning them among different parallel jobs. This is based on the widespread use of spacesharing in parallel processing systems, possibly in combination with other strategies.[15,48] We do not consider the classes of scheduling strategies that combine spacesharing with different forms of timesharing, where the servers are shared by rotating them among a set of jobs in time. See Refs. 42, 44, 54 and 56 and the references therein for a stochastic analysis of various scheduling strategies based on both spacesharing and timesharing.

A number of empirical studies have demonstrated the benefits and superiority of dynamic spacesharing over other forms of spacesharing strategies in single-class parallel processing systems where jobs are statistically identical and have sublinear speedup characteristics, and no prior knowledge of service time characteristics is available or used in scheduling decisions; refer to Refs. 13, 19, 26, 27, 32 and 60 and the references cited therein. We therefore focus on this important class of scheduling strategies in which the number of servers allocated to a parallel job can be adjusted dynamically throughout its execution in response to changes in the state of the system. In particular, dynamic spacesharing tends to decrease the number of servers allocated to jobs with increasing system loads in order to increase the efficiency of parallel execution at heavier traffic intensities. The assumption that parallel applications are malleable, in the sense that their server allocations can be changed at any time, provides the greatest flexibility with respect to the scheduling of such applications. (See Refs. 15 and 48 and the references therein for a discussion on other types of parallel application models.) This flexibility and its benefits, however, are gained at some cost as the reallocation, or reconfiguration, of the servers among a set of jobs under dynamic spacesharing causes the system to incur various overhead penalties. In fact, the fundamental parallel scheduling tradeoff between the benefits of dynamic spacesharing and its costs is central to the design and performance of dynamic scheduling in parallel processing systems.

The memory requirements of parallel applications are another critical factor in the design and performance of dynamic scheduling in parallel processing systems; refer to Refs. 28, 33, 34, 36 and 43 and the references cited therein. More specifically, the working set size of a parallel job on each of the servers allocated to it increases with reductions in the size of this server allocation, since the job's memory requirements are spread over fewer servers. Reducing the number of servers allocated to a sufficiently large job below a certain point can cause excessive memory overhead as the job's working set on each server no longer fits in the server's local memory, thus increasing the number of page faults incurred by the job. While dynamic spacesharing strategies decrease the server allocation size with increasing system loads, memory considerations in parallel processing systems tend to argue in the opposite direction. Hence, there is a fundamental tradeoff between the impact of program efficiency towards allocating fewer servers to jobs at heavier traffic intensities and the performance impact of memory requirements towards larger allocations. This tradeoff is also central to the design and performance of dynamic scheduling in parallel processing systems. We therefore derive stochastic modeling and related queueing-theoretic results on the memory requirements of parallel applications at each of the servers allocated to them in our analysis of dynamic spacesharing.

In this chapter, we formulate a general stochastic model of parallel processing systems under dynamic spacesharing. An exact matrix-analytic analysis of this model is derived, which yields closed-form solutions under certain instances of the model based on their probabilistic structure. We also derive expressions for several performance measures of interest, including the tail distribution of the queue length process and its asymptotic decay rate, the mean sojourn time of parallel jobs, and the long-run proportion of time the system spends reconfiguring the allocation of servers among the jobs. These stochastic modeling and analysis results generalize and extend those presented in Ref. 51. In this chapter, we also formulate and derive an analysis of a general nearly completely decomposable model of parallel program memory reference behavior that introduces and analyzes the inter-locality miss ratio which includes the memory overhead caused by the reloading of pages upon return visits to localities (especially in iterative programs), as well as a more accurate representation of the page faults due to transitions between localities. This stochastic analysis solves a fundamental problem with previous nearly completely decomposable models and analyses that had remained open since the early 1970s. The results of our analysis are then used to construct a probability distribution for the total memory overhead incurred by a parallel program as a function of its server allocation, which can be directly incorporated in our analysis of parallel processing systems under dynamic spacesharing. These stochastic modeling and analysis results generalize and extend those presented in Ref. 36.

The remainder of the chapter is organized as follows. In Sec. 2, we present our parallel processing system model. A matrix-analytic analysis of this model and a nearly completely decomposable analysis of the corresponding memory overheads are derived in Secs. 3 and 4, respectively. Our concluding remarks are provided in Sec. 5. Throughout the chapter, we shall use $\mathbb{Z}^+$ and $\mathbb{Z}_+$ to denote the set of positive and non-negative integers, respectively, with $\mathbb{R}^+$ and $\mathbb{R}_+$ denoting the corresponding subsets of real numbers. Furthermore, the term *partition* will be used to refer to a (disjoint) set of servers allocated to a single parallel job.

2. Model of Parallel Processing Systems

Consider a parallel processing system that consists of P identical servers, each having its own local memory, under a single-class parallel application workload with sublinear speedup characteristics. The servers are scheduled according to a dynamic spacesharing strategy that attempts to equally allocate the servers among a set of parallel jobs, where no information about service time characteristics is used in making scheduling decisions. Let U denote the minimum number of servers allocated to any parallel job, and therefore the maximum number of server partitions is given by $N = \lfloor P/U \rfloor$. Upon the arrival of a job when the system is executing i jobs, $0 \leq i < N$, the P servers are repartitioned among the set of $i+1$ jobs such that each job is allocated a server partition either of size $\lfloor P/(i+1) \rfloor$ or of size $\lceil P/(i+1) \rceil$. Arrivals that find $i \geq N$ jobs in the system are placed in a first-come first-serve infinite-capacity queue to wait until a server partition becomes available. When one of the i jobs in the system departs, $2 \leq i \leq N$, the system reconfigures the server allocations among the remaining $i-1$ jobs such that there are only partitions of sizes $\lfloor P/(i-1) \rfloor$ and $\lceil P/(i-1) \rceil$. A departure when the system contains more than N jobs simply causes the job at the head of the queue to be allocated the available server partition, and no reconfiguration is performed. Every parallel job is executed to completion without interruption and all of the servers in the partition are reserved by the application throughout this duration.

Parallel jobs are assumed to arrive from an exogenous source according to a Markovian Arrival Process (MAP)[21,31] having descriptors $(\mathcal{S}_0^A, \mathcal{S}_1^A)$ of order $m^A < \infty$ with (positive) mean rate $\lambda = (\mathbf{x}\mathcal{S}_1^A\mathbf{e})^{-1} < \infty$, where $\mathbf{e}$ denotes the column vector of appropriate dimension containing all ones and $\mathbf{x}$ is the invariant probability vector of the generator $\mathcal{S}^A = \mathcal{S}_0^A + \mathcal{S}_1^A$, i.e., the (unique) solution of $\mathbf{x}\mathcal{S}^A = \mathbf{0}$ and $\mathbf{xe} = 1$. (Our results can be easily extended to handle a batch MAP (BMAP) arrival process using standard methods.[21,31,51]) The parallel service times depend upon the number of servers allocated to the jobs. When executed on partitions of size p, the service times of the parallel jobs are assumed to be independent and identically distributed (i.i.d.) following an order $m_p^B < \infty$ phase-type distribution[21,30] with parameters $(\underline{\beta}_p, \mathcal{S}_p^B)$ and (positive) mean $\mu_p^{-1} = -\underline{\beta}_p(\mathcal{S}_p^B)^{-1}\mathbf{e} < \infty$, $p \in \{U, \ldots, P\}$. The times required to repartition the servers among the i jobs to be executed (either due to a departure when the system contains $i+1$ jobs or an arrival when the system contains $i-1$ jobs) are assumed to be i.i.d. according to a phase-type distribution having parameters $(\underline{\zeta}_i, \mathcal{S}_i^C)$ of order $m_i^C < \infty$ with (positive) mean $\gamma_i^{-1} = -\underline{\zeta}_i(\mathcal{S}_i^C)^{-1}\mathbf{e} < \infty$, $i \in \{1, \ldots, N\}$. All of the above stochastic processes are assumed to be mutually independent.

The execution behavior of the parallel jobs on each possible server allocation is an important aspect of any parallel processing model. Our formulation takes the general approach of modeling the execution behavior of the parallel jobs by a separate probability distribution for each possible number of servers p, $p \in \{U, \ldots, P\}$. This supports the inclusion of any factors that may affect the execution behavior of the parallel applications of interest (e.g., see Refs. 14, 23, 37, 38, 47 and 48 and the references therein), especially given the known closure properties of phase-type distributions such as the convolution of a finite number of phase-type distributions being phase-type.[21,30] The only requirement we have is that there exists a probabilistic mapping from the residual life of the service demands on each server allocation at the point of a reconfiguration to any other possible server allocation within the same collection of phase-type distributions. Using this mapping, the details of the relatively complex server allocation decisions that can be made by the dynamic spacesharing strategy in each case, as well as the overheads of making these decisions and of reconfiguring the applications involved, are captured in the probability distributions and the state transitions of the corresponding stochastic process. Moreover, the memory overheads incurred by a parallel job as a function of the dynamic scheduling decisions can be captured directly in the corresponding service time distributions as described in Sec. 4.

The use of MAPs and phase-type distributions for all model parameters is of theoretical importance in that we exploit their properties to derive an exact solution of our general parallel processing model. It is also of practical importance in that, since the class of phase-type distributions is dense within the set of probability distributions on $[0, \infty)$, and since the class of MAPs provides a similar general framework for capturing the dependence structure and variability of a process, any stochastic process on this space for the parallel processing systems of interest can in principle be represented arbitrarily closely by a MAP or a phase-type distribution. Moreover, a considerable body of research has examined the fitting of phase-type distributions and MAPs to empirical data, and a number of algorithms have been developed for doing so; refer to Refs. 1 and 22 and the references cited therein. This includes recent work that has considered effectively approximating long-range dependent and heavy-tailed behaviors with instances of the classes of MAPs and phase-type distributions in order to analyze performance models. By appropriately setting the parameters of our model, a wide range of parallel application and system environments can be investigated.[15,48] In particular, the subexponential tails of the marginal interarrival distribution and the dependence structure of the interarrival process found in some parallel processing systems[55] can be captured by a MAP. Furthermore, most of the results of our analysis in the next section will continue to hold when the order of the MAP and phase-type distributions m^A, m_p^B and m_i^C are infinite, under a proper formulation.

3. Analysis of Dynamic Spacesharing

The parallel processing model of the previous section can be represented by a continuous-time stochastic process $\{X(t); t \in \mathbb{R}_+\}$ on the state space given by $\Omega = \bigcup_{i=0}^{\infty} \Omega_i$, where $\Omega_0 \equiv \{(0, \bar{j}^A) \mid \bar{j}^A \in \omega^A\}$, $\Omega_i \equiv \{(i, \bar{j}^A, \bar{j}_{-,\ell}^B, \bar{j}_{+,\ell}^B, \bar{j}_\ell^C) \mid i \in \mathbb{Z}^+, \bar{j}^A \in \omega^A, \bar{j}_{w,\ell}^B \in \omega_{w,\ell}^B, w \in \{-,+\}, \ell = \min\{i, N\}, j_\ell^C \in \{0, \ldots, m_\ell^C\}\}$, $\omega^A \equiv \{(j_c^A, j_h^A, j_p^A) \mid j_c^A \in \{1, \ldots, m_c^A\}, j_h^A \in \{1, \ldots, m_h^A\}, j_p^A \in \{1, \ldots, m_p^A\}\}$, $\omega_{w,\ell}^B \equiv \{(j_{w,\ell,1}^B, j_{w,\ell,2}^B, \ldots, j_{w,\ell,m_{\hat{n}}^B}^B) \mid j_{w,\ell,k}^B \in \{0, \ldots, \mathcal{P}_w^\ell\}, k \in \{1, \ldots, m_{\hat{n}}^B\}, \sum_{k=1}^{m_{\hat{n}}^B} j_{w,\ell,k}^B = \mathcal{P}_w^\ell, \hat{n} = n_w^\ell, w \in \{-,+\}\}$, $n_+^\ell \equiv \lceil P/\ell \rceil$, $n_-^\ell \equiv \lfloor P/\ell \rfloor$, $\mathcal{P}_+^\ell \equiv \mod(P/\ell)$, $\mathcal{P}_-^\ell \equiv \ell - \mathcal{P}_+^\ell$, for $\ell \in \{1, \ldots, N\}$. The state-vector variable i denotes the total number of parallel jobs in the system; $\bar{j}^A$ denotes the state of the MAP arrival process; $j_{w,\ell,k}^B$ denotes the number of jobs executing on n_w^ℓ servers whose service time process is in phase k; and j_ℓ^C denotes the phase of the reconfiguration overhead process when $j_\ell^C \in \{1, \ldots, m_\ell^C\}$ and it indicates no reconfiguration when $j_\ell^C = 0$ (i.e., the ℓ parallel jobs are executing). Moreover, n_-^ℓ and n_+^ℓ represent the two partition sizes when the system contains i jobs, for $\ell = \min\{i, N\}$, and $\mathcal{P}_w^\ell$ denotes the number of such partitions of size n_w^ℓ, for $w \in \{-,+\}$.

Let $x_{i,d} \in \Omega_i$, $d \in \{1, \ldots, D_i\}$, $i \in \mathbb{Z}_+$, be a lexicographic ordering of the elements of Ω_i, and define $D \equiv \sum_{i=0}^{N-1} D_i$, where $D_i = |\Omega_i|$. The set Ω_i is also called the ith level of the process. We then define $\boldsymbol{\pi} \equiv (\boldsymbol{\pi}_0, \boldsymbol{\pi}_1, \boldsymbol{\pi}_2, \ldots)$, $\boldsymbol{\pi}_i \equiv (\pi(x_{i,1}), \pi(x_{i,2}), \ldots, \pi(x_{i,D_i}))$ and $\pi(x_{i,d}) \equiv \lim_{t \to \infty} \mathbb{P}[X(t) = x_{i,d}]$, $i \in \mathbb{Z}_+$, $x_{i,d} \in \Omega_i$, $d \in \{1, \ldots, D_i\}$. The limiting probability vector $\boldsymbol{\pi}$ is the stationary distribution for the stochastic process $\{X(t); t \in \mathbb{R}_+\}$. Assuming this process to be irreducible and positive recurrent, the invariant probability vector is uniquely determined by solving the global balance equations $\boldsymbol{\pi}\mathbf{Q} = \mathbf{0}$ together with the normalizing constraint $\boldsymbol{\pi}\mathbf{e} = 1$, where $\mathbf{Q}$ is the infinitesimal generator matrix for the process.

The generator matrix $\mathbf{Q}$, organized in the same order as the elements of $\boldsymbol{\pi}$, has a structure given by

$$\mathbf{Q} = \begin{bmatrix} \mathbf{B}_{00} & \mathbf{B}_{01} & 0 & 0 & 0 & \cdots \\ \mathbf{B}_{10} & \mathbf{B}_{11} & \mathbf{A}_0 & 0 & 0 & \cdots \\ 0 & \mathbf{A}_2 & \mathbf{A}_1 & \mathbf{A}_0 & 0 & \cdots \\ 0 & 0 & \mathbf{A}_2 & \mathbf{A}_1 & \mathbf{A}_0 & \cdots \\ \vdots & \vdots & \vdots & \vdots & \vdots & \ddots \end{bmatrix}, \quad (1)$$

where $\mathbf{B}_{00}, \mathbf{B}_{01}, \mathbf{B}_{10}, \mathbf{B}_{11}$ and $\mathbf{A}_n$, $n = 0, 1, 2$, are finite matrices of dimensions $D \times D$, $D \times D_N$, $D_N \times D$, $D_N \times D_N$ and $D_N \times D_N$, respectively. The matrices corresponding to the non-homgeneous boundary of the state space Ω have the structures

$$\mathbf{B}_{00} = \begin{bmatrix} \Psi_0 & \Lambda_0 & 0 & 0 & \cdots & 0 & 0 \\ \Phi_1 & \Psi_1 & \Lambda_1 & 0 & \cdots & & \\ 0 & \Phi_2 & \Psi_2 & \Lambda_2 & \cdots & \vdots & \vdots \\ \vdots & \vdots & \vdots & \vdots & \ddots & & \\ 0 & 0 & 0 & 0 & \cdots & \Phi_{N-1} & \Psi_{N-1} \end{bmatrix}, \quad \mathbf{B}_{01} = \begin{bmatrix} 0 \\ 0 \\ \vdots \\ 0 \\ \Lambda_{N-1} \end{bmatrix}, \quad (2)$$

$$\mathbf{B}_{10} = \begin{bmatrix} 0 & 0 & \cdots & 0 & \Phi_N \end{bmatrix}, \qquad \mathbf{B}_{11} = \Psi_N, \quad (3)$$

where Φ_i, Ψ_i and Λ_i have dimensions $D_i \times D_{i-1}$, $D_i \times D_i$ and $D_i \times D_{i+1}$, respectively. The matrix Φ_i defines the transitions from states in Ω_i to states in Ω_{i-1}, $i \in \{1, \ldots, N\}$, Λ_i defines the transitions from states in Ω_i to states in Ω_{i+1}, $i \in \{0, \ldots, N-1\}$, and the off-diagonal elements of Ψ_i define the transitions between states within Ω_i, $i \in \{0, \ldots, N\}$. These level-dependent matrices define the exact server allocation behavior of the dynamic spacesharing strategy under consideration, the arrival, service and reconfiguration processes of the workload being modeled, and the various interactions of each of these aspects of the system. The same holds true for the $\mathbf{A}$ matrices with respect to the homogeneous portion of the state space.

Let $sp(\mathbf{C})$ denote the spectral radius of a matrix $\mathbf{C}$ and let $\mathbf{I}$ denote the identity matrix of appropriate dimension. The stationary probability vector

$\boldsymbol{\pi}$ of the process $\{X(t); t \in \mathbb{R}_+\}$ with generator $\mathbf{Q}$ then can be obtained from the following standard matrix-analytic results (see Theorems 1.7.1 and 1.5.1 in Ref. 30).

Theorem 1. *Let $\mathbf{Q}$ be irreducible and in the form of (1). This stochastic process is positive recurrent if and only if $sp(\mathbf{R}) < 1$, where $\mathbf{R}$ is the minimal non-negative matrix that satisfies*

$$\mathbf{R}^2\mathbf{A}_2 + \mathbf{R}\mathbf{A}_1 + \mathbf{A}_0 = \mathbf{0}. \tag{4}$$

Furthermore, there exists a positive vector $(\boldsymbol{\pi}_0, \boldsymbol{\pi}_1, \ldots, \boldsymbol{\pi}_N)$ such that

$$(\boldsymbol{\pi}_0, \boldsymbol{\pi}_1, \ldots, \boldsymbol{\pi}_N) \begin{bmatrix} \mathbf{B}_{00} & \mathbf{B}_{01} \\ \mathbf{B}_{10} & \mathbf{B}_{11} + \mathbf{R}\mathbf{A}_2 \end{bmatrix} = \mathbf{0}. \tag{5}$$

The remaining components of the invariant probability vector $\boldsymbol{\pi}$ are then given by

$$\boldsymbol{\pi}_{N+n} = \boldsymbol{\pi}_N \mathbf{R}^n, \quad n \in \mathbb{Z}_+, \tag{6}$$

where $(\boldsymbol{\pi}_0, \boldsymbol{\pi}_1, \ldots, \boldsymbol{\pi}_N)$ is normalized by

$$(\boldsymbol{\pi}_0, \boldsymbol{\pi}_1, \ldots, \boldsymbol{\pi}_{N-1})\mathbf{e} + \boldsymbol{\pi}_N(\mathbf{I} - \mathbf{R})^{-1}\mathbf{e} = 1. \tag{7}$$

The time and space complexities of computing (5) and (7) can be significantly reduced with the use of the following matrix-analytic results.[17,18,50,56]

Theorem 2. *Let $\mathbf{Q}$ be irreducible and in the form of (1) through (3). If the minimal non-negative solution $\mathbf{R}$ of (4) satisfies $sp(\mathbf{R}) < 1$, and if there exists a positive probability vector $(\boldsymbol{\pi}_0, \ldots, \boldsymbol{\pi}_N)$ satisfying (5), then the components of this probability vector are given by*

$$\boldsymbol{\pi}_n = -\boldsymbol{\pi}_{n+1}\Phi_{n+1}\tilde{\mathbf{R}}_n^{-1}, \quad n \in \{0, \ldots, N-1\}, \tag{8}$$

$$\boldsymbol{\pi}_N = -\boldsymbol{\pi}_{N-1}\Lambda_{N-1}\tilde{\mathbf{R}}_N^{-1}, \tag{9}$$

where $\tilde{\mathbf{R}}_0 \equiv \Psi_0$, $\tilde{\mathbf{R}}_n \equiv \Psi_n - \Phi_n\tilde{\mathbf{R}}_{n-1}^{-1}\Lambda_{n-1}$, $n \in \{1, \ldots, N-1\}$, $\tilde{\mathbf{R}}_N \equiv \Psi_N + \mathbf{R}\mathbf{A}_2$. Furthermore, when $N > 1$, the vector $\boldsymbol{\pi}_{N-1}$ can be determined up to a multiplicative constant by solving

$$\boldsymbol{\pi}_{N-1}[\Psi_{N-1} - \Phi_{N-1}\tilde{\mathbf{R}}_{N-2}^{-1}\Lambda_{N-2} - \Lambda_{N-1}\tilde{\mathbf{R}}_N^{-1}\Phi_N] = \mathbf{0}, \tag{10}$$

$$\boldsymbol{\pi}_{N-1}\mathbf{e} = \theta, \quad \theta > 0. \tag{11}$$

Otherwise, when $N = 1$, the vector π_1 can be determined up to a multiplicative constant by solving

$$\pi_1[\tilde{\mathbf{R}}_1 - \Phi_1 \tilde{\mathbf{R}}_0^{-1} \Lambda_0] = \mathbf{0}, \tag{12}$$

$$\pi_1 \mathbf{e} = \theta, \quad \theta > 0. \tag{13}$$

In either case, the vector $(\pi_0, \pi_1, \ldots, \pi_N)$ then can be obtained from (8), (9) and the normalizing equation (7).

3.1. Irreducibility and stability criterion

While the irreducibility of the stochastic process $\{X(t); t \in \mathbb{R}_+\}$ is often obvious, it can be verified for any specific instance of our model by determining whether the first $N+2$ levels of the state space (the boundary plus the first level of the homogeneous portion) and the corresponding transitions among these states, when viewed as a directed graph, is strongly connected. This follows directly from the fact that transitions between the states of levels $N+1$ and $N+2$ are identical to those between the states of levels N and $N+1$, and the fact that the process is skip-free to the right and to the left with respect to levels. Hence, upon verifying that the non-homogeneous boundary plus the first level of the homogeneous portion is irreducible, it follows that the entire process is irreducible.

The stability conditions for the system are provided in Theorem 1. When the generator matrix $\mathbf{A} \equiv \mathbf{A}_0 + \mathbf{A}_1 + \mathbf{A}_2$ is irreducible, Neuts[30] determined the following necessary and sufficient conditions for $sp(\mathbf{R}) < 1$.

Theorem 3. *Let the generator $\mathbf{A}$ be irreducible. Then $sp(\mathbf{R}) < 1$ if and only if*

$$\mathbf{y}\mathbf{A}_0 \mathbf{e} < \mathbf{y}\mathbf{A}_2 \mathbf{e}, \tag{14}$$

where $\mathbf{y}$ is the stationary probability vector of $\mathbf{A}$.

3.2. Special case: Exponential model parameters

We now consider instances of the model where U evenly divides P and the interarrival time, service time and reconfiguration overhead distributions are all exponential, and obtain closed-form expressions for the elements of the $\mathbf{R}$ matrix satisfying (4). In this case, we have $\mathbf{A}_0 = \lambda \mathbf{I}$, $\mathbf{A}_1 = \begin{bmatrix} -(\lambda + \mu_N) & 0 \\ \gamma_N & -(\lambda + \gamma_N) \end{bmatrix}$ and $\mathbf{A}_2 = \begin{bmatrix} \mu_N & 0 \\ 0 & 0 \end{bmatrix}$. Note further that the generator $\mathbf{Q}$ has the form given in (1) with $D_0 = 1$, $D_i = 2$, $i \in \{1, \ldots, N\}$, and $D = 2N - 1$.

The probabilistic significance of the element $r_{u,v}$ of the matrix $\mathbf{R} \equiv [r_{u,v}]_{u,v \in \{0,1\}}$ is the expected amount of time spent in the state $(i+1, v)$ before the first return to any state of level i, expressed in units of the mean sojourn time for the state (i, u), given that the process started in state (i, u),[30] $i \geq N$. Upon uniformizing $\{X(t); t \in \mathbb{R}_+\}$ to obtain an equivalent discrete-time version $\{X_t^0; t \in \mathbb{Z}_+\}$ with the corresponding $\mathbf{R}^0 \equiv [r_{u,v}^0]_{u,v \in \{0,1\}}$, where

$$r_{u,v} = \left(\frac{r_{u,v}^0}{\delta_{v,v}}\right)\delta_{u,u}, \quad u,v \in \{0,1\}, \tag{15}$$

and $\Delta \equiv [\delta_{u,v}]_{u,v \in \{0,1\}} = -\mathbf{diag}(\mathbf{A}_1)$, the probabilistic interpretation of the element $r_{u,v}^0$ is the expected number of visits to the state $(i+1, v)$ before the first return to any state of level i, given that the process started in state (i, u),[30] $i \geq N$. We then have the following result for the exponential case of our parallel processing model.

Theorem 4. *Let $\mathbf{Q}$ be irreducible and in the form of (1), under exponential distributions for the model parameters and with U evenly dividing P. Then this stochastic process is positive recurrent if and only if*

$$\frac{\lambda}{\mu_N} < 1, \tag{16}$$

and the elements of the minimal non-negative matrix $\mathbf{R}$ satisfying (4) are given by

$$r_{0,0} = \frac{\lambda}{\mu_N}, \tag{17}$$

$$r_{0,1} = 0, \tag{18}$$

$$r_{1,0} = \frac{\lambda}{\mu_N}, \tag{19}$$

$$r_{1,1} = \frac{\lambda}{\lambda + \gamma_N}. \tag{20}$$

Proof. Equation (18) follows directly from the probabilistic interpretation of $r_{0,1}$ and the fact that there are no paths from the state $(i, 0)$ to the state $(i+1, 1)$, which do not first visit a state of level i, $i > N$. Now consider the uniformized process $\{X_t^0; t \in \mathbb{Z}_+\}$ starting in state $(i, 0)$, $i > N$, observing that the only transitions involving the probabilistic interpretation of $r_{0,0}^0$

in this process are from $(v,0)$ to $(v+1,0)$ with probability $\lambda(\lambda+\mu_N)^{-1}$ and from $(v,0)$ to $(v-1,0)$ with probability $\mu_N(\lambda+\mu_N)^{-1}$, $v \geq i$. The expected number of visits to $(i+1,0)$ before the first return to $(i,0)$ in this case is then given by $\mu_N(\lambda+\mu_N)^{-1}\sum_{n=0}^{\infty} n(\lambda/(\lambda+\mu_N))^n$, and thus $r_{0,0}^0 = \lambda/\mu_N$, which in combination with (15) yields (17). Next consider the uniformized process $\{X_t^0; t \in \mathbb{Z}_+\}$ starting in state $(i,1)$, $i > N$, and note that this process makes 0 visits to state $(i+1,0)$ before returning to level i with probability $\gamma_N(\lambda+\gamma_N)^{-1}$ and otherwise makes $1+n$ visits to state $(i+1,0)$ before returning to level i with probability $\lambda(\lambda+\gamma_N)^{-1}\mu_N(\lambda+\mu_N)^{-1}(\lambda/(\lambda+\mu_N))^n$, $n \in \mathbb{Z}_+$. The expected number of visits to $(i+1,0)$ before the first return to level i in this case is then given by $\lambda(\lambda+\gamma_N)^{-1}\mu_N(\lambda+\mu_N)^{-1}\sum_{n=0}^{\infty}(n+1)(\lambda/(\lambda+\mu_N))^n$, yielding $r_{1,0}^0 = \lambda(\lambda+\gamma_N)^{-1}[\lambda/\mu_N+1]$ from which, together with (15), we obtain (19). Now consider the uniformized process $\{X_t^0; t \in \mathbb{Z}_+\}$ starting in state $(i,1)$, $i > N$, observing that this process makes 0 visits to state $(i+1,1)$ before returning to level i with probability $\gamma_N(\lambda+\gamma_N)^{-1}$ and otherwise makes only 1 visit to state $(i+1,1)$ before returning to level i with probability $\lambda(\lambda+\gamma_N)^{-1}$. Hence, $r_{1,1}^0 = \lambda(\lambda+\gamma_N)^{-1}$, which in combination with (15) yields (20). Finally, the matrix $\mathbf{R}$ is lower triangular, and thus its eigenvalues are given by its diagonal elements. Since $r_{1,1}$ is always less than 1 with $\gamma_N > 0$, it follows from Theorem 1 that the stability criterion is given by (16). □

Intuitively, the condition $\lambda < \mu_N$ ensures a positive recurrent process because, given $\gamma_N > 0$, the expected drift of the system in the homogeneous portion of the state space is toward level N when $\lambda < \mu_N$.

3.3. Performance measures

Using the components of the invariant vector $\boldsymbol{\pi}$, we can obtain various performance measures of interest. In particular, the tail distribution of the queue length process can be expressed as

$$\mathbb{P}[Q > z] = \begin{cases} \sum_{n=z+1}^{N-1} \boldsymbol{\pi}_n \mathbf{e} + \sum_{n=N}^{\infty} \boldsymbol{\pi}_n \mathbf{e} = \sum_{n=z+1}^{N-1} \boldsymbol{\pi}_n \mathbf{e} + \boldsymbol{\pi}_N(\mathbf{I}-\mathbf{R})^{-1}\mathbf{e}, \\ \qquad 0 \leq z < N-1, \\ \sum_{n=z+1}^{\infty} \boldsymbol{\pi}_n \mathbf{e} = \boldsymbol{\pi}_N \mathbf{R}^{z+1-N}(\mathbf{I}-\mathbf{R})^{-1}\mathbf{e}, \\ \qquad z \geq N-1, \end{cases} \quad (21)$$

with the corresponding expectation given by

$$\mathbb{E}[Q] = \sum_{n=1}^{N-1} n\pi_n \mathbf{e} + \sum_{n=0}^{\infty} (N+n)\pi_{N+n}\mathbf{e} = \sum_{n=1}^{N-1} n\pi_n\mathbf{e}$$
$$+ N\pi_N(\mathbf{I}-\mathbf{R})^{-1}\mathbf{e} + \pi_N\mathbf{R}(\mathbf{I}-\mathbf{R})^{-2}\mathbf{e}. \qquad (22)$$

The expected sojourn time of a job can then be calculated using Little's law[59] and (22), which yields

$$\mathbb{E}[T] = \lambda^{-1}\left(\sum_{n=1}^{N-1} n\pi_n\mathbf{e} + N\pi_N(\mathbf{I}-\mathbf{R})^{-1}\mathbf{e} + \pi_N\mathbf{R}(\mathbf{I}-\mathbf{R})^{-2}\mathbf{e}\right). \qquad (23)$$

The asymptotic decay rate of the tail distribution of the queue length process is another measure of interest. Let η denote this decay rate, which is also called the caudal characteristic.[31] Note that $\eta = sp(\mathbf{R})$ under the assumptions of this chapter. Let $\mathbf{u}$ and $\mathbf{v}$ be the left and right eigenvectors corresponding to η that are strictly positive and normalized by $\mathbf{ue} = 1$ and $\mathbf{uv} = 1$. Under the assumptions herein, it is well known that[40]

$$\mathbf{R}^z = \eta^z \mathbf{v}\cdot\mathbf{u} + \mathrm{o}(\eta^z), \quad \text{as } z\to\infty,$$

which together with (6) yields

$$\pi_{N+z}\mathbf{e} = \pi_N\mathbf{v}\,\eta^z + \mathrm{o}(\eta^z), \quad \text{as } z\to\infty. \qquad (24)$$

It then follows that

$$\mathbb{P}[Q \geq N+z] = \frac{\pi_N\mathbf{v}}{1-\eta}\eta^z + \mathrm{o}(\eta^z), \quad \text{as } z\to\infty, \qquad (25)$$

and thus

$$\lim_{z\to\infty}\frac{\mathbb{P}[Q\geq N+z]}{\eta^z} = \frac{\pi_N\mathbf{v}}{1-\eta}, \qquad (26)$$

or equivalently

$$\mathbb{P}[Q \geq N+z] \sim \frac{\pi_N\mathbf{v}}{1-\eta}\eta^z, \quad \text{as } z\to\infty, \qquad (27)$$

where $f(z) \sim g(z)$ denotes that $\lim_{z\to\infty} f(z)/g(z) = 1$. Hence, in addition to providing the stability criterion for the parallel processing system, η is indicative of the tail behavior of the stationary queue length distribution.

Note that the caudal characteristic can be obtained without having to first solve for the matrix $\mathbf{R}$. Define the matrix $\mathbf{A}^*(s) \equiv \mathbf{A}_0 + s\mathbf{A}_1 + s^2\mathbf{A}_2$, for $0 < s \leq 1$. When the generator matrix $\mathbf{A}$ is irreducible, this matrix $\mathbf{A}^*(s)$ is irreducible with non-negative off-diagonal elements. Let $\chi(s)$ denote the spectral radius of the matrix $\mathbf{A}^*(s)$. Then, under the above assumptions, η is the unique solution in $(0, 1)$ of the equation $\chi(s) = 0$. This solution can be directly computed, although more efficient methods have been developed.[3]

Another performance measure of interest is the long-run proportion of time the system spends executing reconfigurations. This can be expressed as

$$p_r = (\pi_0, \pi_1, \ldots, \pi_{N-1})\nu_b + \sum_{n=0}^{\infty} \pi_{N+n}\nu_r$$
$$= (\pi_0, \pi_1, \ldots, \pi_{N-1})\nu_b + \pi_N(\mathbf{I} - \mathbf{R})^{-1}\nu_r, \qquad (28)$$

where the vth position of the vector ν_b (respectively, ν_r) contains a 0 if $j_\ell^C = 0$ in the corresponding state of the boundary (respectively, homogeneous portion) and contains a 1 otherwise (i.e., when $j_\ell^C \in \{1, \ldots, m_\ell^C\}$).

4. Analysis of Memory Reference Behavior

Our analysis of dynamic spacesharing in the previous section does not explicitly include the memory requirements of parallel applications as a function of the number of servers allocated to the applications. This requires a stochastic analysis of the memory reference behavior of the parallel programs at each server allocated to them, which in turn depends upon the parallel processing system and parallel applications of interest.

In this section, we derive such an analysis for a general class of parallel processing systems and parallel applications whose memory reference behaviors are consistent with the findings of many empirical studies since the early 1970s of serial applications on single-server systems. Specifically, the parallel program behavior tends to consist of (not necessarily disjoint) locality phases that clearly dominate the fraction of total memory references and transitions that account for a considerable fraction of the program's page faults. Phase periods tend to be of much longer duration than transition periods, but both phases and transitions are of equal importance in the program's memory reference behavior. While these properties may differ from those found in parallel environments where the entire memory reference set at each server must be entirely loaded in the physical memory of the server,[6,28,33,34,43] they indeed have been shown to hold for an important class of computationally-intensive parallel applications that consist of numerical computations on large amounts of data in an iterative manner.[35,36]

A classical approach to derive a stochastic analysis of memory reference behavior consists of formulating a nearly completely decomposable model of program behavior that exploits its locality properties and obtaining an approximate solution of the model using the methods of decomposition and aggregation; see Refs. 2 and 9 and the references therein. The model solution is based on extensions of the Simon–Ando approximations for the stationary probabilities of the corresponding Markov chain. This solution is then used to estimate the miss ratios of a program as a function of the physical memory capacity, which are computed as weighted sums of the miss ratios for the individual locality phases where the weights correspond to the long-run proportion of time the program spends in the respective localities. Error bounds also can be obtained within this framework, e.g., refer to Refs. 10 and 57.

On the other hand, the iterative nature of the parallel applications of interest cause program localities to be visited multiple times in some, potentially non-deterministic, manner. This aspect of parallel programs is not taken into account in any of the previous models of program behavior, even though the impact of this behavior on system performance can be quite significant.[36] The reason for this is easily illustrated with a simple example. Consider a program consisting of multiple localities whose sizes are individually less than, but cumulatively greater than, the physical memory capacity. Previous modeling approaches, including those in Refs. 2 and 9 and their references, will yield a miss ratio of zero in this case because the miss ratio for each locality is zero and thus the weighted sum (for any set of weights) is zero. However, if the program iterates among the different locality phases then it can experience a significant memory overhead as potentially large portions of each locality are reloaded upon return to the locality. This represents a fundamental problem with previous nearly completely decomposable models and analyses of the memory reference behavior of programs that remained open since the early 1970s until it was first observed and addressed in Ref. 36. While our focus here is on parallel processing systems and parallel applications, our solution to this longstanding open problem and corresponding results are completely general and can be applied in any computing environment with the foregoing program behavior properties, especially given the large size of physical memory in contemporary computer systems.

4.1. *Program behavior models*

We now develop models of memory reference behavior that are used to approximate the paging overhead incurred by a program on each server allocated to it. This consists of modeling the memory reference behavior of the program at each server and deriving approximations for the corresponding miss ratio realized by the program when executed with a finite capacity memory. The page replacement policy defines which page currently residing in memory will be replaced upon the reference to a page that is not in memory, and thus it determines the set of pages that are in memory at any given time. Computer systems, including the servers comprising parallel processing systems, often employ (or approximate) the least recently used (LRU) replacement algorithm in which the page chosen for replacement is the one that has not been referenced for the longest time. We therefore assume an LRU page replacement algorithm.

There has been a significant amount of research concerning the stochastic modeling and analysis of the page reference behavior of programs; see Refs. 2, 8, 9, 11, 12 and 49 and the references therein. The independent reference model (IRM) has many advantages from the mathematical modeling viewpoint, but this model can produce very poor approximations in practice because it does not capture any concept of locality. In fact, IRM goes to the other extreme by assuming that the probability of the next page reference is independent of the page currently being referenced. The LRU stack model (LRUSM), on the other hand, specifies the distribution for the inter-stack distances in an LRU stack. While this model can be parametrized to give a high probability for referencing the pages at (or near) the top of the stack, it still does not capture the idea that there could be sudden jumps between localities, which has been empirically shown to occur in real programs, nor does it capture changing locality sizes. In our study, we use the Markov reference model (MRM) of program behavior because it captures quite well the concepts of program locality and dynamic transitions between localities during program execution.

The page reference string generated by a program, denoted by a sequence $\{Y_n; n \in \mathbb{Z}_+\}$, is assumed to be a realization of a time-homogeneous Markov process with irreducible page transition matrix $[p_{ij}]$ where

$$p_{ij} = \mathbb{P}[Y_{n+1} = j \mid Y_n = i].$$

The miss ratio is defined as the ratio of the total number of page faults to the total number of references. Let $LRU(n)$ denote the set of all pages in the LRU stack after the nth reference. Then we can calculate the page fault probability as

$$\lim_{n \to \infty} \mathbb{P}[Y_{n+1} \notin LRU(n)].$$

Assuming the measurement interval to be sufficiently long, the miss ratio converges to the page fault probability.

Computing the page fault probability directly from the probability transition matrix $\mathbf{P} = [p_{ij}]$ can be prohibitively expensive both in terms of time and space. This is due to the fact that the computation involves a sum over each of the states of the LRU stack, which grows exponentially. This direct approach, however, ignores the important properties of program behavior. The structural properties of this behavior result in a type of system that has been termed nearly completely decomposable by Simon and Ando.[9] We reduce the complexity of the problem at hand by exploiting these structural properties to facilitate our analysis of the dynamic behavior of parallel programs.

Assume for the moment that the program localities are disjoint and that no additional pages are referenced in transition from one locality to the next. Arrange the rows and columns of the probability transition matrix $\mathbf{P}$ such that the pages of each locality are grouped together consecutively. We then block partition $\mathbf{P}$ according to these locality sets, which yields the following structure

$$\mathbf{P} = \begin{bmatrix} \mathbf{P}_{11} & \mathbf{P}_{12} & \cdots & \mathbf{P}_{1L} \\ \mathbf{P}_{21} & \mathbf{P}_{22} & \cdots & \mathbf{P}_{2L} \\ \vdots & \vdots & \ddots & \vdots \\ \mathbf{P}_{L1} & \mathbf{P}_{L2} & \cdots & \mathbf{P}_{LL} \end{bmatrix},$$

where $\mathbf{P}_{IJ}$ defines transitions from pages in locality $I \in \{1, \ldots, L\}$ to pages in locality $J \in \{1, \ldots, L\}$, and L denotes the number of program localities. It follows from the locality property of program behavior that the submatrices along the main diagonal (i.e., $\mathbf{P}_{11}, \ldots, \mathbf{P}_{LL}$) consist of relatively large probability measures, while the elements of the other submatrices are very small in comparison (i.e., $\mathbf{P}_{IJ} \approx \mathbf{0}, J \neq I$).

Matrices of this type are called nearly completely decomposable.[9] In general, the matrix $\mathbf{P}$ can be written in the form

$$\mathbf{P} = \mathbf{Q}^* + \varepsilon \mathbf{C}, \tag{29}$$

where $\mathbf{Q}^* = \mathbf{diag}(\mathbf{Q}_1^*, \mathbf{Q}_2^*, \ldots, \mathbf{Q}_L^*)$, the matrices $\mathbf{Q}_I^*$ are stochastic, $I \in \{1, \ldots, L\}$, ε is small compared to the elements of $\mathbf{Q}^*$, and $|c_{ij}| \leq 1$. The matrix $\mathbf{Q}^*$ is said to be completely decomposable because all elements off the main diagonal of submatrices are zero. We refer the interested reader to Ref. 9 for a comprehensive treatment of completely and nearly completely decomposable matrices and their solutions.

Intuitively, we decompose the probability transition matrix $\mathbf{P}$ into a macro model and L individual micro models. This is consistent with the use of macro and micro models in Ref. 12. The key idea is that the macro model characterizes the transitions between localities, while each micro model characterizes the references within a particular locality. From this perspective, the matrices $\mathbf{Q}_I^*$ are the probability transition matrices for each of the individual micro models. The macro model is defined by the matrix $[\hat{p}_{IJ}]$ of dimension $L \times L$ whose elements represent the probability of referencing some page in locality J on the next memory reference, given that the current reference is to some page in locality I. More formally, we have

$$\hat{p}_{IJ} = \mathbb{P}[Y_{n+1} \in J \mid Y_n \in I].$$

Note that the subscripts are capitalized to emphasize that they refer to the macro model. Letting $\underline{\psi}_I$ denote the invariant probability vector of the matrix $\mathbf{Q}_I^*$, the elements $\hat{p}_{IJ}$ are then computed as

$$\hat{p}_{IJ} = \sum_{i \in I} \sum_{j \in J} \psi_{I,i} \, p_{ij} \, . \tag{30}$$

In the interest of conserving space, we do not describe here our approaches for adding within the above framework the case of overlapping localities and of pages that are referenced in transitions between localities. These technical details can be found in Ref. 35. We note, however, that the page faults due to transitions between localities, together with those resulting from multiple visits to localities in an iterative manner, are included in our analysis of the macro model (see Sec. 4.3).

As a consequence of the Simon–Ando theorems,[9] we can make the following important observations regarding the model of program behavior developed above. In the short-term period, equilibrium is (approximately) reached separately by each locality $\mathbf{Q}_I^*$. These equilibrium states are (approximately) preserved over the long-term period such that the distribution of references among the different localities approaches the distribution $\tilde{\boldsymbol{\pi}} = (\tilde{\pi}_1, \tilde{\pi}_2, \ldots, \tilde{\pi}_I, \ldots, \tilde{\pi}_L)$, where $\tilde{\pi}_I$ is the stationary probability that a memory reference is directed to locality I.

We next consider the miss ratio and memory overhead realized by the program at each server within the context of our program behavior model. Let M denote the number of pages comprising the finite capacity memory available to a parallel application at each of the V servers allocated to it. To elucidate the exposition, we divide the page faults incurred by a program at each server into two different classes. The first consists of faults that occur within each locality, whereas the second class of page faults consists of those resulting from transitions between localities and from the iterative nature of parallel programs in which localities are visited multiple times in some (non-deterministic) fashion. We refer to the miss ratios and memory overheads due to these different types of page faults as the intra-locality and inter-locality miss ratios and memory overheads, respectively, and consider each type in turn. These methods are then used to approximate the total memory overhead incurred by a parallel application as a function of its server allocation.

4.2. Intra-locality memory overhead

Given a nearly completely decomposable model of program behavior with irreducible page transition matrix $\mathbf{P} = [p_{ij}]$ of the form in (29), we compute the intra-locality miss ratio $\mathcal{R}^{w\ell}$ (i.e., the miss ratio within a locality) under the LRU page replacement algorithm as follows. Let $F(\mathbf{P}, M)$ denote the stationary page fault probability for a program model $\mathbf{P}$ and a finite memory of M pages. More formally,

$$F(\mathbf{P}, M) = \lim_{n \to \infty} \mathbb{P}[Y_{n+1} = i \mid i \notin LRU(n)].$$

It follows from the properties of the nearly completely decomposable matrix $\mathbf{P}$ that the page fault probability can be approximated as

$$F(\mathbf{P}, M) \approx \sum_{I=1}^{L} \tilde{\pi}_I F(\mathbf{Q}_I^*, M), \qquad (31)$$

the accuracy of which is known to be (at least) within $O(\varepsilon)$.[9] Due to the locality property exploited in the construction of the matrix $\mathbf{P}$, such errors are expected to be very small. The intra-locality miss ratio is then obtained from (31) by recalling that $\mathcal{R}^{w\ell}$ converges to $F(\mathbf{P}, M)$ for sufficiently long measurement intervals.

The intra-locality miss ratio of the program model $\mathbf{P}$ is therefore obtained by solving L much smaller micro models to calculate their corresponding miss ratios (i.e., $F(\mathbf{Q}_I^*, M)$, $I \in \{1, \ldots, L\}$) and combining these results with the solution to the macro model (i.e., $\tilde{\pi}$). If the matrices $\mathbf{Q}_I^*$ are fairly small, then the intra-locality page fault probability can be computed by analyzing the Markov chain over the state space of all possible LRU stacks. While this Markov chain is also irreducible, since the $\mathbf{Q}_I^*$ are irreducible, and a closed-form solution exists for the page fault probability, the state space can become prohibitively large even for moderate size $\mathbf{Q}_I^*$ matrices. Some of the methods in Sec. 3 can be exploited to address this problem when the appropriate structure exists. However, it is important to note that there is significant evidence[2,12,35] suggesting that in the short-term (micro model) the IRM and LRUSM assumptions may be satisfied.

This is especially the case for the LRUSM in part because sudden jumps between localities are directly handled outside of the micro model for each locality. We further note that closed-form expressions exist for $F(\mathbf{Q}_I^*, M)$ when $\mathbf{Q}_I^*$ corresponds to the IRM or LRUSM.[2]

The intra-locality memory overhead of the program model $\mathbf{P}$ as a function of the memory capacity M on each of the V servers allocated to the program, $\mathcal{M}_{VM}^{w\ell}$, is then obtained in terms of the corresponding miss ratio as

$$\mathcal{M}_{VM}^{w\ell} = \mathcal{R}_{VM}^{w\ell} R_{VM} \mathcal{C}, \tag{32}$$

where R_{VM} is a non-negative discrete random variable representing the total number of memory references for the program, and $\mathcal{C}$ is the cost to load a page in memory. Note that the product $R_{VM}\mathcal{R}_{VM}^{w\ell}$ represents the number of page faults incurred by the program.

Equation (31) is a very valuable result in that it greatly simplifies the computation involved in calculating $\mathcal{R}^{w\ell}$. This approximation, however, does not account for the page faults generated during repeated visits to each locality. The importance of these effects were previously noted above, although now the problem can be understood even more precisely. Consider a program that visits each of its localities multiple times, where every locality fits in memory but the total number of pages far exceeds the capacity of memory. Thus, $F(\mathbf{Q}_I^*, M) = 0$, $I \in \{1, \ldots, L\}$, and from (31) the miss ratio $F(\mathbf{P}, M)$ is equal to 0, which is clearly not correct given the multiple visits to localities with the number of pages comprising the program far exceeding M. We capture this important aspect of program behavior in the inter-locality miss ratio and memory overhead.

4.3. Inter-locality memory overhead

We develop an approximation to the inter-locality miss ratio $\mathcal{R}^{a\ell}$ and inter-locality memory overhead $\mathcal{M}^{a\ell}$ (i.e., the miss ratio and memory overhead *across* *l*ocalities) under LRU page replacement based primarily on the macro model. Since the program reference behavior is assumed to be Markovian, the process repeats itself (i.e., regenerates) on each return to locality I. Thus, the measures we need to consider concern the number of pages in locality I that must be reloaded on return to locality I.

Let C_I be a non-negative discrete random variable that represents the number of pages in locality I that have to be reloaded on return to I, and let N_I^* be a non-negative discrete random variable that represents the number of returns to locality I, for $I \in \{1, \ldots, L\}$. The inter-locality memory overhead then can be calculated as

$$\mathcal{M}^{a\ell} = \sum_{I=1}^{L} \sum_{j=1}^{N_I^*} C_{I,j}, \qquad (33)$$

where $C_{I,1}, C_{I,2}, \ldots, C_{I,N_I^*}$ is a sequence of i.i.d. random variables such that $C_{I,j} \stackrel{d}{=} C_I$, $j = 1, 2, \ldots, N_I^*$. Under the assumptions herein, the random variable N_I^* is a stopping time for this sequence and thus the moments of $\mathcal{M}^{a\ell}$ can be determined by applications of Wald's equation; e.g., see Ref. 59. Dividing the inter-locality memory overhead by the total number of references yields the corresponding inter-locality miss ratio. All that remains is the calculation of measures of the random variables N_I^* and C_I, $I \in \{1, \ldots, L\}$.

4.3.1. Calculation of N_I^*

We can calculate measures of N_I^* from the distribution of first passage times and the corresponding recurrence time random variable $\mathcal{T}_I^*$ representing the elapsed time between first entry into locality I and the next return to I. Following Ref. 36, we focus on the recurrence time $\mathcal{T}_I^*$. Let $\{Z_n; n \in \mathbb{Z}_+\}$ be a Markov chain with one-step transition matrix corresponding to the macro model of Sec. 4.1, defined over the state space $\mathbf{S} = \{1, 2, \ldots, L\}$ of localities. The mean recurrence time to state I, $\mathbb{E}[\mathcal{T}_I]$, is then defined as

$$\mathbb{E}[\mathcal{T}_I] = \sum_{n=1}^{\infty} n \mathbb{P}[Z_n = I, Z_\nu \neq I, 0 < \nu < n \mid Z_0 = I]. \qquad (34)$$

Note that $\mathcal{T}_I$ is not the measure we are interested in because it includes events of the form $[Z_1 = I \mid Z_0 = I]$, which clearly do not imply any change of locality, and because it does not include the time spent in locality I upon first entry. Instead we need $\mathcal{T}_I^*$ whose expectation is defined by

$$\mathbb{E}[\mathcal{T}_I^*] = \sum_{n=1}^{\infty} n \mathbb{P}[Z_n = I, Z_\nu \neq I, 1 < \nu < n \mid Z_1 \neq I, Z_0 = I]$$

$$+ \sum_{n=1}^{\infty} n \hat{p}_{II}^n (1 - \hat{p}_{II})$$

$$= \sum_{n=1}^{\infty} n \mathbb{P}[Z_n = I, Z_\nu \neq I, 1 < \nu < n \mid Z_1 \neq I, Z_0 = I]$$

$$+ \frac{\hat{p}_{II}}{1 - \hat{p}_{II}}.$$

Equation (34) can be rewritten as

$$\mathbb{E}[\mathcal{T}_I] = \mathbb{P}[Z_1 = I \mid Z_0 = I] + \sum_{n=2}^{\infty} n\mathbb{P}[Z_n = I, Z_\nu \neq I, 0 < \nu < n \mid Z_0 = I]$$

$$= \hat{p}_{II} + \sum_{n=2}^{\infty} \{n\mathbb{P}[Z_n = I, Z_\nu \neq I, 1 < \nu < n \mid Z_1 \neq I, Z_0 = I]$$
$$\times \mathbb{P}[Z_1 \neq I \mid Z_0 = I]\}$$

$$= \hat{p}_{II} + (1 - \hat{p}_{II})\left(\mathbb{E}[\mathcal{T}_I^*] - \frac{\hat{p}_{II}}{1 - \hat{p}_{II}}\right),$$

from which it follows that

$$\mathbb{E}[\mathcal{T}_I^*] = \frac{\mathbb{E}[\mathcal{T}_I]}{1 - \hat{p}_{II}}. \tag{35}$$

For a recurrent Markov chain, $\mathbb{E}[\mathcal{T}_I] = 1/\tilde{\pi}_I$, where $\tilde{\pi}_I$ is the invariant probability for state I of the Markov chain Z_n. Upon substituting for $\mathbb{E}[\mathcal{T}_I]$ in (35), we obtain

$$\mathbb{E}[\mathcal{T}_I^*] = \frac{1}{\tilde{\pi}_I - \tilde{\pi}_I \hat{p}_{II}}. \tag{36}$$

4.3.2. Calculation of C_I

The calculation of measures of C_I can be obtained exactly or approximately by an analysis of the program reference matrix $\mathbf{P}$ and its properties developed above. Since the details of this analysis can depend upon the specific details of the matrix $\mathbf{P}$, in what follows we calculate general upper and lower estimates of the moments of C_I.

To illustrate our general approach, consider a particular sample path that takes us through the localities $K_1, K_2, \ldots, K_r$ in any order and any number of times, before returning to locality I. Since $\mathbf{P}$ is an irreducible and nearly completely decomposable Markov reference matrix, it is reasonable to assume that the program spends enough time in each of the localities $K_1, K_2, \ldots, K_r$ to have referenced all of their pages at least once. Let $\mathbf{G} = \{K_1, K_2, \ldots, K_r\}$, and define $\|\mathbf{G}\|$ to be the number of distinct pages in all of the localities comprising $\mathbf{G}$. Observe that if all of the localities in $\mathbf{G}$ were referenced at least once before a return to locality I, then $\|\mathbf{G}\|$ pages would have been loaded in memory. If $\|\mathbf{G}\| + \|\{I\}\| \leq M$, no pages need to be reloaded on return to locality I, whereas if $M - \|\{I\}\| < \|\mathbf{G}\| < M$, then the number of pages to be reloaded on return to locality I is between

$\|\mathbf{G}\| + \|\{I\}\| - M$ and $\|\{I\}\|$. Finally, if $\|\mathbf{G}\| \geq M$, then all $\|\{I\}\|$ pages have to be reloaded on return to I.

More precisely, we define a lower estimate of the overhead $\alpha_I^l(\mathbf{G})$ as

$$\alpha_I^l(\mathbf{G}) \equiv \begin{cases} 0, & \|\mathbf{G}\| + \|\{I\}\| \leq M, \\ \|\mathbf{G}\| + \|\{I\}\| - M, & M - \|\{I\}\| < \|\mathbf{G}\| < M, \\ \|\{I\}\|, & \|\mathbf{G}\| \geq M, \end{cases}$$

and an upper overhead estimate $\alpha_I^u(\mathbf{G})$ as

$$\alpha_I^u(\mathbf{G}) \equiv \begin{cases} 0, & \|\mathbf{G}\| + \|\{I\}\| \leq M, \\ \|\{I\}\|, & \text{otherwise.} \end{cases}$$

Now let $_\mathbf{G}\xi_{II}$ denote the probability that upon leaving locality I, all (and only) the localities in $\mathbf{G}$ are visited in any order and any number of times before returning to locality I. More formally,

$$_\mathbf{G}\xi_{II}^{(n)} = \mathbb{P}[Z_n = I, \{Z_\nu : 1 < \nu < n\} = \mathbf{G} \mid Z_1 \neq I, Z_0 = I],$$

$$_\mathbf{G}\xi_{II} = \sum_{n>1} {_\mathbf{G}\xi_{II}^{(n)}}.$$

With this formulation, we can compute an upper and lower estimate for $\mathbb{E}[C_I^k]$ as follows

$$\sum_{\mathbf{G}:\mathbf{G}\subset S, I\notin \mathbf{G}} {_\mathbf{G}\xi_{II}}(\alpha_I^l(\mathbf{G}))^k \leq \mathbb{E}[C_I^k] \leq \sum_{\mathbf{G}:\mathbf{G}\subset S, I\notin \mathbf{G}} {_\mathbf{G}\xi_{II}}(\alpha_I^u(\mathbf{G}))^k. \quad (37)$$

Note that the summation in (37) can be reduced to only those $\mathbf{G}$ for which $\alpha^u(\mathbf{G}) > 0$.

To calculate $_\mathbf{G}\xi_{II}$ we define a measure related to taboo probabilities.[7] Consider a set $\mathbf{H}$ of localities (we are actually interested in $\mathbf{H} = \mathbf{G}^c$). For all $J \in S\backslash \mathbf{H}$ and $n \in \mathbb{Z}^+$, define

$$_\mathbf{H}P_{JI}^{(n)} \equiv \mathbb{P}[Z_n = I, Z_\nu \notin \mathbf{H}, 1 < \nu < n, Z_1 \neq J \mid Z_0 = J]$$

and

$$_\mathbf{H}P_{JI} \equiv \sum_{n \in \mathbb{Z}^+} {_\mathbf{H}P_{JI}^{(n)}}. \quad (38)$$

We then can decompose $_{\mathbf{H}}P_{JI}^{(n)}$ by the method of first entrance (refer to Ref. 7) as follows

$$_{\mathbf{H}}P_{JI}^{(n)} = \sum_{\substack{K \notin \mathbf{H} \\ K \neq J}} \hat{p}_{JK} \sum_{\nu=0}^{n-2} \hat{p}_{KK}^{\nu} {}_{\mathbf{H}}P_{KI}^{(n-\nu-1)}, \quad n \geq 2;$$

$$\sum_{n \geq 2} {}_{\mathbf{H}}P_{JI}^{(n)} = \sum_{n \geq 2} \sum_{\substack{K \notin \mathbf{H} \\ K \neq J}} \hat{p}_{JK} \sum_{\nu=0}^{n-2} \hat{p}_{KK}^{\nu} {}_{\mathbf{H}}P_{KI}^{(n-\nu-1)}, \qquad (39)$$

$$= \sum_{\substack{K \notin \mathbf{H} \\ K \neq J}} \hat{p}_{JK} \sum_{\nu=0}^{\infty} \sum_{n \geq \nu+2} \hat{p}_{KK}^{\nu} {}_{\mathbf{H}}P_{KI}^{(n-\nu-1)}, \qquad (40)$$

$$= \sum_{\substack{K \notin \mathbf{H} \\ K \neq J}} \frac{\hat{p}_{JK}}{1 - \hat{p}_{KK}} {}_{\mathbf{H}}P_{KI}. \qquad (41)$$

Rewriting the left-hand side of (41) in terms of equation (38) yields a system of $\|\mathbf{S} \backslash \mathbf{H}\|$ equations which can be solved for the same number of unknowns. That is, for each $J \in \mathbf{S} \backslash \mathbf{H}$, we obtain

$$_{\mathbf{H}}P_{JI} = \begin{cases} \displaystyle\sum_{\substack{K \notin \mathbf{H} \\ K \neq J}} \frac{\hat{p}_{JK}}{1 - \hat{p}_{KK}} {}_{\mathbf{H}}P_{KI} + \hat{p}_{JI}, & J \neq I, \\ \displaystyle\sum_{\substack{K \notin \mathbf{H} \\ K \neq J}} \frac{\hat{p}_{JK}}{1 - \hat{p}_{KK}} {}_{\mathbf{H}}P_{KI}, & J = I. \end{cases}$$

To compute $_{\mathbf{G}}\xi_{II}$, we actually need

$$\sum_{n \geq 2} \mathbb{P}[Z_n = I, Z_\nu \notin \mathbf{H}, 1 < \nu < n \mid Z_1 \neq I, Z_0 = I] = \frac{{}_{\mathbf{H}}P_{II}}{\mathbb{P}[Z_1 \neq I \mid Z_0 = I]}$$

$$= \frac{{}_{\mathbf{H}}P_{II}}{1 - \hat{p}_{II}}. \qquad (42)$$

Upon substituting $\mathbf{H} = \mathbf{G}^c$ in (42), $_{\mathbf{G}}\xi_{II}$ can be calculated via the following recursion

$$_{\mathbf{G}}\xi_{II} = \frac{{}_{\mathbf{G}^c}P_{II}}{1 - \hat{p}_{II}} - \sum_{\mathbf{F}: \mathbf{F} \subsetneq \mathbf{G}} {}_{\mathbf{F}}\xi_{II}. \qquad (43)$$

Hence, we calculate the upper and lower estimate for moments of C_I by substituting (43) in (37). Once again, we only need to compute $_{\mathbf{G}}\xi_{II}$ in (43) for those $\mathbf{G}$ for which $\alpha^u(\mathbf{G}) > 0$. As previously noted, one can often obtain a more accurate approximation for the moments of C_I by exploiting properties of the matrices $\mathbf{P}$ and $\mathbf{Q}_I^*$ in the above analysis. In fact, exact values of $\mathbb{E}[C_I]$ are obtained for the parallel applications considered in Refs. 35 and 36, and the same approach can be exploited to obtain higher moments of C_I in such cases.

4.4. Total memory overhead

The total memory overhead of the program model $\mathbf{P}$ as a function of the memory capacity M on each of the V servers allocated to the program, $\mathcal{M}_{VM}$, can be expressed in terms of the corresponding intra-locality and inter-locality memory overheads as

$$\mathcal{M}_{VM} = \mathcal{M}_{VM}^{w\ell} + \mathcal{M}_{VM}^{a\ell}. \tag{44}$$

Assuming $\mathcal{M}_{VM}^{w\ell}$ and $\mathcal{M}_{VM}^{a\ell}$ are independent, the moments of $\mathcal{M}_{VM}$ can be obtained from the analysis in Secs. 4.2 and 4.3. We then construct a phase-type distribution with parameters $(\underline{\beta}'_V, \mathcal{S}'^B_V)$ of order $m'^B_V < \infty$ by matching as many moments (and/or density function) of $\mathcal{M}_{VM}$ as are of interest, using any of the best known methods for doing so; e.g., see Refs. 1 and 22 and the references therein.

The total service times of parallel jobs when executed on partitions of size V are comprised of the combination of their corresponding original service requirements and total memory overheads. By exploiting the known closure properties of phase-type distributions,[21,30] this combined service time distribution can be appropriately constructed as a (possibly more compact) phase-type distribution based on $(\underline{\beta}_V, \mathcal{S}^B_V)$ and $(\underline{\beta}'_V, \mathcal{S}'^B_V)$ with mean $\mu'^{-1}_V = \mu^{-1}_V + \mathbb{E}[\mathcal{M}_{VM}]$, $V \in \{U, \ldots, P\}$, and substituted into the dynamic spacesharing model of Sec. 2. The analysis of this dynamic spacesharing model that includes the memory overheads incurred by each parallel application as a function of its server allocation is then directly given by our analysis derived in Sec. 3.

5. Conclusions

In this chapter, we have presented a mathematical analysis of server and memory resource allocation in parallel processing systems. First, a general stochastic model of parallel processing systems under dynamic spacesharing was formulated, and an exact matrix-analytic analysis of this model was derived. Our results included closed-form solutions for certain model instances based on their probabilistic structure and closed-form expressions for several performance measures of interest, such as the tail distribution of the queue length process and its asymptotic decay rate, the mean sojourn time of parallel jobs, and the long-run proportion of time the system spends reconfiguring the allocation of servers among the jobs. Second, a general nearly completely decomposable model of parallel program memory reference behavior was formulated, and a stochastic analysis of this model was derived. Our results included probability measures of the total memory overhead incurred by a parallel program as a function of its server allocation, which in turn can be directly incorporated in our stochastic analysis of parallel dynamic spacesharing systems. Moreover, we solved a longstanding open problem with previous nearly completely decomposable models and analyses by introducing and deriving results for the inter-locality miss ratio in addition to the classical intra-locality miss ratio. The collection of theoretical results presented in this chapter can be exploited to investigate the design and performance space of parallel processing systems with respect to fundamental tradeoffs related to the server and memory allocation strategies and their interactions.

Acknowledgment

This chapter is dedicated to Professor Kenneth Sevcik on the occasion of his 60th birthday and also dedicated to his memory.

References

1. S. Asmussen, Phase-type distributions and related point processes: Fitting and recent advances, in *Matrix-Analytic Methods in Stochastic Models*, eds. S. R. Chakravarthy and A. S. Alfa (Marcel Dekker, 1997), pp. 137–149.
2. O. I. Aven, E. G. Coffman, Jr. and Y. A. Kogan, *Stochastic Analysis of Computer Storage* (D. Reidel, 1987).
3. N. G. Bean, J.-M. Li and P. G. Taylor, Caudal characteristics of QBDs with decomposable phase spaces, in *Advances in Algorithmic Methods for Stochastic Models*, eds. G. Latouche and P. Taylor (Notable Publications, 2000), pp. 37–55.
4. S. C. Borst, Optimal probabilistic allocation of customer types to servers, in *Proc. ACM SIGMETRICS Conf. Measurement and Modeling of Computer Systems* (1995), pp. 116–125.
5. S. L. Brumelle, Some inequalities for parallel-server queues, *Operations Research* **19** (1971), 402–413.
6. D. C. Burger, R. S. Hyder, B. P. Miller and D. A. Wood, Paging tradeoffs in distributed shared-memory multiprocessors, *J. Supercomputing* **8** (1996), 1–30.
7. K. L. Chung, *Markov Chains with Stationary Transition Probabilities* (Springer-Verlag, 1960).
8. E. G. Coffman, Jr. and P. J. Denning, *Operating Systems Theory* (Prentice Hall, 1973).

9. P. J. Courtois, *Decomposability* (Academic Press, 1977).
10. P. J. Courtois and P. Semal, Error bounds for the analysis by decomposition of non-negative matrices, in *Proc. Int. Workshop on Applied Mathematics and Performance/Reliability Models of Computer/Communication Systems* (1983), pp. 253–268.
11. P. J. Denning, The working set model for program behavior, *Communications of the ACM* **11**(5) (May 1968), 323–333.
12. P. J. Denning, Working sets past and present, *IEEE Trans. Software Engineering* **6**(1) (January 1980), 64–84.
13. K. Dussa, B. Carlson, L. Dowdy and K.-H. Park, Dynamic partitioning in transputer environments, in *Proc. ACM SIGMETRICS Conf. Measurement and Modeling of Computer Systems* (1990), pp. 203–213.
14. D. L. Eager, J. Zahorjan and E. D. Lazowska, Speedup versus efficiency in parallel systems, *IEEE Trans. Computers* **38**(3) (March 1989), pp. 408–423.
15. D. G. Feitelson, L. Rudolph, U. Schwiegelshohn, K. C. Sevcik and P. Wong, Theory and practice in parallel job scheduling, in *Job Scheduling Strategies for Parallel Processing*, eds. D. G. Feitelson and L. Rudolph, Lecture Notes in Computer Science, Vol. 1291 (Springer-Verlag, 1997), pp. 1–34.
16. D. W. Fife, Scheduling with random arrivals and linear loss functions, *Management Sci.* **11**(3) (1965), 429–437.
17. D. Gaver, P. Jacobs and G. Latouche, Finite birth-and-death models in randomly changing environments, *Adv. Appl. Prob.* **16** (1984), 715–731.
18. J. L. Hellerstein, T. S. Jayram and M. S. Squillante, Analysis of large-scale distributed information systems, in *Proc. Int. Symp. Modeling, Analysis, and Simulation of Computer and Telecommunication Systems* (July 2000).
19. N. Islam, A. Prodromidis and M. S. Squillante, Dynamic partitioning in different distributed-memory environments, in *Job Scheduling Strategies for Parallel Processing*, eds. D. G. Feitelson and L. Rudolph, Lecture Notes in Computer Science, Vol. 1162 (Springer-Verlag, 1996), pp. 244–270.
20. L. Kleinrock, *Queueing Systems Volume II: Computer Applications* (John Wiley and Sons, 1976).
21. G. Latouche and V. Ramaswami, *Introduction to Matrix Analytic Methods in Stochastic Modeling* (ASA-SIAM, Philadelphia, 1999).
22. G. Latouche and P. Taylor, *Advances in Algorithmic Methods for Stochastic Models* (Notable, 2000).
23. S. Majumdar, D. L. Eager and R. B. Bunt, Characterisation of programs for scheduling in multiprogrammed parallel systems, *Performance Evaluation* **13**(2) (1991), 109–130.
24. A. M. Makowski and R. D. Nelson, Distributed parallelism considered harmful, Technical Report RC 17448, IBM Research Division (December 1991).
25. A. M. Makowski and R. D. Nelson, Optimal scheduling for a distributed parallel processing model, Technical Report RC 17449, IBM Research Division (February 1992).
26. C. McCann, R. Vaswani and J. Zahorjan, A dynamic processor allocation policy for multiprogrammed shared-memory multiprocessors, *ACM Trans. Computer Systems* **11**(2) (May 1993), 146–178.

27. C. McCann and J. Zahorjan, Processor allocation policies for message-passing parallel computers, in *Proc. ACM SIGMETRICS Conf. Measurement and Modeling of Computer Systems* (May 1994), pp. 19–32.
28. C. McCann and J. Zahorjan, Scheduling memory constrained jobs on distributed memory parallel computers, in *Proc. ACM SIGMETRICS Conf. Measurement and Modeling of Computer Systems* (May 1995), pp. 208–219.
29. R. D. Nelson, D. Towsley and A. N. Tantawi, Performance analysis of parallel processing systems, *IEEE Trans. Software Engineering* **14**(4) (April 1988), 532–540.
30. M. F. Neuts, *Matrix-Geometric Solutions in Stochastic Models: An Algorithmic Approach* (The Johns Hopkins University Press, 1981).
31. M. F. Neuts, *Structured Stochastic Matrices of M/G/1 Type and Their Applications* (Marcel Dekker, 1989).
32. K.-H. Park and L. W. Dowdy, Dynamic partitioning of multiprocessor systems, *Int. J. Parallel Programming* **18**(2) (1989), 91–120.
33. E. W. Parsons and K. C. Sevcik, Benefits of speedup knowledge in memory-constrained multiprocessor scheduling, *Performance Evaluation* **27&28** (October 1996), 253–272.
34. E. W. Parsons and K. C. Sevcik, Coordinated allocation of memory and processors in multiprocessors, in *Proc. ACM SIGMETRICS Conf. Measurement and Modeling of Computer Systems* (May 1996), pp. 57–67.
35. V. G. Peris, M. S. Squillante and V. K. Naik, Analysis of the impact of memory in distributed parallel processing systems, Technical Report RC 19336, IBM Research Division (October 1993).
36. V. G. Peris, M. S. Squillante and V. K. Naik, Analysis of the impact of memory in distributed parallel processing systems, in *Proc. ACM SIGMETRICS Conf. Measurement and Modeling of Computer Systems* (May 1994), pp. 5–18.
37. E. Rosti, G. Serazzi, E. Smirni and M. S. Squillante, The impact of I/O on program behavior and parallel scheduling, in *Proc. ACM SIGMETRICS Conf. Measurement and Modeling of Computer Systems* (June 1998), pp. 56–65.
38. E. Rosti, G. Serazzi, E. Smirni and M. S. Squillante, Models of parallel applications with large computation and I/O requirements, *IEEE Trans. Software Engineering* **28**(3) (March 2002), pp. 286–307.
39. L. E. Schrage and L. W. Miller, The queue M/G/1 with the shortest remaining processing time discipline, *Operations Research* **14**(4) (1966), 670–684.
40. E. Seneta, *Non-Negative Matrices and Markov Chains*, 2nd Edn. (Springer Verlag, New York, 1981).
41. J. Sethuraman and M. S. Squillante, Optimal stochastic scheduling in multiclass parallel queues, in *Proc. ACM SIGMETRICS Conf. Measurement and Modeling of Computer Systems* (June 1999), pp. 93–102.
42. J. Sethuraman and M. S. Squillante, Analysis of parallel-server queues under spacesharing and timesharing disciplines, in *Matrix-Analytic Methods: Theory and Applications*, eds. G. Latouche and P. Taylor (World Scientific, 2002), pp. 357–380.

43. S. K. Setia, The interaction between memory allocation and adaptive partitioning in message-passing multicomputers, in *Job Scheduling Strategies for Parallel Processing*, eds. D. G. Feitelson and L. Rudolph, Lecture Notes in Computer Science, Vol. 949 (Springer-Verlag, 1995), pp. 146–194.
44. S. K. Setia, M. S. Squillante and S. K. Tripathi, Processor scheduling on multiprogrammed, distributed memory parallel computers, in *Proc. ACM SIGMETRICS Conf. Measurement and Modeling of Computer Systems* (May 1993), pp. 158–170.
45. S. K. Setia, M. S. Squillante and S. K. Tripathi, Analysis of processor allocation in multiprogrammed, distributed-memory parallel processing systems, *IEEE Trans. Parallel and Distributed Systems*, **5**(4) (April 1994), 401–420.
46. K. C. Sevcik, Scheduling for minimum total loss using service time distributions, *J. ACM* **21**(1) (1974), 66–75.
47. K. C. Sevcik, Characterizations of parallelism in applications and their use in scheduling, in *Proc. ACM SIGMETRICS Conf. Measurement and Modeling of Computer Systems* (May 1989), pp. 171–180.
48. K. C. Sevcik, Application scheduling and processor allocation in multiprogrammed parallel processing systems, *Performance Evaluation* **19** (1994), 107–140.
49. J. R. Spirn, *Program Behavior: Models and Measurements* (Elsevier, 1977).
50. M. S. Squillante, A matrix-analytic approach to a general class of G/G/c queues, Technical report, IBM Research Division (May 1996).
51. M. S. Squillante, Matrix-analytic methods in stochastic parallel-server scheduling models, in *Advances in Matrix-Analytic Methods for Stochastic Models*, eds. S. R. Chakravarthy and A. S. Alfa (Notable Publications, 1998).
52. M. S. Squillante and E. D. Lazowska, Using processor-cache affinity information in shared-memory multiprocessor scheduling, *IEEE Trans. Parallel and Distributed Systems* **4**(2) (February 1993), 131–143.
53. M. S. Squillante and K. P. Tsoukatos, Optimal scheduling of coarse-grained parallel applications, in *Proc. 8th SIAM Conf. Parallel Processing for Scientific Computing* (March 1997).
54. M. S. Squillante, F. Wang and M. Papaefthymiou, Stochastic analysis of gang scheduling in parallel and distributed systems, *Performance Evaluation* **27&28** (October 1996), 273–296.
55. M. S. Squillante, D. D. Yao and L. Zhang. Analysis of job arrival patterns and parallel scheduling performance, *Performance Evaluation* **36&37** (August 1999), 137–163.
56. M. S. Squillante, Y. Zhang, A. Sivasubramaniam, N. Gautam, H. Franke and J. Moreira, Modeling and analysis of dynamic coscheduling in parallel and distributed environments, in *Proc. ACM SIGMETRICS Conf. Measurement and Modeling of Computer Systems* (June 2002), pp. 43–54.
57. G. W. Stewart, Computable error bounds for aggregated Markov chains, *J. ACM* **30** (1983), 271–285.
58. W. Winston, Optimality of the shortest line discipline, *J. Appl. Prob.* **14** (1977), 181–189.

59. R. W. Wolff, *Stochastic Modeling and the Theory of Queues* (Prentice Hall, 1989).
60. J. Zahorjan and C. McCann, Processor scheduling in shared memory multiprocessors, in *Proc. ACM SIGMETRICS Conf. Measurement and Modeling of Computer Systems* (May 1990), pp. 214–225.

CHAPTER 14

Periodic Task Cluster Scheduling in Distributed Systems

Helen Karatza

*Department of Informatics, Aristotle University of Thessaloniki,
54124 Thessaloniki, Greece
karatza@csd.auth.gr*

This chapter addresses issues of task clustering — the coalition of several tasks into single coarser grain tasks called *task clusters* — and task cluster scheduling on distributed processors. It considers a special scheduling method referred to as *periodic task cluster scheduling*. With this method, processor queues are rearranged only at the end of predefined intervals called *epochs*. The objective is to find an epoch that minimizes the number of queue rearrangements, and that also results in good overall performance, and in fairness in individual job service. Simulation models are used to compare the performance of this method with other task cluster scheduling policies. Simulated results indicate that periodic task cluster scheduling is a good policy to use.

1. Introduction

Scheduling in multiprocessor systems has been a major research goal for many years. However, it is still not always possible to efficiently execute parallel jobs. To achieve this, it is important to partition the program into tasks properly, assigning the tasks to processors and scheduling execution on each processor. Good scheduling policies are needed to improve system performance while preserving individual application performance so that some jobs do not suffer unbounded delays. And indeed many papers exist in the literature that study scheduling in multiprocessor systems. In the references section, we list a few of them.[1-32]

In distributed systems, the efficiency of execution of parallel programs critically depends on the policies used to partition the program into modules or tasks and to schedule these tasks onto distributed nodes. In these systems, communication cost is incurred if two tasks are assigned to different processors.

Several partition algorithms have been proposed in the literature. The goal of them is to divide the program into the appropriate size and number of tasks to balance the two conflicting requirements of low communication overhead and a higher degree of parallelism. One solution that has been proposed is to coalesce several tasks into single coarser grain tasks called task clusters. Upon construction, task clusters are scheduled on their assigned processors. Therefore, task clustering is a pre-process step to scheduling.

Typically, a set of tasks that represents a distributed program corresponds to nodes in a directed graph with node and edge weights. Each vertex in a graph denotes a task and a weight, which represents its processing time. Each edge denotes the precedence relation between the two tasks, and the weight of the edge is the communication cost incurred if the two tasks are assigned to different processors.

Many authors have studied the clustering problem and they have proposed various algorithms based on graph scheduling and heuristics.[19-26] Two fundamental scheduling strategies are used in clustering: scheduling independent tasks in one cluster (non-linear clustering) and scheduling tasks that are in a precedence path of the directed graph in one cluster (linear clustering). Linear clustering fully exploits the parallelism in the graph while non-linear clustering reduces the parallelism by sequentializing independent tasks to avoid high communication.

In this chapter, we consider linear clustering. A simple probabilistic task clustering method is employed for coalescing tasks into task clusters. Emphasis is given to the study of the subsequent cluster scheduling within processor queues. Tasks in a cluster must be executed sequentially on the same processor without preemption.

Task cluster scheduling has been studied in Ref. 27 while I/O scheduling and task cluster scheduling have been studied in Ref. 28. Those papers consider closed queuing network models with a fixed number of jobs. Both papers show that from all task cluster scheduling methods that they examine the Shortest-Cluster-First (SCF) method yields the best performance. However, the SCF policy has two disadvantages: (a) it involves a considerable amount of overhead because processor queues are rearranged each time new clusters are added, and (b) it is possible to starve a cluster if its service time is large.

Most research into distributed system scheduling policies has focused on improving system performance where scheduling overhead is assumed to be negligible. However, scheduling overhead can seriously degrade performance. First-Come-First-Served (FCFS) is the simplest scheduling method and it is fair to individual jobs but often it results in sub-optimal performance. This method results in no overhead.

In this chapter, along with the FCFS and SCF scheduling methods, we also consider periodic task cluster scheduling. With this policy, processor queues are rearranged only at the end of predefined intervals. The time interval between successive queue rearrangements is called an epoch. At the end of an epoch, the scheduler recalculates the priorities of all clusters in the system queues using the SCF criterion. Therefore, our method is Periodic SCF (PSCF). We aim to find an epoch that performs close to SCF but minimizes the disadvantages of SCF as much as possible, which means that it significantly reduces the number of queue rearrangements and is fairer than SCF.

This type of epoch scheduling is different from epoch scheduling that is studied in McCann and Zahorjan.[29] In that paper, only policies that provide co-scheduling are considered and all nodes are reallocated to jobs at each reallocation point.

We study and compare the task cluster scheduling policies for various workloads and for different epoch sizes. Comparative results are obtained using simulation techniques. The results of this study apply to both loosely coupled multiprocessor systems and networks of workstations connected to support parallel applications.

In previous papers,[30,31] we also studied epoch scheduling. However, none of these two papers examines scheduling of task clusters. This chapter is an extension of our previous work[32] which considers epoch task cluster scheduling. That paper considers that the number of tasks per job is described by the uniform distribution while in this work we examine the normal distribution as well as the uniform distribution for the number of tasks per job. Furthermore, Ref. 32 considers only the exponential distribution for task service demand while in this chapter we also consider task service demand with high variability. The author has found no evidence that this type of scheduling has previously been applied to this system operating under these workload models.

The structure of this chapter is as follows. Section 2.1 specifies system and workload models, Sec. 2.2 describes scheduling strategies, Sec. 2.3 presents the metrics employed while assessing performance of the scheduling policies, and Sec. 2.4 describes model implementation and input parameters. Simulation results and performance analysis are presented in Sec. 3, and Sec. 4 contains conclusions and suggestions for further research.

2. Model and Methodology

The technique used to evaluate the performance of the scheduling disciplines is experimentation using a synthetic workload simulation.

2.1. *System and workload models*

An open queuing network model of a distributed system is considered (Fig. 1). $P = 16$ homogeneous processors are available, each serving its own queue. A high-speed network connects the distributed nodes. The effects of the memory requirements and the communication latencies are not represented explicitly in the system model. Instead, they appear implicitly in the shape of the task execution time functions. By studying different distributions of task service demands, we believe that various architectural characteristics will be represented.

We consider the problem of task cluster scheduling. There is a two step approach to scheduling: (i) clustering, and (ii) scheduling the clusters.

Jobs are partitioned into $n \geq 1$ tasks that can be run either sequentially or in parallel. We assume that the number of tasks of jobs is in the range of $[1 \cdots P]$.

A simple probabilistic clustering method is employed to coalescing tasks into task clusters. Processors are characterized by numbers $1, 2, \ldots, P$. Tasks are assigned random numbers that are uniformly distributed in the range of $[1 \cdots P]$. We consider that assignment is realized in such a way that tasks of a job with precedence constraints are assigned the same number and perform a cluster that is mapped to the processor labeled with this number. The number of tasks of a job j is represented as $t(j)$. The number

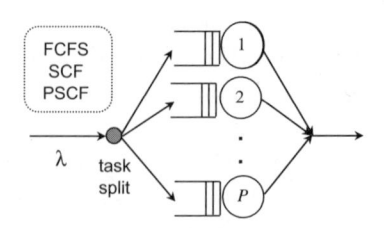

Fig. 1. The queueing network model. FCFS, SCF, PSCF are the scheduling methods, and λ is the mean arrival rate of jobs.

of clusters of a job j is represented as $c(j)$ and is equal to the number of processors $p(j)$ required by job j. Therefore, the following relations hold: $t(j) \leq P$, and $c(j) = p(j) \leq t(j)$.

The scheduling problem is equivalent to determining a mapping of the clusters to processors and then determining an ordering of the clusters within each processor queue.

Tasks are executed according to the cluster scheduling method that is currently employed. No migration or preemption is permitted. Once a task of a cluster starts execution, then this task and all other tasks belonging to the same cluster will also run to completion without interruption. Although tasks scheduled on two different processors may communicate with each other, we do not model any communication overhead, and we consider it as part of task execution time.

On completing execution, a task waits at the join point for its sibling tasks of all clusters of the same job to complete execution. Therefore, synchronization among tasks is required. The price paid for increased parallelism is a synchronization delay that occurs when tasks wait for siblings to finish execution.

The workload considered here is characterized by three parameters: the distribution of job arrival, the distribution of the number of tasks per job, and the distribution of task service demand.

Distribution of Job Arrival. Job inter-arrival times are exponential random variables with a mean of $1/\lambda$.

Distribution of the Number of Tasks per Job. Two different types of distribution of the number of tasks per job have been utilized:

Normal Distribution. We assume a "bounded" normal distribution for the number of tasks per job with mean equal to $\eta = (1 + P)/2$. We have chosen standard deviation $\sigma = \eta/4$.

Uniform Distribution. We assume that the number of tasks of jobs is uniformly distributed in the range of $[1 \cdots P]$. Therefore, the mean number of tasks per job is equal to the $\eta = (1 + P)/2$.

It is obvious that jobs of the uniform distribution case present larger variability in their degree of parallelism than jobs whose number of tasks is normally distributed. In the normal distribution case, most of the jobs have a moderate degree of parallelism (close to the mean η).

Distribution of Task Service Demand. We examine the impact of the variability in task service demand on system performance. A high variability in task service demand implies that there is a proportionately high number of service demands that are very small compared to the mean service time and there are a comparatively low number of service demands that are very large. When a cluster that has a task with a long service demand starts execution, it occupies a processor for a long interval of time and, depending on the scheduling policy, it may introduce inordinate queuing delays for other task clusters waiting for service. We examine the following cases with regard to task execution time distribution (μ represents the mean processor service rate):

- Task execution times are exponentially distributed with a mean of $1/\mu$.
- Task execution times have a Branching Erlang distribution[33] with two stages. The coefficient of variation is C, where $C > 1$ and the mean is $1/\mu$.

We assume that there is no correlation between the different parameters. For example, a job with a small number of tasks may have a large computational demand.

2.2. Scheduling strategies

We examine only non-preemptive cluster scheduling policies. All tasks belonging to the same cluster must finish execution before any other task starts processing. Tasks within a cluster are executed sequentially.

First-Come-First-Served (FCFS). With this strategy, each cluster is scheduled into the assigned queue in the order of its arrival. This policy is the simplest form of cluster scheduling and also is the fairest scheduling method.

Shortest-Cluster-First (SCF). This policy assumes that *a priori* knowledge about a cluster is available in the form of cumulative service demand of all its tasks. When such knowledge is available, clusters in the processor queues are ordered in a decreasing order of total service demand.

It should be noted, however, that *a priori* information is not often available and only an estimate of task execution time can be obtained. In this study, task execution time estimated is assumed to be uniformly distributed within $\pm E\%$ of the exact value.

With this scheduling strategy, it is possible to starve a cluster if its cumulative service demand of tasks is too large. Since processor queues are rearranged each time a new task cluster is inserted to them, some jobs may result in unbounded delays.

Table 1. Notation.

Parameter	Definition
λ	Mean job arrival rate
$1/\mu$	Mean task service demand
C	Coefficient of variation of task service demand
U	Mean processor utilization
RT	Mean response time
MRT	Maximum response time
NQR	Number of queue rearrangements
E	Estimation error in service time
D_{RT}	Relative (%) decrease in RT when the SCF or the PSCF method is employed instead of FCFS
D_{NQR}	Relative (%) decrease in NQR when PSCF scheduling is employed instead of the SCF policy
MRT Ratio	The ratio of MRT in the SCF or PSCF scheduling case over MRT in the FCFS case

Periodic SCF(PSCF) – Epoch = x. With this policy, processor queues are rearranged only at the end of epochs, where the size of each epoch is x. Then the scheduler recalculates the priorities of all task clusters in the system queues using the SCF criterion.

2.3. Performance metrics

We define response time of a random job as the interval of time from the dispatching of these job clusters to processor queues to service completion of the last task of the last cluster of this job. Parameters used in simulation computations are shown in Table 1.

RT represents overall performance, while *MRT Ratio* provides an indication of fairness in individual job service.

2.4. Model implementation and input parameters

The queuing network model described above is implemented with discrete event simulation[34] using the independent replication method. For every mean value, a 95% confidence interval was evaluated. All confidence intervals were found to be less than 5% of the mean values.

We have chosen mean processor service time $1/\mu = 1$, which means mean service rate per processor $\mu = 1$.

Since there are on average 8.5 tasks per parallel job $((P+1)/2)$, if all processors are busy, then an average of $P/8.5 = 1.88235$ parallel jobs can be served each unit of time. This implies that we had to choose $\lambda < 1.88235$, and consequently $1/\lambda > 0.531$. For this reason, we set mean inter-arrival time $1/\lambda = 0.56, 0.58, 0.60, 0.62$, which corresponds to arrival rate $\lambda = 1.786, 1.724, 1.667, 1.613$.

Epoch size is 5, 10, 15, and 20. We chose epoch length 5 as a starting point for the experiments because the mean processor service time is equal to 1, and also because with this epoch size NQR is smaller than in the SCF case. Therefore, we expected that larger epoch sizes would result in even smaller NQR. In all cases, we have also examined service time estimation error $E = \pm 10\%$ and $\pm 20\%$.

3. Simulation Results and Performance Analysis

The results that follow represent the performance of the different policies. Mean processor utilisation for all mean inter-arrival times is given in Table 2.

Simulation experiments accessed the impact of service time estimation error on the performance of the scheduling methods. The simulation results (not shown here) indicated that estimation error in processor service time slightly affected performance when $E = 10, 20$. This is in accordance with other results reported in the literature that are related to estimation of service time.[2] For this reason, in this chapter we present results of the $E = 0$ case only.

3.1. *Normal distribution case*

We present first the simulation results for the case where the number of tasks per job follows the normal distribution. Results for $C = 1, 2$, and 4 are included.

$C = 1$. In Fig. 2, we observe that the worst performance appears with the FCFS policy because this method yields the highest mean response

Table 2. Mean processor utilization.

$1/\lambda$	U
0.56	0.94
0.58	0.91
0.60	0.88
0.62	0.85

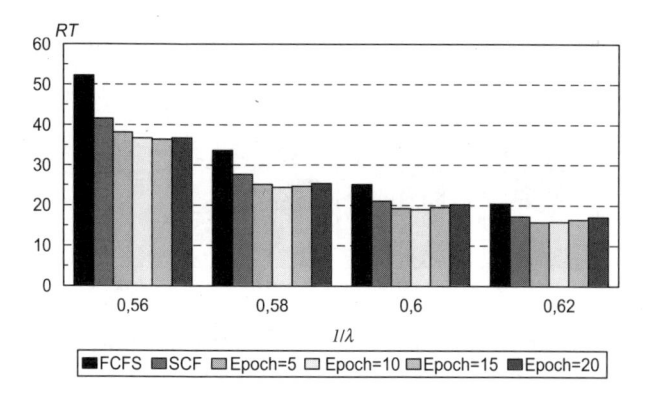

Fig. 2. RT versus $1/\lambda$, $E = 0$, $C = 1$, normal distribution.

time. It is obvious that with FCFS scheduling, clusters with small cumulative service demand get blocked behind a cluster that has a large service demand and is waiting in the queue. Blocking behind a large cluster introduces inordinate queuing delays and also synchronization delay to the sibling clusters.

PSCF for all epoch sizes that we examine yields mean response time that is lower than that of the SCF method. This is contrary to intuition, as we expected that SCF would perform best. This is due to the following reason. With the SCF method, clusters that have a small cumulative service demand do not delay behind a large cluster. However, this does not necessarily mean that the job to which they belong will have a shorter response time. This is because some sibling clusters of the same job may have to delay longer in other queues due to the SCF criterion. This may result in increased synchronization delay of sibling clusters and therefore in increased response times of the respective jobs.

In Fig. 2, we also observe that for $1/\lambda = 0.56, 0.58, 0.60$ RT first slightly decreases with increasing epoch size and then increases after a certain epoch size, which is different at each load. In these cases the smallest RT are observed for epoch sizes of 15, 10, 10, respectively. For $1/\lambda = 0.62$, RT increases with increasing epoch size.

In Fig. 3, we observe that with all methods, D_{RT} decreases with increasing mean inter-arrival time. This is because there are fewer clusters in the queues when $1/\lambda$ is large than when it is small and therefore there are then fewer opportunities to exploit the advantages of the SCF and PSCF strategies over the FCFS method.

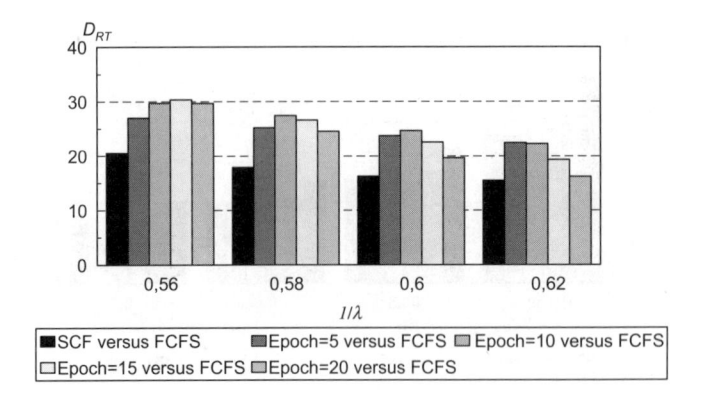

Fig. 3. D_{RT} versus $1/\lambda$, $E = 0$, $C = 1$, normal distribution.

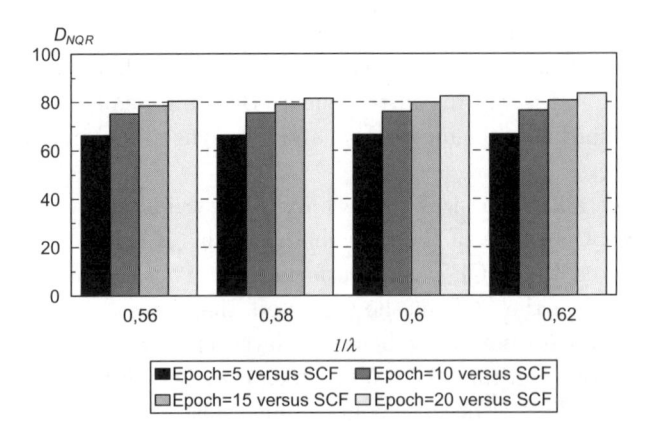

Fig. 4. D_{NQR} versus $1/\lambda$, $E = 0$, $C = 1$, normal distribution.

For all λ, the relative decrease in the number of queue rearrangements due to epoch scheduling is significant (Fig. 4). Actually, for all epoch sizes D_{NQR} varies in the range of 66.25–83.6%. For each λ, D_{NQR} increases with increasing epoch size. D_{NQR} increase is larger when epoch size is small compared to when it is large. For example, in all cases the difference in D_{NQR} between epochs 5 and 10 is larger than the difference between epochs 15 and 20. For each epoch size, D_{NQR} generally very slightly increases with increasing mean inter-arrival time.

In Fig. 5, it is shown that SCF and PSCF yield larger maximum response time than the FCFS method does. This is due to the fact that

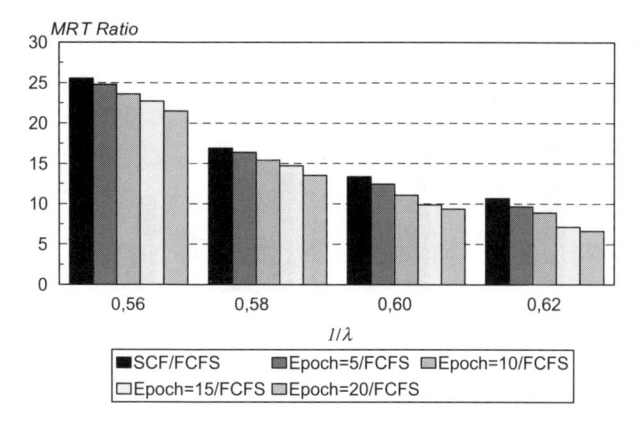

Fig. 5. MRT Ratio versus $1/\lambda$, $E = 0$, $C = 1$, normal distribution.

with the SCF and PSCF policies, some clusters with large cumulative service demands may suffer long delays in their respective queues and this results in large synchronization delays of their sibling clusters and therefore in large response times of the respective jobs.

In all cases, the PSCF method is fairer than the SCF because the former method prevents clusters from long delays. For any λ, the *MRT Ratio* decreases with increasing epoch size. Therefore, fairer service is provided to jobs when queue rearrangements take place after long epochs than after small ones.

From the results presented in Fig. 5, it is also shown that with each of the SCF and PSCF methods, the *MRT Ratio* decreases with increasing mean inter-arrival time. This is due to the fact that when a cluster has a large cumulative service demand, then it is more probable to be bypassed by many clusters when the system load is high, then when the system load is low.

$C = 2$. As shown in Figs. 6 and 7, the superiority of each of SCF and PSCF over FCFS is more significant in the $C = 2$ case than in the $C = 1$ case. This is due to the fact that as C increases the variability in task service demand increases too and this results in better exploitation of the SCF and PSCF strategies abilities. Also the results reveal that RT increases with increasing epoch size, and that in all cases PSCF for epoch size 5 performs slightly better than SCF, while for epoch size 10 in most cases performs close to SCF. The SCF method performs better than PSCF

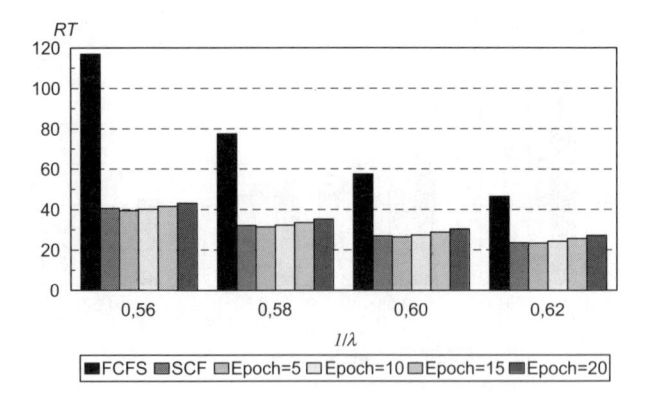

Fig. 6. RT versus $1/\lambda$, $E = 0$, $C = 2$, normal distribution.

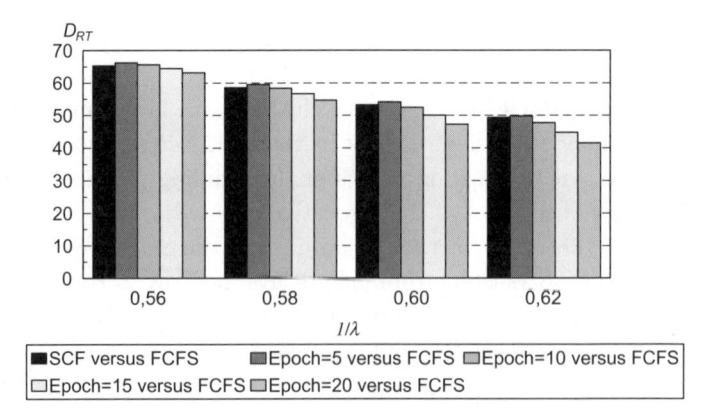

Fig. 7. D_{RT} versus $1/\lambda$, $E = 0$, $C = 2$, normal distribution.

when epoch size is 15 and 20. As in the $C = 1$ case, the results for $C = 2$ show that D_{RT} also decreases with increasing mean inter-arrival time.

For all λ, the relative decrease in the number of queue rearrangements due to periodic scheduling is a little smaller than in the $C = 1$ case (Fig. 8). For all epoch sizes D_{NQR} varies in the range of 63.7–79.7%. For each epoch size, D_{NQR} is almost the same for all mean inter-arrival times. The remaining observations for D_{NQR} that hold for the $C = 1$ case also hold for $C = 2$.

In Fig. 9, it is shown that the observations about *MRT Ratio* that hold for the $C = 1$ case generally also hold for $C = 2$. By comparing the results presented in Fig. 5 and Fig. 9, we observe that *MRT Ratio* decreases with decreasing load in a larger degree in the $C = 1$ case than in the $C = 2$ case.

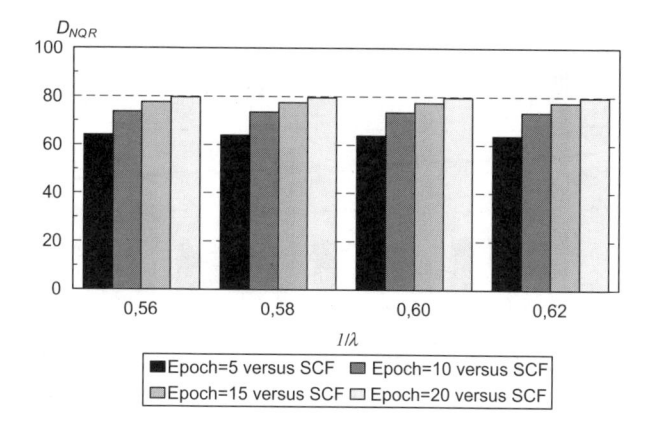

Fig. 8. D_{NQR} versus $1/\lambda$, $E = 0$, $C = 2$, normal distribution.

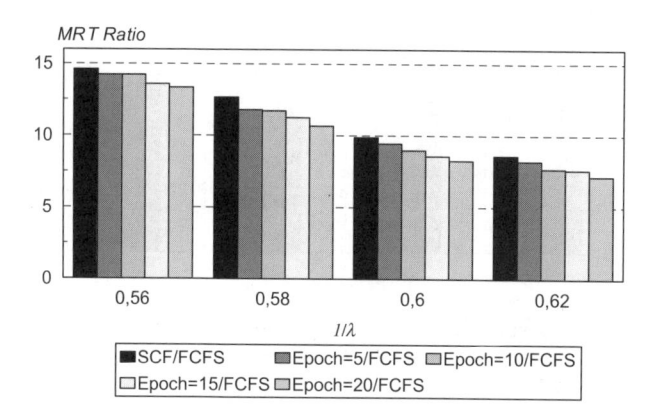

Fig. 9. $MRT\ Ratio$ versus $1/\lambda$, $E = 0$, $C = 2$, normal distribution.

This is because as C increases the majority of task service demands are very small while there are few very large task service demands which result in very large response times and make the effect of the load less significant.

$C = 4$. As shown in Figs. 10 and 11, the superiority of each of SCF and PSCF over FCFS is more significant in the $C = 4$ case than in the $C = 2$ case. This is because task service demand variability is larger in the $C = 4$ case than in the $C = 2$. Also the results reveal that RT increases with increasing epoch size, and that in all cases PSCF for epoch size 5 performs slightly better than SCF, while for epoch size 10 performs close to SCF. The SCF method outperforms PSCF when epoch size is 15 and 20. As in

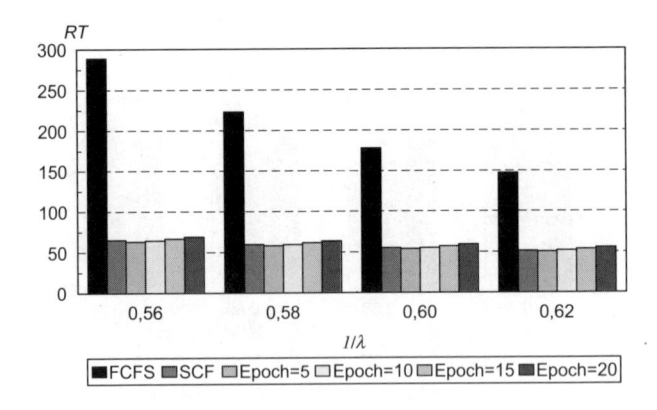

Fig. 10. RT versus $1/\lambda$, $E = 0$, $C = 4$, normal distribution.

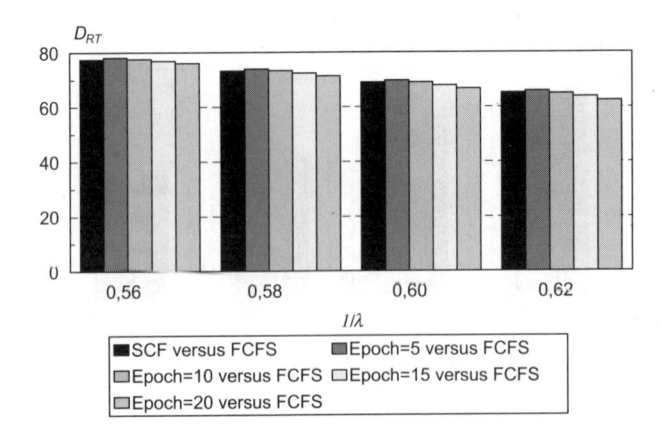

Fig. 11. D_{RT} versus $1/\lambda$, $E = 0$, $C = 4$, normal distribution.

the other C cases, D_{RT} also decreases with increasing mean inter-arrival time.

In Fig. 12, it is shown that for all λ, the relative decrease in the number of queue rearrangements due to epoch scheduling is a little smaller than in the $C = 2$ case. For all epoch sizes D_{NQR} varies in the range of 62.1–78.0%. The remaining observations for D_{NQR} that hold for the $C = 2$ case also hold for $C = 4$.

In Fig. 13, it is shown that the observations about *MRT Ratio* that hold for the $C = 2$ case generally also hold for $C = 4$. However, for $C = 4$ at each load the difference in fairness between different epochs is very small.

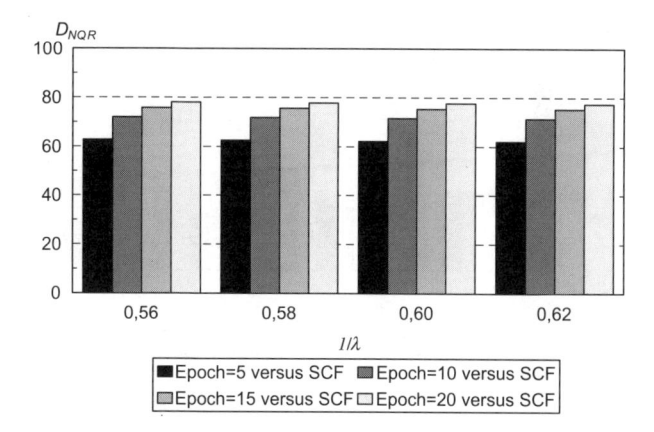

Fig. 12. D_{NQR} versus $1/\lambda$, $E = 0$, $C = 4$, normal distribution.

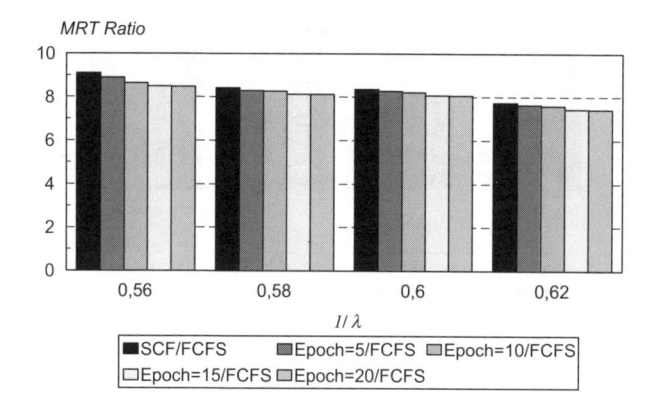

Fig. 13. *MRT Ratio* versus $1/\lambda$, $E = 0$, $C = 4$, normal distribution.

MRT Ratio decreases with decreasing load in a larger degree in the $C = 2$ case than in the $C = 4$. This is because the variability in task service demand is larger in the $C = 4$ case than in the $C = 2$.

3.2. Uniform distribution case

In the case of the uniform distribution for the number of tasks per job the simulation results have shown that the performance of the scheduling algorithms follows a similar pattern with that of the normal distribution case. For this reason we present here only the results for the $C = 2$ case (Figs. 14–17).

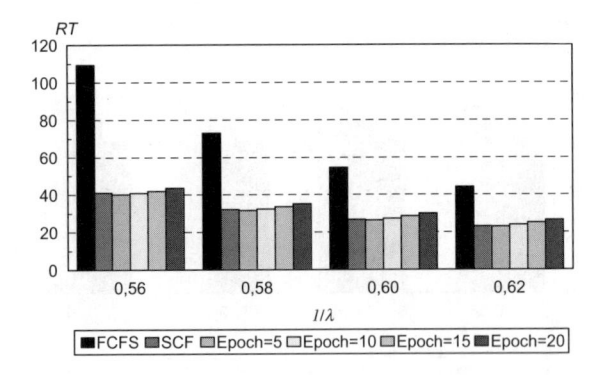

Fig. 14. RT versus $1/\lambda$, $E = 0$, $C = 2$, uniform distribution.

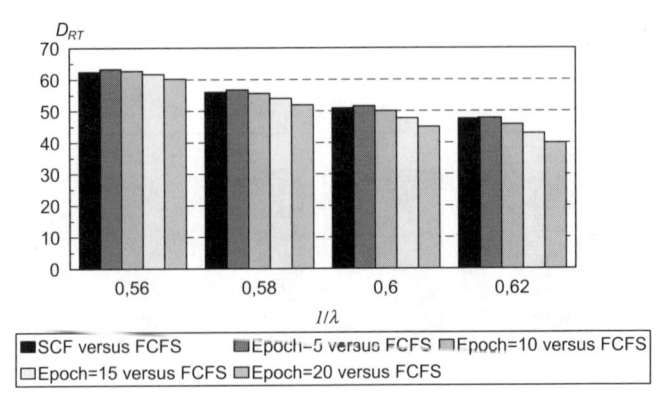

Fig. 15. D_{RT} versus $1/\lambda$, $E = 0$, $C = 2$, uniform distribution.

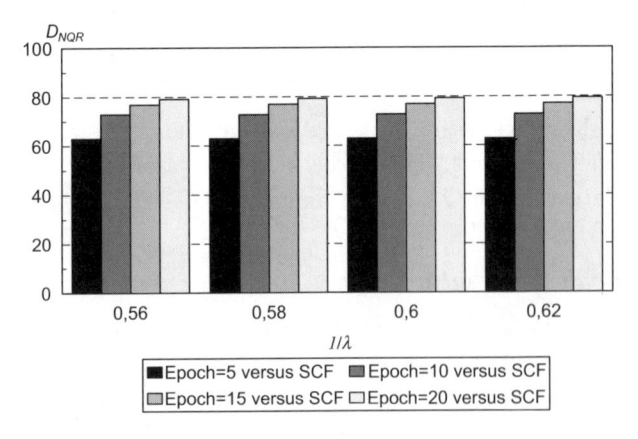

Fig. 16. D_{NQR} versus $1/\lambda$, $E = 0$, $C = 2$, uniform distribution.

MRT Ratio

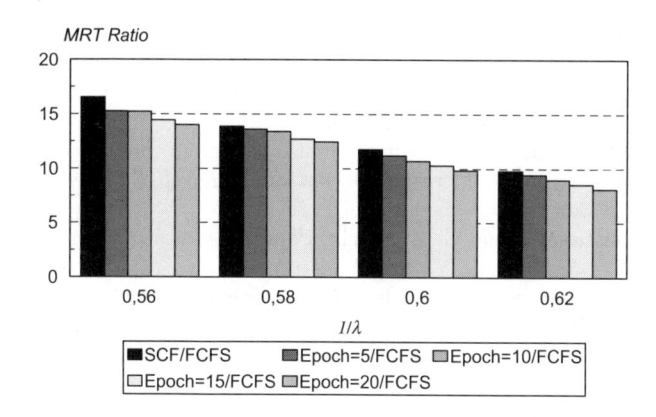

Fig. 17. MRT Ratio versus $1/\lambda$, $E = 0$, $C = 2$, uniform distribution.

4. Conclusions and Future Research

This chapter studies performance issues related to task clustering in a distributed system. Simulation is used to generate results needed to compare different configurations. Periodic Shortest-Cluster-First (PSCF) scheduling is studied along with other task cluster scheduling methods (FCFS, SCF).

The normal and the uniform distribution have been examined for the number of tasks per job. Simulation results reveal that for some epoch sizes that depend on the workload, PSCF performs better than SCF in terms of overall performance, fairness, and overhead. FCFS is the fairest method but it performs worse than SCF and PSCF. Simulation results show that large epochs involve a smaller overhead than short epochs. In most cases, large epochs result in fairer service of individual jobs than short epochs. In the remaining cases, mostly observed when task service demands are highly variable, large epochs do not differ significantly with smaller epochs in fairness.

Future research is directed towards applying periodic task cluster scheduling over heterogeneous distributed systems operating under time varying workload.

References

1. K. C. Sevcik, Application scheduling and processor allocation in multiprogrammed parallel processing systems, *Performance Evaluation* **19** (1994), 107–140.

2. S. P. Dandamudi, Performance implications of task routing and task scheduling strategies for multiprocessor systems, in *Proc. IEEE-Euromicro Conference on Massively Parallel Computing Systems* (IEEE Computer Society, Los Alamitos, CA, 1994), pp. 348–353.
3. D. G. Feitelson and L. Rudolph, Evaluation of design choices for gang scheduling using distributed hierarchical control, *J. Parallel Distrib. Comput.* **35** (1996), 18–34.
4. S. V. Anastasiadis and K. C. Sevcik, Parallel application scheduling on networks of workstations, *J. Parallel Distrib. Comput.* (Special Issue on Workstation Clusters and Network-based Computing), **43**(2) (1997), 109–124.
5. L. W. Dowdy, E. Rosti, G. Serazzi and E. Smirni, Scheduling issues in high-performance computing, *Performance Evaluation Review* **26**(4) (1999), 60–69.
6. M. Harchol-Balter, K. Sigman and A. Wierman, Asymptotic convergence of scheduling policies with respect to slowdown, *Performance Evaluation (Proceedings of IFIP Performance 2002)* **49** (2002), 241–256.
7. J. H. Abawajy and S. P. Dandamudi, Suheduling parallel jobs with CPU and I/O resource requirements in cluster computing systems, in *Proc. 11th IEEE/ACM Int. Symp. Modeling, Analysis and Simulation of Computer and Telecommunications Systems* (IEEE Computer Society, Los Alamitos, CA 2003), pp. 336–343.
8. S. P. Dandamudi, *Hierarchical Scheduling in Parallel and Cluster Systems*, 1st Edn. (Kluwer Academic/Plenum Publishers, New York, 2003).
9. J. B. Weissman, L. R. Abburi and D. England, Integrated scheduling: The best of both worlds, *J. Parallel Distrib. Comput.* **63** (2003), 649–668.
10. E. Frachtenberg, D. G. Feitelson, F. Petrini and J. Fernandez, Flexible CoScheduling: Mitigating load imbalance and improving utilization of heterogeneous resources, in *Proc. Int. Parallel and Distributed Processing Symp.* (IEEE Computer Society, Los Alamitos, CA, 2003), p. 85b [full paper in IEEE Computer Society Digital Library].
11. H. Dail, F. Berman and H. Casanova, A decoupled scheduling approach for grid application development environments, *J. Parallel Distrib. Comput.* **63** (2003), 505–524.
12. Y. Yang and H. Casanova, UMR: A multi-round algorithm for scheduling divisible workloads, in *Proc. Int. Parallel and Distributed Processing Symp.* (IEEE Computer Society, Los Alamitos, CA, 2003), p. 24b [full paper in IEEE Computer Society Digital Library].
13. D. S. Nikolopoulos and C. D. Polychronopoulos, Adaptive scheduling under memory constraints on non-dedicated computational farms, *Future Generation Computer Systems*, **19** (2003), 505–519.
14. G. Sabin, R. Kettimuthu, A. Rajan and P. Sadayappan, Scheduling of parallel jobs in a heterogeneous multi-site environment, in *Job Scheduling Strategies for Parallel Processing,* Lecture Notes in Computer Science, Vol. 2862, eds. D. Feitelson, L. Rudolph and W. Schwiegelshohn (Springer-Verlag, Berlin Heidelberg, 2003), pp. 87–104.
15. M. Gong and C. Williamson, Quantifying the properties of SRPT scheduling, in *Proc. 11th IEEE/ACM Int. Symp. Modeling, Analysis and Simulation of*

Computer and Telecommunications Systems (IEEE Computer Society, Los Alamitos, CA, 2003), pp. 126–135.
16. H. D. Karatza and R. C. Hilzer, Parallel job scheduling in distributed systems, *Simulaton: Transactions of the Society for Modeling and Simulation International* **79** (2003), 287–298.
17. Y.-K Kwok, On exploiting heterogeneity for cluster based parallel multithreading using task duplication, *J. Supercomputing* **25** (2003), 63–72.
18. A. Legrand, L. Marchal and H. Casanova, Scheduling distributed applications: The SimGrid simulation framework, in *Proc. 3rd IEEE/ACM Int. Symp. Cluster Computing and the Grid* (IEEE Computer Society, Los Alamitos, CA, 2003), pp. 145–152.
19. A. Gerasoulis and T. Yang, A comparison of clustering heuristics for scheduling directed acyclic graphs on multiprocessors, *J. Parallel Distrib. Comput.* **16** (1992), 276–291.
20. T. Bultan and C. Aykanat, A new mapping heuristic based on mean field annealing, *J. Parallel Distrib. Comput.* **16** (1992), 292–305.
21. A. Gerasoulis and T. Yang, On the granularity and clustering of directed acyclic task graphs, *IEEE Trans. Parallel and Distributed Systems* **4**(6) (1993), 686–701.
22. T. Yang and A. Gerasoulis, DSC: Scheduling parallel tasks on an unbounded number of processors, *IEEE Trans. Parallel and Distributed Systems* **5**(9) (1994), 951–967.
23. L. C. McCreary, A. A. Khan, J. J. Thomson and M. E. McArdle, A comparison of heuristics for scheduling DAGS on multiprocessors, in *Proc. 8th Int. Parallel Processing Symp.* (IEEE Computer Society, Los Alamitos, CA, 1994), pp. 446–451.
24. A. Gerasoulis, J. Jiao and T. Yang, Experience with scheduling irregular scientific computation, in *Proc. 1st IPPS Workshop on Solving Irregular Problems on Distributed Memory Machines* (IEEE Computer Society, Los Alamitos, CA, 1995), pp. 1–8.
25. M. A. Palis, J.-C. Liou and D. S. L. Wei, Task clustering and scheduling for distributed memory parallel architectures, *IEEE Trans. Parallel and Distributed Systems* **7**(1) (1996), 46–54.
26. J. Aguilar and E. Gelenbe, Task assignment and transaction clustering heuristics for distributed systems, *Information Sciences* **97**(2) (1997), 199–219.
27. H. D. Karatza, A simulation model of task cluster scheduling in distributed systems, in *Proc. 7th IEEE Workshop on Future Trends of Distributed Computing Systems* (IEEE Computer society, Los Alamitos, CA, 1999), pp. 163–168.
28. H. D. Karatza, Task cluster scheduling and I/O scheduling in a workstation cluster, in *Proc. 15th European Simulation Multiconference* (SCS Europe, Ghent, Belgium, 2001), pp. 705–709.
29. C. McCann and J. Zahorjan, Scheduling memory constrained jobs on distributed memory parallel computers, in *Proc. 1995 ACM Sigmetrics Conf.* (The Association for Computing Machinery, New York, USA, 1995), pp. 208–219.

30. H. D. Karatza, Epoch scheduling in a distributed system, in *Proc. Eurosim 2001 Congress* (Eurosim, Delft, Netherlands, 2001), pp. 1–6.
31. H. D. Karatza, A comparison of load sharing and job scheduling in a network of workstations, *Int. Journal of Simulation: Systems, Science & Technology* **4**(3&4) (2003), 4–11.
32. H. D. Karatza, Epoch task cluster scheduling in a distributed system, in *Proc. 2002 Int. Symp. Performance Evaluation of Computer and Telecommunication Systems* (SCS, San Diego, CA, 2002), pp. 259–265.
33. G. Bolch, S. Greiner, H. De Meer and K. S. Trivedi, *Queueing Networks and Markov Chains* (J. Wiley & Sons Inc., New York, 1998).
34. A. Law and D. Kelton, *Simulation Modelling and Analysis* (McGraw-Hill, New York, 1991).

DATE DUE

SCI QA 76.9 .E94 C68 2006

Computer system performance
modeling in perspective